Something in the Air:
Corporate Power and the Environment

ANDREW BLOWERS

Harper & Row, Publishers
London

Cambridge   San Francisco
Hagerstown   Mexico City
Philadelphia   São Paulo
New York   Sydney

First published 1984

Harper & Row Publishers Ltd
28 Tavistock Street
London WC2E 7PN

British Library Cataloguing in Publication Data

Blowers, Andrew
    Something in the air.
    1. Industry—Environmental aspects—Great
    Britain   2. Great Britain—Industries
    I. Title
    304.2'8'0941   TD186.5.G7

    ISBN 0-06-318279-3

Typeset by Acorn Origination, Bournemouth.
Printed and bound by Butler & Tanner Ltd., Frome and London.

Something in the Air:
Corporate Power and the Environment

For my father and to the memory of my mother

CONTENTS

Preface   ix
Chapter 1   Industry and the Environment   1
Chapter 2   The Creation of Corporate Power   16
Chapter 3   The Opening Round — The Failure of
             Negotiation   56
Chapter 4   Deadlock   112
Chapter 5   The Conflict Resolved   162
Chapter 6   Corporate Power and Local Politics   209
Chapter 7   Politics, Environment and the State   260
Chapter 8   Pollution — Theory and Policy   296
Sources and Bibliography   336
Index   347

Preface

The relationship between industry and the environment is a major subject of political and academic debate. Over the past few years proposals for new airports, coal mines and nuclear power stations have encouraged protest from environmental groups seeking either to prevent development or to mitigate its consequences. To an extent technological progress has contributed to environmental improvement. But there remain many cases where control has been resisted by industry on the grounds that it is either too costly or impracticable. At a time of economic recession the ability of industry to resist control is reinforced by fears of unemployment. The conflict between demands for a clean and attractive environment and the need for production, profit and jobs is dynamic, responding to economic, social and technological change. It is a conflict between powerful opponents creating and reflecting a changing political environment.

This book tells the story of such a conflict. When I first arrived in Bedford I was made aware of the impact of brickmaking on the local environment. There were the scars on the landscape, the deep pits with hummocky, partly flooded floors, the abandoned works and the fuming chimneys of the plants still in production. The emissions from these chimneys produced a distinctive and unpleasant smell, and were the cause of concern about damage to crops, vegetation, animals and possibly human health. But the brickworks were a major and long–established local employer and, like most people, I grew accustomed to their impact as an inevitable, if undesirable, aspect of living in an industrial society. Later, as a member of Bedfordshire County Council, I was conscious of the tacit acceptance by the authorities of the problem, and the general feeling that the brick companies were beyond their control.

Towards the end of the 1970s the situation changed. The London Brick Company announced plans for the redevelopment of its brickworks in the Marston Vale. Public concern was aroused, and there were demands for a clean–up of the landscape and the air in return for new planning permissions. This began for me a political and academic adventure lasting five years. It is the story of this book.

I observed and participated in the brickfields debate in a state of political and theoretical ambiguity. This ambiguity is expressed in my title, *Something in the Air*. Not only does it represent the uncertainty surrounding the case (whether or not the emissions from the works were dangerous, whether or not they could or should be controlled), it also indicates a theoretical problem. How far can such a case be interpreted from different theoretical perspectives? Does one perspective offer a more plausible explanation than another? Are the perspectives viewing different aspects of the case? Can they be reconciled? I attempt to provide answers to such questions in this book.

The account is drawn from diaries which recorded meetings, conversations, and interviews. I have drawn on reports, agendas, minutes, correspondence and newspaper files covering the issue. This evidence is put together in a chronological account, which is presented in the first part of the book. My evaluation of this evidence forms the second, theoretical, section of the book. I recognise that this separation of evidence and theory will not satisfy everyone. There are those who argue that theory and evidence are so intertwined they must be presented as an integrated whole to establish the virtues of a particular theory. I consider that this view smacks of theoretical indoctrination. Nor do I take the view, expressed by one of my colleagues, that 'the truth is not pluralist, nor élitist, nor structuralist; it is just the truth'. Truth is not an absolute concept but a matter of interpretation. To suggest otherwise is to suffer the delusion of certainty. In rejecting these views I have not attempted a grand reconciliation of theories or a consensus. Instead I have tried to explore the evidence from different perspectives and to reach conclusions which, to me, seem persuasive in the current state of theoretical knowledge.

The research has depended on the help of many people, some of whom figure in the story. Among those I would mention are Peter Goode and James Aldridge who developed the environmentalists' case; James Bristow, John Wright and Stuart Meier who provided London Brick's defence; and Tony Griffin, County Planning Officer, whose insight and power of argument forced me to think clearly about the issues. My thanks are also due to the many other participants — councillors, brickworkers, action groups, journalists — too numerous to mention by name, who, through their actions and words, contributed to the story.

I am especially indebted to those friends who read the various drafts and whose comments were a constant source of stimulation, criticism and encouragement. I would especially like to thank my colleagues at the Open University, Frank Castles, Tony Walton, Doreen Massey, Phil Batten and Allan Cochrane and David Vogel of the University of California at Berkeley. The research was supported by a grant from the Open University which made possible interviews, surveys and a visit to the United States to gather comparative evidence. Above all I owe my thanks to my research assistant, Shan Hunt, whose persistence in following up every avenue and whose knowledge of the political process had a major influence on the research. My thanks also to Michelle Kent and Eve Hussey who typed an evolving manuscript so quickly and accurately and to John Hunt whose maps add much to the interpretation of the story.

Finally, I must thank my family who bore the brunt of a long and sometimes unsociable enterprise and especially my wife, Gill, who began this research with me and whose constant advice, reading of drafts and support kept it going. They, like me, can at last leave the story of London Brick for others to read.

Bedford
April, 1984

CHAPTER 1
INDUSTRY AND THE ENVIRONMENT

The Marston Vale in 1978

For about 70 miles, stretching across eastern England, lies a belt of Oxford Clay from which nearly half the nation's bricks are produced. Large brickworks with their characteristic forest of chimneys and surrounding clay pits emerge in a predominantly rural but flat landscape across the area (Figure 1·1). In the south are the Calvert and Bletchley works in Buckinghamshire, in the centre the works in Bedfordshire and in the north the constellation of old works with more modern ones east of the city of Peterborough. It was here, towards the end of the nineteenth century, that the village of Fletton gave its name to the 'fletton process', the manufacture of cheap bricks using the peculiar properties of the Oxford Clay. Since then the fletton industry has grown and, by a process of merger and amalgamation, has become dominated by one company: London Brick.

The Marston Vale in Bedfordshire is in the heart of London Brick country (Figure 1.2). Picture the scene in 1978 when the story described in this book begins. The traveller, turning north from junction 13 on the M1 motorway, is immediately aware of the overwhelming presence of brickmaking. At the junction is the Ridgmont works, the second largest of all London Brick's works. From its 24 chimneys, set in parallel lines up to the crest of Brogborough Hill, belch fumes creating the characteristic brickworks smell of burning rubber — a smell which causes many motorists to stop their cars in the belief that their tyres are overheating. Just off the road, at the top of Brogborough Hill, is a picnic site overlooking the Marston Vale as it stretches for ten miles up to Bedford. The view from this site leaves much to be desired. Below, in a huge excavated pit partly filled with water, refuse has been dumped, and is pecked at by myriad gulls. Along the roadside a row of poplar trees has been planted but, as yet, fails to hide the pit from view. On the other side of the road excavations have begun in an even larger pit (Brogborough No. 2); the clay transported to the Ridgmont works on conveyor belts. Beyond these pits are others, partly worked or

1

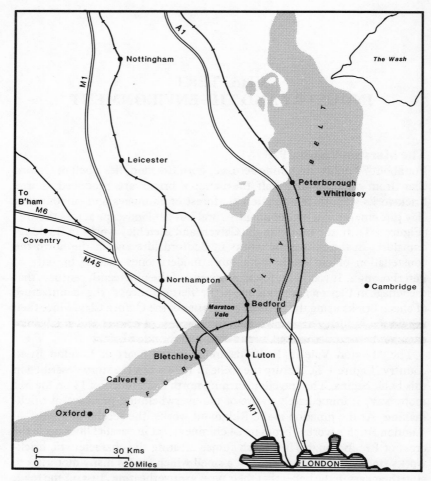

Figure 1.1: The Oxford Clay Belt

awaiting future extraction. Further on still is Stewartby Lake, an exhausted pit now filled with water and used for water sports.

In the centre of the Vale another group of chimneys heralds Stewartby, 'the largest brickworks in the world'[1], the flagship of London Brick. Near the works, between the railway lines to London and to Bletchley, are the great pits of Coronation and Rookery, each with an eerie moonscape on its

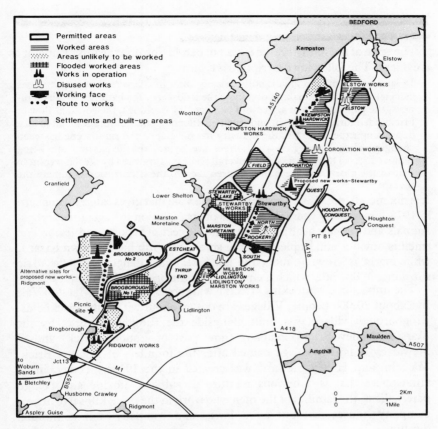

Figure 1.2: The Marston Vale in 1978
Source: Bedfordshire County Council, *Minerals: appraisal and issues*, map 2.1 March 1978

floor, worked then abandoned with no hint of restoration. Dragline excavators and conveyor belts claw out the remaining clay of Rookery and deliver it to the works. Further on, towards Bedford, is a small works at Kempston Hardwick working on clay from a nearby pit. The three operating works of Ridgmont, Stewartby and Kempston Hardwick are capable of producing 25 million bricks a week. But production in the Vale has been declining since the peak years of the early 1970s. There is evidence of decline in the Marston works in the south and at Coronation in the north where the chimneys are cold, the works silent. At Elstow the works have been recently demolished.

The scene in 1978 is a mixture of industrial activity, abandoned works and workings, of new extraction and past neglect.

The scale of the industry, the extent of dereliction and the loss of amenity is evident. The following description is typical:

> In land-use terms the area is still basically rural in character but the activities associated with brickmaking dominate the landscape; the batteries of tall chimneys, the gaping holes of active and derelict clay workings, the constant flow of brick-laden lorries, the sight and smell of effluent from the chimneys; all in all a depressing experience. As the industry has developed the rural scene has been changing also. Trees have died, trees are dying, the hedgerows are being removed . . . The poorness of the overall scene is aggravated by the flat terrain so that in the absence of trees the features alien to the countryside dominate the picture.[2]

It is not merely the visual appearance of the Vale that gives cause for concern in 1978. Over many years the dangers of air pollution to vegetation, crops, animals and human health has been the subject of reports and fears. The smell is obvious and unpleasant, the smoke and sulphur a known hazard, while alarm is growing about the less researched danger from the toxic substance of fluoride, which is emitted from the brickworks' chimneys.

The impact of brickmaking affects a wide area. Within the Marston Vale live about 20,000 people. Villages are dotted about within the brickfields. Brogborough village was built alongside the Ridgmont works by the Marston Valley Brick Company (now part of London Brick) and at Stewartby a garden village named after the founders of London Brick, Malcolm and Halley Stewart, was created in the 1930s. 'Today, in an atmosphere that is a curious mixture of sulphur dioxide and benign paternalism, the families of the men who work in the brick kilns live in neat company houses, set out amid lawns and company-built communal dwellings.'[3]

Elsewhere, in the centre of the Vale, Marston Moretaine and Lidlington are villages with a mixed population of brickfields' workers and newcomers in new housing estates. Just outside the brickfields to the north–west are the large commuter villages of Wootton and Cranfield, the latter close to the Cranfield Institute of Technology, a centre for research in engineering and aeronautics. Over in the eastern side of the Vale is Houghton Conquest, originally an agricultural settlement, but with new housing adjacent to a pit designated for future clay extraction. At the northern end of the Vale is Elstow, famous for its association with John Bunyan, close to a derelict pit used for waste disposal — the initial cause of the conflict which is the subject of this book. Elstow is on the southern fringe of Bedford, which, with Kempston, has a population of about 100,000. Bedford is a mixed community, the county town, a market centre, with old established and modern industries, a substantial commuting population and a large multi-ethnic community, many of whom originally came to the town to work in the brickfields. At the other end of the Vale, across the M1 from Ridgmont, are the middle class commuter villages of Aspley Guise and Woburn Sands set in the sandy, wooded ridge formed by the Lower Greensand. The Marston Vale and its surroundings is a changing and growing community containing those who earn a living from brickmaking and those who are affected by the environmental problems caused by the industry.

During the years of growth up to the early 1970s the companies had recruited labour, often from overseas. The work was unskilled and unattractive.

> Labour conditions in early works were very harsh. Although this has changed there are still many problems associated with employment in this industry. It is a highly cyclical seasonal trade and it is inefficient and undesirable to keep hiring and laying off people. It is also very dirty work, and many of the jobs are hot, heavy, unskilled and highly repetitive. Most workers stack bricks, drive transporters or mind machinery. A more skilled job is supervising the kiln firing; but the need to operate kilns long periods or continuously means employees must work unsociable hours.[4]

In addition to poor working conditions and job insecurity, there has been a long term decline in employment in the brickworks brought about by higher productivity and a falling demand for the product. The workforce in the company as a whole declined from 9,557 to 7,036 during the years 1972-83. Relationships between workers and companies have been relatively good and their cooperation is one of the interesting features of this case study. This relationship stems in part from the strong identification of the company owners and managers with brickmaking. Unlike many modern corporations, the fletton brick industry is still run by people who have grown up in the traditions of the industry. The familiar family names in the fletton industry — the Stewarts, the Rowes, and the Bristows — were involved in brickmaking from the nineteenth century.[5] This family tradition is an interesting and somewhat unusual feature in modern capitalist firms.

A management style that blends the paternalistic and the modern is embodied in the first chairman of London Brick, Sir Malcolm Stewart. 'He was a generation ahead of his time in management–labour relations. Welfare and pension schemes, joint consultation, profit sharing, holidays with pay, all these he introduced . . . with the result that stoppages and strikes were almost unknown.'[6]

By the late 1970s significant changes were bringing about a transformation in the company's image. It remained a major employer and its wage bill and contribution to the local rates had a significant impact on the local economy.[7] But the power of the brick industry both in terms of its market and employment was declining. Its reputation for secretiveness and lack of concern for environmental damage was ill–suited to combat growing public anxiety about its activities. A large population, many of them newcomers to the area, had no stake in the industry but experienced its detrimental effects. There was developing an environmental opposition to the company sufficiently strong to mount an effective challenge.

This changing balance of power between economic and environmental interests will be explored in Chapter 2. The conflict between these opposing forces which had festered for many years became inflamed during 1978-83, and is the subject of this book. It is a theme of considerable relevance at a time when anxiety about environmental damage is matched by anxiety about economic prosperity and the survival of manufacturing industry. The case of London Brick raises some major theoretical questions central to contemporary debates about the exercise of power, the nature of issues, the role of interests, the determination of outcomes and the relationship between the state and the private sector.

Questions and Themes

Empirical studies of conflicts between economic and environmental interests have been relatively rare. 'Very little attention has been given to the consequences of the interventions in the urban system by large private corporations.'[8] In the USA Lindblom[9] has set out a general thesis on the privileged position of business, and there are specifically empirical studies of the environmental impact of industry such as Bartlett's analysis of pollution in Lake Superior.[10] There have been a few studies which combine empirical observation with theoretical insight. The two best examples, by Crenson on pollution in Gary, Indiana[11] and that by Gaventa on the impact of mining in Appalachia have focused on the questions of why environmental issues have been subdued or repressed.[12] Environmental conflicts raise a series of questions which, when addressed to the evidence, may both support and contradict theoretical assumptions about the nature of power, its exercise and outcomes. This book analyses one conflict in depth in order to evaluate the strengths and weaknesses of various theoretical perspectives and to reveal areas of theoretical controversy.

The underlying questions for this study are, 'Why did the conflict occur?'

'Why did it take the course it did?' and 'What were the consequences of the conflict?' Such questions revolve around the nature of power, a concept which is discussed in Chapter 6. In the conflict considered here a number of agencies were involved and the role of each raises important questions. First, there is the company, London Brick — did it possess greater power than its adversaries? How far was its power dependent on factors external to the local conflict? Among these were the economic climate, the role of central government, and decisions taken in other authorities. Second, there were the officials through whom negotiations between the company and its opponents were communicated. Did they play a determining role or were they simply intermediaries reflecting the balance of the conflict? Third, there were the interest groups and individuals including politicians. Did they have a decisive impact on the course of the conflict and its outcomes or was their role a marginal one when viewed in the wider context? There is a central theoretical question at issue here, namely whether the exercise of power was dependent on the role of agencies operating in the circumstances of the conflict, or was determined by structures external to the conflict. It is the classic debate between theories which argue the importance of agencies and those which are based on a recognition of structural forces.

Another set of theoretical questions concerns the role of interests in pursuing their objectives. Whose interests did the various agencies involved in the conflict really serve? What were the relationships between the environmental groups, the company, its workers and the decision makers? What accounts for the conflicts of interest which appear to contradict class allegiances and political alignments? Did the various agencies each have equal access to the decision making process? How far did the decision makers respond to the pressures of these various agencies? These questions lead us to consider the more fundamental question of whether power was dispersed among a variety of agencies each able to mobilise interests and influence outcomes or was instead concentrated among élites possessing superior power and ability to achieve their objectives.

Other theoretical questions are suggested by the type of issues which are the cause of conflict. Environmental issues have tended to increase in political prominence over recent years. Why is this? Are environmental issues related to party political or other kinds of conflict? Environment embraces a series of issues such as amenity or pollution. It is frequently in conflict with economic issues which include investment and employment. There are other issues also competing for a place on the decision making agenda such as social welfare or education. This competition among issues poses a further series of questions: Why are some issues raised rather than others? How important are certain issues when related to other competing issues? Why do certain issues get raised at a particular time? Such questions are clearly related to the theoretical problem of whether agency or structure is responsible for conflicts and their outcomes and whether power in a community is concentrated or dispersed.

The fourth group of questions investigated in this study concerns the theoretical problem of outcomes. Once again the problem can be polarised in terms of structure and agency. Was the outcome unpredictable, a matter of changing and unforeseen circumstances manipulated by agencies? Or was the outcome, at least in general terms, predictably being determined by underlying structural factors? One view argues that where the resources and capabilities of one side in a conflict are greater than another's the outcome is 'predictable and unvarying'.[13] The opposing view is that outcomes depend on conditions ouside the agent's control and that 'outcomes are produced in the course of the struggle itself'.[14]

This debate can only be resolved, if resolved at all, through close inspection of evidence.

Theory and evidence

The various questions posed by a conflict between environmental and industrial interests will be raised at different points in the case study which follows (Chapters 2-5). They are designed to stimulate theoretical speculation as different aspects of the case are examined. The problems which arise through an analysis of the case are confronted in the theoretical chapters (Chapters 6 and 7) later in the book. In attempting to bring together theory and evidence I am aware of the problem described by Saunders, 'In gratefully making good our escape from the devil of "abstracted empiricism", we must beware of the deep blue sea of "grand theory".'[15] In Chapter 6 various theoretical perspectives are used to interpret the evidence of the case. They are not put forward as clearly defined sets of hypotheses capable of being supported or falsified by the evidence. Rather, they must be seen as ways of viewing the world. Nor are they necessarily comparable, so that one set of explanations derived from a particular perspective may be regarded as somehow superior to another. In practice each tends to identify certain aspects of the case and to ignore others.

Three broad perspectives are examined. The first, the pluralist, with its focus on conflicts of interest and its emphasis on a responsive policy providing access to all participants in a dispute, expresses the course of the struggle once it is exposed on the agenda for decision making. By contrast the élitist perspective recognises the hidden agenda, the ability to prevent issues arising and the privileged access of particular groups to decision makers. Finally, the structuralist perspective is concerned with the underlying forces which bring about outcomes which favour particular classes engaged in social conflict. Thus each perspective gives prominence to particular aspects of the story. But they are not merely complementary. It is not simply a matter of choosing specific aspects of different perspectives in order to construct some composite explanation of the events and outcomes described. The theoretical perspectives are at too abstract a level and are too incompatible for such *legerdemain* to be compatible. What is needed is the provision of mediating concepts which relate broad theoretical perspectives to empirical reality.

> Theories must also have the capacity to *return to the real complexities*. The abstractions they contain must be able to produce more complex formulations which approach the real world more closely. That is, theories do not 'jump' from their most abstract formulations to particular events. They build a series of intermediate steps.[16]

In Chapter 7 I attempt to provide these intermediate steps by introducing concepts which, though related to broad theories, enable a closer interrogation of the empirical evidence. I also indicate conclusions which offer an explanation that is consistent with the evidence of this case.

The conclusions depend, to an extent, on the analysis of a single case. This raises two problems. The first concerns the adequacy of one case. The advantages of taking one case are that it 'allows the observer to dig deeply into the social psychology or political science of a particular dispute'.[17] Such probing is only possible through a detailed study and is necessary 'to illustrate generalisations which are established otherwise, or to direct attention towards such generalisations'.[18] In this sense the London Brick case can be used to provide empirical illustration for the various theoretical perspectives discussed in Chapter 6. But, it may be argued, such generalisations are insecure unless supported by comparative evidence from similar studies undertaken elsewhere. Quite aside from the problem of locating or creating genuinely comparable material, the comparative method is unable to provide extended analysis and so is liable to reach either partial or superficial conclusions. Indeed it can be argued that the deep probing of particular cases is a necessary prerequisite to comparative theoretical enquiry. Dunleavy makes the point that 'it can usefully serve as the basis for the comparative assessment of theoretical approaches, the exposition of gaps in the analyses, the testing of hypothesised relations in an empirical context, and the assessment of the different approaches' utility in empirical research'.[19] This is the task I have attempted in Chapter 7. The single case study must therefore be seen as complementary to comparative analysis. It assists in the sieving out and defining of issues for comparative survey.

In the final chapter (Chapter 8) I have provided evidence from comparable studies of environmental conflicts in order to relate this case to a wider empirical and theoretical context.

The second problem with the case study approach is the basis for selection of the case itself. I take the view that any case, provided its subject matter is relevant to the theoretical problems under discussion, should be appropriate for study. The idea that cases should be specifically selected to illustrate theoretical propositions clearly denigrates the principles of disinterested theoretical enquiry. The selection of a case, therefore, depends on its availability and the access to evidence afforded the researcher. The London Brick case presented itself by virtue of my role on a local authority giving me access to information that would otherwise be hard to unearth. This serendipitous circumstance was one I could hardly ignore.

My role in the case deserves some comment. It might most aptly be described as a case based on participant observation. I was a local politician, a member of the County Council, which was the decision making body involved. I was appointed to the various committees which dealt with various aspects of the case.[20] As a result of the part I played I was invited to join one of the major environmental pressure groups which figures in the case.[21] I had access to the planning officials, participated in meetings with pressure groups, parish councils, trade unions, political groups, and met with company officials from time to time. Some of these meetings were held in public, and I have compiled the evidence from reports, minutes, transcriptions of meetings and newspaper articles which are matters of public record. Other meetings were confidential and I have culled evidence from observation, interviews and conversations with participants. Throughout the conflict I kept a diary detailing what transpired and noting opinions on the course of events. My record is therefore detailed and derived from first–hand evidence. There were, of course, aspects of the process I could not penetrate. I was unable, for obvious reasons, to observe the company's decision making process. This was partly compensated for by interviews with company management which enabled a reconstruction of the positions adopted by the company. In this way I have tried to present as comprehensive a view as possible of a complex case involving many participants and many meetings over a period of five years.

There is the danger that an overlap of political and academic roles will prejudice the enquiry, providing a particular slant by celebrating the endeavours of one set of combatants. I have tried to avoid this by standing back from the case and describing events, where possible, through the actions and words of the participants. I have eschewed the interposition of personal observations and tried to place my own role in the story on the same terms as others. Thus, in the narrative I refer to Councillor Andy Blowers who is, of course, one and the same as the author of this book. The conscious attempt to separate my political and academic roles was a chastening experience. At times I found myself as an academic in strong sympathy with those who had criticised my political role. This, I hope, provides some reassurance to those who feel it is impossible to provide a reasonably neutral analysis from the position of 'insider'.

I have made no attempt to provide a story line based on a particular theoretical position. The case presented in the ensuing chapters is presented as a resource for theoretical interpretation. At the outset I had few notions about the most appropriate theories and simply followed the case as it unfolded. In hindsight the pattern may appear clear but, at the time, the story was always capable of new and dramatic twists and turns. I have used the case to reach my own conclusions about the processes involved. Others, using the same material, may venture different interpretations and conclusions.

The political environment of decision making

The conflict between London Brick and its opponents which is the subject of this book was transmitted through a political process which transformed the signals it received into policies and decisions. Conceptually it may be helpful to visualise this decision making process as a system, used as a descriptive device rather than as an explanatory device as advocated by systems theorists.[22] The system here consists of a political organisation with power to take decisions interacting with a political environment which exerts influence on the organisation (Figure 1.3).

The *political environment* is created by conflict between different sets of values represented by different groups of interests. In this case the interests are aggregated with labour predominantly concerned about employment, environmental interests concerned about pollution and dereliction, and industry concerned with investment. These issues are fed into the *political organisation* as inputs or pressures urging particular courses of action. These inputs are then converted by the decision makers (in this case local

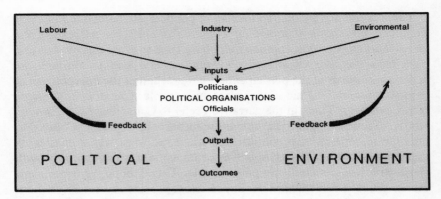

Figure 1.3: The political environment

politicians and their professional advisers, the planners) into outputs which
take the form of recommendations for action. These outputs may require a
further round of interaction (represented by feedback) which may alter the
political environment and the resulting inputs and outputs. Once the
process of negotiation, bargaining and debate has been concluded and a final
decision taken, the result is an outcome. The outcome represents the stage
at which a decision is accepted by all parties to a conflict, whether or not they
agree with the decision. In the London Brick case various stages in decision
making were outputs in the sense that they were challenged, and redefined.
The outcome was the point at which both sides acknowledged a conclusion
had been reached and the conflict died away.

Figure 1.4 expresses the specific interrelationships within the political
organisation and the impact of external pressures from the surrounding
political environment. The political organisation with which this case is
primarily concerned is Bedfordshire County Council. The Environmental
Services Committee consists of 22 elected members (politicians) advised by
various officials. The committee constitutes the local planning authority
responsible for preparing development plans containing policies covering
all aspects of the environment within the county. It is also the authority
which grants or refuses applications to extract minerals and the development of associated industries such as brickmaking plants. In preparing
these plans and deciding on applications for development the committee
will receive inputs from the external political environment. There is a
tendency for these inputs to reach the committee by different channels. A
developer, in this case London Brick, will make proposals through the

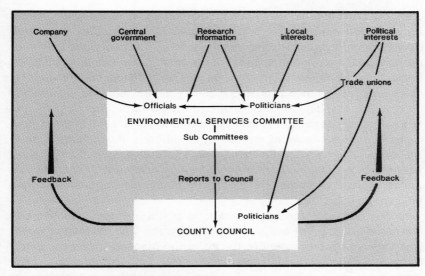

Figure 1.4: The political organization

planning officials. These officials will also receive messages from central government departments on the likely attitude of government ministers. During the course of this conflict it became clear that central government, while sympathetic to the company, was not prepared to intervene, but would leave the decision to the local planning authority. The local politicians receive considerable information and pressure from locally–based organisations, whether statutory, like the parish councils, or pressure groups concerned with specific issues such as pollution or dereliction. They are also sensitive to party political pressures, and trade unions may exert their influence on the politicians. These channels of communication are not mutually exclusive. For example the company, from time to time, sought to gain influence with the politicians, and local interests applied pressure on officials. Advice in the form of commissioned reports is received by both members and officials. The media also plays a part in both creating and reflecting public opinion. On the basis of these various inputs from the political environment the officials prepare reports and recommendations. Through the interaction of officials and politicians within the committee (or, as in this case, specially constituted sub-committees) policies are prepared and recommendations made.

In most cases the committee would be the effective authority, acting with delegated powers on behalf of the full Council of elected members. In this instance the conflict was so profound that it was referred to the County Council for decision. During this period the Council consisted of 83 members, each representing a part of the county, and was predominantly Conservative. The Council received the recommendations of the committee and some of its members experienced direct pressure from local interests and the trade unions. The procedures of Council meetings preclude participation by officials in debate. Normally, in conditions of majority party rule, Councils endorse decisions reached by committees on the basis of party allegiance. This traditional model did not apply in this case. The divisions within the Council, and between it and the Environmental Services Committee, were a significant factor in determining the outputs, if not the outcome, of the conflict.

In 1978 there were few intimations of the conflict that was about to divide and dominate the Council for over three years. The dereliction of the landscape and the pollution of the air in the Marston Vale were widely accepted as the inevitable consequence of one of Bedfordshire's major industries. The power of the London Brick Company to neglect the environmental impact of brick production appeared to be firmly entrenched. The source of that power is the subject to which I now turn.

Notes

1 Collier, L.J. 'The world's largest brickworks', *Bedfordshire Magazine*, (Vol.9. No.65. Summer 1963, pp.18-20).

2 Bedfordshire County Council *Bedfordshire Brickfield*, (October, 1967, p.i).

3 Bugler, J. *Polluting Britain: a report* (Harmondsworth, Penguin, 1972, p.115).

4 Bollard, A.E. *Brick Work: small plants in the brick industry* (Alternative Industrial Framework for the UK, Report, 1962, No.3. Intermediate Technology Development Group, pp.13-14).

5 Halley Stewart was the leading figure in the Bedfordshire firm of B.J. Forder and Son Ltd., one of the companies which merged to form the London Brick Company. His son, Malcolm, was Chairman of London Brick. J.W. Rowe began in the Peterborough area and a member of his family is the present Chairman of London Brick. James Bristow developed the fletton process, his grandson was Managing Director and Deputy Chairman of London Brick, and his great grandson is now Managing Director of the company.

6 Hillier, R. *Clay that Burns: a history of the fletton brick industry* (London Brick Company Ltd., 1981, p.70).

7 In 1981 London Brick Company employed 8358 people, had a wage bill of £52,716,000 and contributed £1,400,000 to the rates in the counties of Bedfordshire, Cambridgeshire and Buckinghamshire.

8 Dunleavy, P. *Urban Political Analysis* (London Macmillan, 1980, p.120).
9 Lindblom, C.E. *Politics and Markets* (New York, Basic Books, 1977).
10 Bartlett, R.V. *The Reserve Mining Controversy* (Bloomington, Indiana University Press, 1980).
11 Crenson, M.A. *The Un-Politics of Air Pollution: A study of non-decision making in the cities* (Baltimore, The Johns Hopkins Press, 1971).
12 Gaventa, J. *Power and Powerlessness: Quiescence and Rebellion in an Appalachian Valley* (Urbana, University of Illinois Press, 1976).
13 Benton, T. '"Objective" interests and the sociology of power', *Sociology*, (15, 1981, p.177).
14 Hindess, B. 'Power, interests and the outcomes of struggles', *Sociology*, (Vol.16. No.4. November 1982, p.505).
15 Saunders, P. *Urban Politics: a sociological interpretation* (Hutchinson, Penguin edition, 1980, p.13).
16 Clarke, J. and Costello, N. 'The production of social divisions', *Social Sciences: a foundation course*, Unit 13 (The Open University, 1982, p.55).
17 Gladwin, T.N. 'Patterns of environmental conflict over industrial facilities in the US, 1970-78', *Natural Resources Journal*, (Vol.20. No.2. April, 1980, p.244).
18 Eckstein, H. *Pressure Group Politics* (London, Allen and Unwin, 1960, p.15).
19 Dunleavy, P. *The Politics of Mass Housing in Britain 1945-1975* (Oxford, Clarendon Press, p.182).
20 During this period I was a member of the Environmental Services Committee responsible for dealing with minerals planning applications. I was also on the Brickfields sub-committee initially appointed to negotiate a planning agreement with the company and subsequently dealing with various issues arising from the brickfields issue. Later I was appointed to the research committee investigating techniques of pollution control. In 1981 I was nominated to represent Bedfordshire County Council on the Fletton Brickworks Liaison Committee, composed of local authorities in the brickfields area. These committees are mentioned at various points in the story.
21 Public Review of Brickmaking and the Environment (PROBE). The composition of this group is given in Chapter 3.
22 Easton, D. *A Framework for Political Analysis,* (Englewood Cliffs, Prentice-Hall, 1965).

CHAPTER 2
THE CREATION OF CORPORATE POWER

London Brick — the economic context

The concentration of brickmaking in the Bedford-Peterborough area is a result of geographical and technological factors. In the early nineteenth century new types of kiln were introduced employing a downdraught system which recirculated the air, enabling even heating and high temperatures and thus quality control. But the brickmaking process was slow until, in 1858, the Hoffman Kiln was patented. This enabled continuous firing using connected chambers through which the fire passed, so that all stages of the brickmaking process could operate simultaneously. As a result bricks could be loaded in one part of the kiln, fired in another, dried in another and emptied once dried.[1] The economies of scale made possible by Hoffman kilns were fully realized by the discovery of the 'fletton process' in 1881, which created 'a revolution which outdated the traditional brickworks overnight, and which was to transform the landscape of Bedfordshire's central vale, while turning the county into a major brickmaking centre'.[2] This process used the lower Oxford Clay, which is 10–30 metres deep, is virtually exposed in the area and has properties peculiarly conducive to cheap brick manufacture. The beds are uniform, and with a granular formation and a water content of 18–20 per cent, making it easy to press, and strong for stacking without initial drying. The clay also has the right lime content to prevent cracking and contains few impurities. Above all it contains 10 per cent carbonaceous material which, once heated, enables the bricks almost to make themselves,[3] thus saving 75 per cent of fuel costs in an industry where energy normally accounts for a high proportion of operating costs.[4] The cheap production, allied to the scale economies of Hoffman kilns and a location astride the main north-south railway routes, ensured the fletton industry a national market for its brick products.

The growth of the fletton industry hastened the decline of smaller works employing traditional methods using surface clays — by the First World War the major fletton companies were in embryonic form. By 1920 there were four major groupings in the fletton industry. During the 1920s there was a series of mergers and takeovers which eventually led to the emergence of London Brick Company Ltd. in 1936. After the Second World War London Brick achieved a monopoly over fletton brickmaking by virtue of its takeover of the Marston Valley Brick Company (1968-71) based on Ridgmont and Lidlington in Bedfordshire with 14 per cent of the fletton market;[5] Redlands (1971) operating in the Peterborough and Bedford (Kempston Hardwick) areas with 8 per cent; and the absorption of the small National Coal Board operation at Whittlesey Cambridgeshire) in 1974. London Brick had been approached by these companies. The Monopolies Commission 'found nothing to suggest that LBC had set out to obtain a complete monopoly as a matter of policy'[6] but also remarked that 'LBC's dominance of fletton brickmaking has given it substantial additional market power'.[7] But it was power in a declining industry and in a market which the company could not control and which left London Brick vulnerable to takeover.

London Brick is in competition with the non-fletton industry. Here, too, there has been a process of concentration through takeover or closure of smaller producers. The number of brick plants in the UK has fallen from 1150 in 1938, to 780 in 1951 and to about 248 in 1976. Several medium sized brick chains have emerged such as Redland, Butterly, Ibstock, Steetley and Scottish Brick, most of them part of companies involved in a wide range of activities. There also remain around 140 small plants in the country.[8]

The brickmaking industry as a whole faces the problem of cyclical fluctuations in demand combined, since the early 1970s, with a long-term decline in demand for its products. The all-time peak of brick deliveries nationally was reached in 1964 with just over 8000 million bricks, of which 3200 million were flettons (2129 million from London Brick). A further peak was reached a decade later with production over 7000 million and in 1973 London Brick, now with a monopoly of flettons, produced its highest ever total of 3000 million. Since then fluctuations in production have occurred (Figures 2.1 and 2.2) within a general decline, with the lowest national total of 3566 million (LBC 1610 million) flettons recorded in 1981. The brick industry suffers heavily in recession since the construction industry is among the first to feel the cut–backs. Scarcity of mortgage funds and cuts in public sector housing depress the house building industry, which accounts for 70 per cent of the brick market. Quite aside from the effects of the deep recession in the late 1970s the industry has experienced competition from other building materials, especially concrete blocks,

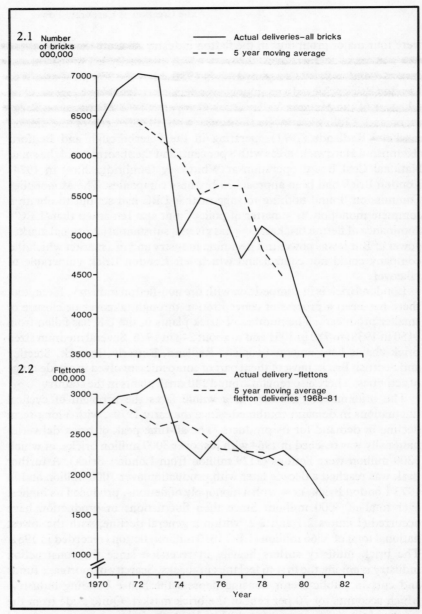

Figure 2.1: Production of all bricks, 1970–1982 and five year moving averages
Source: Department of the Environment, Housing and Construction Statistics
Figure 2.2: Production of fletton bricks and five year moving averages
Source: London Brick plc

which have eroded the market for 'commons' (i.e. bricks produced by the firing process without any further treatment). Consequently brickmakers have switched to the higher quality 'facing' bricks used on the exposed walls of buildings. Commons account for about 35 per cent of the market, facings for 57 per cent, the rest being made up of engineering bricks. London Brick has responded to the changing pattern of demand and its modern works are capable of producing up to 100 per cent facings (Figure 2.3). There has been some recent revival in the commons market used in foundations and for factories. London Brick, developing its cheap production process[9] and improving its handling and transportation,[10] has sustained its position in a declining market by producing 42 per cent of the total house building bricks delivered in 1981.

The overall decline has compounded the problems of coping with fluctuations in the business cycle. In a normal downturn of the cycle the industry would adjust production levels, first, by a reduction of overtime, by closing marginal plant used only for peak production, then by the introduction of short term working at the remaining works,[11] and finally by closure of kilns or complete works. The industry would also allow its stocks of bricks to build up in anticipation of a recovery in the market later.

Stockpiling creates problems of cash–flow and space, and there is the risk that stocks will deteriorate over the long term and that, if the market does not recover, they will remain unsold for long periods. Capacity reduction may bring problems and is inflexible in that it takes time to bring plant back into operation when demand begins to rise. In a recession the industry must still bear its high fixed costs, and there are high costs in laying off labour.

In the long term, investment in new plant may be justified on grounds of the scale economies and savings in labour costs that can be achieved. Replacement of ageing works which have been in continuous production since the inter-war years also becomes necessary on grounds of obsolescence. New works enable the company to reduce the labour force by increasing productivity. The capital-labour ratio in the brick industry is estimated to have been rising by 7.2 per cent per annum.[12] New works have improved working conditions which must, in part, account for the marked lack of resistance by trade unions to the pace of job losses in the industry.

During the late 1960s London Brick embarked on a modernisation programme which would require at least 20-25 years to recover the capital outlay and would therefore need a secure (and national) market. The first of its 'new generation' works were opened near Peterborough at King's Dyke (1969) and New Saxon (1972), with capacities of 250 million and 125 million bricks per year respectively. In 1978 the company proposed a second phase

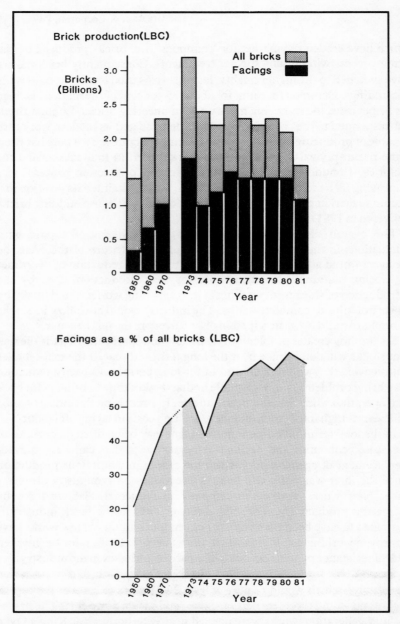

Figure 2.3: London Brick: production of 'commons' and 'facings' and graph showing percentage growth of facings to commons
Source: London Brick plc

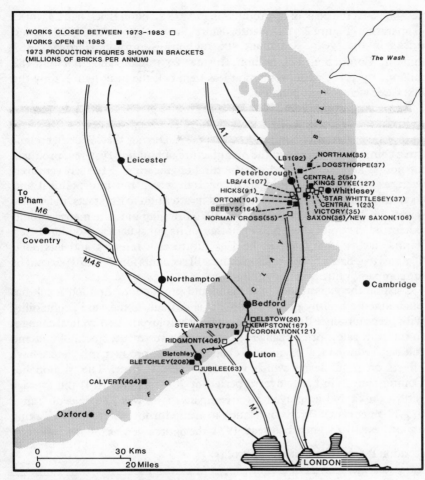

WORKS CLOSED BETWEEN 1973–1983 □
WORKS OPEN IN 1983 ■
1973 PRODUCTION FIGURES SHOWN IN BRACKETS
(MILLIONS OF BRICKS PER ANNUM)

The Wash

Leicester

To
B'ham
M6

Coventry

M45

Northampton

LB1(92)
NORTHAM(35)
DOGSTHORPE(37)
Peterborough
CENTRAL 2(54)
LB2/4(107)
KINGS DYKE(127)
HICKS(91)
Whittlesey
ORTON(104)
STAR WHITTLESEY(37)
BEEBYS(164)
CENTRAL 1(23)
NORMAN CROSS(55)
VICTORY(35)
SAXON(36)/NEW SAXON(106)

Cambridge

Bedford
ELSTOW(26)
STEWARTBY(738)
KEMPSTON(167)
CORONATION(121)
RIDGMONT(406)

Bletchley
BLETCHLEY(208)
Luton
JUBILEE(63)

CALVERT(404)

Oxford

0   30 Kms
0   20 Miles

LONDON

Figure 2.4: London Brick brickworks, 1973–1983
Source: Monopolies and Mergers Commission (1976) *Building Bricks: A report on the supply of building bricks*, HMSO

at King's Dyke to bring its capacity up to 500 million bricks per year and at two similar works (500 million per year) at Stewartby and Ridgmont in Bedfordshire. The controversy surrounding these latter two works is the subject of the story which follows.

As the recession deepened, the plans looked excessively optimistic and the problem became one of closing down existing works rather than creating new ones. At the peak of its production in 1973 London Brick had 23 works in operation (Figure 2.4). In Bedfordshire, Stewartby produced 738 million bricks in that year, Ridgmont 406 million, Kempston Hardwick 167 million, Coronation 121 million, Elstow 26 million and Marston 182 million. By 1981, with production less than half the peak figure, only the first three were left in operation.

By the beginning of the 1980s brickmaking displayed all the symptoms of an industry in decline. In an effort to reduce dependence on its basic product the company has tried to diversify. During the 1970s it bought three companies engaged in the manufacture of building systems, products for homes and gardens and in structural engineering.[13] It even ventured overseas with a brickmaking plant in Iran which ran into political and economic difficulties. It has also turned its attention to its 'assets' in land by setting up London Brick Landfill in 1970 bringing in waste material to fill exhausted clay pits at a profit. Another of its subsidiaries, London Brick Farms, farms 1400 hectares held as future clay reserves and lets 3400 hectares to tenants.[14] But brickmaking still accounts for about 70 per cent of the company's turnover and profits.

Despite the vicissitudes in demand and production, London Brick has maintained a healthy profits record. It is difficult to measure profitability with precision since different bases may be employed. Also cyclical changes in interest, sales, price changes, the cost of investment, stockholding and release, redundancy payments, changes in the product mix, etc., have effects on profit levels which vary from year to year. The Monopolies Commission found that over a period of 20 years (1955-74) the average return on capital employed on a company basis was 22 per cent (range 8.3-29.5 per cent). Profits in relation to group turnover were lower. Taking a good year, 1973, and a bad year, 1974, the figures were as follows:

London Brick – Comparison of Profits

	Company Basis Ave. cap. employed*	Profit Before loan stock interest and tax	Return on cap. employed	Group turn-over	Profit as % of turn-over
	£M.	£M.	%	£M.	%
1973	36.357	8.927	24.6	45.5	19.8
1974	41.231	3.399	8.3	45.1	6.9

*Includes a revaluation of fixed assets in 1968 which increased capital employed from a historic figure of £18.8M. to £25.6M.
Source: Monopolies and Mergers Commission (1970) *Building Bricks,* HMSO para 152.6, 8 Appendix 6.

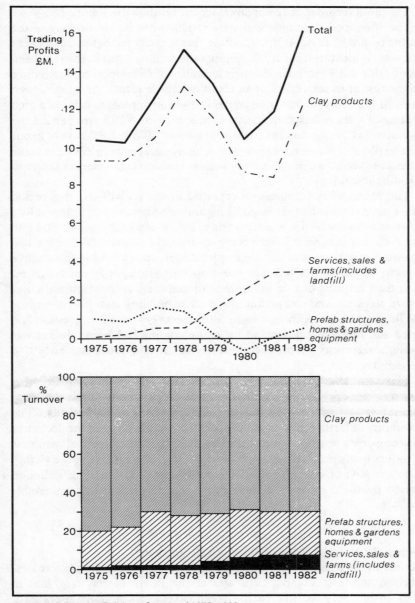

Figure 2.5: London Brick profits record 1875–1982
Source: London Brick plc Annual Reports and Accounts

The profit record of the company since 1975 is shown in Figure 2.5.

The Monopolies Commission were struck with the consistency of the profits record of London Brick, noting that it rarely fell below 20 per cent and was resilient in recovery. It appears the company has in the past been able to ride out a recession through its ability to raise prices and to reduce production at its least efficient and least profitable plants. At times of high demand the company has been content, it would appear, to achieve a high volume of sales rather than charge excessive prices. This strategy led the Monopolies Commission to conclude as follows: 'While LBC has not in our view exploited its monopoly position to charge excessive prices or to make excessive profits, we nevertheless consider that it has the market power to do both these things'.[15]

The Monopolies Commission reported in the mid-1970s, at a period when the company had achieved its highest production ever, followed by a downturn from which it was recovering. By the end of the decade and into the 1980s the prospects for the company looked ominous. Production had slumped, stocks were at the highest level ever, the bulk of its productive capacity was in old works that had been operating for up to 50 years or more; with the prospects of new investment diminishing as the combination of severe recession and competition from other building materials depressed the future outlook. Although some future recovery once the recession had eased and the pent–up demand for housebuilding had been released was likely, a return to the production levels of the mid 1960s and early '70s appeared remote.

This rapid change in the late 1970s in the fortunes of the company from relative prosperity to rapid decline coincided with a major public challenge from environmental groups and the County Council in Bedfordshire. The possibility of further investment provoked the challenge, and the decline in the company's prospects eventually defeated it. The commercial weakness of the company proved in the end its source of strength in wresting a victory from the jaws of defeat. But, at the outset, dereliction and air pollution caused by the company's activities appeared to place it in a vulnerable position.

Dereliction — the local costs of a national asset

An inevitable consequence of fletton brickmaking is the progressive destruction of the landscape. Estimates of the extent of clay workings in Bedfordshire vary according to the likelihood of excavation. An appraisal of the area in 1978 gave the total area with permissions for clay extraction (plus areas worked prior to 1948 before permissions were required) as 1681 hectares (ha.) of which 572 ha. had been worked. The brick company indicated that they would be unlikely to work 281 ha. of the remaining area, leaving 828 ha. still to be worked.[16] By the time of a further survey in 1982 it was estimated that over 700 ha. had been worked. The amount of reserves permitted and likely to be worked at this time stood at 667 ha., sufficient for the Stewartby works to operate for at least 25 years, Ridgmont for 35-40 years and Kempston Hardwick for 30 years.[17] Such estimates carry a great deal of uncertainty and the closure of both Ridgmont and Kempston Hardwick in the early 1980s and the possible development of a new works obviously affects the potential life and locations of future workings.

Until these closures London Brick excavated about 5 million cubic metres of clay annually creating (after allowance for density of the clay and remaining overburden) about 3 million cubic metres of empty space each year, while the rate of filling was only about 600,000-700,000 cubic metres per year. Thus there was a problem that grew annually to add to the 80 million cubic metres of empty space potentially available for filling already created. To restore that space to ground level would require about 50 million tonnes of domestic refuse or 80 million tonnes of colliery waste plus 2-3 million tonnes each year to keep pace with the increase in extraction. Some idea of the size of the problem can be gained from the estimate that 3 million tonnes annually of colliery waste would require 50 train loads a week.[18] Even with two works closed in 1982 and only Stewartby operating in the county the annual increase in empty space is over 1 million cubic metres a year, while the current rate of filling of just over 600,000 cubic metres, though impressive, does not bridge the gap (Figure 2.6). By 1992 the rate of fill is likely to have increased to 809,000 cubic metres; but by that time the rate of extraction is likely to have increased following an upturn in the market and the opening of new works. Figure 2.7 illustrates the problem and shows that only on the most optimistic (and probably quite unrealistic) assumptions of future fill (from domestic sources and possibly colliery waste from the Vale of Belvoir) and the most pessimistic forecasts of production will it be possible to decrease the empty space by the end of the century.

The problem of huge pits has been compounded by the lack of consistent or comprehensive landscaping or restoration effort. Although ultimate restoration to ground level and reclamation of the landscape for agriculture is an idealistic long-term aim it is recognised that the goal is impossible. Hence the local authorities have emphasised the need for intermediate plans

Waste	1982 cubic metres	1992 cubic metres
Local Arisings	202,000	215,000
Current/Committed imported waste	402,000	594,000
Possible future imports;		
Belvoir colliery spoil (max.)		1,200,000
Other possible future imports		151,000[2]
Minimum		809,000
Maximum	604,000	260,000

1   Includes contract with Hertfordshire County Council commencing 1983.
2   Estimated maximum further GLC waste
     Source: Bedfordshire County Council, Oxford Clay Draft Subject Plan, September
     1983.

Figure 2.6: Current and projected rates of fill
Source: Bedfordshire County Council, *Oxford Clay Subject Plan*, Table 6.1, September 1983

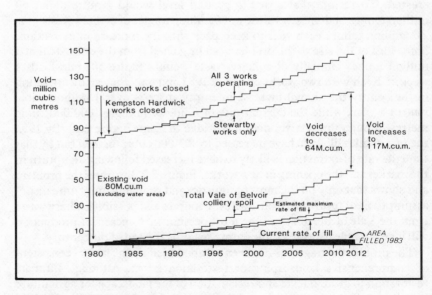

Figure 2.7: Estimated void and net shortage of fill
Source: Bedfordshire County Council, *Oxford Clay Subject Plan*, Figure 6.2, September 1983

for low-level restoration, recreational uses, and careful landscaping to mitigate the most offensive aspects of the dereliction created. But, for many years, London Brick appeared to adopt a cavalier attitude, failing to undertake even minimal landscaping and regarding the pits as part of the company's assets 'and the filling of them a privilege to be bought at what they consider to be a reasonable price'.[19] This attitude runs totally against the idea that dereliction is imposed on the local community, and that the costs of reclamation should be borne by the company as part of its production costs. This is the 'polluter pays' principle arguing that brick companies 'having obtained the profits from brick manufacture and being able to look forward to the benefits from the after use of the restored land, should be prepared to reclaim the land at their own expense provided that the costs are not too high'.[20]

The issue of dereliction has been stressed in various planning reports, conferences, and in the media. The company has been accused of wilful neglect and of placing profit before any environmental considerations. Over three decades after the Second World War the hostility developed; the company did little to soothe the public concern; and the authorities seemed impotent in the face of the company's intransigence. It was not until the late 1970s that the issue really became a matter not merely for debate but for action. Until then the company had undertaken minimal cosmetic treatment to the landscape and filled pits only when it suited its commercial interest. Explanation for the indifference of the company and the ineptitude of the local authorities on the dereliction issue rests in the nature of the planning permissions granted in the years immediately after the Second World War. It raises the question central to this study of whether industry enjoys a special, privileged position in relation to government compared to other local interests. The evidence suggests that it does.

Early permissions — a charter for dereliction

Figure 2.8 shows the various permissions granted for clay extraction in the period 1947-71. Prior to the Town and Country Planning Act of 1947 some working had been carried out at Stewartby and Elstow. By far the most extensive permissions were those granted by the Minister (of Town and Country Planning and later in the 1950s of Housing and Local Government) who 'called in' the applications since they were of national importance. The size of these permissions reflects the emphasis placed on post-Second World War reconstruction and the part that brickmaking was seen to play in it, as

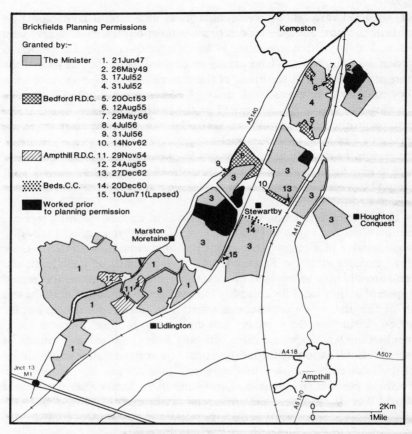

Figure 2.8: Early planning permissions
Source: Bedfordshire County Council

the major permission granted to the London Brick Company shows:

> The importance of the proposals from the national aspect both as regards land use generally and the maintenance of brick supplies over a long term period has been carefully considered by the Minister. In the light of the information supplied to him, he has come to the conclusion that the proposed extension of the workings in this area with the facilities for brick production that are desirable, is in the national interest . . . [21]

The national interest at a time of housing shortage was overriding, but implied a commitment which would last many years into a time when values and circumstances were profoundly different. [22]

By the mid 1960s it was clear that the permissions had stressed the national interest to the neglect of the local environment. 'Whilst the conditions attached to the early permissions may have been in accord with the national need for cheap building materials they have so far proved in practice to be of detriment to the Bedfordshire landscape'.[23] At the time the permissions were granted it was difficult to foresee or imagine the extent of devastation that would be caused. It was also a time when national needs were paramount and environmental concern was weak and ill-organised. Although conditions designed to protect the environment were applied they were few, ambiguous and, as was soon evident, incapable of implementation. The problem was clearly recognised but regarded as insoluble:

> . . . the resulting excavation will be too deep and the bottom too infertile to enable any use of the land to be made without arrangements for filling the excavation. [The Minister] is not aware of any supply of filling material which can be made use of for this purpose at any reasonable cost, and he does not therefore consider that any steps can be taken at the present time with regard to the treatment of the land after the extraction of the clay.[24]

The conditions which were applied varied a little but were designed to address the problems of landscape and restoration.[25]

Landscaping

The landscape conditions were evasive and inadequate. For example: 'The Company shall to the satisfaction of the Minister plant trees, shrubs and grass for the concealment of the working.'[26]

In the later permissions the idea of a landscaping scheme and the involvement of the local authority were incorporated: 'The workings shall be screened by the planting of trees or shrubs or by the construction of banks or ridges in accordance with a scheme prepared within 12 months.'[27]

These loosely worded conditions in permissions granted by the Minister covered 86 per cent of the total area granted to the companies for clay working. The various permissions subsequently granted by the local authorities (see Figure 2.7) merely consolidated the permissions, adding small parcels of land to the major pits. The greater degree of local environmental concern is evident in these permissions which attached a larger number of more explicit conditions.[28] The later permissions by the County Council at least have the appearance of concern for the local environment even if the aim 'to secure the restoration of the site and to preserve the visual amenities of the area' seemed unlikely to be fulfilled.[29]

Loosely worded conditions granted piecemeal would have posed problems of implementation even had there been willingness to undertake the landscaping in a consistent and comprehensive manner. Some planting of trees was undertaken and some of the pits were screened. Some experimental planting was carried out in the early 1970s to identify which species could best survive the conditions in the Vale and contribute to the improvement of its barren landscape.[30] But poor soils, expense and lack of maintenance led to the failure of several schemes, and to adverse comment. In 1973 it was estimated that 60 per cent of the Vale could be classed as in the lowest possible category of landscape.[31] But the brickmaking industry is not entirely responsible. Changes in agricultural practice and especially the shift from mixed husbandry to extensive arable farming has led to the loss of hedges and trees and the creation of large fields and open landscape. Dutch Elm disease has added its toll to the poor appearance of the Vale. Even without the brick industry the area would have suffered a deteriorating landscape. The conflict between economic and environmental interests present in the brick industry has strong echoes in the controversy now raging over the devastation caused by agriculture.[32] The Marston Vale suffers from both agricultural change and mineral extraction. The change in agricultural landscape is a gradual, almost insidious process while brickmaking is obvious and more dramatic. Significantly, agriculture remains outside the planning process whereas the brickmaking industry requires planning permissions. Public opinion can therefore exert pressure on the planning authorities to assert control over the brick industry. The planners have responded with increasingly elaborate planning conditions; but their powers of implementation remain feeble unless the industry cooperates.

Restoration

Planning powers are even weaker in the case of restoring the brick pits where resources of landfill and finance are largely absent. The conditions on restoration applied by the Minister were all broadly the same. The following is typical:

> The land shall be filled to such level and the surface restored at such time and in such stages and with such materials as the Minister considered to be suitable and practicable having regard to the availability of suitable materials at reasonable prices and to any representations made by the undertakers that suitable materials at a reasonable price are not available at the time in question.[33]

It was quite clear from this that initiative largely rested with the company. The phrase 'reasonable terms' was ambiguous in the extreme and could be construed by the local authorities as a reasonable cost to the company, or, as the company preferred to interpret it, as meaning 'reasonable charge rather than payment'.[34] Thus for many years scarcely any filling occurred beyond sporadic and small-scale waste disposal. A few pits, notably Stewartby Lake and later Brogborough No.1 (Figure 1.2), were allowed to fill with water, thus creating some recreational use and amenity, but the rest were left without any effort at improvement. The Minister's permissions made a half-hearted gesture towards the need to improve the pits and in some of the permissions schemes were required for dealing with the slope of the pit sides, the methods of working, levelling and the use of overburden, and topsoil. But the methods of working, whereby callow and blue clay are dumped on the floor of the pit, gave rise to the typical 'moonscape' topography, and no effort was made to conserve topsoil. As a result 'the excavations are extremely unsightly and are of no use whatever unless completely filled with water'.[35] The local authorities were not blameless either and appeared to make few efforts to implement the conditions. Indeed in 1953 the county planning committee actually agreed to delete a condition requiring the separate removal and storage of topsoil.[36]

The brick pits would appear to fall comfortably within the government's criterion of derelict land: 'land so damaged by industrial or other development that it is incapable of beneficial use without treatment'.[37] Ironically the pits are excluded from this classification since they are 'subject to conditions attached to planning or other statutory arrangements providing for after treatment'. Although the pits are clearly useless and unlikely to be reclaimed the idea that they could be is sufficient to preclude them being designated. Thus a problem created in the national interest can attract no national funds. The local authorities in the area bearing the costs of dereliction can hardly be expected, even if their strained resources would permit, to subsidise a private company to remove the problem.

Dereliction remains, fundamentally, a problem of resources both financial and landfill. Where profits can be made then London Brick has been anxious to fill its pits. London Brick Landfill has won contracts with London boroughs, Northamptonshire County Council, and later with Hertfordshire County Council, bringing domestic refuse in by rail and road. The first phase of a four phase restoration at 'L' field is completed and another pit, Brogborough 2, is under restoration. But these are insufficient to keep pace with the problem. The really impressive contracts, such as that secured in the Peterborough area bringing in pulverised fuel ash from the Central Electricity Generating Board's (CEGB) Trent-side power stations,[38] have proved elusive in Bedfordshire. In the 1960s the prospect of

moving 3.2 million tonnes of colliery waste by rail 80 miles from Nottinghamshire to fill up Brogborough No.1 in four years foundered when it
became clear that 'the cost of the operation would be far above the benefit
obtainable in terms of saving agricultural land in Nottinghamshire and
returning land to productive use in Bedfordshire'.[39] Neither the NCB nor
London Brick were prepared to pay the bill.[40] In the late 1970s a somewhat
similar scheme was floated to bring colliery waste from the putative Vale of
Belvoir coal field in Leicestershire to fill Brogborough No.2. The maximum
amount available would be about 1.5 million cubic metres, enough with
other sources of landfill to keep pace with excavations (Figures 2.5 and 2.6),
but the more likely amount would be 800,000 cubic metres. Even that
would only become available if permission was granted for coal mining in
the Vale of Belvoir; if a condition required the transport of the spoil from the
Vale; and if — the most unlikely of all — either the NCB or London Brick or
both could be persuaded to bear the costs of transport.

Air Pollution — a cause for concern?

Throughout the 30 years or so from the end of the Second World War to the
conflict of the late 1970s the problem of air pollution — and specifically the
offensive odours — was a source of comment and complaint. Yet it never
achieved the salience of the problem of dereliction. Furthermore, whereas
dereliction was obvious, visible and quantifiable, air pollution was a less
tangible problem. The quantity of the emissions was not known with any
precision, the exact extent of the problem was uncertain, and the possible
risks to crops, animals and people was a matter of controversy.

Although air pollution was widely recognised it failed to reach the
political agenda as a major issue throughout this period. The company
continued to pollute the air and experienced no serious challenge to its
activities. There are three sets of explanations for the relative security of the
company on the air pollution issue over this period:
1. The local authorities had limited powers in the area of air pollution and
failed to attempt control until the later part of the period.
2. Scientific and medical research concluded that there was only a minimal
problem. It was, for them, really a non-issue. In addition methods of
pollution abatement were either unknown, or ineffective and too expensive.
3. There is evidence that the air pollution issue was suppressed and
opposition deflected. It was not until the 1970s that public concern was
sufficiently aroused to generate organised and powerful opposition to the
company on the air pollution issue.

These three areas of explanation need to be explored a little more fully since they help to establish the context in which the conflict of the late 1970s and early 1980s took place.

The lack of control

The inability or unwillingness of the authorities to control pollution once again suggests that industry possesses a special relationship with government. Planning authorities possess powers to determine land usage and may attach conditions to a permission designed to mitigate the environmental effects of the activity. But the major planning permissions for clay working in the Marston Vale were granted, as we have seen, by the Minster and reflected the national need for bricks and the lack of public concern for the environment current in the period just after the war. The Minister's conditions on restoration were limited and difficult to implement, and conditions on air pollution were nonexistent. The only reference to air pollution in the four permissions granted by the Minister comes in his letter to London Brick granting permission for excavation for its Elstow Works on 26 May 1949. In this he 'observes that your Research Department is working to eliminate to the greatest degree the possibility of damage to the countryside from injurious fumes . . . .'[41] None of the subsequent permissions granted by the local planning authorities mention the subject, being entirely concerned with the problems of dereliction, landscape and restoration. The County Development Plan does not mention air pollution.[42] It was not until the mid 1960s that the issue was first discussed in some depth by the county planners, where the known research into the effects of the pollutants was reviewed.[43] No specific proposals were made either in this report or the subsequent Aspect report[44] and Appraisal,[45] which also limited themselves to rehearsal of the available evidence. By the time of the latter document the planners had established a policy on air pollution in the Structure Plan which was submitted in 1977 and approved in 1980. The policy states:

> When considering applications for new, or additions to existing, brick manufacturing works, the local planning authorities will need to be satisfied as to the location and appearance of the proposed works and their effect on the level of offensive emissions from the brickworks of the Marston Vale.[46]

Subsequently an Oxford Clay Subject Plan was developed and published for consultation in 1982.[47] By the time these plans were being drafted and debated public anxiety about pollution had begun to exert pressure on the planners. This was consequently reflected in the increased interest shown in the planning documents.

Until the late 1970s the planners had regarded the control of pollution as substantially a matter for the Alkali Inspectorate. Under the Alkali and Works Regulation Act (1906) certain processes including brickmaking are registered and subject to control.[48] Section 7 of the Act states that the owner of a scheduled works:

> shall use the best practicable means for preventing the escape of noxious or offensive gases by the exit flue of any apparatus used in any process carried on in the works, and for preventing the discharge, whether directly or indirectly, of such gases into the atmosphere, and for rendering such gases harmless . . .

This is the kernel of the pragmatic and flexible approach to pollution control in Britain. From the public's point of view it is difficult to know how control is being enforced, what criteria are being used and what pressure is being exerted on industry to improve its production process to avoid air pollution. Reports are published annually but provide little insight into the process of control. In general, it appears 'the Inspectorate chooses to pursue a policy of close cooperation with industry and only rarely resorts to formal enforcement procedures'.[49] Much of the information on pollution levels and abatement technology is possessed by industry and questions of the cost of abatement are clearly relevant in discussions between the Inspectorate and individual polluters. 'Pollution is not simply a technical matter; fundamentally it is concerned with weighing the benefits derived from pollution-generating activities against the costs imposed by that pollution'.[50]

For many years the methods of control exercised by the Alkali Inspectorate, removed as they were from close public scrutiny, were enough to keep the issue off the public agenda. But as time went on the secretive nature of the Inspectorate's work, its close ties with industry and lack of accountability, together with its bland pronouncements on pollution dangers led to growing public concern about whether enough was known or was being done.

A rising lack of confidence in the methods of control being exercised by the planners and the Alkali Inspectorate was a major factor in the strength of the opposition to London Brick in the late 1970s.

The lack of evidence

The apparent indifference of the authorities to establishing or heeding evidence on pollution hazards further reinforces the concept of a special relationship between government and industry. There are three major pollutants emitted from the brickworks; sulphur dioxide (SO_2) caused by the thermal decomposition and oxidation of pyritic and sulphate materials within the clay; fluorides caused by reactions within the clay; and odours (mercaptans) which arise from the combustion of the organic materials. It is estimated that overall the Stewartby and Ridgmont works produced 43,000 tonnes of SO_2 per year which compares with the 100,000 tonnes which could be expected from a 2000 megawatt coal burning power station. The fletton industry contributes about one per cent of the national total of SO_2, the electricity industry 50 per cent. Although amounts vary according to wind and weather conditions, a report on the brickfields concluded that 'so far as pollution by sulphur gases is concerned the situation of the brickmaking area may be compared to that of a small industrial town'.[51] Fluorides are produced in much smaller absolute quantities but the amount from Stewartby and Ridgmont, estimated at 430 tonnes per year, is higher than the 360 tonnes which could be expected from a 2000 megawatt (MW) power station. The precise amounts and variations in the incidence are not known with any great precision since the monitoring has been spasmodic, uncoordinated and, according to two authoritative reports, inadequate.[52] The organic materials produce an offensive and distinctive smell rather like burning rubber. They are difficult to identify and to measure, but their presence is obvious and gives rise to complaint. Not surprisingly the problem of removal of odour has received most attention, but so far no practicable techniques have been found to deal with any of the emissions — so the gases have been emitted untreated into the atmosphere.

From time to time concern has been expressed about the possible damage to crops, vegetation, animals and human health from the acid gases, sulphur dioxide and fluoride. Most of the official reports have attempted to remove anxiety by arguing the problem is minimal. Thus the annual reports of the Alkali Inspectorate present a consistent picture of unconcern on the health issue. For example, in 1965 the Annual Report stated: 'There is no evidence of any public health hazard due to emission of sulphur oxides or fluorine compounds.'[53] Occasionally awareness of public concern has been evident, as in 1971: 'There has been a noticeable revival of public concern about emissions from fletton brickworks and several general area complaints against the industry have been received. In these cases it has not been possible to do more than assure complainants that the problem is still being actively studied, though no early solution is in sight.'[54] The reports consistently state that ground level concentrations of sulphur and fluoride are 'satisfactorily low', yet no fluoride samples were taken by the Inspectorate themselves since, they argued, 'The pattern of fluoride emissions is now well-established'.[55]

A similar complacency is evident in the medical research relevant to the problem. The Area Health Authority says it has found, after repeated enquiries of medical practitioners in the area, no evidence of harm to human health. Various small enquiries have been made of dental mottling (as an index of high fluoride levels) and respiratory disorders (possibly linked to sulphur oxide) but they have scarcely qualified as attempts at serious scientific research and their results have been inconclusive. A local GP intended to undertake a study to identify the correlation with peak emissions and chest complaints but found that Dr. Alfred Lobban, the local Medical Officer of Health was uncooperative. 'He is against upsetting the brickworks and has suggested that the study is a waste of time and money.' Belief that there is no positive evidence of harm to human health persists at the highest levels. 'This is also the opinion of Professor P.J. Lawther of the Medical Research Council Toxicology Unit, an internationally recognised expert on the subject of air pollution and is also the opinion of the Department of Health and Social Security.'[56] It has to be acknowledged that the problems involved in carrying out research into long-term health effects are prodigious. They involve problems of sampling, diagnosis, isolation of a welter of possible causes, the need for adequate control groups, levels of statistical significance and interpretation.

Only one piece of medical research has tried to grapple with some of these problems in order to discover a possible link between brickworks emissions and human health. This was the Brothwood report (1960) undertaken by two medical researchers on behalf of the County Medical Officer of Health in Bedfordshire. Part of the report was a clinical investigation of respiratory disorders in adults aged 45-64 in the brickfield village of Lidlington where pollution is high compared to a similar population in the village of Riseley in the north of Bedfordshire free from brickworks pollution. Although the incidence and complaints of chest symptoms were higher in Lidlington, the incidence of smoking was higher there also. A relationship between heavy smoking and sensitivity to pollution was inferred but the problem of controlling for the small sample size and estimating the significance of the findings led to a predictably tentative conclusion: 'The investigation shows that while it is possible that sulphur fumes in the air in the Lidlington area are partly responsible for the higher incidence of chest symptoms, it is in no way conclusive'.[57]

The problem of 'statistical significance' was commented on by a chest expert at Bedford Hospital:

That phrase has bedevilled discussions over the brickworks pollution. It has been taken to mean that there is little difference between the two villages. What it really means is that, given the size of sample and the variation in smoking habits, the differences are well within the zone of sampling error. If the same results were found on a larger sample, they would become significant and show a marked increase in chest ailments among people living near the brickworks.[58]

This research related only to the problem of sulphur dioxide, recognised to be low compared to major cities though given to occasional very high levels. On the much more difficult area of fluoride–related ailments the report was only able to quote the evidence of a survey at Fort William[59] and some dental evidence in Bedfordshire and concluded 'It would seem reasonable to conclude . . . that no harm is likely to result from the emission of fluorine to the persons living in the Brickworks' Valley, but the matter is not absolutely free from doubt'.

By the late 1970s medical research evidence was fragmentary and inconclusive, leaning heavily on research carried out elsewhere from which to make inferences about the local situation in Bedfordshire. The lack of hard evidence, and a growing public concern about the possible, though unknown, dangers arising from long term ingestion of toxic substances such as fluoride created an atmosphere of doubt, and lack of confidence in the placatory conclusions from medical experts. This anxiety played a major part in fuelling opposition to the brick company and in identifying fluoride as the major issue.

Research findings on the potential dangers to animals and crops, though equivocal, were somewhat more positive. Grazing animals may be subject to a disease usually called 'fluorosis' caused by the ingestion of excessive amounts of fluoride. The disease is insidious, its causes are complex and diagnosis may be difficult. There is the problem of determining the precise levels of fluoride intake which may lead to the disease. Its symptoms are dental mottling and lesions, and, as fluoride accumulates in the skeletal structure, thickening of the joints results in lameness, stiffness and a decline in milk yields of the animal. Calves and dairy cows are the most vulnerable and there is a considerable literature on the extent and nature of the problem. The presence of fluoride in herbage appears to be a factor in the development of fluorosis. It is difficult to isolate the effect of fluorides from brickmaking from other factors such as the use of certain artificial fertilisers especially phosphates. Nevertheless, the few surveys undertaken in Bedfordshire provide a strong inference that the higher levels of fluorosis in cattle experienced there are associated with the emission of fluoride from brickworks and its accumulation in the soil and on herbage.

An early account[60] identified a 'mysterious lameness in cattle' in Bedfordshire and related it to the intake of fluoride from industrial emissions. The most significant evidence was provided by a comparative survey undertaken from 1954-7 by the Ministry of Agriculture.[61] The survey covered 832 farms in 21 industrial districts, and found damaging fluorosis on 170 farms in 17 districts. In Bedfordshire 19 out of 43 farms surveyed were affected. In a report (30 September 1957) the Veterinary Research Laboratory of the Ministry of Agriculture, Fisheries & Food (MAFF) stated:

> The evidence from the Bedford brickfield shows that the typical clinical signs of fluorosis occur in the livestock. Analytical data show the presence of fluorine in amounts high enough to be deleterious to animal health. There can be no doubt that damaging fluorosis occurs in the Bedfordshire brickfield.

By 1965 the Alkali Inspector was confirming a farming hazard.[62] Since the period of the mid 1960s the problem as manifested in complaints from farmers has reduced dramatically, only two cases being brought to the MAFF's attention in the 1970s. Changes in husbandry with the switch from grazing to cereals, the reduction in the use of certain fertilisers containing phosphates, and the decline in emissions as brickmaking has entered recession may account for the apparent absence of fluorosis. A lack of complaint is not conclusive evidence of a lack of problem but may result from an unwillingness to complain or suppression of evidence as we shall see in a moment. Certainly the claims of one farmer that his cattle were suffering damaging fluorosis as a result of the brickworks was a major factor in the strength of the hostility towards London Brick which developed at the end of the 1970s. Although the evidence against the company was not conclusive there appeared to be widespread acceptance that fluorosis in cattle could be caused by excessive ingestion of fluorides arising from the brickworks.

The shift towards cereal farming in Bedfordshire is part of a wider change towards extensive, almost monocultural, farming, occurring all over eastern England. Concern about the effect of pollution on crop yields has led to research conducted in the brickfields by the Rothamstead Experimental Station. This research designed to take place over seven growing seasons focused on the effects of air pollution on barley, which is recognised as a sensitive crop. Crops grown in closed and open clear plastic chambers with filtered air were compared to those grown in unfiltered air. There are variables to be considered including climatic variation affecting pollution levels and crop growth; the problem of isolating the effects of individual pollutants; the strain of barley used and so on. Obviously given these problems and the absence of similar research elsewhere the conclusions are tentative but seem to indicate a relationship between crop yield and pollution:

Our investigations have emphasised the large number of environmental factors which influence cereal growth and yield, and the difficulty of removing one of these — aerial pollutants — without altering others. However, we believe that, by the use of two contrasting chambers which modify the environment within the chambers in different ways, it is possible to draw conclusions about the effect of pollutants. We believe it is significant that in both types of chamber filtration results in an increase in yield . . . .[63]

Indeed, the researchers felt confident enough to pronounce that 'there is a strong indication that pollutants at levels previously regarded as acceptable may be causing significant yield losses in British agriculture'.

The effects of pollution on certain sensitive plants and trees have also been a source of debate and criticism of the brick company. 'The existing picture is one sparse in hedgerows and trees, but in addition many of the trees that do still stand are dead, or dying and stag-headed, so that there is visible decay to stand testimony to the decline in the quality of the landscape.'[64] Much of the loss of trees and hedgerows is due to changing agricultural practice but stag-heading is a sign of premature decline. Little research has been undertaken to assess the impact of air pollution in the Marston Vale on plant life. But some effort has been made to assess which species may best survive the conditions there.[65] It would appear that most damage to plants is done at times of peak pollution, particularly of SO_2 rather than as a cumulative effect.

Considering the large area affected by London Brick's operations, and the widespread criticism of the company, the paucity of research into the effects of air pollution in the Marston Vale was surprising. What research there was was highly qualified, offering some armour for London Brick's defence and providing some ammunition for the company's opponents. The lack of any really conclusive evidence helped to justify London Brick's lack of control over emissions. Although it had undertaken research into abatement technology, it claimed none of the systems it investigated were feasible or economic. London Brick was more concerned about the odours than the acid gases. In this it was supported by the Alkali Inspector. 'It is our considered opinion that any process which did not at the same time remove the odour from the gases would not justify the expense of treatment.'[66] He had concluded that tall stacks were the best practicable means of abatement and would provide sufficient dispersion to remove the problem of effluent gases.

The questions of evidence and technology were at the heart of the controversy. On the one hand London Brick, supported by the Alkali Inspectorate and influential research opinion, claimed that there was no evidence of significant damage to human health, and the evidence on crop and animal damage was inconclusive and, in the case of animals, indicated a decline in the problem. There was no justification, therefore, in applying expensive control technology which, in any case, had not been found. In new works the problem would be virtually eliminated by the use of tall chimneys. This, in essence, was the case which London Brick deployed and sustained throughout the controversy which is the subject of the following chapters. For it air pollution was a non-problem. On the other hand opponents emphasised the lack of in-depth research especially when the research which had been done indicated there were grounds for concern. They argued that so long as the problem was disregarded, little resource or attention would be devoted to adequate pollution control. The secrecy surrounding the company's operations gave rise to the suspicion that the true extent of the problem lay hidden.

The 'hidden' evidence

Here we encounter another of the major questions raised by this study — Why do certain issues fail to get raised on the decision making agenda? In previous sections one possible explanation, the privileged relationship between government and industry, has been suggested. Backed by the government stressing the national need for bricks, armed with planning permissions that left the company relatively free to excavate large areas without paying too much attention to restoration, supported by the Alkali Inspectorate in their claims that treatment of effluent gases was not possible, the company could continue its activities unhindered. Its opponents possessed no legal means by which to sustain any challenge.

Another, related, explanation may be that industry possesses sufficient power to ensure issues inimical to its interests are not agitated. Matthew Crenson (1971) has argued that the air pollution issue in Gary (USA) failed to reach the public agenda because the mere reputation for power of the dominant industry, United States Steel, was sufficient to ensure that it was suppressed. 'The mere reputation for power, unsupported by acts of power, has been sufficient to inhibit the emergence of the dirty air issue.'[67] His thesis that industry can succeed through inaction cannot really be tested,[68] but the possibility that industry acts behind the scenes to prevent the pollution issue emerging certainly exists.

There is some evidence that London Brick, far from remaining inactive and relying on its permissions, sought to secure its position in other ways. In particular it was able to silence any challenge from agricultural interests.

The company was a major landowner in its own right, farming large areas on which it has permissions for future clay extraction. Over the years the company has boasted of its success at both dairy and arable farming. Prizes had been won and yields were high, enabling the company 'to demonstrate that dairy farming using normal methods of good husbandry can be successfully undertaken in the shadow of the brickworks'.[69] The inference is that those farmers who have claimed damaging fluorosis in their herds are guilty of not using normal methods of good husbandry. The apparent success of London Brick's farming enterprise is one way of disposing of the case against the company.

Another method is to employ a tenancy agreement with London Brick's tenant farmers by which all claims for damage against the company are waived. The clause (15) is comprehensive:

> To waive all rights and claims against the Landlords on account of any damage howsoever arising (whether directly or indirectly to the Tenant his servants or agents or to the farm or other lands and premises occupied by the Tenant or to any crops, animals, farming stock or farming equipment or any other moveable property used in connection with the farm or such other lands and premises) which may be caused by water smoke fumes dust noise vibration of machinery or in any other way whatsoever arising out of or in the course of or occasioned by the working use or occupation of any present or future manufactury or works by the Landlords or by their tenants agents or subsidiaries.

Such a clause cannot prevent claims against the company but is typical of agreements intended to assert the primacy of industry over other activities.

Apart from London Brick's own farming operations and those of its tenants in the Vale there is a considerable acreage farmed by owner–occupier farmers in the vicinity of the brickworks. Over the years there have been a number of cases of farmers seeking redress from the company for damaging fluorosis which they attribute to the works. Details of the cases are difficult to trace but some are recorded at least in outline. An early example was during the 1940s when the then Duke of Bedford commenced an action against the company for damage caused by fumes, but his death and low production rates during the war led to the abandonment of the action.[70] Another instance was of a tenant of the Duke's who began an action against the company, but was forced to settle when he found the farm had been sold over his head and he had become a tenant of the Marston Valley Brick Company.

There was also the case of Mr Borland of Lidlington whose farm was bought out and he was given a tenancy with the condition preventing claims against the company attached. The case of Mr George Patrick of Houghton Conquest who claimed that more than 200 of his cows had been destroyed because of fluorosis is quoted by Bugler[71]: 'London Brick know I haven't got enough money to fight them. They've bought up, or are going to buy up, all the farms from here to Kempston, so what can I do?'[72] Another long–running battle took place in the Peterborough area and was finally settled by an out of court settlement in 1979 with the NFU claiming that thousands of pounds had been paid out through the NFU by London Brick to a farmer's widow.[73] 'We got a gentlemanly settlement although there was no direct cash compensation.'[74] By the end of the 1970s the only dairy farms left around Whittlesey were in the hands of London Brick.

Perhaps the most celebrated case, in terms of public attention, was that of Farmer Dunkley of Houghton Conquest who began an action in 1954 which was later taken over by the local Branch of the NFU. 'But I had to sign a promise to abide by whatever settlement they reached.'[75] He claimed that he was silenced by the Official Secrets Act and was warned that 'I'll be in serious trouble if I disclose anything'.[76] The action, having been to the Court of Appeal, was suddenly settled in 1968 when one of the companies (London Brick or Marston Valley) paid over a 'substantial sum'. Farmer Dunkley claimed he received nothing, but James Bristow of London Brick says: 'a sum of £5000 was paid over to the NFU.'[77] No liability was admitted and London Brick commented after the settlement: 'It is interesting to note that we purchased the farm in question from Mr Dunkley and his partners in September 1959 and since that date have farmed it successfully, winning many prizes with cattle from the farm.'[78]

The local NFU's policy was to deal with cases separately, agreeing with the brick companies that no precedents should be set. Publicity was to be avoided and confidentiality maintained in the interests of achieving settlement out of court. The NFU says 'We always advise the brick companies to go for an out of court settlement, to purchase the farmer's land, pay compensation, then release the land to the farmer with some conditions attached so that should he have further trouble, setttlements can be reached.'[79]

These policies of applying the tenancy clause, buying up farms or settling out of court without admitting liability may be construed as evidence of the company's need to suppress the pollution issue. Conversely, the generous price offered for farms might be regarded as a means of maintaining goodwill and recognising the company's responsibility. But out of court settlements incorporate mutual advantages. London Brick avoids too much adverse publicity and the farmers gain some recompense without the risk and cost of court action.[80] The lack of a consistent legal challenge to London

Brick perhaps illustrates the lack of real evidence. The role of the NFU is ambiguous. It has acted on behalf of its members but has also shown willingness to negotiate with London Brick rather than pursue litigation. More recently the local NFU has taken a more public and aggressive stance on the pollution question, for reasons which are explored in later chapters.

There is also the 'hidden evidence' that is possessed by the company and not released to the public. For many years the monitoring of emissions conducted by the company was not released. Also the company's research into pollution control was confidential. Work on air pollution carried out between London Brick, the Alkali Inspectorate and Warren Springs Laboratory (responsible for the national air pollution survey) has not been published and 'most of the information obtained is confidential and not available to the county planning department'.[81] This reflects the traditional secrecy of government departments and the fact that research commissioned remains the property of the company. The particular research dealing with experimental attempts to remove odour proved inconclusive and, though levels of odour were reduced, the laboratory tests were not applied in conditions comparable to the brickworks.[82] The collection of data on emissions and research into their control remains largely in the hands of London Brick. Whatever the reasons for the lack of public information on research and monitoring, suspicion grew that there was more to be known than had been revealed. This was a powerful component in the case against the company in the late 1970s. One of the outcomes of that conflict was greater dissemination of information and the involvement of the local authority in the research programme.

The developing challenge

The ability of London Brick to scar the landscape and pollute the air may be explained in terms of its relationship with government and its suppression of the issues but it found itself, at the end of the 1970s, facing a powerful challenge from environmental interests. Why, after so many years when little was done to control the industry, should the issue suddenly erupt and dominate the decision making agenda in Bedfordshire? The explanation lies in the fact that latent hostility developing over the years at last found an opportunity to express itself in terms that the company could no longer contain or ignore.

During the 1970s there were signs that the company recognised it could not sustain a secretive, almost complacent, attitude towards its activities and that, in the face of growing environmental awareness, a more open approach was necessary. The change in its public profile manifested itself first as a defensiveness, an injured innocence, and a lack of recognition of the hostility that had been gradually fostered in the local community among those who were not dependent on London Brick but experienced the undesirable aspects of its activities. In part there was a natural antipathy to the large corporation achieving substantial profits, and apparently able to dispense with surplus workers at will.

The company, during its period of rapid expansion in the 1950s, had recruited low cost labour from overseas. First came Poles and other East Europeans after the war, then Italians from 1950, West Indians from 1955 and lastly Asians (Indians and Pakistanis) from 1958. This policy contributed substantially to the multi-ethnic population of Bedford — by 1970 about half the total of 4000 workers were from ethnic minorities.[83] Apart from the higher cost and shortage of local labour a major reason for this recruitment lay in the nature of the work which is 'hard, dirty and unattractive', and does not appeal to the indigenous work force at times of high employment.[84]

A singular feature of London Brick's poor public image is that it is held by those who would normally uphold capitalist enterprise as well as those who would condemn it. To many in the local population the company seemed unwilling to undertake restoration of the landscape or abatement of pollution which 'would provide a reasonable recompense for providing the nation with millions of bricks'.[85] This stereotyped image, based on past neglect by the industry, failed to reflect the company's more sensitive approach to environmental questions which were becoming evident in the late 1970s. The company found itself embattled, a prisoner of its past. The time lag in public attitudes is a crucial element in the explanation for the controversy.

Public concern had been ventilated on a number of occasions in the past. An inquiry in 1966 into a proposal by Redland Bricks Ltd. to develop a brickworks at Woburn Sands on the Bedfordshire-Buckinghamshire border provided a platform for debate about the pollution issue. This case has been well documented.[86] A year later a Brickfield Conference was held in Bedford and again the major issues, but particularly dereliction, were aired.[87] The frustration felt by many at the company's use of the empty pits as commercial assets was likened by one speaker to 'a pick-pocket selling back the wallet after he had emptied it'. With the company in a secure position little was likely to be achieved by debate. As the local MP commented: 'I think it raises a great pitch of enthusiasm and thinking that tends, as the weeks go by, to die away, until nothing is left again but all the excuses we heard before as to why nothing whatever can be done'.[88] But the Conference demonstrated, if such was needed, profound dissatisfaction with the situation and indicated a broadly–based and growing opposition to the environmental impacts of the brick industry in Bedfordshire.

During the next decade the opposition became focused around the debates over the various plans being developed by the County Council which was responsible for the preparation and implementation of plans for mineral working and for waste disposal policy. The County Council was seen, and saw itself, as the authority arbitrating the economic and environmental interests by exercising powers over the extent of clay workings, the location of new works and, by extending its environmental concern, to the issue of air pollution. It both stimulated and indulged the public appetite for participation and afforded environmental interests a platform which they readily seized and which eventually threatened to engulf the brick company. Thus the encouragement of public participation assisted the orchestration of opposition to London Brick, which precipitated the confrontation at the end of the decade.

The County Council prepared both its structure plan[89] covering the whole range of strategic policies for the county and, subsequently, a more detailed Minerals Subject Plan.[90] This had specific proposals for dealing with landscape and pollution problems arising from the development of minerals, of which Oxford Clay was the most important.[91] Public reaction was both predictable and familiar. There was disquiet over the flouting of the planning conditions: 'the companies took acount of restoration costs when working of the areas commenced and they should be made to finish the job off rather than wriggle out of loosely worded agreements'.[92] For this the Council were, in part, to blame in not challenging the company's interpretation of the conditions. 'A reasonable interpretation of the restoration clause would thus seem to be that restoration will take place, but that its standard will depend on materials available and cost to the company. If restoration could be speeded by abolishing charges or even paying for tipping, then, subject to legal advice, the County should challenge LBC.'[93] The principle that the company should pay for restoration was a recurrent theme. This sense of unleashed anger tinged with a feeling of impotence was everywhere: 'The loss of fertile topsoil was a disgrace, the pollution by sulphur and fluorine compounds was an outrage to surrounding villages and the absence of restoration at many worked out pits was a continuing affront to the whole of society.'[94] The demand for intervention by the County

Council was strident and imperative:

> In other countries there is a rapidly advancing movement towards the assessment of the relative value to the public and shareholders of the products of a company. This is judged in relation to the company's total exploitation of all forms of natural resources, i.e. labour, capital, fuel, *land*, water, air and amenity. The County Council could begin to give a lead in this direction by making an audit on some of the extractive industries. The Fletton brick industry is a prime candidate for an early investigation.[95]

Public reaction concentrated largely on questions of landscape and restoration. This reflected the planners' own perception of the major problems as discussed in the planning documents and the public perception of the role and powers of the planning authorities.

Although the County Council, in its various planning documents, extended its environmental concern to the issue of air pollution, this was an area where responsibilities were shared among a number of authorities.[96] These included the three County Councils in the fletton area, seven District Councils, which as Environmental Health Authorities collected information on air quality, the Area Health Authorities responsible for public health, the Alkali Inspectorate and the London Brick Company.[97] In the early 1970s these bodies established a Fletton Brickworks Liaison Committee, whose task was to consider information on air pollution, the prospects of research and technology for pollution control and to recommend action to remedy or to mitigate the effects of pollution. Its first term of reference was 'to keep local authorities and the public generally informed of the work being done on the control of air pollution'. But its decision to keep its minutes and papers confidential made this task difficult. The secrecy, and anodyne press pronouncements emanating from the committee hardly contributed to public knowledge of the issue or created confidence in the activities of the committee. Later, when the conflict with the company raised air pollution as the central issue, the Liaison Committee began to respond to public pressure and played a more active role in developing more comprehensive monitoring of pollution.

Throughout these debates London Brick's defence was restrained, emphasising the efforts being made to deal sensitively with environmental problems and indicating a willingness to cooperate — provided it did not impede the company's production plans. 'We accept that it is the operator's problem to ensure that land is restored effectively and to allow an appropriate after–use'.[98] They were in favour of the review and updating of planning conditions. They were prepared to extend the system of monitoring, 'providing that it can be demonstrated that the work would form an essential part of an overall clinical investigation'.[99] This moderate placatory tone represented the company's efforts to improve its public image and the real efforts it had made to deal with some of the effects of its activities. It indicated the company's vulnerable position, as it was about to present its case for a complete redevelopment programme which would involve a comprehensive revision of the whole operation in the Marston Vale. Public opinion, for long relatively dormant, was at flood tide and was now presented with an opportunity to achieve its objective — the control of London Brick in the interests of the environment. Over many years the company had exercised power through inaction; now it found that that inaction had produced forces which threatened that very power.

The seeds of conflict

It is possible to conceptualise the development of the dereliction and pollution issues in terms of three phases through which they passed. Each phase raises questions about the relative power of the company and its environmental opponents.

The first was a *dormant* phase when the issues gave rise to no conflict. This was a relatively short period after the Second World War when the planning permissions were granted. As the scale of the problem became evident, so the potentiality for conflict emerged and the issues became matters of public concern and debate.

They entered a *passive* phase marked, for example, by the Brickfields Conference and the later debates over the structure plan. If the problems were so obvious why did they not become a matter for public decision making? The explanation for this, as suggested earlier, lies in the superior power which the company enjoyed during the period. It was a company able to supply the nation with cheap bricks at a time of national reconstruction. The private interest of the company was therefore effectively concealed behind claims to support the national interest. 'We are an industrial country, we live by industry and this area is now very largely an industrial one and we hope that nothing . . . will prevent our continued growth and prosperity.'[100] As a result of this overriding national interest the company had been given very lax planning conditions which enabled it to resist efforts to control its activities. Its position was further protected by the lack of conclusive information on the dangers of pollution, enabling the company, supported by the Alkali Inspectorate and the medical authorities, to claim there was no cause for concern. Even if proven, there was no feasible technology to prevent the emissions entering the atmosphere. But the company did not simply depend on its powerful relationship with government authorities. There is some evidence that it was able to influence the emergence of information that might damage its case through tenancy agreements, purchase of farms, and settlements out of court. Its strength was also apparent in the lack of effective opposition. During the passive phase there were complaints; there was public response to the debate on the structure plan; and there was sporadic Press coverage of the problem. But at no time was there a concerted opposition able to mobilise enduring political support or to challenge the company's position.

For all these reasons the company was able to carry on largely unhindered. At the end of the 1970s there was a marked change when the conflict entered its *active* phase and could no longer be contained, but expressed itself in a form demanding resolution through political action. The challenge which it met in 1978 and subsequent years did not just strike suddenly or even unexpectedly. Over the years there had been a subtle shift in the balance of power between corporate and environmental interests. The company's position in the late 1970s was perceptibly weaker and its opponents stronger and more determined. What accounts for this change?

The company's power was largely dependent on factors beyond its control. By the end of the 1970s the national demand for bricks was no longer such a persuasive issue. Although the need for housing remained great, it ceased to be a major national political issue. Public expenditure cuts, which particularly hit the construction industry, brought about a major decline in the number of new housing projects. There was a switch of emphasis towards rehabilitation, and the brick industry was meeting competition from alternative materials. All this made the fletton industry a less critical factor in the national calculation on housing. By the late 1970s overcapacity was the main problem for the brick industry. The fact that cuts in production brought less pollution and a slower clay extraction rate did not diminish the strength of the opposition.

It was claimed that the conditions on the original planning applications, weak as they were, had been abused by the company. The failure to landscape the workings or to conserve the overburden and topsoil provoked criticisms which were only partially stilled when efforts at tree planting were belatedly begun. Above all the policy of making charges for filling the pits, rather than bearing 'reasonable costs', was widely regarded as a cavalier interpretation of the planning conditions, placing corporate profit above environmental benefits. The lack of evidence on the dangers of pollution, for long used as a shield by the company, became a weapon of attack upon it. Evidence was lacking because insufficient monitoring had been undertaken and medical research was inadequate. What evidence there was should have been used not to exonerate the company but to indicate that there were grounds for growing anxiety about health risks, animal disease and crop damage. The secrecy surrounding the company's operations fuelled rumours that information was being witheld. The relationship between the Alkali Inspectorate and the company ensured a monopoly of information about control technology and could, it was argued, inhibit the application of techniques from other industries. Whether or not justified, these feelings were a factor in gaining public sympathy and support for a major offensive against the company.

Opposition was not an isolated event, an attack on the presumed abuses of one company. It was part of a shift in values throughout the advanced industrial countries. The social costs of economic growth were being increasingly debated, and environmental groups were offering a more sustained and coordinated opposition to major companies.

This growing environmental movement is usually seen as a consistent trend, with industry thrown increasingly on the defensive. David Vogel argues from American experience that there are signs of industry resisting the tide and fighting back, using tactics similar to those of its opponents.[101] There is, as we shall see, some support for this line of argument in the case of London Brick, but up to the point where the conflict began there seems to have been a gradual, but accelerating, public hostility towards the company.

As the conflict developed so the issues became more focused. For a long time the problem of dereliction had occupied the most prominent position. It was a visible and obviously growing problem as the pace of clay extraction far exceeded restoration. It was a problem which clearly fell within the competence of land use planning, though the solution lay with the company and not with the local authorities. The authorities sought by persuasion to gain improvements and had marginal successes, but the financial and landfill resources required precluded restoration. Thus the issue of dereliction remained a source of debate which contributed to the political environment of conflict.

It was the problem of air pollution which proved a far more effective political issue. Although the smell was obvious and offensive and the plumes were clearly visible, the problem was less tangible. Here the company was on weak ground as the dangers were unknown, largely unmonitored and only crudely researched. It was possible to fan public disquiet into anxiety and anger that nothing was being done. The environmental groups and, later, the politicians seized on pollution as the key issue, and identified fluoride as the area of specific concern since its dangers were least known and most worrying. This may well have been a non-issue in the sense that there was no danger and no grounds for alarm. But it provided the platform for those who considered the company's power too great and too damaging to local interests. Once the conflict had become politicised the desire to exert power became an end in itself for the company's opponents as well as a means to achieve environmental objectives.

The three decades or so after the Second World War were a period in which London Brick consolidated its power within the fletton industry and created dereliction and pollution largely without interference. In the absence of challenge and with the support of central government, and its agency the Alkali Inspectorate, there was no incentive for the company to do other than produce bricks at the cheapest possible cost. From its viewpoint investment in reclamation or pollution control, even if feasible, would have been unjustified. It could claim that it had made some effort to improve the landscape and was conducting some research into control measures as required by the Alkali Inspectorate. Once brick production became a less salient issue the external support for the company began to weaken. This coincided with a strengthening of elements in the local community intent on exercising more control over the company. This history poses questions of central theoretical relevance to this study. Why was the company opposed so vigorously? How far does the relative power of industry and environmental interests reflect external economic factors? How far are external factors responsible for the outcomes of a conflict between these interests? The theoretical interpretation of this case depends on the answers given to these questions.

In 1978 the company still appeared largely impregnable. Opposition was aroused but awaited an opportunity to measure its strength against the company. That opportunity came first with a local conflict over toxic waste disposal and then with the much larger conflict over the company's plans for the complete redevelopment of its brickmaking activities in Bedfordshire.

Notes

1 Descriptions of the brickmaking process and the historical development of the brickmaking industry will be found in, Alan Cox (1979) *Brickmaking: A History and Gazeteer*, Bedfordshire County Council and Royal Commission on Historical Monuments (England), Survey of Bedfordshire; and Richard Hillier (1981) *Clay that Burns: a history of the fletton brick industry*, London Brick Company Ltd. Collier.

2 Cox (1979) op. cit. p.50.

3 The dry weight of the clay includes 10 per cent water, 5 per cent fuel, 14 per cent chalk, 45 per cent silicon, 16 per cent alumina, and 5.5 per cent iron. The mechanically held water content of around 20 per cent is removed during drying.

4 In small non-fletton brickworks it has been estimated that energy costs are 29 per cent of total production costs. See, Bollard, A,E. (1982) *Brick Work: small plants in the brick industry*, Alternative Industrial Framework for the UK, Report No.3, Intermediate Technology Development Group.

5 The take-over offer of £3½ million was challenged on grounds that the offer was unfair, by a group of ordinary shareholders holding 5.8 per cent of the ordinary stock of Marston Valley Brick Company. They claimed the value should have been much higher given the assets especially of clay, though the offer was 35 per cent over the Stock Exchange quotation. Their challenge was not upheld.

6 Monopolies and Mergers Commission (1976) *Building Bricks: A report on the supply of building bricks*, HMSO, p.32 para.108.

7 Ibid, p.69. para.237.

8 Bollard (1982) op. cit.

9 The fletton industry has low fuel costs but high capital costs. In 1973 LBC's ex-works costs consisted of: manufacturing wage 46 per cent; manufacturing materials (excluding clay) 3 per cent; electricity and fuel 9 per cent; overheads and other costs 43 per cent. Source Monopolies and Mergers Commission (1976) op. cit. p.19. fn. Large kilns with a capacity of 125 million bricks per year represent the development of conventional technology to take advantage of scale economies and a more flexible product mix.

10 Among these innovations were the introduction of fork-lift trucks to handle bricks during production, 'Selfstak' lorries for unitised delivery, and 'Fletliner' rail services for long distance rail haulage.

11 Short time working is expensive since kilns still have to be maintained and fuelled at the same rate, though fewer bricks are made.

12 Wragg, R. and Robertson, J. (1978) *Post war trends in employment*, Research Paper No.3, Department of Employment.

13 Banbury Alton Ltd., The Croydex Co. Ltd., and Midland Structures Ltd. Banbury Alton was sold in 1983.

14 A restructuring of the company in 1982 produced 6 divisions, each with a Managing Director — London Brick Products, Engineering, Property, Landfill, Croydex, and Banbury Alton.

15 Monopolies and Mergers Commission (1976) op. cit.72 para.251.

16 Bedfordshire County Council (1979) *Minerals: Appraisal and Issues*, March Table 2.1., p.16.

17 Bedfordshire County Council (1982) *Oxford Clay Subject Plan* Consultation Draft, May, p.19, para.4.2, Table 4.1: Bedfordshire County Council (1983), Brickfields Sub-Committee, 31 January, Agenda item 4.
18 Bedfordshire County Council (1978) *Minerals: Appraisal and Issues,* op. cit. p.31.
19 Bedfordshire County Council (1972) *County Review Minerals Aspect Report,* Consultation Draft, March, p.21.
20 Bedfordshire County Council (1967) *Bedfordshire Brickfield* op. cit. p.36.
21 Letter on behalf of Minister to Estates Manager, London Brick Company Ltd., 17 July 1952. (No.3 figure 7).
22 The length of time of these early permissions was very long term, possibly 60 years, and the scale was also large. 'The Minister does not consider a permission covering an area of that magnitude is inappropriate, having regard to the scale of brick production and the capital involved in this enterprise.' (letter on behalf of Minister to Managing Director, Eastwoods, 31 July, 1952). (No. 4 figure 7).
23 Bedfordshire County Council (1972) *Minerals Aspect Report* op. cit. p.20.
24 Letter on behalf of Minister to The Clerk, Ampthill RDC, 21 June, 1947.
25 The number of conditions was very small. That granted in 1947 to Marston Valley Company had 4 conditions (No.1, figure 7), that to London Brick in 1949 had 3 (No.2, figure 7), that to London Brick in 1952 had 4 (No.3, figure 7), and that to Eastwoods in 1952 had 5 (No.4, figure 7). This contrasts with the complex set of conditions and the planning agreement that were prepared for the permissions in the new generation works at Stewartby and Ridgmont, which are discussed in later chapters.
26 See note 24.
27 See note 22.
28 For example, a small permission for part of the Brogborough 2 site (No.12 on figure 7) contained 10 conditions applied by Ampthill RDC.
29 Permission granted by Bedfordshire County Council to London Brick Company Ltd., 20 December, 1960, (No.14, figure 7).
30 This scheme covering 50 acres and planting 50,000 trees in 5 years was jointly financed by London Brick (50 per cent), the Countryside Commission (37½ per cent) and Bedfordshire County Council, who managed the scheme and planted the trees (12½ per cent).
31 Bedfordshire County Council (1978) *Minerals: Appraisal and Issues,* op. cit. p.23.
32 See, for example, Marion Shoard (1980) *The Theft of the Countryside,* Temple Smith, London: Joan Davidson and Gerald Wibberley (1977) *Planning and the Rural Environment,* Oxford, Pergamon: Howard Newby (1979) *Green and Pleasant land?,* Harmondsworth, Penguin: Countryside Review Committee, Discussion Papers, especially *The Countryside — Problems and Policies,* 1976 and *Food Production in the Countryside,* 1978, HMSO.
33 See note 24.
34 Bedfordshire County Council (1978) *Minerals: Appraisal and Issues,* op. cit. p.33.
35 Bedfordshire County Council (1972) *Minerals Aspect Report,* p.21.

36 Resolution (23 September 1953) deleting condition 1 of permission for Eastwoods 1952 permission (No.4, figure 7).
37 Ministry of Housing and Local Government Circular 68/65, Appendix B, 1 October 1965, *Derelict Land*.
38 A £3.5 million contract completed in 1973 converted an old clay pit covering 112 acres to farmland using fly ash from the CEGB. But subsequently fly ash proved a valuable resource for making building blocks.
39 Bedfordshire County Council (1967) *Bedfordshire Brickfield*, op. cit. p.36.
40 A former Chairman of the Planning Committee, commenting on a meeting with Sir Ronald 'Brickie' Stewart, commented 'I was appalled to find that London Brick Company wanted to charge NCB 16 shillings a ton to tip. I charged "Brickie" with profiteering and have not discussed the matter with him since'. (Conversation with Harold Trusting, June, 1980).
41 Letter on behalf of the Minister to Estates Manager, London Brick Company Ltd., 26 May 1949 (site 2, figure 7).
42 Bedfordshire County Council, (1952) *County Development Plan, Written Analysis*.
43 Bedfordshire County Council, (1967) *Bedfordshire Brickfield*, op. cit. ch.4.
44 Bedfordshire County Council, (1972) *Minerals Aspect Report*, op. cit.
45 Bedfordshire County Council (1978) *Minerals: Appraisal and Issues*, op. cit.
46 Bedfordshire County Council, (1980) *County Structure Plan*, Policy 66, p.52.
47 Bedfordshire County Council, (1982) *Oxford Clay Subject Plan*, op. cit.
48 Brickworks were registered in 1958.
49 Graham Bennett (1979) 'Pollution Control in England and Wales: A Review', *Environmental Policy and Law*, 5., p.95.
50 Ibid. p.95.
51 Bedfordshire County Council (1960) *Report on Atmospheric Pollution in the Brickworks Valley* (The Brothwood Report), Health Department, 1960.
52 Cremer and Warner (1979) *The Environmental Assessment of the Existing and Proposed Brickworks in the Marston Vale, Bedfordshire*, see Chapter 3 for full discussion.
    Department of the Environment (1980) *Air Pollution in the Bedfordshire Brickfields*. Discussed in Chapter 4.
53 Department of the Environment *102nd Annual Report on Alkali, and C Works 1965*, London, HMSO.
54 Department of the Environment, *108th Annual Report on Alkali, and C Works 1971*, London, HMSO p.54.
55 Department of the Environment, *107th Annual Report on Alkali, and C Works 1970*, London, HMSO p.48.
56 Bedfordshire County Council (1982) *Oxford Clay Subject Plan*, op. cit. p.75.
57 See note 51.
58 Quoted in *Bedfordshire on Sunday*, 15 October 1978.
59 Agate, J.N., Bell, G.H., Boddie, G.F. et al (1949) 'A study of the hazard to man and animals near Fort William, Scotland', Medical Research Council, Memorandum No.22, Industrial Fluorosis, HMSO. The study concluded that effects on human beings were noticeable but did not lead to clinical problems. Children had fewer dental caries than elsewhere in Scotland.

60 Blakemore, F., Bosworth, F.J. and Green, H.H. (1941) *Proceedings of Royal Society of Medicine* 34, 611.
    Blakemore, F., et al (1948) 'Industrial fluorosis of farm animals in England, attributable to the manufacture of bricks, the calcining of ironstone and to enamelling processes', *Journal of Comparative Pathology*, 58, pp.267-301.
61 Burns, K.N. and Allcroft, Ruth (1964) 'Fluorosis in cattle: Occurrence and effects in industrial areas in England and Wales', *Animal Disease Surveys Report* No. 2 PO. 1, Ministry of Agriculture, Fisheries and Food, HMSO, London.
62 Reports of fluorosis occurred elsewhere and at the 1966 inquiry into Redland Bricks application for a brickworks at Woburn Sands in neighbouring Buckinghamshire evidence of cattle fluorosis was produced. One farmer claimed nine cows were affected in 1957 from the Bletchley brickworks. See *Environmental Pollution and Public Health*, 'Planning and Pollution, Areas of Concern', Open University Course PT272, Unit 16, p.34. See also note 53.
63 Brough, A., Parry, M.A., and Whittingham, C.P. (1978) 'The influence of aerial pollution on crop growth', *Chemistry and Industry*, 21 January, pp.51-53.
64 Bedfordshire County Council (1967) *Bedfordshire Brickfield*, op. cit. p.18.
65 See note 30.
66 Quoted in Bedfordshire County Council (1967) *Bedfordshire Brickfield*, op. cit. p.15.
67 Matthew Crenson (1971) *The Un-Politics of Air Pollution: A Study of Non-Decisionmaking in the Cities*, Baltimore, The Johns Hopkins Press.
68 Crenson's argument and criticisms of it are fully discussed in Chapter 6.
69 London Brick Company Ltd. (1979) *Report and Accounts*, p.22.
70 Personal Communication from Lyne and Martin, Public Analysts, Reading, 17 October 1979.
71 J. Bugler 'Bedfordshire Brick', in B.J. Smith (Ed) (1975) *The Politics of Physical Resources*, Penguin, Ch. 4, p.134.
72 *Bedfordshire Times*, 24 November 1972.
73 This case is discussed in Chapter 3.
74 Interview with Peter Morrison of NFU Peterborough.
75 *Bedfordshire on Sunday*, 19 November 1978.
76 Interview with David Dunkley.
77 Dunkley made his claim to *Bedford on Sunday*. James Bristow's claim was given as a personal observation.
78 *Bedfordshire Times*, 9 August 1968.
79 Interview with Mr Oliver of national NFU, London.
80 Ibid.
81 Bedfordshire County Council (1967) *Bedfordshire Brickfield*, op. cit.
82 The reports referred to here are:
    P. Clayton (1970a) 'Brickwork odours — a subjective evaluation of a removal process' — Warren Springs Laboratory, Department of Technology, LR 131 (AP).
    P. Clayton (1970b) 'Brickwork odours — a laboratory investigation of their production, evaluation, and removal' — Warren Springs Laboratory, Department of Technology, LR 122 (AP).
83 J. Brown (1968) *The Un-melting Pot*
    Barr, J. (1964) 'Napoli, Bedfordshire', New Society, 2 April.

R. Skellington (1978) *The Housing of Minority Groups in Bedford;* (1980) *Council house allocation in a multi racial town,* Open University, Faculty of Social Sciences, Occasional Paper Series.

84 Bedfordshire County Council (1972) *Minerals Aspect Report,* op. cit. p.16

85 Alan Cox, (1979) Brickmaking: *A History and Gazetteer,* Bedfordshire County Council, p.59.

86 Porterous, A., Attenborough, K., and Pollitt, C. (1977) *Pollution: The Professionals and the Public,* 'Air Pollution and Visual Amenity', Article 3 'An account of the public inquiry into the appeal by Redland Bricks Ltd.', prepared by The Woburn Sands District Society, The Open University Press, p.77. See also references to the inquiry in Richard Crossman (1975) *Diaries of a Cabinet Minister,* Hamish Hamilton and Jonathan Cape, Vol.1, 1 August 1975, p.310, and Vol.1, p.310, August 1966, p.625.

87 See Bedfordshire Brickfield Conference, Transcript of Proceedings, Bedfordshire County Council, 8 January 1968, p.33.

88 Ibid. p.33.

89 The Bedfordshire County Structure Plan was prepared during 1974-77. Public participation took place in 1976 and the plan was submitted in 1977. It was examined in public at the end of 1977 and finally amended and approved by the Minister in 1980. A full discussion of the history of this plan is given in Andrew Blowers (1980) *The Limits of Power,* Oxford, Pergamon, Ch. 7.

90 Bedfordshire County Council (1978) *Minerals, Appraisal and Issues,* op. cit. The plan itself took the form of specific policies for each mineral excavated in the county.

91 Bedfordshire County Council (1982) *Oxford Clay Subject Plan* Draft. The plan was finally adopted by the Council in 1984. May.

92 Bedfordshire County Council (1978) *Minerals, Appraisal and Issues,* Public *Consultation* — submission by Elstow Parish Council, p.23.

93 Ibid, submission for Ramblers' Association, p.88.

94 Ibid, submission for Bedfordshire Preservation Society, p.83.

95 Ibid. p.70.

96 The powers of the various authorities responsible for pollution control are discussed in Chapter 8.

97 The full membership is: County Councils — Bedfordshire, Cambridgeshire, Buckinghamshire; District Councils — North Bedfordshire Borough, Mid-Bedfordshire, Aylesbury Vale, Milton Keynes Borough, Fenland, Huntingdon, and Peterborough City; Milton Keynes Development Corporation; Area Health Authorities; Health and Safety Executive (Alkali Inspectorate); and London Brick Company.

98 Bedfordshire County Council (1978) *Minerals, Appraisal and Issues.* Public Consultation, p.114.

99 Letter from J. Rowe, Deputy Chairman, London Brick, to Clerk of Bedfordshire County Council, 4 July, 1973.

100 Bedfordshire Brickfields Conference, Transcript of Proceedings, Statement by J.P. Bristow for London Brick, 8 January, 1968, p.6.

101 David Vogel (1981) 'How business responds to opposition, corporate political strategies during the 1970's', draft paper.

CHAPTER 3
THE OPENING ROUND —
THE FAILURE OF NEGOTIATION

'Now I saw in my dream, that just as they had ended this talk, they drew nigh to a very miry slough that was in the midst of the plain; and they being heedless, did fall suddenly into the bog. The name of the slough was Despond.'

(John Bunyan, *Pilgrim's Progress*)

The 'L' field debate

The brickfields issue — or rather bundle of issues — emerged from its passive to its active phase during 1977-8. Until that time there had been a groundswell of debate about dereliction, pollution and the failure of the company to respond to environmental interests. From time to time this was punctuated by deeper public concern, as at the time of the Brickfield Conference, or over the problem of fluorosis. But at no time did the issue reach the decision making agenda. During 1977 and 1978 the company, for the first time since the early 1950s, wanted new planning permissions in order to redevelop its major brickworks in the Marston Vale. This provided the stimulus which brought latent public hostility to life. The issue began with a phase of *negotiation* as opponents and advocates of the company took up their positions. Certain compromises were reached, but the central problem of pollution could not be settled by compromise, and so the issue deepened into conflict and eventually into *confrontation*. It was a relatively minor and peripheral matter which served as the spark to light the tinder which was to inflame the local community for a period of three years, 1978-1981. The incident was significant in that it raised public consciousness about the role of the company just at the time when London Brick was about to bring forward its major redevelopment plan.

Tipping of notifiable wastes (toxic materials in liquid form) had been undertaken in a brick pit near Elstow village just south of Bedford, where clay extraction had ceased in 1969.[1] Tipping was allowed in part of this site not covered by conditions excluding notifiable wastes. By 1976 this site was saturated, and unauthorised tipping, including notifiable wastes, began elsewhere on the site and was discovered by routine inspection. For some time there were complaints about the tip from the residents of Elstow. 'These complaints mainly allege nuisance from smell and flies and have become more vociferous, particularly since the acceptance of liquid wastes has increased.'[2] It was clearly in the interests of the company which offered a comprehensive waste disposal service to industry to regularise its tipping and, if possible, find an alternative, less controversial site.

Such a site was 'L' field, an exhausted clay pit near the Stewartby works covering 77 hectares (190 acres) which had been worked for clay between 1947 and 1963. A legal agreement in 1974 had allowed tipping of industrial and domestic waste here but excluded notifiable wastes. Contracts had been signed with Northamptonshire in 1975 and, more significantly, with the Greater London Council (GLC) in 1977 for domestic waste to be brought to 'L' field.[3] Under the Control of Pollution Act, 1974 a site licence for tipping was required, which enabled the County Council to exercise control over the tipping operation. The County Council, since 1974 responsible for all waste disposal, was faced with a major problem in the northern part of the county where its landfill sites, one of which was Elstow, were nearing exhaustion. It so happened that there was further room at Elstow if the County Council could secure the land from London Brick. Thus three major problems could be solved if toxic waste dumping could be transferred to 'L' field. The village of Elstow would be relieved of a major nuisance attributed to toxic dumping; London Brick would be able to continue the disposal of toxic wastes from surrounding counties and the County Council could gain sufficient land to solve its landfill problems in the north of the county. All that was needed was for London Brick to trade its land at Elstow for a permission to dump toxic wastes at 'L' field.

A proposal was accordingly drawn up allowing London Brick to dispose white and grey notifiable wastes in the part of 'L' field capable of taking the current 57,000 gallons a day.[4] This could rise to possibly 120–150,000 gallons per day, with the domestic waste acting as 'blotting paper'. In return London Brick were prepared to provide the County Council an option to lease or to purchase their land at Elstow for domestic refuse disposal. In addition a Department of the Environment Research Station staffed by the UK Atomic Energy Research Establishment (UKAERE) would be established to monitor the interaction of the various wastes dumped in 'L' field.

The proposal unleashed a storm of criticism. Objections to the idea of toxic waste disposal were made by local villages and amenity groups. In particular Bedfordshire Action Committee Against Pollution (BACAP) argued the nuisance caused would be far greater than had been experienced at Elstow; that enforcement of conditions would be difficult; and that Bedfordshire should not be made responsible for the country's 'foetid industrial droppings' and could well become a giant 'Pitsea'[5] in future.[6] The mention of the UKAERE gave rise to quite unjustifiable apprehensions about nuclear waste dumping. Thus what seemed a perfectly sensible and desirable package deal to the Council's officers became, in the eyes of some local interests, a suspicious and even sinister proposal.

These feelings were echoed by some members of the County Council. The report to the Environmental Services Committee, which had recommended the deal, received objections and criticism. Though it was passed by a majority at the committee stage it was referred to the full Council for a final decision.[7] At the Council meeting on 20 April, 1978 the various doubts and fears were aired — the probable escalation of toxic dumping at 'L' field; the problem of controlling the operation; the heavy and dangerous traffic that would be generated; and the general environmental nuisance that would be caused. The Conservative Leader of the Council, Philip Hendry, who was later to play a prominent role as the adversary of London Brick, described the company's operations as 'the unacceptable face of capitalism'. His attempt to prevent the proposal and to obtain conditions 'which are more capable of being enforced than those before this Council today and give greater protection to the interests and safety of the public of Bedfordshire' was unsuccessful.[8] A motion to restrict expansion of the operations at 'L' field and to prevent more dangerous wastes than those envisaged in the site licence was carried. In this preliminary skirmish the antagonism towards the company was manifested, local opinion had been mobilised and prominent members of the County Council had declared their position. This made the company's next moves more difficult to negotiate and exposed them not merely to the planning committee but to the full County Council of 83 members.

First stirrings — summer and autumn 1978

'No part of the Great War compares in interest with its opening . . . the first collision was a drama never surpassed'.

(Winston Churchill)

As in all great conflicts, the opening stages of the battle between London Brick and its opponents established the framework for all the later developments. The positions were taken up, the key issues were identified and the room for manoeuvre was circumscribed. It is clear that right from the outset, however, both sides were in reality in entrenched positions, though each appeared willing to make small concessions. There was a willingness to negotiate but, when compromise proved impossible, both sides were prepared to adopt uncompromising lines. Although the conflict involved various interest, and shifted its emphasis from one issue to another, the basic objectives of the two sides remained unaltered. Ultimately it was the impact of external circumstances that altered the political environment decisively and brought about a resolution of the conflict.

London Brick's terms

By the summer of 1978 the proposals of London Brick were clear. They required permission for two new works, one in the south of the Vale to replace Ridgmont, the other in the centre as a successor to their largest works at Stewartby. (See Figure 1.2, Chapter 1). Each works would be constructed in two units, each unit having a production capacity of 5 million bricks per week. The units would consist of four Hoffman kilns (with a capacity of 1.25 million bricks per week), regarded as the economically optimum size, linked to a chimney 400 feet above the surrounding terrain. Each unit would incorporate provision for a third flue which could handle gases from the 'main dryer' and 'coming hot' chambers, the stages at which the gases were emitted from the kilns (Figure 3.1). The third flues would only be constructed, however, if monitoring and research proved that pollution was harmful and if a suitable means of treating the gases could be discovered. In addition to the kilns and chimneys there would be 16 loading sheds, four press sheds, and two pan sheds and ancillary buildings at each new works. The proposed layout is shown in Figure 3.2, and some idea of the scale of the new developments can be gained from Figure 3.3.[9]

In return for permissions for these new works, London Brick appeared willing to make a number of significant concessions. But these were more apparent than real, and it is clear from the correspondence that the company's position was largely predetermined. Indeed, it is interesting to note how little its position changed during the course of the debate. They first approached the planning officials of the County Council in August 1977. A year later informal meetings occurred between the company and the Chairman of the Environmental Services Committee, Councillor Keith White. In a letter dated 10 October 1978, the County Planning Officer

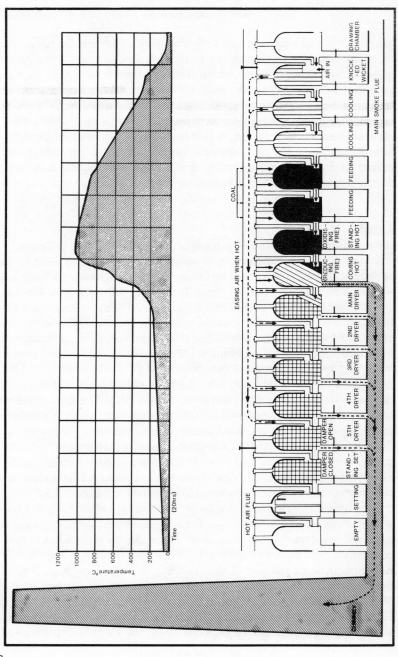

60

welcomed the proposals 'as an opportunity to secure important environmental improvements to this part of the Marston Vale'. He outlined the improvements he would expect.[10] Three issues were to dominate the conflict: the siting of the new works in the south of the Marston Vale; the problem of dereliction and restoration; and the question of anti-pollution measures. On the first, the site of the Ridgmont replacement works, the company appeared to be flexible. They were prepared to consider four possible sites (see Figure 3.4). One of these, a site in an excavated pit, seemed mutually acceptable to the company and the planning officials and to offer more planning benefits and have fewer planning objections than the others, but it had aroused vociferous local objections from the residents of the nearby large village of Cranfield. The company professed its indifference on the question of siting and was quite willing for the planning authority to make the choice. In this way the company could appear quite flexible and prepared to accommodate local pressures.

On the second issue, the problem of dereliction, the company was already prepared to entertain a number of concessions long sought by the County Council. As part of the redevelopment programme, three existing but disused works would be demolished and landscaped, topsoil would be carefully removed, and the existing planning permissions wouuld be modified to ensure 'stand-off zones' between clay extraction areas and nearby villages. The company was prepared to enter into a Section 52 Planning Agreement[11] which would commit it to a whole series of environmental improvements in the Vale. Thus, even before serious negotiations began, the company had demonstrated its willingness to accept a more sensitive

---

Figure 3.1: The brickmaking process
Source: Department of the Environment, *Air Pollution in the Bedfordshire Brickfields*, Directorate of noise, clean air and waste, 6/80, Figure 1, 1980
The diagram shows the kiln cycle in a Hoffman kiln. The bricks remain in each chamber and pass through the various stages indicated. The 'green' bricks are set in an empty chamber and then dried, a process which takes about 120 hours. Warm air from the cooling chambers is conducted through the drying chambers. Drying and combustion gases are carried down into the stream flues and out via the chimney. Once dried there is a rapid rise in temperature during the 'coming hot' phase. Once 'hot' cold air is admitted to 'ease' the bricks. Subsequently coal is fed in to achieve the necessary soaking time of about 35 hours above 900°C. The fired bricks are then cooled and withdrawn. It takes about 10–14 days to dry, fire and cool the bricks. A typical time-temperature curve is superimposed above the diagram. Sulphur oxides are released when the temperature rises above 250°C, with the main emissions between 450°C and 600°C, and fluorides are emitted at temperatures up to 900°C. The diagram indicates that the majority of polluting emissions occur during the 'main dryer' and 'coming hot' stages of the process.

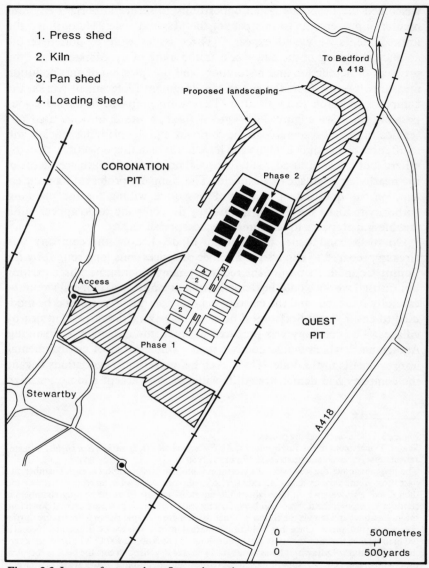

1. Press shed
2. Kiln
3. Pan shed
4. Loading shed

To Bedford
A 418

Proposed landscaping

CORONATION
PIT

Phase 2

Access

QUEST
PIT

Phase 1

Stewartby

A 4118

0   500metres
0   500yards

Figure 3.2: Layout of proposed new Stewartby works
Source: Bedfordshire County Council, *Oxford Clay, Subject Plan,* Draft, 1982, **appendix,**
Figure A3.1

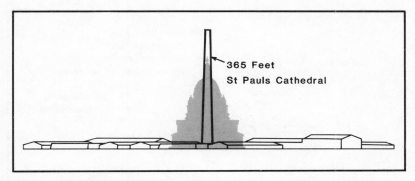

Figure 3.3: Scale of new works

treatment of the landscape as a condition for acceptance of the planning permissions. Although this was, later, to be argued as a major concession, it was not wrung from the company by negotiation but conceded at the outset.[12] But the major issue of restoration by the importation of waste material would still be dependent on terms that were commercially acceptable to the company.

On the third issue in the controversy, the problem of air pollution, the company was not proposing any concessions. It simply stated its position which was to be reiterated with monotonous regularity throughout the debate: 'The replacement brickworks will be designed to incorporate all the current requirements of the Alkali Inspectorate and, of course, provision will be made to enable the future installation of equipment to meet any subsequent requirement of that Inspectorate.'[13] The company regarded the Alkali Inspector as the authority to which it should respond on the pollution question and, in providing for a third flue in the new works, it was conforming precisely to his requirements. At no point in the debate did London Brick deviate from its determination to secure permissions which would avoid the need for costly, and, in its view unnecessary and impracticable, anti-pollution devices.

The Council's reaction
In these early stages the planning officials undertook the negotiations with the company, seeking endorsement for their views through the planning committee. One of the questions raised in this study is the extent to which

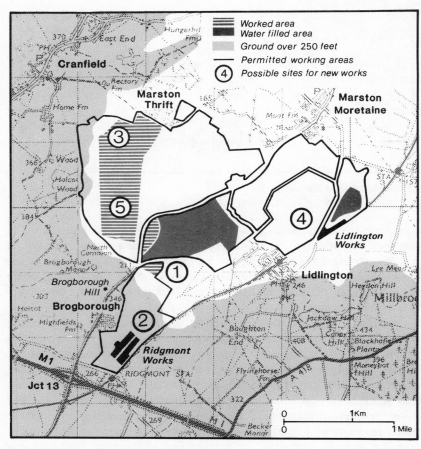

Figure 3.4: Sites for the Ridgmont works
Source: Bedfordshire County Council, planning department

officials are able to exercise power by virtue of their relationship with both
the company and the politicians. Does this position provide them with the
information and influence that enables them to secure their preferences, or
are they merely acting as intermediaries reflecting the state of conflict
between opponents?

Apart from the informal discussions between the company and the
Chairman of the Environmental Services Committee (ESC) the early stages

of debate within the County Council were conducted through the Planning Advisory Group (PAG), an informal body consisting of members and officers who undertook detailed study of specific issues in order to make policy recommendations to the main committee. This group held a series of meetings during the autumn of 1978, focused around the Minerals Subject Plan but entirely devoted to the negotiations with London Brick and its forthcoming planning applications. Here the political reactions to the proposals could be gauged and the council's negotiating stance identified. The general basis of negotiation would seek to relate 'improvements that are needed, to requirements of the London Brick Company'.[14] From the Council's point of view there was a need to modify the existing permissions, to achieve landscape improvements and to reduce air pollution. These might be secured in return for permissions which would secure the long term operation of London Brick in the Marston Vale. It was clear that the decisions being contemplated would affect the area well into the next century.

Undoubtedly the issue which most concerned the planning officials was dereliction and restoration, where there had been no progress and much deterioration since excavations began. 'In short, the restoration problem in the Oxford Clay area is massive, and its scale dwarfs the problems elsewhere in the country. The options open to the County Council vary from adopting a passive role, accepting the London Brick Company view and leaving restoration entirely in the hands of the operator, to the adoption of a positive role involving the purchase of pits and eventual implementation of schemes.'[15] Positive action might include modifying existing permissions, challenging the interpretation of conditions in the courts, seeking the importation of waste from elsewhere, coordinating action with other authorities, seeking government assistance, and financing restoration schemes. The planners concluded that without the company's cooperation, action through the courts would be protracted and revolve around the interpretation of ambiguous conditions. Any attempt to purchase and lease sites would require considerable investment by the Council, and the prospect of a tax on the operator would require government action. The planning officials clearly felt that progress was more likely where the voluntary agreement of the company could be assured and which would not involve the Council in expenditure. The best hope lay in the company's willingness to review and update its existing planning consents without payment of compensation. This should be taken as the starting point for negotiations which would promote short term restoration, identify pits for imported wastes, and rationalise existing workings to avoid impinging on villages in the Vale. Recourse to the courts might be held in reserve and the Council might make 'more forceful overtures to Central Government, British Rail and potential "exporting" authorities, especially on the need to create a more favourable climate for transporting waste material.'[16]

A renegotiation of existing permissions was outlined (see Figure 3.5).

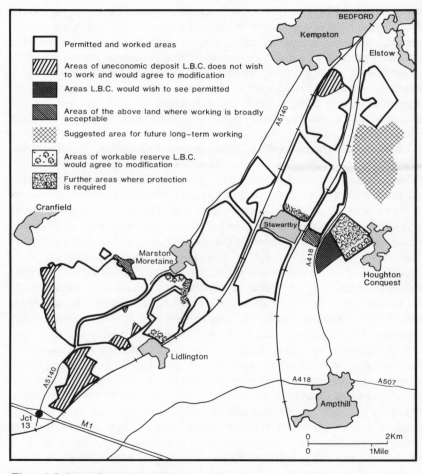

Figure 3.5: Areas of negotiation, 1978
Source: Bedfordshire County Council, planning department

Areas which London Brick no longer needed were deleted and areas without permission which the company would like to work were identified. 'Stand-off' areas near the villages of Stewartby, Marston Moretaine, Lidlington and Houghton Conquest would meet one of the Council's major concerns. The offer to the company of a 'consultation area' covering a wide area to the east of existing permissions where future development would be restricted in order to protect the Oxford Clay reserve was put forward as a 'negotiating stance' but found little favour with councillors even though it was revived and agreed over three years later. Contemporary restoration schemes covering the whole area would also be negotiated with the company. Although regarded as a major step forward and a positive gain to the Council in return for the planning permissions, these proposals represented a position the company was perfectly willing to yield. While bringing some relief to hard–pressed villages, and the promise of better landscaping, it could not guarantee effective restoration of the pits unless vast quantities of waste could be found on terms acceptable to the company.

The air pollution issue was to prove more intractable. The planning officers proposed that 'it would be possible to include a policy in the plan requiring either facilities for, or the actual installation of, equipment to remove any noxious or offensive elements from new brickworks'.[17] But they regarded their status as limited, since it was the Alkali Inspector that had legal standing on pollution control. Arguably, however, the Council could 'do more to draw attention to the brickfield pollution problem with the aim of persuading the Inspectorate to adopt a more positive and effective stance'.[18] The Council could refuse permission on grounds of unacceptable pollution, but to do so it would require support from an independent expert if it was to sustain its case. A consultant would have to answer two questions — is it technically possible to reduce pollution and is it practical financially to advocate control measures given the possible economic effects on brick-making?

In this early stage of negotiation a number of points were already clear. London Brick had more or less settled terms on which it was pre-pared to negotiate. These terms were largely acceptable to the planning officials since they offered the prospect of greater local authority involve-ment and control through the renegotiation of the existing planning permis-sions and agreement over a number of environmental matters. The com-pany was apparently indifferent to the precise site for the Ridgmont works while the planners preferred a site in an existing clay pit known as 'Marston Thrift' near the village of Cranfield. On the air pollution issue the company was leaning on the support of the Alkali Inspector, who had approved tall stacks as the best practicable means of abatement. The planning officials were prepared to seek outside advice but they were not noticeably anxious on the matter. It was public opinion and the views of the elected members of the Council that would thrust the pollution issue forward as the key issue that was to dominate the debate over the next two years. In these early months public and political views were being crystallised and all the possible implications of the redevelopment proposals were being explored.

The emergence of pressure groups

Over the years public opinion had occasionally been stirred into life, especially when opportunities for participation arose. The Press had maintained an interest in the company's operations, contributing to the general climate of suspicion and even hostility towards the visible damage caused by the extraction of clay, and the potential hazards of pollution. But the outbursts tended to be ephemeral, opinion was disorganised with long periods of quiescence. The problem of Elstow and 'L' field had provided BACAP with a focus for its pressure and, as the scale and local impact of the company's proposals became clear during 1978 other local pressure groups flared into life. The Press renewed their interest and the local papers covered both specific issues and provided extensive features on London Brick. The development of public opinion through pressure groups and the media became a most potent weapon in the hands of those who wished, for a variety of reasons, to oppose the company's plans and to ensure that permission was granted only with stringent conditions on air pollution.

The emergence of opposition in the form of pressure groups introduces a further theoretical question for this study. Was their influence and effectiveness dependent on the pressure they could exert through the organisation of support and the action of individuals or was it simply a reflection of the company's relative vulnerability at this point?

Once the company's plans were announced in September 1978, the local action groups had specific targets to aim for. BACAP had already succeeded in their battle over the Elstow pit and could now take up more general pollution issues. In nearby Houghton Conquest another ad hoc group with the onomatopoeic acronym GASP (Group Action to Stop the Pit), led by the charismatic Ray Young, began a campaign against the company's plans to extract clay from pit 81 adjacent to the village (see Chapter 1, Figure 2). The group hoped that, as part of the renegotiation of the planning permissions, this land could be exchanged for land nearby, but further from the village.

At the very least they hoped to achieve a 'stand–off' zone. Over in Cranfield another action group, The Cranfield Action Committee (CAC), also led by a personable figure, Trevor Barber, focused opposition to the proposal to build a new works near the village in the Marston Thrift. CAC pointed out that the site was only a mile away, and owing to the rising ground the chimney would only be 160 feet above the village.

The local parish councils in the area also began to react to the proposals. On 15 December a public meeting attended by 43 people from the parishes was held at Marston Moretaine. A major issue was the siting of the new works, over which there was clear disagreement. While Cranfield argued that the Marston Thrift site would disfigure a beautiful area other speakers opposed sites close to their villages. Those villages most dependent on the industry for employment — Marston Moretaine, Brogborough and Stewartby — favoured the company's proposals since they offered future job security. Already the internal politics of the Brickfields was illustrating the diverse interests involved; the company could take some comfort from the divisions evident and the support it received from its dependent villages. Although the employment issue played little part in the early debate it was to prove a decisive influence on its concluding stages.

The divisions evident at the Marston meeting were clearly straining relationships between the various pressure groups. A meeting designed to coordinate opposition to the company had been called off on the grounds that CAC's campaign was one of expediency and self-interest. BACAP claimed that 'the Cranfield Group is more or less in the pockets of LBC and that so long as they get what they want they don't care about the rest of the problem'.[19] Trevor Barber's response seemed to justify this view: 'I think we are going to get what we want because we are prepared to talk to London Brick, to meet them in the corridors . . . I have found London Brick very helpful. I think the villains of the piece are the politicians. I think it is awful some of the things they have decided behind our backs.'[20] With each action group fighting its own corner and little prospect of a combined and united effort a group less based on specific local issues able to orchestrate a more generalised opposition was needed. Such a group was shortly to emerge and become the main focus of opposition to the company.

The growth of public concern

These more general concerns were expressed at the Marston meeting and were the subject of the various Press reports that were published during the autumn. Several reports reviewed the problem as a whole and took a critical and sceptical view of London Brick. The hostility of the media to the company is a noticeable feature of this case. It suggests two possible explanations. One is that the media was, largely on its own initiative, articulating a long standing and deeply held resentment against the company's neglect of the environment. The other is that the media was responding to influence and that London Brick was less successful in promoting its cause, whereas the company's opponents showed considerable resource in exploiting the opportunities presented for publicity. These explanations are not mutually exclusive and both appear plausible at different points in the story.

Bedfordshire on Sunday, a free newspaper run by Frank Branston, an investigative journalist, ran a major review article exposing the company's past neglect, and claiming that London Brick was 'pretty well alone in interpreting the condition of their planning consents as meaning that filling the pits is dependent on there being organisations willing to pay a charge for the use of the pits as a dumping ground'.[21] The article reviewed the various deals with farmers which had helped to suppress the pollution issue and quoted medical opinion that contradicted the more complacent interpretations made on the research evidence by the official medical experts. Similar ground was covered in *The Guardian*, the one national newspaper which took a consistent interest in the issue and adopted a highly critical stance towards LBC. In two articles it underlined the lack of medical research, lack of effective monitoring and lack of concern felt despite growing evidence of dangers to animals and people from surveys produced in the United States.[22] The more traditional local weeekly newspaper, the *Bedfordshire Times*, with its stablemate the *Bedford Record*, ran articles on various aspects of the problem during the autumn of 1978 covering local meetings, and new reserch findings on crop yields.[23] A third local newspaper, the free *Bedfordshire Journal*, also joined in what appeared to be a campaign of remarkable unanimity against the company, publishing stories which challenged statements from the Fletton Brickworks Liaison Committee and which followed developments in local protests.[24]

All these newspapers highlighted a story which was to have a major impact on the environmentalists' campaign. A local farmer, Peter Goode, owner of Brogborough Manor Farm near the Ridgmont works, claimed that his pedigree cattle were suffering from damaging fluorosis. As *The Guardian* graphically put it, one cow 'rapidly took on the bovine appearance of a Belsen victim'.[25] Pictures of stricken cows were published and farmer Goode threatened to sue the company for damages. He asserted that London

Brick had previously offered to rent him a 259 acre farm in Buckingham provided he dropped any claim for compensation for the loss of cows. The deal was rejected and was a major factor in Peter Goode's sustained and relentless campaign against the company. He devoted most of his time to building up a formidable case against the company, collecting evidence from a variety of sources — academic and medical reports, company reports, Press cuttings and government publications. He was articulate, single-minded and possessed powers of persuasion and organisation which enabled him to gather together a group of people who were to provide London Brick with unrelenting and sophisticated opposition over the next three years.

Throughout the autumn of 1978 both the company and the county planners still appeared ready to negotiate, but flexibility was rapidly diminishing. It appeared that a mutually acceptable agreement on dereliction might emerge through the proposed Section 52 Agreement. For the moment this issue, though much favoured by the county planners, was pushed into the background. As a new year opened the force of public and political opinion had placed two other issues firmly on the agenda for debate. One was the problem of the site for the new Ridgmont works, the company's first priority in its redevelopment programme. The other, more far reaching and longer lasting, was the issue of pollution control. These two issues were the subject of an informal but significant meeting at County Hall, Bedford, in early January, 1979.

1979 — The conflict deepens

Public opinion

During the early months of 1979 the County Council groped its way towards its first tentative decisions on the company's proposals. These concerned the site of the new Ridgmont works and the problem of air pollution. Throughout this period the climate of public opinion was being influenced by successive Press reports and by the local pressure groups. Articles in the newspapers covering the wider issues of the proposals continued to be produced. One, by *Counter Press* based on Milton Keynes, was virulent in its hostility to the company describing it as 'one of the old breed of unreconstructed, unashamed capitalist exploiters'.[26] More influential were the sober local and national papers such as the *Bedfordshire Times* covering the problem of inadequate monitoring and throwing doubt on the claims made about the harmlessness of current pollution levels.[27]

The Guardian, in common with local papers, ran a story about health checks on brickworks employees based on the anxiety of one employee with symptoms similar to those found in cattle suffering from fluorosis: 'It's like having toothache in my legs all the time. My muscles seem completely bound up.' As a result of these claims and a list of 12 fellow sufferers, the Health and Safety Executive decided to undertake checks on the air and dust at the works. The checks apparently revealed that fluoride levels were 100 times lower than the recommended individual exposure level. But, opponents countered, the safety levels accepted by the Alkali Inspectorate were 100 times above what some American scientists now considered to be safe. As always, the guidelines were questionable, and the monitoring unpublished, leaving the way open for claim and counter claim.

One of the most forthright attacks on the company was presented by Thames TV in a programme entitled 'Something in the Air' transmitted on 6 April, 1979. This covered the well worn ground of past settlements with farmers, lack of comprehensive monitoring, and the controversy over the effects of pollutants and acceptable levels. It poured doubt on the company's claim that fluorides were harmless, emphasising the secrecy with which it conducted its operations:

London Brick Company own all the brickworks in the Marston Valley. We asked them to take part in this film. They declined to be interviewed, but gave us information on the company and the brick burning process. They told us how much fluorine leaves the chimneys. But although they have figures for fluorine levels in the air surrounding the brickworks, they would not let us have those figures. They simply say that the levels of fluorine are no cause for alarm.

The programme created a powerful image of local environmental campaigners combating an indifferent and secretive industrial giant.

The gathering propaganda of London Brick's opponents drew a response. In a Press statement printed in the local newspapers the company stated:

London Brick Company is most concerned that the Thames Television report 'Something in the Air' . . . may have caused needless anxiety by giving a distorted view of the situation and by ignoring important facts on emissions from the chimneys.

It went on to quote 'authoritative' statements and research on human and cattle health reinforcing its claims that the levels were harmless, and denied that there was any secrecy about its monitoring statistics which had been discussed with Thames TV. London Brick was now drawn into the public debate, and over the next months made increasing efforts to defend its position by public appearances of its managing director rather than simply relying on statements about the safety of its operations and the benefits of the new works.

Locally, the pressure groups were stepping up their campaigns. Ray Young, Chairman of GASP based on Houghton Conquest, had conducted a detailed correspondence with the Department of the Environment (DoE) and the County Council, accusing the latter of a 'furtive approach' in conducting its negotiations with London Brick in secret.[28] Geoffrey Cowley, the County Planning Officer, like London Brick over Thames TV, was stung into reacting, 'There has been no more secrecy in our discussions with the company than there would be in any possible application for a new house, a factory or whatever.'[29] Young responded by accusing the County Council of failing to challenge the operation of the post-war planning conditions and detailing the public concerns about inactivity on the Council's part. 'Can you blame them for mistrusting any sort of reassurances when the record tells an entirely different story?'[30] This correspondence reflected a widely held view that not only was London Brick, a capitalist concern whose motive was profit, indifferent to its environmental impact, but the County Council, responsible for the public interest in the environment, had manifested a singular lack of energy in asserting that interest.

Ray Young portrayed the political bargaining process in which the concerns of Houghton Conquest were only a small part of a much wider theatre of negotiation.

> The whole point is, London Brick Company are negotiating on many levels for many things. We can't divorce this pit from other negotiations going on for new brickworks, or pollution control, for waste disposal, for the erection of toxic treatment plant, and so on. There's an awful lot of dealing goes on, behind closed doors. It's not illegal, but the whole point is London Brick Company will not make a proposal public until they've first gone to the Bedfordshire County Council and said 'This is what we want to do. How does this proposal fit into your plans?' Bedfordshire County Council may say 'No, we don't like it too much, you'd better go back and think about it again.' Or, perhaps, 'We can do a deal on two different things: you enter a Section 52 Agreement on this particular pit and we'll let you have your brickworks', and so on. It's not just a simple question of going to the County Council and saying, 'Stop this pit, and tell London Brick Company to leave it alone', because it just won't work like that. You've got to deal on something else. This is the compromise part of it.

This showed an impressive insight into the developing debate and the processes at work and proved also to be prophetic. Ray Young argued the role of the local group was to press its own concern, not to become submerged in the wider debate that was being conducted throughout the brickfields.

This marked the climax of the GASP campaign. Little more was heard of it, and Ray Young left the village shortly afterwards. The village viewpoint was left to the parish council. But the group had left its mark on the debate. In the negotiations that followed the possibility of an exchange of land was considered, which would mean the company would abandon their interest in pit 81. This proved impossible, but in the subsequent Section 52 Agreement one of the proposals was the revocation of existing planning permissions, including pit 81, and their substitution by new conditions which, among other things, would ensure adequate screening and a 'stand-off' zone between the workings and the village.

At the other end of the Marston Vale the Cranfield Action Committee focused on the problem of the site for the new Ridgmont works. They, too, had drawn blood, for London Brick announced that it preferred the site at the top of Brogborough Hill (site 2 on Figure 3.4) near the existing works, 'on environmental grounds'—though it had previously seemed happy to accept the county planners' preference for a site in the excavated part of the Brogborough No.2 pit (site 5). This drew a reaction from Councillor Hendry: 'I do think the company are a bit daft to have asked the Council for advice where to put the works and then go completely against it when it is given'.[31] This put the Council in the invidious position which several councillors had feared — of either accepting the company's preference or selecting their own and leaving themselves open to public criticism from CAC.

Dramatis personae

One of the problems with some theories of power is that the role of individual action is either neglected or discounted. Individual action is seen as contingent on the role of interests, or peripheral to a course of events beyond individual control. Theoretically, the possibility that individuals can define a conflict, influence its development and determine its conclusion cannot simply be discounted. Therefore, a question raised by this study is whether individual action plays a determining role or is conditioned by events. Why do certain individuals assume leading roles? Do they believe their actions are significant? In other words, does individual action matter in a conflict of power?

During these early months of 1979 most of the actors who were to figure prominently in the debate had emerged and adopted an attitude towards the conflict. Some had not finally made up their minds, but the trend of their thinking was clear. Once a position has been adopted it is difficult to draw back especially if public credibility is at stake. Up to the point when a choice is made an actor is open to influence from all sources to make up his mind. Once the choice is made he is seeking information that will reinforce his adopted position — he selects evidence, emphasising that which favours his cause, discounting or undermining that which points in another direction.

Of the county officials two were particularly prominent. Although Geoffrey Cowley, the Chief Planning Officer, put his name to all reports and favoured the company he left most of the running to his Deputy and (in 1981) his successor, *Tony Griffin*. Mr Griffin was anxious to make significant environmental gains, achieve greater planning control for the future, and ensure that the matter was decided locally without the necessity for the company to appeal to the Secretary of State. He was dubious about the Council's role in pollution control. With these objectives in mind he favoured detailed negotiation with the intention of wresting significant gains from the company through agreement and planning conditions. He was anxious to avoid a breakdown in negotiations which might force the company to appeal or which might vitiate investment plans of great long term benefit to the county. Though cynical about London Brick's strategy he was opposed to the environmentalist lobby which he regarded as élitist, unrealistic and likely to jeopardise the outcome. The Deputy County Secretary, *John Dawson*, was immersed in the minutiae of planning law, and presented an inscrutable, enigmatic public image notable for his precise but idiosyncratic turn of phrase. He was responsible for the detailed legal negotiations and for ensuring that the Council's interests were protected. On legal points he was virtually unassailable but it was possible to perceive in him a pragmatic if cautious attitude towards the negotiations.

Among the politicians *Councillor Philip Hendry*, leader of the dominant Conservative Group (71 of 83 members of the Council) played the leading role. Although not a member of the ESC he took from the outset a deep interest in the affair, possibly because it affected his brickfield constituents (in Stewartby and Wootton). He was anxious to retain his prominence in a matter which dominated the Council's affairs for three years. He was highly suspicious of the company's motives and concerned to refuse permission for new works unless there was adequate pollution control. He argued 'We must use this as the one-off opportunity that we get to put all the conditions attached to the planning that we want'.[32] He appeared wary of his Deputy Leader and Chairman of ESC, *Councillor Keith White*, a Luton member. Councillor White was intellectual, naturally sympathetic to a major private enterprise, willing to undertake protracted negotiation and consultation, and concerned that everyone should have time to make up his mind. His wish to be seen to be even-handed was a handicap and combined with an occasional diffidence and failure to take opportunities could prove fatal to his cause. On occasion he revealed passion, conviction and force of argument but his performances lacked consistency and contributed to a major defeat later in the debate. Of the other Conservatives two were significant figures. One, *Councillor Michael Kemp*, whose constituency covered the southern part of the Vale (Cranfield, Marston Moretaine and Lidlington), possessed the critical power of a legal mind but also its tendency to equivocation, at least in the early stages of the conflict. Later, when his seat was at stake, he revealed a subtle, determined and ultimately decisive ability to grasp opportunity. *Councillor Allan Chapman*, the third brickfields member representing the Ridgmont area and the middle class districts around Aspley Guise and Woburn, was able to react to situations and capable of producing polemical, persuasive and sometimes highly effective speeches, as he had done some years before during a debate over the mining of fullers' earth at Woburn Sands.[33] Finally, *Councillor Andy Blowers*, leader of the small group of nine Labour members was a former Chairman of ESC reflecting his party's environmentalist concerns and its antipathy to major private enterprises which failed to pay the social costs of their operations.[34] The small Labour group, unlike the Conservatives, was united, and its block of votes proved decisive in the major debates in the County Council, although its close relationship with the trade unions was to weaken its position in the decisive phase in the conflict.

There were other prominent figures outside the Council. Among these were *Peter Goode*, already described, whose campaign against London Brick was responsible for creating a powerful group of opponents.

The major figure from London Brick's side was its managing director, *James Bristow*. He came from a family involved in the fletton industry since the last century and his father had been Deputy Chairman of the Company. James Bristow was accessible, charming, and easy going in nature, enjoying good relations with the workforce, promoting the more friendly, less remote and paternalistic image that the company was intent on fostering. His bland, almost casual manner combined with an air of naiveté which was revealed from time to time. He was the public face of the company in its negotiations with the Council but was backed by able colleagues such as John Wright, the unassuming Estates Manager.

All these actors were involved throughout the conflict. Others were important, sometimes decisive at certain points in the development of the issue. Although theoretical explanations tend to focus on structural factors or on conflicts between groups, explanations focusing on the role of certain actors should not be neglected. An understanding of the role of individuals and their influence on groups provides some antidote to abstract notions of historical inevitability or structural determinism.

The site of Ridgmont works

The early negotiations had been confined to the planning officials and the company. From now on public concern pushed the company's proposals further into the political arena and defined the sources of conflict. Although the influence of the planning officials was still strong, initiative was passing out of their hands. As it did so new issues were emerging and negotiations with the company were paralleled by negotiations which excluded the company.

A meeting at County Hall on 11 January 1979 brought together 12 members of Bedfordshire County Council, six county planners, and three other officials including the Deputy County Secretary; one member and two officers from mid-Bedfordshire District Council in whose territory Ridgmont is located; Dr. Brothwood, responsible for the report on the effects of pollution on public health (see Chapter 2, p.36); Professor Lawther of the Medical Research Council Toxicology Unit; and Dr. Atherton, the Alkali Inspector covering Bedfordshire. Thus many of the leading figures in the debate were present, though notable absentees were representatives of London Brick and Peter Goode. It was an informal meeting intended to discuss the issues and to assess the options available to the County Council as it developed its response to the planning proposals.

The question of where to site the new Ridgmont works had already aroused bitter criticism in the Brickfields area, notably from CAC. So far four sites (see Figure 3.4) had been put forward by London Brick with site 3 (Marston Thrift) being preferred by the planners, though, as we have seen, the company was prepared to negotiate on any of the sites and had indicated a preference for site 2 on Brogborough Hill. This put the County Council in a dilemma. If the Council proposed a site it would be able to take the initiative and to advocate its preference if the issue went to a public inquiry. Conversely, delay in deciding a site would have the advantage of time for further consultation. The case was unusual in that the company was not proposing a specific site but prepared to let the location 'float' until a mutually agreed solution could be found. If the Council delayed and London Brick proposed a site then it might not meet the planners' criteria while London Brick could still claim it had been willing to negotiate. The planners were thus placed in a cleft stick facing the unpalatable alternatives of adverse public reaction if they chose, or a less satisfactory site if they did not. They put forward 11 criteria for site selection and identified an area (see Figure 3.4) remote from surrounding settlements, within which the site would be acceptable. The precise location should avoid visual impact and sterilising agricultural or clay–bearing land. They concluded-that a new site at Marston Thrift — site 5 — in the bottom of the excavated pit at Brogborough would meet these criteria and 'would appear to raise least objection' on grounds of pollution, intrusion and land use.[35] It was clear at the meeting that councillors were not ready to draw a firm conclusion on the siting and would want further consultation, though there were hints from some members that site 5 would *not* prove acceptable and that a site near the existing works (site 2) would be preferable. The planners argued that all four sites (1-4) proposed by London Brick were unacceptable according to their planning criteria.

The decision on the siting of the Ridgmont works went through three stages: an informal discussion by the Planning Advisory Group (PAG) on 19 February, a recommendation by the Environmental Services Committee (ESC) on 1 March and endorsement by the County Council on 26 April. The PAG meeting seemed to show a slight preference for site 2, but at the ESC the planners made their bid for site 5 in the clay pit.

Expert advice on the impact of tall stacks was presented by Mr D.H. Lucas of the Central Electricity Generating Board (CEGB) to the ESC on 1 March. He concluded that the proposed London Brick chimneys would render sulphur dioxide (SO_2) pollution 'negligible', the strong smell would disappear, and the fainter smell at greater distances would not be affected (though smell could be eliminated if the stacks were 390 metres high instead of the proposed 125). He also found that topographical features in the area were minor and would have no appreciable effects on air pollution and consequently 'there will be no marked localised effects and no particular site need be rejected for air pollution reasons'.[36]

Given this assurance the county planners decided to advance the case for site 5 in the Marston Thrift on environmental grounds. They argued that site 2, preferred by CAC and now by London Brick, 'would have a catastrophic impact on the landscape' and would 'perpetuate the close relationship between existing Ridgmont works and Brogborough village i.e. its immediate visual impact and possible noise and nuisance'.[37] By contrast sites 3 or 5 'are as remote from residential areas as possible and have the advantage of using excavated areas and avoiding agricultural land or clay-bearing areas. The accommodation of a brickworks on either of these sites would provide excellent opportunities for assimilating development into the area by reason of the ground levels'. The members of the committee were less enthusiastic and although they supported the planners' recommendations a number felt it advisable to show no preference.

Their fears were borne out when the predicted attack from CAC came. At a meeting held as early as 26 October 1978 between the Chairman and Vice-Chairman of the ESC, the Chairman and Vice-Chairman of the three parishes Cranfield, Lidlington and Marston Moretaine and Michael Kemp, County Councillor for the area, CAC were able to put across their view that sites in Marston Thrift were unacceptable to Cranfield. Such sites would bring a chimney to within a mile of the village and, owing to rising ground, only 200 feet above it. In a circular letter they identified a series of omissions in the planners' report, stressing the proximity to villages, and the overwhelming local support in favour of the Ridgmont site. The letter ended with a strong statement referring to Tony Griffin the Deputy Planning Officer whom CAC regarded as the architect of the decision: 'This is a Griffin folly to hide it from the motorists and he is hanging on the theory of put it where no one can see it. The tall chimney policy is the only practical one (Alkali Inspectorate) and is best for Marston Vale'.[38] This was followed by a letter to the local Press, which underlined CAC's attack on the planning officials:

> The County Planning Officers . . . remain oblivious to the opinions of the people in the area. Their dogmatic insistence on putting the new works in a hole . . . has been endorsed by the Environmental Services Committee based on a report by the Planning Office which saw fit not to mention anything about local opinion despite clear statements of preference from all affected parishes.[39]

Just before the Council met CAC indicated that they would do 'everything in our power to ensure a public inquiry'.[40]

At the County Council meeting in April the decision to advise London Brick of the Council's preference for site 5 in Marston Thrift was presented as a recommendation for comment but not for endorsement. By this time there were indications that London Brick had shifted its siting strategy once again. A report in *Bedfordshire on Sunday* revealed that the company was now placing its first priority on the replacement of the works at Stewartby.[41] The ostensible reason for the switch was the need to open up new workings at the Quest pit (see Chapter 1, Figure 1.2) since Rookery pit, on which the present works depended, was nearing exhaustion. By the time the new works was built, in the base of Coronation pit, it would be possible to connect it to the new workings.[42] Another reason was the delay already experienced in trying to get agreement on the site of the Ridgmont works. At the County Council meeting Councillor White, Chairman of ESC, admitted it was likely that London Brick would now pursue its plans for Stewartby rather than Ridgmont.

How far the company saw this as a tactic to achieve a permission at the least controversial site is a matter for speculation, but from this point on the focus of attention was on Stewartby as the first works, though the Ridgmont problem still remained to be solved. At the meeting members expressed doubts about the ESC recommendation for site 5, Councillor Kemp in particular arguing the preference for site 2. Others felt the Council was unwise to show its hand since this let London Brick off the hook and transferred public opposition to the County Council. For the present the county planners had got their way over the site, but their position was rapidly eroded.

The CAC had been dismayed by the decision of ESC to prefer the Marston Thrift site to the new Ridgmont works but did not feel defeated. They marshalled experts in an effort to influence opinion on the Council as the application for the works was felt to be imminent. They were supported by Mr Ian Harris, a Senior Lecturer in Wind Engineering, who provided a detailed critique of the Lucas report on the effects of the new tall chimneys. He concluded that Marston Thrift would show a higher maximum of pollution at ground level, spread over a wider area, and that Cranfield would be vulnerable in certain climatic conditions. 'A chimney at Ridgmont would produce no such problems anywhere in the area.'[43] In addition CAC used two further pieces of evidence. They quoted the Alkali Inspector's opinion on the siting question: 'It was and still is, that the existing works at Ridgmont be demolished and replaced on the same site.'[44] The other was the view of Cranfield Institute of Technology that a site in Marston Thrift might cause aviation problems though objections were only likely to be raised against site 3, no longer seriously regarded as an option.[45]

Armed with this evidence CAC produced a detailed analysis of the siting issue and circulated it to county councillors. It was designed to undermine the planners' view: 'We have become increasingly concerned about the motives of the County Planning Officers in pursuing their interest in the Marston Thrift Site and the amount of bias which has been evident'.[46] The document quoted from the planners' report to ESC and showed point by point how the planners had selected evidence omitting points favourable to Ridgmont (e.g. public reaction), presenting evidence favourable to Marston Thrift (e.g. does not invade the skyline) and by providing their own interpretation of the evidence. For example the planners stated that Marston Thrift was 'as remote from residential areas as possible' though it was well within a mile of both Cranfield and Marston Moretaine. They had claimed that Ridgmont would have 'catastrophic effect on the landscape', failing to point out that the existing 24 chimneys would be replaced by two. The CAC report then went on to take each of the planners' 11 criteria in turn, demonstrating that in the case of ten of them Ridgmont was the best relative site. They indicted the planners on two grounds:

1. The attempt to force a new brickworks and its obnoxious side effects onto an hitherto unaffected residential area despite a mountain of evidence against such a course of action and the biased selection of evidence to promote this plan.
2. The blatant lack of consultation with local representatives and other affected parties with the resultant avoidance of evidence contrary to the course of action being promoted.

This document was supported by a circular entitled 'We are backing London Brick Company', urging public support for CAC's campaign. A 'mass of "behind the scenes" dealings by the County Planners' had been uncovered. The need was for the tallest possible chimney at the highest point, not Marston Thrift but Ridgmont. CAC's activities reached a climax in the summer just before the applications were made by London Brick. When the applications were made it was clear that CAC had achieved partial success. London Brick, despite the advice in favour of Marston Thrift given by the ESC, decided to apply for permission on both sites, as alternatives. The company, once again, demonstrated its political dexterity in removing itself from the conflict. It took nearly another two years before the issue was finally resolved, but there is little doubt that the single-minded energies of CAC were responsible for the ultimate defeat of the planners on the siting issue.

Pollution — the key issue

A theoretical problem for this study is why certain issues become matters for political conflict. At the outset there were several potentially controversial issues. Dereliction, the issue which concerned the planners and which had been the source of concern for many years, receded as the conflict developed. Similarly those issues of most concern to localised pressure groups, the location of clay workings and the siting of new works, achieved an early prominence and then faded. By the middle of 1979 air pollution was the prime issue, and opposition to the company had passed from local action groups concerned with specific issues to a campaign against pollution waged on a much broader front. The escalation of the conflict implies that the company was facing powerful forces that could not be contained within conventional channels of negotiation.

A major report was produced by the planners, which acknowledged the views of members 'that the pollution issue is the main consideration'.[47] The report stressed the primary role of the Alkali Inspector in controlling pollution but rehearsed the main criticisms made of his role — his lack of accountability, his close cooperation with industry, the lack of justification for decisions made and the lack of pollution guidelines. The potential role of the County Council was set out in the report of the Royal Commission on Environmental Pollution:

> If the planning authority, using air quality guidelines consider that an unacceptable amount of pollution is likely to be emitted from a proposed plant when the Alkali Inspectorate's requirements have been met their sanction should be the refusal of planning permission not the imposition of planning conditions designed to control emissions.[48]

However, the planners reached a somewhat pusillanimous conclusion on the Council's ability to influence pollution control:

> There would be nothing to prevent the County Council from taking a positive lead in monitoring, coordinating and disseminating information on pollution, and using its influence to achieve modifications and improvements in both practice and procedures.[49]

The report reviewed the current state of knowledge on the effects of brickwork pollution. It reiterated the medical experts' claims that the pollution may not cause illness but could aggravate existing illnesses. It emphasised the problem of monitoring sulphur dioxide (SO_2) and pointed out the tendency to short term, high–peak pollution levels undetected by 24 hour average measurements. Inversions which trapped pollution near the ground were common, especially at night and during the winter. It seemed clear that relatively low concentrations of SO_2 would affect vegetation, and there was general acceptance that 24 hour means, of the type occasionally found in the brickfields, would exacerbate chronic health conditions.

What is interesting is that opponents of London Brick devoted little attention to the question of SO_2. Although monitoring was randomly located and short term peaks could not be measured, knowledge of this pollutant was relatively good and monitoring was part of the UK National Survey of Air Pollution.[50] Although the levels of SO_2 in the Marston Vale were high for a rural area they were not apparently abnormally high compared to urban areas, and there was much less particulate matter in the atmosphere. Levels in the Bedford area had been reduced as smoke control orders spread but those in the Vale varied according to the levels of production in the brickworks. At the January meeting Professor Lawther repeated his view that the levels in the Vale were well below danger level and there was little medical evidence of abnormally high risks. 'There are undesirably high peaks at times, but these have acute and not chronic effects which can, at times, affect the vulnerable but are not the cause of illness.' Lack of emphasis on SO_2 by the environmentalists can perhaps be explained by the fact that its effects were broadly known, that Bedfordshire's problem was not unique, and, more cynically, that the problem had less impact on interests concerned about damage to farming, though it must be said the research by Rothamsted referred to earlier (see Chapter 2, page 38) identified SO_2 as a possible cause of crop damage.

The pollutant that attracted the environmentalists' attention was fluoride. Much less was known both about the incidence and effects of fluorides. There were only two monitoring stations in the Vale capable of detailed analyses and results were not published. Little was known about the local effects on animals beyond the research already quoted (see Chapter 2, page 37) and evidence on human health effects was much more speculative and circumstantial. Clearly the evidence on fluorides was contestable, and government sources seemed to differ on the subject. Thus the Department of Health and Social Security claimed that current information 'gives no cause for concern at present that they are harmful to human health'[51] — a view apparently contradicted by a Junior Health Minister about the same time, stating that long exposure to fluorides 'may cause skeletal changes or if exposure occurs during the period of tooth development, an increased prevalence of dental mottling'.[52] The planners referred to research in the United States which indicated that even small amounts of fluoride could affect the bone structure of human beings, a report publicised in the local Press.[53] The planners felt unable to draw any conclusions on fluoride. The fact that the fluoride problem was specific to Bedfordshire (its occurrence elsewhere is also localised and associated with aluminium smelters in Anglesey and Fort William) provided the environmentalists with a case that was difficult to contradict with evidence from elsewhere.

The offensive odour caused by the organic compounds in the clay – mercaptans – is peculiar to fletton brickmaking. Here, too, it would appear that opponents of London Brick had a case worth pursuing, especially as the problem was widespread, frequent, perceptible and the subject of complaint. Even miniscule amounts (one volume per 50 billion volumes of air) are detectable and so tall chimneys which would disperse and dilute other pollutants might actually increase the area over which the smell persisted. Throughout the debate London Brick maintained that odour was the major problem and that its research efforts should be devoted to its removal as the first priority. In this it was, once again, reflecting the views of the Alkali Inspector, who argued that any process which did not remove the odour would not justify the expense of treatment.[54] Clearly, London Brick considered it necessary to endorse the views of the Inspector responsible for pollution control and considered that the removal of odour would remove complaints and thus reduce opposition to the company. Opponents accepted the view that the odours were harmless, and felt their removal would be largely cosmetic, reducing the force of opposition but not removing the main problem, which they considered to be fluorides.

The main dimensions of the debate about pollution had now become clear. The problems of SO_2 were known and generally accepted but not given great attention by either side. London Brick recognised the problem of smell whereas opponents focused on fluoride. This resulted in a dialogue of the deaf in which each side failed to recognise (or, more likely, chose to ignore) the claims of the other.

The impasse was evident at the meeting of 11 January. Professor Lawther was adamant in his view that there were few dangers and that the Alkali Inspectorate was 'one hundred years in advance of any other institution in the world dealing with pollution'. Dr. Atherton, the Alkali Inspector, argued that the best practicable means of reducing pollution was by tall chimneys which would reduce peak ground level concentrations by a factor of 8, provide lower concentrations elsewhere, and nowhere would future levels reach those currently experienced. This claim was supported by evidence from the CEGB:

> Tall stacks are sometimes criticised because they only spread the pollution problem further afield. This implies that distant regions receive additional pollution so that nearer regions can be spared. If the pollutant is a gas, which is not absorbed by the ground, the implications is false. . . . If a chimney is used there is an area close to the source where the very high concentrations become zero, a middle region where the concentrations are greatly reduced and a far region where the already small concentrations are reduced a little. There is no region where the concentrations are increased.[55]

This point was much contested during the course of the debate by opponents who claimed that 'what goes up must come down'. They pointed to the phenomenon of 'acid rain' caused by long-distance transfers of sulphur from tall stacks. Tall chimneys would merely spread the problem affecting more people, even those in Scandinavia. The counter claim, that tall chimneys would greatly reduce existing pollution levels achieved far less prominence. Complex arguments about pollution levels were reduced to simplistic assertions. The company's opponents focused on fluoride to gain local support and on sulphur dioxide to raise an international dimension to their arguments.

Council strategy

Air pollution had become undeniably the prime issue. But opponents of the company needed to define their objectives more clearly, to gather together appropriate expertise and to exert their influence on the relevant decision makers. At the PAG meeting in February the need to acquire an independent appraisal of the problem to establish and, if necessary, defend the Council's position was accepted. A number of consultants were considered and the members accepted the planners' view that Cremer and Warner, with international experience of the environmental pollution field, should be retained. It was recognised that much of the expert knowledge was concentrated, some of it within the industry. Nevertheless, Cremer and Warner were highly regarded as independent experts with both experience and knowledge of fields akin to the brickworks.

A 'whole gamut of pollution issues' would be put to the consultants. These included the severity of pollution in the Marston Vale and its effects on animals, crops annd human beings; the technical feasibility and cost of pollution control measures; the design of kilns which could be retrofitted in the event of control measures being practicable; and the possibility of alternative manufacturing methods which would reduce emission levels. There was unanimity over the appointment of Cremer and Warner at a cost of £25,000. Supporters of the company hoped that the consultants would endorse the tall stacks proposal whereas opponents anticipated recommendations which would enforce stricter control measures.

Concurrently the Fletton Brickworks Liaison Committee (FBLC) was also reacting to public pressure for more action over pollution. This committee appeared as a rather toothless watchdog with varying degrees of commitment by the various member authorities (see Chapter 2, p.46). During the autumn of 1978, when interest in the brickfields proposals first aroused concern, the committee had been content to issue one of its periodic bland Press releases arguing that 'evidence indicates fluoride emissions are not a hazard to humans'. This release had been subjected to detailed public criticism by Roger Tagg, Lecturer in Technology at the Open University, who was setting up a monitoring station, and conducting research into fluoride emissions, and who had been providing advice to the County Council on the issue. He argued that emission levels had fallen owing to a decline in production and this in no way indicated the problem had gone away. The same could be said of better husbandry methods which could veil the problem. 'Just a statement that it is safe means nothing unless evidence is produced to show it is safe.'[56]

In a further Press release on 18 April, 1979, the FBLC had clearly responded to public anxiety and announced that it had asked the DoE to carry out a 'comprehensive review of all the available information on the environmental effects of the Fletton brickworks' emissions to the atmosphere'.[57] The statement reiterated the view that there did not appear to be any evidence of harm to health, and stressed the monitoring being undertaken and the availability of the results. Much appeared to hinge on the eventual publication of these two reports by Cremer and Warner and the DoE, but more than a year was to elapse before the latter was published. When it did come it was important not so much for its content as for its timing.

By the spring of 1979 London Brick's strategy was becoming clear. Although anxious to gain permission it seemed prepared to bide its time while the Council made up its own mind. Already it had shifted its preference from one Ridgmont site to another and from Ridgmont to Stewartby. It maintained its position on the pollution question but raised no objection to the employment of consultants. It showed no anxiety to appeal if permission was refused and tried to promote a public image of a company anxious to provide environmental benefits providing it did not impede the investment programme.

The Council's strategy was less clear and several options seemed available. It could refuse the application, but if it did so it must state the reasons and be able to substantiate them. The evidence provided by the consultants would be crucial here as London Brick had the support of the Alkali Inspector and an Industrial Development Certificate. Refusal ran the risk of an appeal by the company, which might result in the Council securing less attractive conditions than if it decided the matter itself. If the Council took no decision this would amount to a deemed refusal, with the difference that the Council would not have stated its position and would be free to adopt its stance later when (and if) the company appealed. The same outcome would result if the Minister decided to call the matter in for his own decision for then the Council would be one of the objectors. The alternative course was to continue with negotiations in the hope of a mutually acceptable solution both as to site and to conditions. The Council would be able to secure a Section 52 Agreement providing for environmental benefits in return for the permission. This was the course favoured by the plannners. Indeed Geoffrey Cowley, the County Planning Officer, urged the members to 'be nice to London Brick. You need good relations for waste disposal. These are strong cards and we want a good clean fight.' He criticised those members who had exposed the Council by their fierce opposition to the company. 'We set out to get the best deal. You've blown our cover. We can't sell the Section 52 now. They'd laugh us down the road. They've no reputation to be sullied.'

While few would echo sentiments quite so extreme it was clear that the politicians were becoming increasingly divided. Outside the committee other forces were at work which were shortly to have a profound influence on the course of events.

The opposition — a new focus

The months following the County Council debate in April into the summer of 1979 were relatively quiet on the political front. Two events were awaited — the submission of the planning application and the report of the Council's consultants. But it was a period during which local anti-pollution campaigners were busy attracting publicity and preparing for an organised assault on the company once the plans were presented and open to formal public debate. During this period fears about the danger to human health, regarded as the strongest weapon against the company, if also the most difficult to prove, were fostered.

A rather ghoulish incident brought the health issue to the fore. A campaigner against the fluoridisation of water, the Hon. Miss Elizabeth Keyes of Tingewick in Buckinghamshire, was trustee for the body of her friend, Miss Emily Jones, who died aged 82 in 1978. Miss Jones had suffered for 14 years before her death from fluorosis-like symptoms assumed to be caused by drinking from a well with a high fluorine content. After considerable delay, during which the body was kept in deep freeze, an investigation revealed a level of fluoride within the expected range for a person of that age.[58] This unremarkable finding would have had no impact had it not coincided with the brickfields debate at a critical point when the health issue was emerging. It was not the findings but the lack of interest in, or facilities for, research on fluoride that was at issue. Dr. Wix of South Bank Polytechnic, who had undertaken the examination, said that the evidence of bone samples from Miss Jones was inconclusive but 'that does not mean there is not a problem that needs looking at in much greater depth. As far as I am concerned, as a scientist, the present monitoring system of brickworks emissions is totally inadequate when it comes to gauging fluoride effects'.[59] He urged long term clinical research. The allegations of inadequate research were passed to the Fletton Brickworks Liaison Committee who responded with one of their periodic Press releases. They were passing on the information to the Department of the Environment which 'has informed the committee that a review will be carried out in consultation with other departments to see whether there is a problem of damage to health and to determine the need, if any, for further environmental monitoring'.[60] The same release quoted the Area Health Authority's view that there was no local evidence of fluoride deposition in bones X-rayed over many years. The Liaison Committee also took the opportunity to state that the recent television programme (see page 72) 'was felt by most members to have been presented in a biased and distorted way'. In the minds of London Brick's critics the Press release as a whole demonstrated the company was using the Liaison Committee for a public relations exercise.

The Jones case pinpointed the lack of research into the health effects of fluorides. It suggested that the authorities were vulnerable and that, confronted by other expert evidence, they might find their denial of a problem hard to sustain. The local environmentalists had noted this weakness and began to assemble their own expertise to challenge the opinions of the official 'experts'.

CAC had already demonstrated the use of expertise when producing evidence about the effects of tall chimneys at alternative locations. The public debate about the brickfields had covered a number of issues but air pollution was clearly the one causing most anxiety. And it was the effects of flurides, unresearched and damaging to cattle and potentially human beings, that had attracted more attention than either SO_2 or the odours. The fluoride question was taken up in the summer of 1979 by a group which over the next year was to provide sustained, versatile and effective opposition.

Peter Goode, who had suffered the loss of two cows the previous year through suspected fluorosis, discovered similar symptoms in another of his prize herd.[61] For the past months he had been amassing evidence and writing to the authorities about the problem. He decided more concerted action was necessary and gathered together a group of influential people to form the nucleus of a new pressure group. The group met for the first time on 25 July in the House of Commons. Those present included the three local Conservative MPs, Councillors Philip Hendry and Allan Chapman, two academics with relevant expertise, Roger Tagg and Professor John Loxham, a local businessman, Anthony Stanbury, David Parish, and Peter Goode. The chairman was the Marquis of Tavistock, the major landowner of the county with his seat at Woburn Abbey. The committee also included a general practitioner, Dr. David Rhodes, to give medical advice, and later Councillor Andy Blowers, the Labour Group Leader was invited to join to provide a broader political base. The committee eventually chose the acronym PROBE (Public Review of Brickmaking and the Environment) with a symbol (see Figure 3.6) of smoking chimneys.[62]

The name indicated the main objective of the committee. 'We believe that there is too little information available to review, and that in view of the totally conflicting statements a full scale investigation is called for. We further believe that pending the outcome of a full and thorough investigation no new planning permissions should be granted for works unless filtration processes are installed from the commencement of operations.'[63] The meeting considered a report from Roger Tagg indicating the lack of

Public Review of Brickmaking and the Environment

Figure 3.6: PROBE logo
Source: Public Review of Brickmaking and the Environment

local information on pollution in contrast to increasing and worrying data from other countries.[64] Peter Goode presented papers summarising some of the research and emphasising the possible dangers of airborne fluorides. The committee agreed to send a small deputation to meet Jeremy Rowe, Chairman of London Brick, to impress upon him the strength of local feeling and the need for the company to clear up its emissions. The MPs agreed to put pressure on the Minister. A Press release announcing the formation of the committee was published on 15 August, almost coinciding with London Brick's planning application. The release stated they 'were not opposing the building of new brickworks but that they were demanding a very significant reduction in the amount of pollutants spewed into the atmosphere by the company's chimneys'.[65] The committee now began a series of meetings, Press announcements, appearances on TV, and lobbying both at Westminster and on the County Council with the aim of ensuring that, if the new works were built, they would have pollution controls from the outset.

London Brick — the applications are made

After months of private discussion with planning officers and a year of public debate and negotiation, the planning applications for the new brickworks were finally made in August 1979. The applications when they came reflected both the agreements already reached and the areas of debate and uncertainty that still remained. The company hoped it had done enough to allay suspicion and to secure a favourable result. Just before the applications were lodged, the company burnished its image with a major public relations exercise highlighting its new found role in restoration and waste disposal. In June 'Operation Landfill' was launched and widely reported in the local Press. This marked the beginning of a contract with the GLC for the disposal of 800-2000 tonnes each day of domestic refuse from North London, using a specially constructed transfer station at Hendon, hiring trains from British Rail, and disposing in 'L' field. Although the scheme was widely welcomed it also aroused the festering suspicions of the company's ability to profit from the dereliction it had caused. The contract was worth £40 million over twenty years with a charge of £11.50 per tonne disposed, and was intended to yield 'a "modest" but undisclosed profit'.[66] From London Brick's viewpoint the publicity was worthwhile since it promoted the image of a company anxious to secure restoration and was a valuable prelude to its planning applications.

London Brick had a further card to play, the significance of which went unremarked at the time. As well as applying for permission for new works in Bedfordshire, the company simultaneously applied for a new works at Whittlesey in Cambridgeshire. The site was at Kings Dyke, next to the new works already opened there in 1969, and close to the new Saxon works opened in 1972. Thus, Cambridgeshire already had new works, so clearly London Brick did not anticipate much of a problem with its applications there since the precedent had already been set.

A further attraction of the Kings Dyke proposal was that it would create new employment rather than reduce it as was the case in Bedfordshire. The new works was intended to replace disused old works at Central 1 and 2 nearby, and LB 1 at Peterborough, whose 150 workers would be transferred. The new works, with a 5 million bricks per week capacity, would require 340 employees, an increase of about 190 jobs. The application, supported by the Alkali Inspector, provided for demolition of old works and 18 chimneys. It would be located in the base of an excavated pit and would have one chimney with provision for a third flue.[67]

It was part of a progressive replacement policy already underway in the area and, as such, unlikely to meet with anything like the opposition already aroused in Bedfordshire. As we shall see it met with few problems and later this fact had considerable bearing on the outcome of events in Bedfordshire.

The Bedfordshire applications were made on 13 August, 1979, and, reflecting the concern in the county, were rather more elaborate affairs than in Cambridgeshire. As had been anticipated, the company applied for two new works each with two units with a combined capacity of 10 million bricks per week. One was to be located in the base of Coronation pit at Stewartby, but for the other the company put in two mutually exclusive applications at sites in Marston Thrift and Ridgmont. The applications proposed extensive demolition of existing works. But there were also detailed proposals and comments which reflected the issues raised in the public debates. CAC's protests had led to the alternative applications for the Ridgmont works. The planners' concern about the environmental impact was met by detailed proposals for demolition (including about 100 existing chimneys) and a lengthy report on landscaping commissioned from consultants. There would be careful conservation of topsoil, and reclamation 'would depend on the availability of suitable filling materials but would be actively undertaken with such things as refuse and colliery shale wherever possible'.[68]

The new works would be screened by trees and banking, and the company indicated their willingness to plan the landscape in the longer term. Although restoration to existing levels for agriculture would be preferable, low level agricultural restoration was a possibility. Extensive tree planting throughout the Vale was envisaged using hardwoods 'in place of the preponderance of poplars and willows'.

These were important gains from the planners' viewpoint, offering a new era of cooperation, but the proposals on future excavation were even more significant and represented a success for the efforts of groups such as GASP to mitigate the effects of clay working on villages. The company agreed that, in return for planning consent, it would 'make no objection to the revocation by the County Council without compensation' (page 19) of all its existing mineral consents. In effect this meant that the clay extraction areas could be rationalised, stand-off areas agreed, and new consents be granted with modern and more comprehensive conditions than the loose and vague conditions which had been the source of so much friction over the years. Specifically, the company excluded part of its old permission near Houghton Conquest to safeguard the amenity of the village and, if other suitable land could be found nearby, was willing to exclude the whole area of pit 81.

On the air pollution question the company was not able or prepared to make any significant concessions. Although a third flue would be provided for future possible abatement the company reiterated its familiar themes about the value of tall chimneys for dispersion, the lack of alternative technology, and the results of monitoring which had 'produced no evidence indicating that chimney emissions are harmful to human health' (page 12).

The company might have felt it had gone a long way to meet all the criticisms made of its operations. The application promised a greater degree of coherence and cooperation in restoration and the rationalisation of clay extraction. Although the opposition could argue that it had scored some significant successes it is not clear that London Brick had offered any concessions it was not prepared to make from the outset – none of which really had any profound effect on its operations or, more significantly, its profits. The holes would remain if there was insufficient landfill to be gained at a commercial rate, and the renegotiated workings would provide a secure long term basis for brickmaking.

Although the landscaping proposals would require investment by the company, such work had already been undertaken, and, in the interests of promoting goodwill and a favourable image, it would more than repay the outlay. Whatever interpretation is placed on the company's willingness to concede, the landscape improvements represented a major gain for the

Council. Much time was to be spent finalising these proposals but in essence they changed little. London Brick considered enough had been offered to induce a permission. But it still faced an opposition that had fastened on to air pollution and was determined that more should be demanded of the company — more, as it turned out, than the company would yield. For the next year the battle, now fought on a narrower front, increased in intensity as each side sought an outright political victory but one which, they still hoped, could be negotiated.

Autumn 1979 — old themes and new issues

The period between August and November 1979, after the applications were made and before the publications of the consultants' report, was a time of speculation, informal meetings, public response, and preparation for the major debates to come. Debate over the established ground lingered on and some new problems emerged. It was a time to draw breath, to pause before the conflict entered formally and finally the political arena of the County Council.

In the brickfields the local parishes and action groups responded from established positions. In September a meeting at Brogborough, the company village near the Ridgmont works, had voted 27 to 3 in favour of the new works at the existing site, apparently on the grounds that it was convenient for the workforce to get home for lunch. The Cranfield campaign had successfully isolated the county planners as the only supporters of the Marston Thrift site. The village of Wootton also declared in favour of the existing site.[69] Although Mr Griffin still favoured Marston Thrift on environmental grounds he confided that he had given up promoting it, acknowledging that the opposition was too great. He was partly influenced by the anticipated recommendation of the consultants which would marginally favour the Ridgmont site on grounds of the greater dispersion likely from its position on the ridge overlooking the Marston Vale. Over in Houghton Conquest the parish seemed split between those who viewed the works as a 'necessary evil' and those who were opposed to it unless pollution controls were enforced. However, agreement was reached to press London Brick to find an alternative to pit 81 if at all possible.[70]

Outside the county there was another development which had a bearing on the debate. The application for the Kings Dyke works in Cambridgeshire caused much less of a stir. At a public meeting in Whittlesey on 30 August attended by 50 people the dialogue on the pollution issue had a familiar ring:

Questioner: 'Is there a better cleaning process than tall chimneys?'
London Brick: 'Yes, but it requires a lot of money. One system creates another problem and we would finish up with toxic sludge in the pits.'
Questioner: 'Isn't toxic sludge in the pits mores savoury than in the air?'
London Brick: 'No – because we disperse and dilute emissions through higher chimneys.'
Questioner: 'How much of the budget is spent on research?'
London Brick: 'The answer to that is, as much as is necessary.'

Overall the meeting introduced the notes of scepticism and anxiety already evident in the Bedfordshire debate, and close liaison between the two counties was urged so that similar positions could be adopted on the planning applications.

This meeting was practically the only evidence of public concern in the neighbouring county. The contrast suggests a refinement to the question of why certain issues become matters of political conflict. The question is: Why do such issues arise at certain times and in certain places and not others? Certain reasons may seem self-evident. New works had already been built in the Whittlesey area, and would create more employment. But such explanations cannot fully account for the differences between broadly similar applications in 1979. In theoretical terms it will be necessary to examine whether differences relate to role of individuals, interests, or structural conditions in the two counties.

The subtle, but in the end crucial, differences were not initially evident. At a meeting held shortly after the public meeting at Whittlesey, the Fenland District Council stated that 'the discharge of untreated waste gases and its associated effects are of international concern requiring examination in detail, and no decision should be taken until the forthcoming report of the Department of the Environment on the Fletton Brick Industry is issued'.[71] It was clear that the district planners wanted the application to be treated in the same way as those for Bedfordshire so that a common front could be achieved.

Meanwhile in Bedfordshire there was speculation about the outcome of the consultants' report, and the likely attitude of the Department of the Environment (DoE). According to Mr Griffin the DoE were reluctant to call the matter in so that a public inquiry could be held and the decision taken by the Minister. The proposed investment was a good example of prevailing government philosophy supporting the expansion of private sector development. There was a fear that an inquiry would be very protracted. The DoE regarded the application as one that ought to be determined locally.

However, PROBE were beginning to apply pressure on the government to hold an inquiry on the grounds that it was a national, even an international issue. A report in *The Guardian* (29 September) underlined the concern of the Scandinavian countries about trans-boundary pollution from British power stations and the resulting acid rain that had, it was claimed, infected about a fifth of Sweden's lakes and those in southern Norway, depriving them of aquatic life. 'Proposals by the London Brick Company to build two brickworks in Bedfordshire with chimneys four hundred feet high may bring Scandinavian intervention.' An OECD Agreement pledging countries to eliminate long-range pollution was about to be signed in Geneva. *The Observer* (21 October) carried a story about research findings which suggested that the rise of the cancer rate in Birmingham could be traced to the introduction of fluroidisation of water in that city in 1964. Although this was challenged on grounds of statistical evidence it raised anxiety about the possible carcinogenic effects of fluoride. Further evidence of national media interest was presented in a BBC2 TV 'Grapevine' programme transmitted on 20 October, in which the dangers from the brickworks were included along with lead poisoning in West Yorkshire and the hazards from a proposed titanium works at Hartlepool in County Durham. It began to look as if an orchestrated campaign at national and international level might make a 'call in' irresistible. At this point the publication of Cremer and Warner's report for the County Council in October 1979 rehearsed much that was already known or suspected but also introduced new possibilities into the debate over pollution.

The Cremer and Warner report

The brickfields problem had, over the years, stimulated inquiries into the effects of pollution on crops, animals and human health. The findings, though inconclusive, had been summarised in various reports in order to assist judgements on the company's redevelopment plans. Expert advice had been brought in by the planners, and the pressure groups, notably CAC, had gathered their own expertise. It is clear that expert advice may use similar information to support quite different conclusions. The production, dissemination and interpretation of evidence is not simply a matter of disinterested experts contributing rational evaluation to decision making, but is, rather, a part of the political process itself. Questions such as 'what is the purpose of evidence?', 'who controls information?' and 'how is it interpreted? are political questions. By investigating the role of expertise

and information we may gain theoretical insights into the means by which
particular interests exercise power.

The report of the consultants employed by the County Council repre-
sented an attempt to get an independent assessment of the pollution issue.
The Cremer and Warner report, published in two volumes, a General
Appraisal and a Main Report,[72] was intended to be, and was accepted as, a
definitive and substantive statement of the current state of knowledge about
the effects of pollutants and the methods for control in the brick industry.
Its interpretations were challenged but it could not be conclusively refuted.
The problems of evidence and technical feasibility pervaded its conclusions,
and recommendations were based on the consultants' judgement of practicability. It was not possible to remove all doubt, and the way was left open
for continuing equivocation and prevarication on the part of the company
and its opponents. As an aid to decision making, the report served largely to
provide more sophisticated arguments both to reinforce and undermine
positions already adopted by the contestants.

The first remit of the consultants was to assess the severity of existing air
pollution in the Marston Vale and its effects on health, plants, animals and
buildings. An examination of local dispersion (wind direction and speed,
turbulence, temperature and inversions) demonstrated inversions likely to
hold down air for about 10 per cent of the year. Data on existing air quality
in the Vale could be derived from monitoring. There were 14 volumetric
samplers for sulphur dioxide (SO_2) recording *absolute* levels for the National
Survey and 10 lead dioxide candles (mostly operated by London Brick)
which could only give *relative* values. These demonstrated levels above rural
averages. The low seasonal variation, fluctuations over short periods, and
general persistence over time when pollution in urban areas was reducing,
indicated the brickworks were the major source in the area. Monitoring for
SO_2 was adequate for the survey of trends, and any extension to cover the
short period high concentrations would need to be justified — 'so far as it is
known at the present time, there is no known reason why such an analysis is
required' (Main Report, B84). As for fluoride, there were only two sites
using volumetric samplers to measure levels near Stewartby and eight lime
candles and three dust deposit gauges giving only relative values. Levels of
airborne fluoride were about 1 per cent of those for SO_2 and varied widely.
There was no systematic survey of the incidence of fluoride accumulated in
vegetation, although Gilbert[73] had pointed to a strong correlation between
the decline of mature deciduous trees in the Vale and fluoride. Overall
fluoride monitoring was 'extremely limited' (B85). A more comprehensive

survey of short period concentrations, and herbage sampling on a before and after the new works basis, using well established techniques 'will often allay public concern over the development, thus making it acceptable within the community' (B86). There was no measurement of the odours emitted from the chimneys.

A major section of the report was devoted to a survey of the literature on the effects of the various pollutants. Sulphur dioxide produced its effects both in airborne form and through precipitation on water and the soil. Sensitive plants showed both visible and subtle effects, but it was generally concluded that even high concentrations had no adverse effects on farm livestock. The acute health effects of SO_2 during high pollution episodes were well known, especially on those suffering chest symptoms. Although the Brothwood report had been suggestive rather than conclusive on the effects of the brickworks, research undertaken by Petrilli[74] and Donaldson,[75] controlling for such variables as age and smoking, had found correlations between respiratory symptoms and air quality. Longitudinal studies on children[76] had showed a reduction in the effects as air quality improved.[77]

The effect of fluorides on sensitive plant species was identified by leaf injury (necrosis), showing lesions and spotting.[78] Although these symptoms appeared at certain levels of fluoride concentration, 'the paucity of data for the effects of fluorides on plants at low atmospheric concentrations prevents the establishment of stringent air quality standards for fluorides' (B135). In the case of cattle the condition of fluorosis was insidious, affecting teeth and eventually the skeleton, causing lameness and inability to feed properly. The level found in bones was normally between 100 and 1500 parts per million (ppm) and symptoms began to appear at 4000 ppm with levels of 10,000 ppm fairly frequent in affected cattle, with 20,000 ppm being the upper limit. Human intake was largely through water and especially tea. One ppm intake was regarded as the level needed to prevent dental caries, but above this level mottling of teeth could occur and high levels could have effects on the skeleton as fluoride was deposited on the bones and insufficiently excreted. Fluoride absorbed from the air was insignificant, and research conducted near the aluminium smelter at Fort William[79] had not revealed any unusual symptoms. This had been contradicted by other research, and countries such as the USSR and other eastern countries had adopted ambient air standards for fluorides.[80]

A second problem tackled by the consultants was to assess the effects of the new chimneys and to indicate the best site for the new works. To achieve this a dispersion model was constructed and calibrated against known weather and pollution conditions to provide a correspondence between measured and predicted concentrations. This enabled model predictions to be used 'with a fair degree of confidence' (B189). A series of 20 maps was produced showing existing and predicted situations for various statistical measurements of concentration for both SO_2 and fluoride. They confirmed the bimodal distribution of peaks in the Vale around Lidlington and Stewartby with the existing works and showed the persistence of odour at 5 dilutions for 10 hours per year to a distance of up to 85km.[81] The model predicted that the new works with tall chimneys would produce one peak area south of Bedford, but that levels of SO_2 would be reduced by seven or eight times from its previous peak levels in the vicinity of the old works, and would be four times less at Bedford declining to an improvement of two times elsewhere. The fluoride reductions were of the order of five times lower than existing peaks. Although the predicted levels of odour also showed a reduction 'an area including parts of Bedford will still be subjected to odour levels that could well constitute a nuisance' (B195). On the question of siting of the new works the model was agnostic since the overall pattern remained similar. But the consultants argued 'from the dispersion point of view, the Ridgmont 2 site has advantages due to its more exposed location' (B197).

The third major issue covered in the report was the financial and technical feasibility of pollution control using conventional and alternative kiln designs. The consultants reviewed the research already undertaken into pollution removal by London Brick. Attempts to scrub away fluorides and SO_2 presented insuperable problems of odorous sludge, fouling of ducts, extra traffic needed to import lime, and high costs, bringing an estimated 47 per cent increase in the price of bricks. Odour removal through incineration was also very costly in terms of fuel and pilot tests with alternative kilns (tunnel kilns) had led to technical problems and poor quality control. The report entered a note of criticism of London Brick's approach to this research:

> In all the experimental work undertaken, LBC would appear to have relied exclusively on 'in house' expertise with regard to kiln design. C & W have discovered no evidence to indicate that LBC have sought any advice from kiln manufacturers, or attempted to seek knowledge from other sections of the industry who have solved similar odour control problems (B204).

Cremer and Warner argued that the best approach would be to remove the organic compounds producing the odour as a prerequisite to any future removal of fluorides. The problem of removing the acid gases was one of removing sludge, and preventing acid rain effects and could only be justified if there were suitable and saleable by-products (which was unlikely). Current costs were 'unacceptable' although they could be reduced somewhat with heat exchange and a lower level of abatement. Much more promising was the idea of modifying the kilns with an emphasis on odour removal. Cremer and Warner considered tunnel kilns whereby the product moves through the process (instead of the process moving around the product as in Hoffman kilns) offered the best promise of odour destruction by incineration overcoming problems of flue fires and pressure balance. 'An extremely elegant solution to both these problems has been produced by a British kiln construction company for a similar problem in a totally dissimilar industry' (B247) and 'offers excellent prospects for application in the Fletton brick industry' (B248). It could provide a high level of odour destruction, good thermal efficiency, the elimination of volatile constituents, improved quality control and had potential for mass production. It would need to be evaluated and tested in a pilot plant.

The examination of direct incineration using a tunnel kiln was a major recommendation of the report, commenting: 'if the company builds plant that does not incorporate the most up-to-date technology, it may be unable to meet future environmental guidelines without considerable financial loss' (A9).

On the question of odour removal the recommendations of the report were quite explicit. 'Planning permission should be deferred or rejected for the construction of conventional Hoffman kilns as proposed. This action should be taken on the grounds that alternative kilning techniques (or modification to Hoffman kilns) may be utilised which will completely remove one type of pollutant (odour) produced in the firing of lower Oxford Clay' (General Appraisal A23). If examination proved successful then the elimination of odours would prove a preliminary to the reduction of the other pollutants.

Cremer and Warner, however, were not convinced that a need had been established for the elimination of fluorides and sulphur dioxide:

> In summary, it would appear that current sulphur dioxide, smoke and fluoride concentrations would not give cause for concern with respect to average healthy individuals. Sensitive groups, however, could be subjected to additional stress, as the elevated concentrations observed in pollution incidents could exacerbate respiratory and other illnesses. Grazing animals could be at risk due to the accumulation of fluorides in forage, although the severity or otherwise of this problem has not been established. Sensitive plants can be injured by both sulphur dioxide and fluoride. In general, the former is considered to be the greater problem. With the information currently available, the magnitude of this damage cannot be assessed (A15).

Given the doubts about the problem the consultants concluded that 'there is no justification with respect to human health for the introduction of acid gas abatement' (A23). Regarding animals the case for fluoride removal was unproven, and until the problem had been established and the tall stacks assessed research into fluoride removal should be continued. The evidence of need for fluoride abatement could only be gained by an extension of the monitoring network with results made public.

By focusing on odour as the key pollution problem and by casting doubt on the supposed dangers from fluoride Cremer and Warner had provided support for the position adopted by London Brick. Conversely, the arguments favouring greater monitoring and a consequence analysis together with the recommendation to refuse or delay the application favoured the environmentalists' cause. Both sides were to use the report to back their own case. In that sense the report entered into a political engagement already well advanced and did little to alter the balance of the struggle. But it did assist the process of negotiation, first in a minor way by giving tentative endorsement of the Ridgmont site and second by introducing the concept of tunnel kilns as a method of pollution control in the Fletton brick industry.

Reactions to the report

The Cremer and Warner report was presented to the Environmental Services Committee on 1 November. There were 27 councillors present including several prominent members such as councillors Hendry and Kemp not on the committee, and in the crowded public gallery were PROBE members and representatives of London Brick. Cremer and Warner opened with their conclusions on the effects of the pollutants: 'We do not think there is a health risk with SO_2. Fluoride is more difficult — with respect to human health I don't think there is a cause for concern.' The effect on animals left a 'small area of doubt'. The Alkali Inspector, Dr. Howard Atherton, also present at the meeting, had no such inhibitions, arguing that control techniques were unnecessary. 'The new works will have solved the problem by the use of tall chimneys. It is unreasonable to expect people to do something that is unnecessary.' His assertions led to Councillor Hendry arguing that the meeting was considering the views of Cremer and Warner not of Dr. Atherton, which effectively silenced the interruptions of the Alkali Inspector.

Cremer and Warner were concerned that monitoring information was poor and accepted that risk could not be ruled out altogether. 'We have to live with some risk — it is part of the price we pay for living in an industrial society.' The evidence was conflicting – 'It is, of course, possible to do a whitewash or to make a categoric statement that is opposite. On any piece of detailed technical evidence you can get opposing views. It is very difficult to judge some of these. London Brick will never prove to anyone's satisfaction that fluoride is no danger to anyone. The reduction of risk has great merit but it would be wrong to pick on one company when it is a much wider issue. We must recognise the low probability of risk from small emissions. There are others which emit far higher quantities.'

To some members these comments seemed highly equivocal, and provided an opportunity for opponents who were vocal at the meeting to underline the public doubts and anxiety being expressed locally. A succession of speakers, including Councillors Hendry, Blowers and Kemp, wanted greater reassurance and the elimination of doubt by insisting that processes to eliminate pollutants be put into effect. Councillor Chapman went further, attacking the company's evasive and parsimonious attitude to pollution control:

> I personally believe there are very serious hazards caused by fluoride. Nothing I've heard has put my mind at reast. It's no good talking about it after the permission has been passed. The company's approach was: First, there's no problem. Second, if there is a problem we don't know how to solve it. Third, even if there is a way to solve it the industry can't afford it.

This statement encapsulated the whole burden of the opposition case against the company. The committee agreed that its Chairman, Keith White, its Vice-Chairman, Cyril Everard, and Councillor Philip Hendry should meet with London Brick to see if the company were willing to undertake the necessary investigation into pollution control, as suggested by the Cremer and Warner report.

At the meeting the opponents had been most vocal, but there appeared to be considerable sympathy towards the company's proposals among the more silent members of the committee. It was clear that if the matter went to an inquiry the company would receive unequivocal support from the Alkali Inspector, who was officially responsible for ensuring adequate control measures. He felt that Cremer and Warner had not been positive enough, a view taken by Councillor Hendry for opposite reasons: 'I am in an impossible position. We employed Cremer and Warner, who are internationally acclaimed consultants . . . the whole firm would stand by the report, but I just think it is unfortunate they didn't put someone strong up front.'[82] Hendry also complained about the conflict of opinion coming from Cremer and Warner and the Alkali Inspector. Press reaction generally was hostile to the company, as it had tended to be throughout the debate. *The Guardian* (1 November) picked on the failure of the company to seek outside expertise on the control of pollution, and quoted the report's argument that excessive fluoride levels could be harmful, that sulphur dioxide levels were unacceptably high and that odour nuisance would not be removed. Similar criticisms were echoed in the local Press. Overall the debate, fuelled by the Cremer and Warner report, was taking on a more impassioned, if more sophisticated course, with accusation and counter-accusation as the opponents brought to bear on it the evidence culled by the report's findings. As the time for deciding the applications drew near the two camps stepped up their attacks and reviewed their strategies.

Responses — London Brick

The expertise provided by Cremer and Warner was countered by the expertise gathered by London Brick. London Brick responded at two levels. One was to provide a careful appraisal of the Cremer and Warner report, the other was to adopt a higher public profile through a succession of statements and letters to the Press. The meeting between the councillors and London Brick did not take place until 17 December, by which time it had become clear that while the company were prepared to continue research into pollution control as they had always done, they were, nevertheless, determined to pursue their applications. Their position was announced in a Press statement, and carefully argued in their response to the consultants' report. The Press release opened with: 'At last, a completely independent enquiry has confirmed there is no hazard to general human health from brickworks emissions . . . This completely rejects the claims of various local groups who have been trying to create public alarm over fluorides.'[83] The benefits of the redevelopment plans had been endorsed, though the company were 'very surprised' that Cremer and Warner suggested delay or deferral of the plans 'on the sole ground of odour — when this hasn't been a major issue over the planning applications'.

This stance was developed in the detailed technical critique provided by the company on the report, which followed the lines foreshadowed by Councillor Chapman in his remarks to the committee meeting. The assessment began by referring to the consultants' conclusions that there was no known danger from the fumes, leaving the case for fluoride removal unproven at the present time. Certain inconsistencies and omissions were pointed out, such as the implication that airborne fluorides might have an effect on susceptible individuals, when only about 5 per cent of the daily intake came from this source. Cremer and Warner had failed to emphasise the synergistic effects between smoke and SO_2 and the absence of smoke in the Vale. Much of the critique was devoted to a technical analysis to demonstrate that the methods proposed by Cremer and Warner were impracticable. Much research on odour removal had already been undertaken by London Brick, as required by the Alkali Inspector but they 'were unaware of any practicable or proven technology which will permit the realisation of this objective'.[84] The consultants had clearly not understood the need for avoiding oxidation of bricks during the rising temperature, the point at which the organic compounds giving off the smell are generated. 'It is essential to maintain non-oxidising conditions . . . to avoid pre-shrinkage oxidation leading to the production of bricks showing craze-cracking over the surface.' (page 9)

Nor had they understood the problems presented by attempting to modify Hoffman kilns to achieve incineration which would pass hot gases into the lower temperatures needed during the drying process. This would result in cracking and acid attack, which would cause the loss of facing materials on bricks exposed to weathering.

The coup de grâce was applied in the company's comments on the tunnel kiln proposal. This had already been tried and existing techniques were at a much smaller scale and in different industries than fletton brickmaking. Any progress here would face two major obstacles. One was the time needed to test a pilot plant of appropriate scale, which the company estimated would be about 5 years from design to final production designs. The other was the cost, which would increase the investment programme from the £60 million proposed to around £135 million (an increase of £14.50 per 1000 bricks), not including possible extra fuel costs and the costs of special equipment.

> Cremer and Warner have not appreciated the economics of kiln construction, which allows a Hoffman kiln to be built at only about one-fifth of the cost of a Tunnel kiln/Tunnel dryer of equivalent capacity. Even if the major research programme required showed the process to be effective, the whole redevelopment plan with its attendant benefits would be both delayed, and slowed down, while the major increase in cost would have a crippling effect on the national market for bricks: indeed Cremer and Warner have accepted that increases of this magnitude are not justifiable (page 16).

Whatever further compromises might be achieved by negotiation, the company intended to press their application forward on the basis of existing technology. On that there would be no compromise.

There was evidence too that London Brick was beginning to adopt a more aggressive posture through its various pronouncements in the Press. James Bristow, the Managing Director, began to argue that further delay would imperil the whole redevelopment programme. 'We could well carry on with 98 chimneys than with the four planned. There are a few people who hit us as a sitting target.'[85] 'They are obsessed with air pollution and if they succeed in blocking the plans this will have a totally negative outcome.'[86] His father, the former Deputy Director, entered the debate with a long letter intended to promote a very positive image for the company, and ending with a resigned but threatening peroration:

> If I were still on the Board of LBC, faced with all this nonsensical fuss, I would be inclined to say — O.K. we will stay as we are — the smell, if any, will remain the same, the conditions in the works will not be improved, there will be no chance to improve the environment, there will be no chance to hold down the price of bricks; but why bother when they are so much cheaper than anywhere else, so there is plenty of room for manoeuvre.[87]

This new line, that it might not invest after all, was partly in response to what were seen as delaying tactics and partly a means of keeping up the pressure on the Council.

James Bristow elaborated his views in conversation in January 1980. He maintained that the company might withdraw. 'Frankly, we are getting bored with the issue.' He hinted at other options open to the company. It might be possible to go forward on the basis of just one of the new works, Stewartby, using conventional technology. Then a research programme could be undertaken before the second works at Ridgmont was developed. This was to be part of a significant and final concession made by the company. Alternatively, the application for Cambridgeshire was awaiting the Department of the Environment report, but attitudes were more favourable there where people were already enjoying the benefit of two new works. This hint of a possible change in investment priorities, though unremarked at the time, was to prove a telling weapon in the hands of the company a year later. A third possibility, an appeal against refusal by the company was ruled out by Bristow on the grounds that it would cause at least two years further delay and imperil the opening of the Quest pit at the Stewartby works. It might not appeal, in effect saying if you don't want it you can keep things as they are. This may have been a bluff but it was a bluff that, in the event, was not called. Overall, London Brick had considered its position carefully and had decided which conditions would be acceptable to it. Its attitude was a combination of bewilderment at the opposition stirred up, injured innocence at the public hostility it faced, and an underlying confidence in the attractiveness of its proposals. But it had to face an opposition that had chosen the ground on which it wished to fight and that had garnered the expertise and political power for the approaching confrontation.

Responses — PROBE

The opposition to the company's plans was by now focused around the PROBE group. The group was able to provide the arguments and to lobby decision makers both locally and at central government and had easy access to the media. Just as London Brick stepped up its public campaign so PROBE responded with a strategy that was varied and flexible.

The main elements in this strategy were drawn up at a meeting of the group held in Milton Keynes on 16 November. They reviewed the two meetings already held with London Brick and with the Department of the Environment. London Brick 'did not gain so much as they hoped' according to the Marquis of Tavistock. Philip Hendry felt the company had seen it as a public relations exercise. It was clear that the DoE possessed little information on peak levels of concentration and had reached few conclusions. Their forthcoming report would only be a review, but could counteract the Cremer and Warner report by providing little evidence of fluoride danger. The group felt that the medical issue was the one most likely to rouse public opinion — if sufficient alarm could be created then the case against the company's proposals would become very compelling.

The committee decided to focus on the medical evidence by calling on members of the public to come forward with any evidence on the effects of the brick fumes. At the same time pressure would be exerted on the government to ensure the matter was called in for a public inquiry. This would gain the time needed for evidence to be gathered. Questions would be raised in the House of Commons and contacts would be made with BBC 'Panorama' for a major TV programme able to ask the 'nasty' questions. The Press release issued after the meeting led with a call for a public inquiry, and emphasised the lack of information on the effects of pollutants which could only be remedied by a full investigation. PROBE were carrying out their own survey on health effects. 'We would ask anyone with breathing, muscular or arthritic problems to write to the Secretary if they feel they may have been caused or aggravated by the brickwork emissions.'[88]

This was followed by a succession of Press reports about health damage. Peter Goode, PROBE's secretary, presented a 'bundle of letters' he had received,[89] and the *Milton Keynes Gazette* (29 January) published a page of letters headed 'The Bletchley Disease' from residents claiming such symptoms as nausea, stomach trouble, chest ailments, insomnia, sore throats, eye infections, arthritis and other bone symptoms, all attributed directly, or by implication, to the brickworks.

In Bedford the claim by a former brickworker that he was suffering from symptoms similar to fluorosis were denied by the district community physician, Dr. Alfred Lobban. 'I can definitely and categorically state that Mr Rawlings' illness is not fluorosis. His illness has nothing whatsoever to do with brickworks' emmissions.'[90] Such insistence in the face of uncertainty was later exposed by a consultant at King's College London, who argued that human fluorosis was always present where the disease was found in cattle.[91] Later Dr. Lobban 'leaked' the findings of the DoE report claiming there was no danger to human health from fluorides. The DoE had, in fact, only sent him five pages of the draft report in confidence.[92] Dr. Lobban asserted that opponents of the company 'are causing totally unnecessary anxiety to the people of Bedfordshire as far as the effects on human health are concerned'.[93] His unequivocal stance was attacked as irresponsible, and lacking evidence 'when his duty should be to search for evidence to prove the case one way or the other'.[94] The company's opponents were having considerable success in undermining the certainty expressed by official experts such as the Alkali Inspector and the community health physician. The ground work was being carefully laid to emphasise the lack of evidence or interest in research into the effects of fluoride.

Further doubt was cast on the company's claims by a story, widely publicised that 'London Brick Company is poised to add two £3 million "scrubbers" to its plans for new brickworks', which would eliminate fluoride and most of the sulphur dioxide.[95] London Brick regarded this as a publicity leak by the manufacturer, but it added to the public doubts about its willingness to undertake pollution control.[96] A further obstacle the company had to face was opposition to the design proposals for the new works, described by Philip Hendry as 'appalling' and 'absolutely basic'.[97]

The National Farmers' Union weighed in with a claim that tens of thousands of pounds had been paid out to a farmer's widow in Cambridgeshire after a 19 year legal battle to gain compensation for cattle deaths from fluorosis (see Chapter 2, page 42). Again London Brick denied any connection between the payment and the cattle losses: 'The company had decided to buy his house from his widow on humanitarian grounds. In no way did it set a precedent — there was no question of compensation.'[98] This incident, combined with Peter Goode's avowed intention to prosecute the company, and the NFU's insistence that compensation should be paid to farmers, was further evidence of growing and formidable opposition. Press coverage was highly sympathetic to the company's opponents, fastening on to any story that illustrated neglect or indifference on the part of the company. The Press coverage was crucial in the creation of the political environment in which the decision on the application would be taken, since it was bound to have an effect on those councillors who had yet to make up their mind on the issue.

The long period of negotiation stretching from the middle of 1978 to the end of 1979 had considerably narrowed the area of conflict. It appeared that considerable environmental benefits had been conceded by, or wrung from, the company depending on the view taken. The siting of the southern works at Ridgmont had effectively been agreed. Even on the question of pollution the issue had been focused on the potential hazards from fluorides rather than the other pollutants. The detailed discussions, voluminous reports, public meetings, committee debates and informal discussions had contributed to a greater awareness of the issues and of the constraints. It had brought a greater exchange of information and cooperation over policies than had ever existed before between the company and the County Council. It might be thought that enough was known, enough had been done and understanding was sufficiently developed for a solution to be found that was mutually acceptable. But the debate had within it the seeds of a conflict which could not be settled by compromise and agreement. Latent hostility had been aroused, passions unleashed and positions adopted from which there could be no retreat. The debate had created a new and organised environmental lobby; a lobby which, partly through desire and partly through intransigence, could not back away. The phase of negotiation led inevitably and inexorably to a showdown between the contending parties that could only be resolved through the political process.

Notes

1 Defined under the Deposit of Poisonous Wastes Act 1972, Section 3. They are those wastes other than those known to be safe, but include a wide range which are harmless if properly diluted and handled. They are defined in three categories: 'white' — which cause no problems; 'grey' — those which are toxic but rendered harmless before deposit (these were the type proposed for 'L' field); and 'black' — very toxic, potentially dangerous, and requiring special methods of disposal.

2 Report to Environmental Services Committee (ESC), 25 November, 1977, p.4.

3 The GLC contract of 1200 tonnes of domestic waste per day, involving a transfer station in North London and direct rail facilities is described in Chapter 3, page 31.
4 See note 1.
5 Pitsea in Essex was a site for toxic waste disposal including 'black' wastes (see note 1), and fumes had resulted in the death of a lorry driver there.
6 Report to ESC, 25 November, 1977, pp.6-7.
7 Provided a quorum of 6 members 'stood' at a committee meeting a resolution could be referred to the Council in the form of a recommendation.
8 County Council, 20 April, 1978, Minute 78/61.
9 Each works would be nearly 3000 feet long, and over 1000 feet wide.
10 Letter from County Planning Officer to Estates Manager, London Brick Company, 10 October, 1978.
11 Under Section 52 of the Town and County Planning Act, 1971, local planning authorities and developers may agree those matters of a development that are mutually agreeable. Such agreements are legal documents enforceable through the court, and not subject to appeal. The Agreement negotiated with London Brick is discussed in Chapter 4.
12 The Committee on *Planning Control over Mineral Working* (the Stevens Committee) HMSO, 1976 had proposed that planning authorities should have power to review mineral permissions. This was being considered by the government at the time, and may have exerted some influence on the company to make concessions in advance of legislation. But, as is suggested later in Chapter 4, the Section 52 arrangements were likely to prove far more satisfactory to the local authority than the promise of legislation which might be difficult, or expensive, to enforce.
13 Letter from Estate's Manager, London Brick, to County Planning Officer, 23 November 1978.
14 PAG, Minerals Subject Plan, Oxford Clay, Report 19 October, 1978, p.5.
15 Ibid pp.5-6.
16 PAG, Minerals Subject Plan, Oxford Clay, Report 2 November, 1978, p.10.
17 See note 14, p.2.
18 See note 16, p.8.
19 *Bedfordshire on Sunday*, 10 December, 1978.
20 Ibid.
21 *Bedfordshire on Sunday*, 15 October, 1978.
22 *The Guardian*, 4 and 10 November, 1978.
23 *Bedfordshire Times*, 10 and 24 November, 1978.
24 *Bedfordshire Journal*, 19 October and 30 November, 1978.
25 *The Guardian*, 4 November, 1978.
26 *Counter Press, Milton Keynes Socialist Paper*, December 1978, Janaury 1979, 'London Brick: it may smell but it makes money', pp.10-11.
27 *Bedfordshire Times*, 'Are the chimneys harmful?' 27 April, 1979.
28 Letter from Ray Young to County Planning Officer, 30 September, 1978.
29 Letter from County Planning Officer to Ray Young, 17 October, 1978.
30 Letter from Ray Young to County Planning Officer, 20 November, 1978.
31 *Bedfordshire on Sunday*, 18 March, 1979.
32 *Bedfordshire Times*, 10 November, 1978.
33 Described in A. Blowers, *The Limits of Power*, Oxford, Pergamon, Ch.4, 1980.

34 This is, of course, the same person as the writer. The conflict of academic and political roles is discussed in Chapter 1.
35 PAG, The replacement of Ridgmont Brickworks, Report, 11 January, 1979, p.5.
36 Report by Mr D.H. Lucas, Consultant, former Director of the CEGB Research Laboratory.
37 Report to ESC, 1 March, 1979, Agenda item 7 (22) p.178.
38 Letter from T.L. Barber, Cranfield Action Committee, 11 March, 1979.
39 Letter from R.G. Smith, Cranfield Action Committee, Bedfordshire Times, 19 April, 1979.
40 Letter to County Planning Officer, 18 April, 1979.
41 *Bedfordshire on Sunday*, 18 April, 1979.
42 The scheme for working the Quest pit was an integral part of the planning permission for the Stewartby works, and could not be implemented until permission was granted.
43 Letter from R.I. Harris and T.L. Barber, 25 May, 1979.
44 Quoted in a letter to county councillors from R.G. Smith, 16 July, 1979.
45 Letter to County Planning Officer from M.D. Geddes, Cranfield Institute of Technology, 26 April, 1979.
46 Cranfield Action Committee 'A cause for concern — Brickworks modernisation in Ridgmont', 15 July, 1979.
47 *Pollution in the Marston Vale*, Report of County Planning Officer, 11 January, 1979, p.1.
48 Royal Commission on Environmental Pollution, Fifth Report. *Air Pollution Control: An Integrated Approach*, Cmnd 6371, HMSO, January 1976, p.99.
49 See note 28, p.3.
50 The Investigation of Air Pollution: National Survey of Smoke and Sulphur Dioxide. Annual Surveys produced by Warren Springs Laboratory.
51 Quoted in Press release from Fletton Brickworks Liaison Committee, 28 November, 1978.
52 Quoted in *The Guardian*, 4 November, 1978.
53 *Bedfordshire on Sunday*, 26 November, 1978.
54 102nd Annual Report on Alkali and Works, 1965, HMSO, 1966.
55 Central Electricity Generating Board. Clarke, A.J., Lucas, D.H., Ross, F.F. 'Tall stacks — how effective are they?' Paper to Second International Clean Air Conference, Washington, December, 1970.
56 *Bedfordshire Journal*, 30 November, 1978.
57 Fletton Brickworks Liaison Committee, Press release, 18 April, 1979.
58 The findings were revealed in a letter from L.C.A. Nunn to Trustees of Emily Jones, 14 May, 1979, and in a letter from Dr. Paul Wix to J. Rees, 28 September, 1979.
59 *Bedfordshire on Sunday*, 1 July, 1979. Dr. Wix later interviewed a scientist who had been working at the aluminium works in North Wales who hinted that research into the effects of fluorides on people was conclusive (and detrimental). Economic considerations were likely to cause the findings to be suppressed. (The scientist was bound by the Official Secrets Act.)
60 Fletton Brickworks Liaison Committee, Press release, June, 1979.
61 *Bedfordshire Times*, 8 June, 1979.

62 The group was inaugurated as the Fletton Emissions Investigative Committee and decided a suitable acronym and logo were necessary to capture public imagination. The initials CHOKE were suggested but did not elicit a suitable title, so PROBE was chosen instead.

63 PROBE, Notes for Guidance, 25 July, 1979.

64 Tagg later circulated his research report on the effects of fluorides to councillors and other interested people (25 March, 1980).

65 PROBE, Press release, 15 August, 1979.

66 *Bedfordshire on Sunday*, 17 June, 1979.

67 London Brick Company Ltd. Planning Application of New Brickworks at King's Dyke Whittlesey to replace existing Brickworks known as Central 1 and 2 and C.B. 1. July 1979.

68 London Brick Company Ltd. Planning Application for Brickworks at Stewartby (and Ridgmont and Marston Thrift) and associated mineral working and landscaping, August 1979, p.18.

69 *Bedfordshire Times*, 29 September, 1979.

70 *Bedfordshire Journal*, 17 September, 1979.

71 Fenland District Council, Planning and Development Committee, Minute 234/79, 6 September, 1979.

72 Cremer and Warner (1970a and b) *The Environmental Assessment of the Existing and Proposed Brickworks in the Marston Vale, Bedfordshire*. a — General Appraisal. b — Main Report. Prepared for Bedfordshire County Council by Cremer and Warner. Consulting Engineers and Scientists — London and Cheshire.

73 Gilbert, O.L. 'Tree growth in the vicinity of the Ridgmont Brickworks Bedfordshire' (unpublished) 1971-9.

74 Petrilli, R.L. (1960) 'Epidemiological studies of air pollution effects in Genoa, Italy', Arch., *Environmental Health*, 12, 733-40.

75 Donaldson, R.J. (1974) 'Air pollution and health', Medical Officer of Health, Teeside Health Department, Spring.

76 Douglas, J.W.B. and Waller, R.E. (1966) 'Air pollution and respiratory infection in children', *British Journal of Preventive Social Medicine*, 20 (1), pp.1-8.

77 Lunn, J.E. et. al. (1967) 'Patterns of respiratory illness in Sheffield infant school on children', *British Journal of Preventive Social Medicine*, 21, pp.7-16.

78 Among the sensitive species were gladiolus, iris, tulip, azalea, gardenia, Douglas Fir, larch, apricot, peach, plum, and maize. See Cremer and Warner 1979b, Table 4.8.

79 Agate, J.N. et. al. (1949) 'Industrial fluorosis. A study of the hazard to man and animals near Fort William, Scotland'. A Report to the Fluorosis Committee. Medical Research Council, Memorandum 22, HMSO.

80 Kvartovkina, L.K. (1968) 'Effect of discharges from an aluminium works on health of children'. *Hyg. Sanit.* English Edition 33 (4-6), pp.106-08.

81 Five dilutions indicates that five or more volumes of air would be required to reduce the odour concentration to a threshold at which odour is perceptible.

82 *Bedfordshire Journal*, 8 November, 1979.

83 London Brick Company Ltd., Press Notice, 26 October, 1979.

84 London Brick Company Ltd. (1979). Brickworks Redevelopment Plan. London Brick Company Research Laboratories Assessment and Implications of the Cremer and Warner Report prepared for Bedfordshire County Council, p.1.

85 *Bedfordshire Times*, 2 November, 1979.
86 *Bedfordshire Times*, 3 November, 1979.
87 *Bedfordshire Times*, 16 November, 1979.
88 PROBE, Press release, 21 November, 1979.
89 *Bedfordshire Times*, 30 November, 1979.
90 *Bedfordshire Times*, 14 December, 1979.
91 *Bedford Record*, 5 February, 1980.
92 Letter from Richard Dudding, DoE, to Peter Goode, 7 March, 1980.
93 Letter to *Bedfordshire Times*, 21 March, 1980.
94 *Bedfordshire Times*, 14 March, 1980.
95 *Bedford Record*, 18 December, 1979.
96 After meeting the manufacturer, London Brick concluded the claims made for the process were optimistic, *Milton Keynes Mirror*, 9 January, 1980.
97 *Bedfordshire Times*, 28 December, 1980.
98 *Bedfordshire Times*, 21 January, 1980. This was an out of court settlement, neither side willing to cover the costs of establishing its case. See Chapter 2.

CHAPTER 4
DEADLOCK

'Say not, the struggle nought availeth,
The labour and the wounds are vain,
The enemy faints not, nor faileth,
And as things have been, they remain.'

(Arthur Hugh Clough)

The phase of confrontation

Sometime towards the end of 1979 and the beginning of 1980 the debate
took a new turn. The atmosphere shifted from one of negotiation to one of
confrontation. The change was marked by the positions adopted both by the
company and its opponents. Each had reached a point beyond which it was
not prepared to retreat. There now developed a contest which each side was
determined to win. Indeed, it might be said that the desire to win was
paramount, rather than seeking a solution which all parties might find
acceptable. Although politics has often been described as the art of compromise what is often ignored is that compromise might only be achieved
after conflict. It is also the case that some conflicts do not result in
compromise but the victory of one set of ideas and policies over another. In
the brickfields case the conflict was clear, and well defined by the beginning
of 1980, though the outcome was difficult to predict.

Although the opposition was achieving considerable favourable publicity, the advantages possessed by the company were considerable. It had
gained the support of the Council's officers and of a substantial majority of
the Environmental Services Committee by its willingness to make concessions and to provide long sought environmental gains. London Brick could
point to major advances on both the major concerns — dereliction and
pollution. And its final position on both of these was made explicit through
two major developments during February 1980.

The Section 52 Agreement

It had been clear from the outset that London Brick was prepared to accept a complete revision of the planning conditions covering the whole Marston Vale. This had been formally established in the planning applications submitted in August 1979 (see Chapter 3, page 90). What remained was for these environmental improvements to be embodied in a legal and binding agreement drawn up under Section 52 of the Town and Country Planning Act, 1971, and signed by the company. It would be put into effect once planning permission had been granted. In September 1979, a sub-committee of seven members was set up 'to supervise detailed negotiations with London Brick Company and the execution of conditional planning agreements'.[1] The committee met four times (7 and 24 January, and 13 and 19 February 1980) and presented two reports to the main committee (17 January and 28 February). Its members gained considerable detailed knowledge of the whole application and its ramifications. They became informed experts with knowledge far more extensive than that of the main committee, let alone of other members of the Council hitherto uninvolved in the issue.

There were three major reasons for the Section 52 Agreement. First, it would revoke without compensation the old planning conditions, which 'had been an embarrassment ever since' according to County Secretary, John Dawson, by new conditions which would 'do much to clarify the legal obligations of the developers in respect of the land which they will then be working'.[2] Second, the agreement would cover matters outside the conditions applied to the planning permissions, thus enabling those areas no longer wanted for excavation by the company and those near the villages to be omitted altogether. And third, as an agreement acceptable to the company, it would be enforceable through the courts and provide for greater control and flexibility on the part of the planning authority than would be possible through planning conditions alone.

From London Brick's point of view a Section 52 Agreement also had advantages. It narrowed down the area of conflict and provided a set of conditions that would not be the subject of conflict. It would help to promote a favourable image for the company, leaving it free, if it wished, to appeal against refusal on grounds of pollution alone, since all environmental matters had been agreed. It was possible that the company appreciated the impact of proposed legislation arising from the Stevens report, which would allow future revision of existing planning conditions.[3] In the words of Tony

Griffin the county planner: 'They see the writing on the wall.' John Dawson's view was different, pointing out that the Stevens committee had not proposed revocation without compensation. 'I don't believe that such conditions would be anything like as good as those in this agreement.' In any case the legislation was vague and imprecise and it was not clear in what form it would be enacted. 'We are weighing a certainty against a statement of intent which is imprecise.'

The agreement was revised and refined until the members were satisfied. It was a complex legal document which had to take into account various options on sites and kiln design. It would come into effect six months after planning permission unless the company indicated that it did not wish to implement, or that any conditions imposed proved unacceptable to the company. Basically it divided the Vale into two parts, each relating to one of the new works, and identified areas of future working and the areas to be excluded, including the stand–off areas around the villages (Figure 4.1). After considerable discussion over several meetings clause 4 of the document provided for the following agreements:

1. The demolition of all the disused works and other buildings.
2. The removal of debris from the sites and agreement to use them only for agriculture, forestry or amenity tree planting.
3. To accept revocation of existing permission without compensation.
4. To use certain pits for recreation, fishing and wildlife conservation, and to landscape them.
5. To maintain existing hedgerows.
6. To provide a scheme for advance planting of trees.
7. To undertake a programme of research into methods of pollution control including alternative methods of firing bricks. On the insistence of members the following sentence was added to the clause: 'The Council shall be kept fully informed, either directly or through its nominated consultants, on the objectives, timing and progress of the said research programme, and shall be given the opportunity to be represented at all meetings and discussions between the Health and Safety Executive and the Owner which may be called to review the progress and results of the said programme'.[4]
8. To install 'as and when they become available at an economic cost such further practicable refinements for the reduction of pollutants' as may be agreed.[5]
9. To cooperate with the Council on monitoring and to make the results known (another clause introduced by the members).
10. To pay for any highway improvements undertaken by the Council to ensure access for the new works.

The agreement was accompanied by schedules setting out the conditions which would be mutually acceptable in the event of a permission being granted. These covered a series of unexceptional details such as noise,

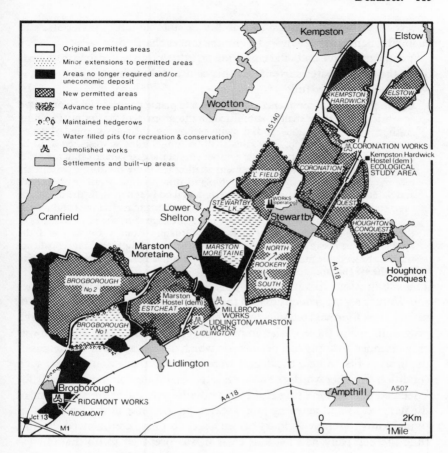

Figure 4.1: Section 52 Planning Agreement
Source: Bedfordshire County Council, *Oxford Clay, Subject Plan,* figures 4.1 and 7.1

removal of machinery, and methods of working the excavations. But they also contained conditions of the highest significance relating to the problems of dereliction and air pollution. Provision was to be made for schemes with fixed time-scales for the restoration and after-use of the pits. These schemes must provide both for temporary and immediate restoration (e.g. low level agriculture) and for final restoration. This was to take account of the uncertainty about the future availability of suitable filling materials, and enabled schemes to be reviewed if circumstances changed.[6]

A comprehensive and vital condition on kiln design was also introduced. Since the later debates surrounded this clause and modifications to it, it is worth quoting here in full:

> Before construction commences of the kilns and plant comprised in the proposed new brickworks there shall be submitted for the approval of the County Planning Authority plans, sections and drawings showing their layout and detailed engineering construction. The kilns shall be tunnel kilns so designed as to be capable of incinerating the organic components of the gases given off in the brick firing processes. This last requirement shall cease to be binding if within six months prior to the submission of such plans, drawings and sections the Health and Safety Executive or such other governmental body as may in future discharge their statutory responsibilities have certified in writing that after the conduct of a research programme by the applicants in accordance with the requirements of the planning agreement between the Bedfordshire County Council and the applicants, the use of such kilns would not at the date of the Certificate constitute the best practicable means of eliminating or minimising the odours which derive from the said organic components.[7]

This was the Council's attempt to apply the recommendations of the Cremer and Warner report, which advised the prior removal of odours by the use of tunnel kilns if proved technically and economically feasible after a research programme. But there was an important qualification. This condition was only intended to apply to a permission which did not approve the details of the brickworks. Where the details were approved there would be no such condition. In other words the way was left open for the company to apply for a detailed permission using Hoffman technology on the first phase of one of the new works and agreeing to a research programme on the feasibility of tunnel kilns to remove odours before a second phase commenced. By this time the company had made it clear it was prepared to do that. It was its final concession in the hope of getting a favourable response and an opportunity to begin construction of the first phase of the Stewartby works.

Despite the company's willingness to accept the agreement, a number of councillors were extremely suspicious, even cynical, about the terms which had been forged.[8] Councillors Hendry and Chapman, members of PROBE, aired their concerns at the Environmental Services meeting on 17 January, and were particularly worried that the company could back out on the grounds that conditions might be introduced which were unacceptable to the company. This turned out to be a prophetic concern. They were warned by John Dawson. 'You run the risk of losing the agreement if you impose major new conditions.'

At a later meeting on 28 February Councillor Kemp voiced his misgivings about the restoration conditions, feeling they were pitifully weak and difficult to enforce. He wanted restoration schemes to be presented in advance of the permissions being granted, otherwise, he felt excavation would increase with nothing being done. London Brick should pay for restoration through its profits. 'We are not making LBC pay nearly enough for the privilege of avoiding a public inquiry which, from their point of view, is what this is all about.' He was supported by Philip Hendry, who considered the agreement was being overplayed since 95 per cent of it was common industrial practice. The officers retaliated saying that London Brick could have got permission (whether via the Council or the Minister) just for the works, but had been persuaded to look at the whole situation. There was the risk of forcing it to revert simply to an application for new works. Nevertheless, the agreement was a powerful card in the hands of the company and its supporters on the Council. A second development, contemporary with the Section 52 Agreement, raised much less local interest, but had an important bearing on the long term environmental improvement of the Marston Vale, and contributed to the overall attractiveness of the plans being put forward by the company. This was unveiled at the Vale of Belvoir public inquiry during late February, 1980.

The Vale of Belvoir Inquiry

Some fifty miles from Bedfordshire, at Stoke Rochford near Grantham, a major public inquiry which had some bearing on the brickfields debate had been taking evidence since the end of October 1979. The major issue was whether to allow the National Coal Board (NCB) to develop three new mines in East Leicestershire in the environmentally sensitive Vale of Belvoir. Bedfordshire clearly was not in a position to judge the central question but it did have an interest depending on the decision finally reached.

> It is concerned solely with the situation in which the Secretary of State might have decided in principle to permit the application in whole or in part and be directing his mind to the question of spoil disposal. The Council has indicated that it will give evidence and make submissions to demonstrate that it is both desirable and practicable in the interests of Bedfordshire residents to remove some or possibly all of the colliery spoil by rail to Bedfordshire where it would be employed to fill and restore to agriculture, forestry or recreational use the exhausted brick pits in the Marston Valley.[9]

In some ways this appeared to be a rerun of the debate about the use of

Nottinghamshire spoil raised during the Brickfields Conference in 1968 (see Chapter 2, page 32). But there were significant differences. Nottinghamshire had been trying to dispose of spoil from working mines, the Vale of Belvoir had yet to be developed; London Brick had since established London Brick Landfill which was endeavouring to fill the pits by offering a waste disposal service, and so could offer the experience and expertise of large scale operations such as that with the GLC (see Chapter 3, page 90); and the County Council and London Brick had joined forces to make a convincing case for the transfer of spoil, should it become available at a time when they were still debating the new planning applications for redevelopment of brickworks. The proposal took up one and a half days of the inquiry (27 and 28 February, 1980).

The County Council had agreed to make representations at the inquiry.[10] Three submissions were put forward, one by Tony Griffin on behalf of the County Council outlining the need for restoration[11]; one by London Brick Landfill describing the feasibility of the operation[12]; and one by the Forestry Commission to demonstrate prospects for forestry in the restored pits.[13]

The County Council's case was, basically, that there were over 750 hectares already worked and 671 hectares still likely to be worked in the Vale, giving sufficient space for 120 million tonnes of Belvoir waste immediately and a further 153 million over the next 30 years. This would be quite sufficient for the entire output over 75 years of the waste likely to arise from the operation of the Vale of Belvoir coalfield (estimated at 304 million tonnes), Chapter 2, page 26 shows the potential input of the Belvoir waste on the brickpits in the Marston Vale expressed in terms of the space that could be filled. London Brick demonstrated that it was feasible to transfer the spoil of one of the mines to the brickpits in the southern Marston Vale provided a rail transfer station was constructed. Reception of all the fill from the three proposed mines would prove more difficult but was possible, although it would require the construction of two or three transfer stations to serve brickpits in other parts of the Vale.

Apart from the question of the feasibility of the proposal, the inquiry revealed two other features of the brickfields debate — the company's attitudes to the costs of restoration and the role of the county planning officials. The company's interpretation of the original planning conditions, a recurring theme of earlier debates (see Chapter 2, pp.44-46), was probed during the inquiry. Mr Needs of London Brick made it clear that the company intended to recover the costs involved in creating a railway terminal, although the space would be offered free of charge. The company felt that 'reasonable costs' did not mean it was obliged to pay for spoil or its transportation in order to conform to the conditions. Indeed it regarded the pits as an asset as the following dialogue makes clear:

> **Question** (*NCB barrister*): Am I right . . . that having created that scar for profit, your company is only prepared to restore the claypits providing that in doing so it can seek to achieve a profit from the exercise?
>
> **Answer** (*Mr Needs*) No . . . My company is willing to do all that is required of them by the Planning Permission or Agreements under which it mines clay. In addition to that, it does budget significant sums of money towards restoration and improving the environment . . .[14]
>
> . . . Is reasonable cost something which London Brick is expected to go out and pay to acquire a commodity to fill, or is it something to do with the cost of all the installations and all the activity and what have you . . . I suspect the Minister really was referring to the fact that the company, in view of what it does, should not be expected to go and pay very much to attract it.[15]

What it came down to was that London Brick would provide a service for the transport of colliery spoil from Leicestershire to Bedfordshire so long as it made a return on its investment and that the costs were borne elsewhere — by which was clearly meant the National Coal Board.

The question of who should pay was raised again in the cross examination of Tony Griffin, the planning officer, and some doubt was cast on the failure of the County Council to ensure the original planning conditions were fulfilled. Tony Griffin felt that responsibility for bearing the cost fell on three parties — the central government, who gave the original planning permission in the full knowledge that dereliction would be created as a result; on the National Coal Board who were creating the waste; and on the London Brick Company, though whether it was enough simply to offer the void space free he was not prepared to say.

It transpired that London Brick regarded the pits as assets and interpreted the concept of 'reasonable terms' as meaning the ability to realise a profit on capital investment. It also left the suspicion that the planning authority could have been more insistent in seeking to get the company to fulfil its obligations. The harmony between the company and the Council's officers, at least on questions of restoration, was clearly evident. The prospect, however distant and however illusory, of Belvoir's spoil filling up the Marston Vale was a further advantage to the company as it entered the critical period of decision making. As Mr Dawson phrased it in his peroration at the inquiry; 'this is a unique opportunity, and I use those words advisedly, to solve one of Bedfordshire's greatest planning problems on the fields of Leicestershire'.[16]

Political developments: PROBE's tactics

In the early months of 1980 the members of the County Council were beginning to make up their minds about the coming decision. It was time to persuade the uncommitted. The opponents urged their arguments both privately and publicly. Although PROBE had so far succeeded in keeping up a varied and prominent Press coverage on the issue, it was aware that London Brick was beginning to seize the initiative by making concessions and adopting a higher public profile. The PROBE committee met on 26 February to review its tactics with a faintly desperate air. The members considered that a 'call-in' by the Minister was unlikely.[17] The Cambridgeshire application was awaiting the DoE report, which members felt would reveal little that was new or helpful to the opposition cause. The prospect of Belvoir spoil and London Brick's agreement to a new condition covering restoration, and to a phased replacement of the works at Stewartby providing an opportunity for research before phase 2, were likely to prove very persuasive with the Environmental Services Committee; and the crucial meeting was only a month away. So far PROBE had managed to prevaricate and delay the decision but time was now running out. What was needed was a more direct appeal to the members of the County Council.

Anthony Stanbury, the businessman member of the group, took up the idea of direct persuasion. He suggested that PROBE capitalise on the prevailing ignorance among members. 'We can appeal on emotional terms — how can you vote for it when you know nothing about it. We must throw caution to the winds.' Other councillors were more circumspect. Allan Chapman the councillor for the Ridgmont area argued: 'We must not be seen as a bunch of cranks who go on opposing when most of the complaints have been met.' It was accepted that the approach must be both factual and emotional. 'We have one final chance of influencing councillors by emphasising pollution' said the Marquis of Tavistock.

The attack would be developed in two ways. One would be by a letter or leaflet distributed to all members of the Council, focusing on the health issue and urging refusal of the application with a call for a public inquiry. This would be followed up by an invitation to all the councillors and their spouses to a meeting on a Sunday evening at the Sculpture Gallery in Woburn Abbey, where direct persuasion could be applied. It was felt that such an invitation to the seat of Bedfordshire's most prominent landowner and noble would prove irresistible, especially if it was accompanied by champagne to be donated by Anthony Stanbury and Peter Goode. Thus

PROBE was already accepting the likelihood of defeat at the first committee stage but hoping to persuade enough councillors who would be able to swing the vote at a meeting of the whole Council. PROBE had no concern for further compromise but saw the issue as a trial of strength which one or other of the adversaries must win outright.

A public debate

Until this point the adversaries had only met informally and in secret. In February a public meeting arranged by the Bedfordshire Preservation Society (who were becoming active on the issue) took place at Ampthill in the centre of the county. Nearly 70 people turned up including six county councillors, five representatives of London Brick, some brickworkers, and representatives of local pressure groups such as GASP and CAC. The three main speakers were James Bristow for London Brick and Philip Hendry and Peter Goode for the opposition. Bristow, appearing confident and assured in his decision to take the offensive, announced: 'We thought the plans would be snatched out of our hands and we'd be told to get on with it as soon as possible.' He stressed all the benefits of the plans — fewer chimneys, less smoke, less traffic and 'less man-made erections'. The new works would guarantee 10,000 jobs, generate £4 million in wages a year, and provide £500,000 in rates for the county. The company took pride in its achievement and would make profits as well as providing great advantages for the community. It was most anxious to get the Stewartby project started.

Peter Goode was diffident and unconvincing. 'I don't want to cross swords with Mr Bristow — he has too much expertise present in the hall.' He had experienced fluorosis in his cattle and the cause was evidently the brickworks. He recognised the need for new works. 'It's not the package I object to but the price', in terms of the high rate of pollution that would continue. 'It's in the air we breathe, killing the vegetation, and is the price we are going to pay for new works.' Philip Hendry was effective with his brand of cheerful sarcasm and selective argument. 'We have seen far more activity from London Brick in the past year than ever before' — presumably because the company now wanted something. 'Just because LBC is a large employer in the county it does not give them carte blanche to despoil it.' Brickmaking using the fletton process was cheap and the new works would last many years. The company could afford to put in the controls demanded.

Among the audience there was concern about the lack of information and a suggestion that the new works with taller chimneys might result in an increase in 'acid rain'. This claim made by Dr. Derek Holloman of the Rothamsted Institute, was taken up by the local Press, and stirred up once again the international concern about the plans from Scandinavia. 'It is very likely that we will suffer pollution from these giant new chimneys. I hope we will claim the right to speak at public inquiries into such schemes', said the Swedish minister for agriculture and the environment.[18] The company's claims that emissions would cause 'relatively small' amounts of sulphuric acid were treated with scepticism, and led the *Bedfordshire Times* in its leader to come out strongly in favour of a public inquiry. 'Opinions and theories are extremely easy to come by but hard facts are somewhat scarce and always, it seems, complicated. Ought we therefore, to act in relative ignorance on such a desperately important environmental issue . . . if there is the slightest danger to health the answer to LBC must be a resounding "No". If councillors feel unqualified to act then the matter should go to a full public inquiry.'[19] It was in this atmosphere of public debate that the scene was set for the climax of the debate.

The political environment

Over the preceding 18 months certain common ground had been established. The landscape and restoration aspects had been embodied in the Section 52 Agreement. Other respects were less clear cut. Although the site of the southern works at Ridgmont looked probable, it was not finally concluded. The compromise on pollution with a phased permission and research before subsequent phases had not achieved a consensus. During the early months of 1980 the arguments gathered intensity, with each side seeking to assert its claims for the attention of the county councillors. London Brick and its supporters (notably the Alkali Inspector and the community health physician) stressed the lack of danger and the improvements provided by new works. Opponents, particularly the PROBE group, were emphasising the lack of evidence, past neglect by the company, and the need to ensure pollution control for such a long term project before it was commissioned. Both sides had invoked experts to support their claims. The political environment created by this sustained and intense debate was one of tension and uncertainty.

By March it had become clear that the decision would probably rest with the County Council. Strident calls for a public inquiry from PROBE and in the local Press, backed by letters, meetings and informal approaches to officials and ministers at the DoE had drawn only a muffled response.[20] The Department had sought advice from the county planners. Tony Griffin's view was that the Council would be 'pissing against the wind' if it thought the DoE would give any support to the opposition since they were firmly behind London Brick. 'All they want is to keep down the price of bricks.' Certainly the planners were in little doubt where they stood. At an inquiry all the cards would be stacked in favour of London Brick, with little expertise to defend the Council's position if it decided to oppose the application. It was far more preferable to consolidate the gains already made and to decide the matter locally. The only outstanding element from the DoE was its long awaited report, and even that was firmly expected to add little to the debate and would if anything add to London Brick's case.

It is impossible to know how or when each councillor made up his or her mind on the issue. Each received different signals and impressions. Some, especially those on the Environmental Services Committee, had been involved in the whole course of the debate. Among these the Chairman and Vice-Chairman had entered discussions with the company. Others, the seven members of the Brickfields sub-committee, had developed a great awareness of all the issues through their detailed negotiation of the Section 52 Agreement. Others still, like Councillor Blowers (and Councillors Hendry and Chapman not on ESC) were deeply committed to the PROBE organisation and therefore aware of all the information coming from the environmentalists' side. Each councillor took his or her decision at a specific time. The process of decision taking can be expressed as a continuum. At either end were those who had made up their minds almost from the outset, and no amount of information or debate was likely to sway them. Among these appeared to be a substantial number of the ESC who favoured the negotiated proposal. Near the middle of the continuum were those who were uncertain, prepared to weigh the evidence before reaching a decision. It was their votes that each side sought to secure. Once they had made up their minds, however painstakingly and marginally, they, too, were unlikely to be dissuaded, and new information would only be used selectively to reinforce the conclusions they had reached. By March, it seemed, most members of the ESC had reached this point. But beyond the committee were the large majority of members, thus far uninvolved in the issue whose views could be swayed one way or another. There were those members right at the middle of the continuum whose votes were uncertain until the last, and liable to change as the debate fluctuated. Their votes were likely to prove decisive, since it had become apparent that the matter was highly likely to be decided by the Council itself.

Although the decision could have been taken by the ESC under its delegated powers as the local planning authority, the majority of members felt that the issue was so substantial that it should be referred to the Council. A survey of opinion undertaken by the *Bedfordshire Times* revealed strong support for this. Eight of the members canvassed considered this was the appropriate democratic forum. Councillor Rex Upchurch expressed their view: 'So many people will be affected by the new works — it is vital that everybody has a say so that the right decision is made'. Others, notably Keith White, the Chairman, and Andy Blowers, the Labour Leader, were more guarded. The accepted the democratic case for a Council decision but were concerned about removing it from the committee which had full knowledge of all the issues. Councillor White argued that all councillors should be fully briefed while Councillor Blowers stressed the significance of the decision. 'Nothing as large as this has been considered by environmental services since the war — this is a decision that will not merely affect this generation but those to come.'[21] At the ESC meeting on 17 January it was agreed by the committee that the matter should be referred to the Council and that a special meeting of the committee, to which all members of the Council would be invited, should decide on the recommendation to be put to the Council.

This surrender by a committee to the Council was somewhat unusual since committees normally guard their independence jealously. References of delegated matters may be frequent in a 'hung' Council where committees are not necessarily representative of the whole Council (and this was to be the case in the 'hung' Council following the 1981 election).[22] It seems that the explanation for the move stemmed from a growing division within the majority Conservative group. Councillor Hendry, the Leader, though not a member of ESC was strongly identified with the opposition to London Brick. He felt his influence over members could only be exerted if it was debated by the Council. Keith White, the chairman of the committee and Deputy Leader of the Conservative Group, was a powerful influence over the committee and therefore, given his sympathies with the application, was likely to secure a decision favourable to the company if the decision was taken by the committee. But he was unable to resist the move to take the matter to the Council and conceded rather than being defeated on the matter. The rift between Hendry and White was becoming apparent, and their power struggle was one of the more interesting political features in the subsequent history of the debate. As it turned out the reference to the Council was to result in an unexpected and controversial twist in the story.

Given the potential split among the Conservatives, it was possible that the small opposition groups might be in the unusual position of exerting a crucial influence on the decision. The Labour Group of nine members considered various alternatives and reached no firm conclusion. Councillor Blowers confessed he had not finally made up his mind and felt it might be better to take no decision on the issue. The group left it to him to decide their position. This, too, proved crucial since the Labour Group subsequently took a united stand which proved decisive when the Council met to take its decision.

Up to this point the debate had been fragmented. London Brick had pursued discussions with the planning officials and, through them, with the planning committee. The opponents had orchestrated public opinion through pressure groups and the media. As the issue became focused around the pollution question the conflict became both polarised and more politicised. It was no longer possible to confine it within the conventional channels of negotiation between officials, the company and the committee. The DoE had signalled their expectation that the matter should be decided locally. The conflict was pushed further into the political arena. There was now a direct and open clash between the two sides beginning with the public meeting at Ampthill and continuing in the Council debates. The decision to refer the matter to the full Council raises a question of theoretical significance. Was this an expression of pluralist politics, or was the more open forum of the County Council a means by which élitist ends could be more effectively pursued?

The First Decision — Environmental Services
After eighteen months of discussion March, 1980, was a month of decision.

Extensive consultations had been undertaken on the applications. Before the ESC met, a consultative meeting was held with the two district councils involved at which the details of the negotiations and agreements were expounded in full.[23] The Mid-Bedfordshire District Council, covering the whole of the southern and a small part of the northern area of the Vale, were generally in favour of the application. Their Environmental Health Officer argued that the only action that could be taken on pollution would be by an injunction on grounds of public nuisance or health hazard; a case difficult to prove on the evidence and in the face of the Alkali Inspector's insistence that best practicable means were being employed. He was of the opinion 'that the proposal will go a long way to alleviate the existing problems'[24] The

District Council were strongly opposed to the Marston Thrift site and pointed out that it would give rise to two industrial areas (the site of the old works and the new one). North Bedfordshire, covering the northern area around Stewartby, had objected to the proposals arguing, along with Cremer and Warner, that controls had been insufficiently researched, that the restoration proposals were inadequate and that the design of the proposed works was of a poor standard.[25] However, at the consultative meeting the North Bedfordshire representatives said they welcomed the package and would prepare a revised statement, and by the time of the ESC meeting had changed their minds and decided to support the views of the county planning officers on the pollution question.[26]

Altogether 50 bodies had been consulted (Figure 4.2), of whom half (24) were particularly concerned about pollution and 13 opposed to the proposed site at Marston Thrift. It is very difficult to categorise the responses, but five, including the prominent opponents of the company such as PROBE, the Bedfordshire Preservation Society and the NFU, favoured total rejection of the proposals in the hope of a public inquiry, and 17, including most of the local authorities and parish councils, argued that steps should be taken at the application stage to ensure adequate pollution safeguards.

Among the parish councils only Cranfield and Wootton were firmly in favour of the proposals. Together with three parishes in the Vale itself (Millbrook, Lidlington and Marston Moretaine) they favoured the Ridgmont site, demonstrating clear local preference on the siting issue. Other parishes were equivocal arguing for specific local measures, alternative techniques and monitoring of emissions. As might be anticipated, the statutory bodies consulted as a matter of routine raised no objections subject to conditions, but only the Alkali Inspectorate and the Area Health Authority were positive in their support of the proposals. The majority of the responses revealed the uncertainty surrounding the issue and some, coming from committed opponents, were bluntly hostile to the proposals.

Cremer and Warner's attitude

On the whole the consultations merely reaffirmed the known attitudes in the debate and were unlikely, in themselves, to influence the adopted position of the councillors. Of more immediate significance was the attitude of Cremer and Warner, whose report had prepared the ground for the negotiation on the pollution issue. Although they were primarily concerned with odour, their argument in favour of rejection or deferral had not been

Figure 4.2a Responses from consultations

Consultees	Comments	No. of responses
i. County Council Depts.	No significant objections.	2
ii Local Authorities	Included 3 District Councils broadly approving the negotiated proposals. 3 Country Councils concerned with pollution effects.	9
iii. Parish and Town Councils	Concerned with pollution and local environmental issues such as site of southern works and clay extration.	10
iv. Statutory and govt. bodies	No objections and Alkali Inspectorate support the proposals.	7
v. Local preservation societies	Object to proposals on pollution grounds.	5
vi. Local ad hoc groups (PROBE, GASP, CAC)	Probe against, CAC in favour, GASP no observations.	3
vii. National groups (FoE, Nature Conservancy, Ramblers, NFU)	Objections from FoE, NFU and Ramblers.	4
viii. Area Health Authority	No health problem.	1
ix. Individuals	Object on pollution grounds	6
x. Others	Cranfield Institute and Civil Aviation Authority concerned about effects of Marston Thrift on aircraft, Open University (report from Roger Tagg).	3
	TOTAL	50

endorsed by the county planners. Instead the idea of a part permission with deferral of the rest had been adopted. If Cremer and Warner could be persuaded to support this view then the hopes of London Brick and its advocates would receive a further fillip. At first it appeared that Cremer and Warner would stick to their guns. They produced a detailed refutation of London Brick's response to the original Cremer and Warner report. They indicated the major differences that existed between their view and that of the company. They believed that odour was a nuisance. They were not satisfied that London Brick had researched all the available technologies for odour removal and considered 'that LBC should demonstrate that all

Figure 4.2b Organisations consulted

Consultees	Comments	No. of responses
i. County Council Depts.	Country Surveyor, Chief Arts and Recreation Officer.	2
ii. Local Authorities	District Councils – North Beds. Mid Beds. South Beds. Country Councils – Bucks., Cambs., Herts., Northants., Norfolk. Milton Keynes DC.	9
iii. Parish and Town Councils	Stewartby, Houghton Conquest, Marston Moretaine, Millbrook, Lidlington, Wootton, Elstow, Ampthill, Kempstone Town and Kempston Rural, Cranfield.	10
iv. Statutory and govt. bodies	Ministry of Agriculture, Fisheries and Food, Anglia Water Authority, Central Electricity Generating Board, Eastern Gas, Health and Safety Executive, British Rail, Department of Transport.	7
v. Local Preservation Societies	Beds., N. Beds., and Leighton Buzzard Pres. Socs., Woburn Sands and District Soc.	5
vi. Local ad hoc groups	PROBE, GASP, CAC	3
vii. National groups	Friends of the Earth, National Farmers Union, Ramblers' Association, Nature Conservancy.	4
viii. Area Health Authority		1
ix. Individuals		6
x. Others	Civil Aviation Authority Cranfield Institute, Open University	3
	TOTAL	50

Source: Bedfordshire County Council, Environmental Services Committee, Agenda, March 27 1980, part 4

available technologies have been tried, and have proved unsuitable for this process before planning permission is granted for the proposed development. Once the present proposed investment is made and construction starts on the new Hoffman kilns, there will be little or no pressure on LBC to evaluate alternative technologies.'[27] This is very much the line taken by the company's opponents. In a technical critique Cremer and Warner asserted that London Brick had not substantiated its claims about the problems of incinerating odours in Hoffman kilns and that the company was not conversant with recent developments in tunnel kiln technology. It appeared that London Brick simply wished to proceed with new works as fast as possible and therefore exaggerated the time needed to investigate new techniques. 'In view of the very long development programme anticipated by LBC, it is clear they do not consider such work as compatible with their present expansion programme.' (p.15) The company had neglected monitoring, relying on the production of data for national surveys rather than for the specific emissions from the brickworks which were high, especially over short periods. Finally, the company's estimate of the costs of tunnel kilns was unsupported by evidence. In Cremer and Warner's view the capital costs could not be established without proper investigation, and other costs and savings such as operating costs, the flexibility of new systems to cope with changing markets and the environmental benefits should be part of a full evaluation. Until this was done the conclusions drawn by the company should not be allowed 'to prevent the development of tunnel kilns in the programme' (p.16).

This hard-hitting rebuttal of London Brick's claims about the technical and financial feasibility of pollution measures may have been inspired by professional pique, but it was potentially powerful support to the pollution lobby. However Cremer and Warner failed to back this strong line at the committee meeting in March. At first their representative, Mr. Rice, seemed inclined to maintain the consultants' line arguing there was not enough knowledge to lead to the approval of Hoffman kilns at this stage. But after the lunch adjournment a different tone was evident, and as the afternoon wore on Mr Rice displayed an increasing degree of enthusiasm for the part permission proposal advocated by the county planners. When asked to react to the wider issues Mr. Rice responded:

> We wouldn't normally give an opinion on the wider aspects but I will give an unofficial and personal view. You must consider the totality of the problem including environmental restoration, amenity and public health compared with other hazards such as the car, alcohol and tobacco. We are all exposed to risks in

an industrial society. Taking all these factors into account I would have been influenced by first, there is an existing operation and we have some kind of measure of what it is producing; second, I would look at the chance presented by [the part permission] to bring about a substantial improvement in the total scene; third, is the pollution level enough to satisfy all demands; fourth, we can't rate the residual risk very highly; fifth, part permission does give control of the situation to the County Council and sixth, it keeps the door open for further improvements. If I were being asked I'd go for part permission — it is a good way forward. I would expect my local representative to do that.

Afterwards Cremer and Warner confirmed this change of heart in a letter to the County Planning Officer, claiming that 'the question became that of deciding whether the loss of some possible, but as yet indeterminate, abatement of odour emission at Stewartby Phase 1 was justified having regard to other long sought environmental improvements that might be secured in the shorter term'. The part permission 'could at worst achieve *almost* all that could reasonably be expected from the recommendations of our October 1979 report, so far as improvement in air quality are concerned'.[28] It appeared that Cremer and Warner had been persuaded to make this apologia during the lunch break. Certainly this intervention was partly responsible for the contrasting moods between the morning and afternoon sessions of the ESC meeting held on 27 March, 1980. During the morning events seemed to be flowing in favour of the company's opponents. The afternoon, when the decision on the application was taken, possessed an entirely different atmosphere.

ESC meeting, March 1980

The special meeting of the ESC was attended by 20 of the 22 members of the committee (16 remaining for the afternoon), and 18 other members of the Council (declining to seven in the afternoon) who were able to participate but not vote. They were presented with a compendious report of 79 pages in ten sections covering all aspects of the debate. The pollution issue comprised several aspects — sulphur oxide, fluorides, odour, public health, control measures, monitoring and the location of works — and the various expert opinions on the subject were quoted and the concerns outlined. On the environmental issues the report reflected the unequivocal welcome given to the proposals on all sides. 'From the local environmental standpoint alone, a detailed examination of the improvements . . . must inevitably lead to the conclusion that there is a great deal to be gained from the granting of planning permission'.[29] From all the evidence and observations the planners concluded there were two broad options available. Option 1 would follow the advice of Cremer and Warner and refuse the applications until research had been completed into the practicability of removing the odour. Option 2 would be to grant a detailed planning permission for a Hoffman kiln on the first phase of one of the new works, while a research programme was undertaken which would dictate the kiln design for the remaining three phases. This was in line with the agreement reached with the company. The first option might lead to an appeal and inquiry affording all parties the opportunities for a wide debate of the problem. But it faced the risk that the company might not appeal or, if it did, the Council would be faced with opposition from the Alkali Inspector. Option 2 offered a guaranteed research programme, monitoring, cooperation with the company and immediate improvements. 'On balance therefore I am firmly of the view that the best option to pursue for the good of Bedfordshire is the second option.'[30]

If this option was followed then other choices had to be made. The remaining three phases could be refused or deferred until the research was complete, running the risk of appeal, or outline permission could be granted on all three phases leaving only the details of the kiln design to be approved later. This would ensure the implementation of the Section 52 Agreement, the research programme and the cooperation of the company and the Alkali Inspector. There was also the choice as to where the first phase permission should be granted. Since it might prove difficult to accommodate two tunnel kilns at Ridgmont, and since the company no longer wished to develop there first it followed that the first phase should be developed at Stewartby. Finally the planners faced the question of the alternative southern sites, outlining the case for and against each of the proposals. 'Having regard to all the factors, therefore, I am of the opinion that, on local grounds, redevelopment of the existing site at Ridgmont would prove overall to be the best location to serve the southern section of the Vale.'[31]

At last the planners had capitulated in the face of the opposition to their preference for Marston Thrift. The planners, after some soul searching, had come down firmly in favour of the negotiated solution and recommended the committee to grant a full planning permission on the first stage of the Stewartby works using conventional kilns; to grant permission for the remaining phase at Stewartby and both phases at Ridgmont excluding kiln designs; and to defer a decision on Marston Thrift pending withdrawal of the application by the company. These permissions would carry with them the full package of conditions and the Section 52 Agreement including, for the later three phases, the significant condition which required tunnel kilns unless the research programme demonstrated they would not constitute the best practicable means of eliminating or minimising the odours. The report concluded: 'In my opinion this total package is, in all the circumstances, the best that can be achieved for Bedfordshire, and there is everything to be gained from granting planning permissions on the basis set out above'.[32]

Tony Griffin spent the first hour of the meeting presenting this report, and the remainder of the morning session was taken up with questions and speeches mainly from non-members of the committee who were hostile to the proposals. The health concerns were prominent and research was inconclusive. As Cremer and Warner put it: 'If you can't identify a medical problem, there is nothing that can go away'. But Allan Chapman waved 67 letters which he claimed were evidence of a medical problem, and Philip Hendry read out a letter on the dangers of acid rain. Other non-members backed this aggressive line with emotional speeches. Councillor Ted Humphreys appealed to the committee on behalf of the people. 'If there is the slightest doubt that there is any danger to one person's health, then vote against it'. But it was not all one way, equally forceful speeches, strong on emotion and short on content, came from the other side. Mrs Phyllis Gershon berated the 'doom merchants', remarked on the healthy appearance of those members like Allan Chapman living nearest the works, and noted that the other two PROBE members present (Blowers and Hendry) caused more pollution with their pipe smoking than London Brick. 'When you consider the amount of good LBC is doing for the county and country why is it taking so long?' In similar vein Charles Cook, an independent member, argued that delay would cause greater pollution. 'We shouldn't hang on any longer — it's talk, talk, talk.' Nonetheless it was generally felt that by lunchtime the opponents of London Brick, led by the three PROBE members — Chapman, Hendry and Blowers — had made most of the running and London Brick's observers in the public gallery felt the meeting would come out against the proposals.

But the opposition had come mainly from non-members of the committee, many of whom had disappeared by the afternoon. The change in Cremer and Warner's position established a different tone during the afternoon, which increasingly favoured the company, as the committee members became more prominent in the debate. There was considerable debate over the options and their implications. The possibilities of refusing on grounds of insufficient evidence or taking no decision were raised, but these were quashed by the Deputy County Secretary, John Dawson, clearly keen to advance the case made by the planners. 'The first point is that you can't give an outright refusal on insufficient knowledge grounds. There are advantages in taking our own decision. Firstly, speed, and secondly, our views and position are clear, so that if the Secretary of State calls the matter in and you've abrogated responsibility for dealing with it, he will have no idea what your view is.' The PROBE members continued to skirmish but had largely exhausted their arguments at this stage. The scene was set for a changing emphasis in the debate and Councillor Cyril Everard, the Vice-Chairman of the Committee, seized his opportunity by saying that there seemed to be a feeling that LBC couldn't be trusted, yet they provided wages, rates and bricks for houses, providing an impact on the local economy and various facilities. The committee should take note of the experts and recognise that the Minister would be bound to support such an industry. Option 2 met all the objections and he moved its acceptance. He was supported by John Hillier, who, as Chairman of the County Council, was a very influential member. Other members fell into line though Roy Sollars, the member representing Houghton Conquest, had been wavering up to this point. He would have liked to see it debated at a public inquiry but was worried about the benefits that might be lost. Reluctantly, though the ideal was option 1, pragmatically he would go for option 2.

Councillor Andy Blowers, Leader of the Labour Group and a member of PROBE, argued that it would be costly to implement controls after a permission and the incentive would be lost, and there might not be time for research before phase 2 was needed. 'Therefore, if we grant phase 1 are we, in effect, granting all four?' He was in favour of a refusal and an inquiry on the grounds of public concern, reasonable doubt and the need for controls to be imposed at the outset. This cut little ice with the committee, however, which had by then made up its mind and voted by 12 to three in favour of the planners' recommendation.

The vote was taken on strict party lines, the three Labour members opposing although no group decisions had been taken over the issue. Councillor Blowers secured a minor victory which had major ramifications later. By a majority of six (three Labour, two Conservative and one Liberal) to four he succeeded in having any decision on the Ridgmont works deferred on the grounds that it was premature.[33] Thus, after a six hour meeting, the committee recommended the Council to permit the first phase of the Stewartby works with no strings, and the second phase only after research programme into kiln design had been carried out. London Brick had surmounted its first major obstacle.

The County Council's first round: before the Council

London Brick was satisfied with the result of the Environmental Services meeting. April was a good month for the company. As the fateful meeting of the County Council approached London Brick was able to announce increased turnover and profits for 1979.[34] The confidence of London Brick was paralleled by disappointment and pessimism in the opposition camp. Publicly the bravado remained. Peter Goode commented 'The decision went through narrowly and I hope it will be rejected by the County Council next month'.[35] But privately the opponents were clearly worried. Philip Hendry was critical of the role played by the ESC: 'ESC are tied to LBC's coat tails. They've been wined, dined and generally socialised by LBC and they come back thinking "They're not such a bad lot, are they?"'[36] He feared the support being provided for the company by the Alkali Inspector was certain to weigh heavily with the Minister, and he felt the Council would endorse the committee's decision. His own resolve to push the issue appeared to be weakening. He candidly admitted to being in two minds and believed considerable gains had already been won. 'We've pushed LBC further than I'd thought or even the officers dreamt they could go, and whatever the outcome I'm satisfied.' But he would, if only for the sake of consistency, press for a public inquiry. Andy Blowers was equally uncertain, aware that the grounds for an inquiry were thin and the Council's case at such an inquiry weak.

This defeatism among the political leaders was counteracted, in public at least, by sustained efforts by the two major environmental lobbies which were the inspiration behind opposition to the company. PROBE's invitation to councillors to visit Woburn Abbey was well attended by councillors and spouses, who were plied with champagne, wine, caviare, salmon and other delicacies. As the social gathering was beginning to wane the Marquis of Tavistock spoke about the important time in the history of the county and his deep concern about the pollution issue. He was followed by Dr. David Rhodes a GP who had practised in the area and was prepared to undertake a study of the medical effects on human beings. Finally, Trevor Skeet, Bedford's MP, made an emotional appeal in favour of rejecting the application and providing the opportunity for a public inquiry. It was an opportunity that would affect the next 20 years or so and he considered that the Council ought not to decide until it had all the facts, and provided a chance for those interests outside the county to present their views.

It is difficult to discern the effect of the meeting. It is possible that some undecided members were persuaded against the application but it was also construed as a cynical piece of arm-twisting. Skeet's appeal for a public inquiry to be decided at a national level was possibly counterproductive, encouraging chauvinistic resentment and a 'Little Bedfordshire' approach — Bedfordshire should decide. The meeting was backed up by a glossy leaflet issued to all members of the Council, posing key questions, providing contrasting quotes from experts and stridently proclaiming 'Members of PROBE are totally in support of the building of new brickworks in the Marston Vale — BUT NOT AT ANY PRICE — Is the price being demanded now too high?'

The other prominent lobby, the Bedfordshire Preservation Society, issued a circular letter to all members of the Council urging members to refer the whole matter to the Secretary of State. The letter argued that London Brick needed the new works and the gains already made would not be sacrificed by an inquiry:

> It is illogical to mortgage the future for the past. A permission granted without insistence on the cleaning of flue gases is unrealistic, for unless this is a firm condition of planning permission, such equipment will always be considered too expensive. There is an ever increasing awareness of the need to control pollution, and flue gas cleansing must be fitted at the time of construction, otherwise the resulting works may well prove impossibly expensive to bring to the required standard at a later date.[37]

Media support for the environmentalists continued unabated during April. At the broader level *The Guardian* (7 April) pursued the international dimension, outlining the worldwide anxiety about trans–boundary pollution and reporting that the Scandinavian countries was contemplating diplomatic protests about the effects of British pollution, including that likely to come from the brickworks, in sterilising lakes. A Swedish soil scientist was quoted as saying that acid rain 'is equivalent to a "chemical war" in which the Swedes are being "bombed" by other nations'. Locally, two newspapers produced editorials on the brickfields issue. *The Bedfordshire Times* (23 March) under the heading 'No time for a gamble' linked the brickfields pollution problem to other problems of public concern such as blue asbestos and high alumina cement and proclaimed 'Our opinion remains unchanged. A safe brickworks involving substantial capital investment will be a direct benefit to the economy of both county and the country. A less than safe installation could become a monument to county councillors who acted in relative ignorance'. *Bedfordshire on Sunday* (20 April) argued that little time would be lost and potentially great benefits could be won if the matter was placed before a public inquiry covering not just the pollution issue but the problems of dereliction as well.

Local MPs joined in the call for an inquiry. Bedford's MP Trevor Skeet made an impassioned plea just before the Council meeting. 'If the decision is left to the County Council the result could be disastrous. This issue is so important it must be examined by a public inquiry which will have the benefit of expert investigation. I will do all I can to persuade county councillors to reject the application before it is too late.[38] The European MP for the area also backed the idea of a public inquiry emphasising the problem of trans–boundary pollution.

Although the local pressure for a public inquiry was mounting, correspondence between ministers and MPs reveals that the government remained unconvinced. In letters to Stephen Hastings, MP for Mid-Bedfordshire, and to William Benyon, MP for Buckingham, the Minister for Local Government, Marcus Fox, made plain his view that the trans–boundary issuue was unlikely to affect the proposals of London Brick. Referring to an agreement on trans–boundary air pollution drawn up by the United Nations Economic Commission for Europe he pointed out that 'the parties to the Convention must take such action as is appropriate "to endeavour to limit and, as far as possible, gradually reduce and prevent air pollution including long-range trans-boundary air pollution". But control measures must be "economically feasible" and "compatible with balanced development". The Convention is therefore a balanced document, the obligation to reduce trans–boundary air pollution being qualified by reference to costs and the state of scientific knowledge.'[39] There was nothing in the Convention 'about tall chimneys as such' and in any case the Alkali Inspectorate were bringing about a reduction of pollution with tall chimneys and insisting on a third flue so that abatement could be incorporated when it became technically feasible.[40] It was clear that the Minister would accede to the advice of the Alkali Inspector and would not impose control measures. 'Certainly, I do not consider that there is at present sufficient evidence of damage to justify more stringent — and potentially very costly — measures by industry.'[41] Thus it was not only unlikely that the Minister would call the matter in, but, in the event of having the matter referred to him on appeal, would be likely to come down firmly in favour of the negotiated proposals endorsed by the Alkali Inspectorate.

With the case for an inquiry looking feeble and its chances of an outcome favourable to the opposition remote, the environmentalists approached the County Council meeting in low spirits. But political confusion and uncertainty was prevalent as a survey of councillors' views published on the eve of the meeting revealed (see Figure 4.3).

The results show that half of those questioned had not made up their

Figure 4.3: Opinion Poll of councillors, April 1980

A total of 70 (out of 83) councillors were asked whether or not they would support the plan for new brickworks at the County Council meeting.

Overall

Yes	23
No	13
Don't Know	31
No Comment	3
Total	70 (83)

By party

	Con	Lab	Lib	Ind	Total
YES	20	0	2	1	23
NO	9	4	0	0	13
Don't know	29	2	0	0	31
No comment	3	0	0	0	3
Total (response)	61	6	2	1	70
Not canvassed	10	3	–	–	13
Total on Council	71	9	2	1	83

By area

North Beds		Mid Beds		South Beds		Luton	
Yes	3	Yes	4	Yes	7	Yes	9
No	6	No	2	No	2	No	3
Don't know	9	Don't know	5	Don't know	5	Don't know	12
No comment	1					No comment	2
Total	19 (21)	Total	11 (16)	Total	14 (17)	Total	26 (29)

Total 70 (83)

Figures in parenthesis denote total number on County Council

Source: Bedford Record, 22 April, 1980.

minds. Among the predominant group of Conservatives (71 of the 83 councillors and 61 of those surveyed) over half had yet to decide, and of those who had come to a conclusion two to one were in favour of the proposals. The other groups were very small, though the Labour members surveyed (six out of the total of nine) were broadly against the proposals, while the two Liberals were in favour. Only North Bedfordshire of the four districts comprising the Council had a majority against the proposals, though in common with Luton more than half the total had not made up their minds. Among the councillors prominent in the debate there were few surprises, with Philip Hendry and Andy Blowers leading those against the proposals and Michael Kemp, who was later to play a prominent role in engineering an outcome of the conflict, declaring in favour.

Given such a division of views compounded by uncertainty it was difficult to predict the outcome of the meeting and the political groups could not enforce a mandate on their members. The Labour Group agreed to stand by the line taken by Councillor Blowers at the ESC meeting arguing for a deferral of the decision and, if support could be found, for a public inquiry. The Conservative Group, with its leadership split, accepted that no decision could be binding on the Group and a free vote should be granted. A possible way out of the impasse facing the group and the Council appeared. Councillor Ian Dixon, the ambitious Vice-Chairman of the Education Committee and a growing force within the group, had declared himself a 'don't know' on the brickfields issue, but was anxious to influence the affair. He argued that until the long promised report on the brickfields being undertaken by the Department of the Environment was available the Council would be taking a decision without examining all the evidence. He therefore indicated that he would put an amendment at the meeting to defer the decision until the report's findings had been examined. Such an amendment, if passed, would provide time for the opposition to regroup and might diminish the chances of the package proposal passing at a time when London Brick's cause seemed in the ascendant.

The Council meeting — April 1980

The arrival of the issue in the full County Council presents a series of questions about the role of politics in the resolution of conflicts. Clearly the issue had crossed conventional party lines, with the Conservatives openly split. The questions here are: Why was the issue not a matter of party politics? Was it the nature of the issue or a clash of personalities that caused divisions within the Conservative Group? How can the antagonism between a substantial number of Conservative members and a major capitalist enterprise be explained? There were other allegiances, other than party or personality which could influence the alignment of members. How far did local constituency pressures affect decisions for example, or how far was there a conflict between the committee and the Council. Beyond these intriguing questions are others. The role played by individual politicians such as the PROBE members, the Chairman of the ESC or Councillor Dixon may have been significant, at least at this stage. There was a prevailing air of indecision among a large group of members who could be influenced in either direction. How far was the outcome unpredictable, depending on changing political circumstances within the Council, influenced by individual action?

The meeting of the County Council on 24 April took place amid an air of expectancy that the day of final decision had at last arrived. For both supporters and opponents of the proposals there were several options available. The leading opponents — councillors Hendry, Chapman and Blowers — conferred before the meeting began. They anticipated that the deferral motion would succeed but felt it did not go far enough. The DoE report was unlikely to shed any new light on the issue, but might provide sufficient evidence to reinforce the proposals. The tide of opposition was probably as high as it would ever be and should be capitalised on by pressing for an inquiry. Tactically, if the inquiry motion was put first and failed it might either raise the prospects of deferral, by casting sufficient doubt on the proposals, or it might diminish the chance of deferral if people felt the Council was temporising and refusing to face a decision. If the deferral was put first it was unlikely that a subsequent attempt to call for an inquiry could succeed. Nevertheless this was regarded as the safest course since at least the issue would be deferred and something gained. Otherwise all might be lost. In a subsequent meeting with Councillor Dixon it was agreed that his motion to defer the matter should be put first, and he promised he would then throw his weight behind a further amendment to place the matter before the Minister. This sequence was politically safer though procedurally illogical.

With the deferral motion gaining support from influential members alternative courses seemed less likely to succeed. The inquiry motion had fewer prospects if put second, and a proposal by Councillor Mick Farley of the Labour Group that would insist that the company install cleaning equipment was regarded as too tough to command much support (though interestingly this was later to be adopted by the opposition to the company).

London Brick's supporters also felt their chances of passing the package of proposals as recommended by the ESC were diminishing. The Deputy Planning Officer, Tony Griffin, had already conceded and the Chairman of ESC, Keith White, by lunchtime had accepted there was a prevailing mood in the Council for deferral.

With so much behind-the-scenes manoeuvring the debate in public was inevitably an anti-climax. Keith White opened, saying the DoE report was still not published but 'If there was anything in the report with grave implications I would have thought the Department of the Environment would have intimated it to me and called the plans in'.[42] He was aware of the mood among members and would be prepared to see the matter deferred, though he was personally quite prepared for a final decision to be taken that day. The Dixon amendment for deferral was passed almost automatically after a desultory debate, though an amendment that, regardless of the availability of the report, the Council should take its decision at the next (July) meeting was also passed by 33 to 30, despite Councillor Blowers' argument that 'If the report is important enough to defer a decision today it is important enough to defer it until we get the report'.[43]

Somewhat reluctantly Councillor Hendry then proposed an alternative that the Secretary of State be invited to call in the applications. 'When our decision will determine the future of the county for 50 years it is right that we should have outside expertise.' He was supported by his fellow PROBE councillors Blowers and Chapman who argued that an inquiry would enable those interests affected by the decision but not represented by the Council to participate in a debate which was not a foregone conclusion. But the resistance to the idea was strong and councillors Kemp, Sollars and Mrs Lennon, a Liberal, argued that the county had the expertise and was quite capable of taking a local decision. In his summing up Councillor White declared that calling for an inquiry was tantamount to rejecting the application and was incomprehensible when the Council had just previously agreed it would make its own decision at its next meeting. 'Will a public inquiry give you a better solution than the hard, steady, silent work of the Environmental Services Committee over the past two years. You are funking a decision.'[44] He had the support of a majority of the Council who rejected the 'call in' motion by 39 to 24, Councillor Dixon, incidentally, abstaining.

The meeting was subsequently portrayed as a day when the Council decided not to decide. 'The company was anxious to forge ahead with its impressive redevelopment programme; the public were waiting to hear the debate of a lifetime; the Press were itching to file long-awaited conclusive copy . . . It was a day which belonged to resolute indecision.'[45] But important gains had been secured by the opposition, aware that they would almost certainly lose if the proposals were determined at the meeting. They had gained time, and with so many councillors clearly undecided there was the chance that opinion could be swayed decisively during the next three months. It was a tactical defeat for London Brick who hinted as much in its comments after the meeting. 'We are disappointed at the further delay although we can understand the Council wanting to wait for the DoE report if available.'[46] No one on either side really expected the DoE report to offer any firm conclusions, and all were aware that it was now a struggle in which the issues were submerged in the effort to gain political mastery. One thing had become clear however and that was the futility of pursuing the call for a public inquiry.[47] It was not only obvious that the Minister was reluctant and would support London Brick, the Council had now decisively rejected the idea. If the opposition were to have any hope of winning the argument they would have to find another tactic.

The battle for votes — 25 April – July 1980

The attitudes of the two camps towards the central government's role appear somewhat paradoxical. The company, vigorously supported by the Alkali Inspector, and with the tacit support of other central departments, seemed to have set its face against a possible appeal. Conversely, its opponents, knowing the company was likely to win, either on appeal or if the matter was called in, nonetheless had argued for a public inquiry. These contrasting positions probably reflected each side's assessment of its chances of winning the debate at the local level. Both had probably calculated that London Brick was likely to win. Therefore, from the company's point of view, there was no point in risking the delays and expense of an appeal, whereas its opponents probably saw government intervention as their best hope of avoiding an immediate defeat. Once that hope had disappeared they devoted their energies to securing victory through the Council. The company, secure in its external support, could afford to engage in the local conflict in the hope of success, but in the knowledge that defeat would not be the end of the road. The fact that central government was likely, ultimately, to favour the company raises the question of how significant the debates at local level might prove in the long run. Were these debates a case of 'sound and fury signifying nothing'? Was the issue likely to be determined eventually by forces outside the Council?

For the present both sides turned their attention to the July meeting of the Council. The general reaction to the outcome of the April Council meeting was that it had been a prelude to a decision in favour of London Brick. The DoE's delay in publishing its report was variously construed as a sign of cunning or incompetence. The three months' interlude between the April and July meetings was devoted to an intense propaganda war between opposing sides. On the one hand, the opponents of the company needed to regroup, try new initiatives and regain their confidence. On the other, London Brick and its supporters needed to consolidate the favourable reaction it had already gained and prevent any erosion of support. Both sides were aware that there were still votes to be won both from those who had not voted in the April debate and from those who had supported the deferral either because they were uncertain or wanted time to ponder their decision. And both sides were able to draw on support that hitherto had been relatively passive. For the opposition the National Farmers' Union began a vigorous attack on the company's plans, while the trade unions representing the brickfield workers began to exert their muscle in favour of the company. However the issue was now polarised between the major protagonists: PROBE ably supported by the Bedfordshire Preservation Society on the one side, London Brick on the other. The earlier debates had been characterised by a plurality of participants, the ad hoc pressure groups, the local councils and amenity societies. This climactic stage was a confrontation between big battalions led by prominent spokesmen engaged in intensive lobbying both directly on councillors and indirectly through the Press. The growing intensity of their efforts is represented in the Press coverage. In May there were 7 articles on the debate in the local Press but in June leading up to the debate the number had quadrupled to 28, and the coverage was as great in the south of the county as in the north.

PROBE recovers lost ground

The despondency in the opposition camp was reflected in statements and letters of PROBE members. Peter Goode, the group's secretary, felt that hope of victory was fading fast. In a letter to Peter Goode, Councillor Andy Blowers argued the case for imposing a condition on the planning permission that would ensure adequate filtration of emissions. But he was not hopeful. 'This inevitably would bring about an inquiry and members will probably conclude that the outcome of an inquiry will be a less satisfactory solution than the one they have already secured. Moreover, it will take control away from the Council. Such an amendment would keep us morally pure but result in a glorious and substantial defeat.'[48]

It seemed that the DoE report would back London Brick, though PROBE viewed its failure to appear with the 'gravest suspicion'[49] and felt it would only be a review not a full scale investigation.[50] Goode felt that the report was deliberately held back, but that the bluff had been called when the Council decided to take a decision in July in any event. *Private Eye* (20 June, 1980) in its black and white 'Colour Section' headed 'Bricks and Slaughter' speculated that, knowing a decision would be taken, the DoE would withhold publication until after the July meeting. The *Luton News* called it 'sheer folly' to go ahead without the report (5 June). What is odd is that if, as all seemed to agree, the report would endorse London Brick the pollution campaigners should be urging its publication. Perhaps the answer is that the report would serve to confuse the issue and offer arguments for both sides, as the Cremer and Warner report had done.

There was an air of general depression at a thinly attended meeting of PROBE held at the Bedford Office in London on 21 May.[51] Efforts by local MPs to get a 'call in' had failed, and the government seemed almost certain to support the company. Peter Goode felt the odds were 10-1 in favour of the Council passing the application. The group outlined their next moves. Pressure at government level would be sustained, and all local MPs should be solicited for support. An attempt would be made to go over the head of Marcus Fox, the Minister for the Environment, by appealing to Michael Heseltine, the Secretary of State. Lord Tavistock agreed to ask Heseltine to dinner — 'I've no worries about doing that'. It appeared there was little hope at the international level, though both Norway and Sweden were prepared to lean on the British delegation at Geneva. The key lay at the local level among the uncommitted members of the County Council. Assuming the nine Labour votes were secure at least 33 Conservatives were needed to ensure the company's defeat. Allan Chapman undertook to confer with Philip Hendry and to apply informal pressure on influential members. A list of targets was discussed. Finally, it was agreed to step up the publicity campaign.

By the end of June support had been canvassed from ten MPs from Bedfordshire and surrounding constituencies plus two Euro-MPs. Lord Tavistock had written to *The Times* (19 June) stating: 'I believe it is time for the country as a whole to be made aware of the ecological and environmental crime that is about to be perpetrated in the name of industrial progress with no regard whatsoever for the health of the population, the well-being of livestock and crops or, for that matter, Britain's signed agreement to participate fully in the abolition of aerial pollution in Europe'. This drew a response also in *The Times* from Jeremy Rowe, Chairman of London Brick (23 June) attacking Lord Tavistock's stance, and a further letter from four members of PROBE urging the need for a full inquiry (3 July). Correspondence with Michael Heseltine and a dinner party with Lord Tavistock had not elicited a favourable response, though PROBE would continue to press him on the matter. 'Failure to place conditions on the application would place an intolerable burden on the people and environment of Bedfordshire for generations to come'.[52]

It was in a slightly more optimistic mood that a small group of PROBE members met again on 22 June at Peter Goode's farm.[53] The two Conservative councillors reviewed their soundings among their colleagues. It was felt that Councillor Sollars, who had displayed considerable uncertainty at the April meeting, had been won over, and Councillor Ian Dixon could be persuaded if it was shown to be in his interest. Further support had been elicited from Lord Campbell, Chairman of Milton Keynes Development Corporation[54] and from Professor Gerald Smart a well known planner.[55]

The National Farmers' Union were adopting a more aggressive posture. It was agreed to put further pressure on councillors Dixon and Whitbread, a prominent landowner in the country; to issue a Press release and to circulate all members of the Council with a list of MPs supporting the campaign, and copies of Tavistock's letter to *The Times* and the article in *Private Eye*. At the Council meeting Philip Hendry would propose an amendment that required filtration of emissions as a prior condition for permission being granted. Although PROBE still expected to be defeated it had been very active in the intervening weeks, and its sustained pressure was felt likely to result in a closer vote at the Council in July than had been anticipated at the end of April.

The opposition was also gaining significant support from other quarters. The Bedfordshire Preservation Society maintained claims about 'acid rain' affecting a wide area, and this created opposition in the south of the county.[56] The Ecology Party added its voice to the protests and circulated all councillors with a questionnaire on the issue, though only one reply was received. More importantly the local National Farmers Union threatened to take out an injunction against London Brick if permission were granted.[57] Their County Secretary, Richard Payne, announced that councillors 'have a heavy burden on their shoulders and I only hope they know what the result of their action will be'.[58] They followed this up with a 'token lobby' of members at the July Council meeting, urging members who had any doubts to 'defer the application for a full investigation into the effects of the proposal on livestock and crops'.[59] A meeting took place between Jeremy Rowe, Chairman of London Brick, and the President of the NFU where it was agreed to work more closely on the effects of the new works.

The Press continued its support for the environmentalists, to the extent that London Brick was moved to comment in its house journal: 'Reading the Bedford Press in recent weeks it has been difficult to believe that the Fletton Brick Industry is one hundred years old . . . from the way people have been reacting to our proposals for new works, one would think that we were introducing new industry to Bedford'.[60] Two of the leading local newspapers the *Luton Post* and the *Bedfordshire Times* inveighed against taking a decision in ignorance. 'It would be irresponsible pomposity for councillors to say yes to this plan unless they have received all the right answers to their questions.'[61] At a national level both *The Times* and *The Guardian* covered aspects of the debate, but it was *Private Eye* which, typically, unleased an unfettered attack on London Brick in the first two of a series of four features ('Bricks and Slaughter'):

LBC owns most of the farms in the area and deals with the problems of pollution and disease by installing tame tenant farmers, whom it compels to sign agreements indemnifying LBC against any claims for damage, however caused. The few remaining independent farmers are in a Catch 22 situation — if they complain that their farms are polluted and their cattle diseased, the farms lose value and the cattle become unsellable. Absence of action by the National Farmers Union may not be unconnected with the fact that LBC is by far the biggest member of the NFU in the area.[62]

The fact that the NFU did take action shortly afterwards is probably unconnected with the article, though *Private Eye's* comments were circulated to councillors, some of whom *Private Eye* later claimed 'were amazed by details of the ride for which they were being taken'.[63]

Private Eye did reveal two aspects of the debate that were not identified elsewhere. One was London Brick's assertion that it was quite content to wait for publication of the DoE report. It appeared therefore that London Brick did not view determination of the issue with such urgency as had been presumed. The second matter was the hint of a power struggle within the Conservative Group. 'Certain ambitious individuals are known to believe that if they can push through the decision they want, favourable to LBC, this display of power will be a big step towards gaining the leadership of the Council.'[64] This was a veiled reference to Councillor KeithWhite, who some

Conservatives believed cherished ambitions for the leadership. Thus this issue, already a struggle for ascendency rather than for principles, between London Brick and its opponents was also possibly a conflict for power over the controlling group in the Council. Therefore much more dependend on the outcome of the July debate than simply whether London Brick would get its planning permission.

London Brick gathers support

After the April Council meeting Deputy Planning Officer Tony Griffin said he was 95 per cent certain the proposal would go through in July. The momentum in favour of London Brick had to be sustained over the three months, and the company began to match its rivals with aggressive publicity. An extensive feature on the company appeared in the *Bedfordshire Times* covering the activities of the company and the social and environmental benefits it produced through brick production, farming and landscape restoration.[65] The improvements to air quality that would result from the new works were explained in simple language and the feature as a whole was designed to give a favourable, progressive image to the company.

Reports of the company's Annual General Meeting on 21 May also gave an impression of an optimistic, forward-looking company. Despite a continuing decline in house building, the trends for 1980 were favourable. 'It may well be that any real volume improvement will have to wait until next year or even the following one, but we are determined to ensure that by stocking — by, in effect, creating and funding our own brick bank — we will be able to match our customers' requirements when higher demand again breaks through as we have seen it do so often in the past.'[66] Later in the year these words were to have a hollow ring. The failure of demand to meet expectations, resulting in excessive stockpiles, would within a few months result in an outcome to the conflict that neither side had apparently foreseen, or dared to contemplate in the spring of 1980.

Favourable publicity for the company came also from unsolicited sources. In May the *Bedfordshire Times* presented a profile of London Brick's Managing Director, James Bristow, together with one of his rivals, Peter Goode, the PROBE secretary. Although both portraits were sympathetic, the feature gave James Bristow an opportunity to air the company's case in his bemused but disarming style, leaving the correspondent to remark: 'If I needed winning over, the James Bristow charm has done its job'.[67] Although the editorial opinion of local newspapers opposed the company, the letter columns provided evidence of support. A letter attacking the PROBE lobby for placing the interests of farmers before the needs of brickworkers was echoed by one from trade union shop stewards arguing the need for a thriving brick industry to overcome the plight of those needing a home.[68] 'Those who live in palaces or Edwardian mansions, like the members of PROBE, never had such problems.'[69] The trade unions had at last begun to throw their weight behind the company.

A meeting between four trade union representatives and seven members of the Labour Group took place on 16 June. Although the Labour Group was small, the trade unions sensed that its vote could be decisive. In the same way that the NFU felt it could exert influence on Conservative members, so the unions believed their links with the Labour Party could be exploited. The meeting had been hailed in the Press as a confrontation, but was, in the event, very amicable. Both sides explained their position. The trade unions argued they were not company stooges and 'would not be hoodwinked into working in conditions which would be harmful'. They had insisted on tests being undertaken to determine the pollution levels in the works, and these had found levels well below the threshold values where dangers might occur. They were convinced that known methods of eliminating pollutants gave rise to other insuperable problems, and that tunnel kilns were difficult to adapt to the fletton process. The new works were likely to result in large job losses over time and tunnel kilns would reduce the workforce even more, but 'if tunnel kilns would eliminate everything — I think we would say, so be it'. The major concern of the workforce was better working conditions and the need to replace ageing plant. 'At present LBC is like an old lorry, it's not going well. We must buy a new lorry.' Already the new works in the Peterborough area had produced a more reliable and higher quality brick. It was clear the company had taken out a number of options so that, if one failed, others were available. In response Labour members argued they had responsibilities to the community as a whole, were aware of strong, if conflicting, evidence on the damage from pollution, and the group felt reassurance could only be gained from a full inquiry.

The union representatives tried applying political pressure on the group. 'Most of our members are members of the Labour Party and we encourage them to pay the political levy and support tote schemes. We are now under pressure from members to withdraw both the levy and the tote scheme.' For the time being the sides parted having agreed new works were necessary, but with the differences over attitudes not resolved. Although the meeting had been friendly and they agreed to issue a joint Press release, the report of the meeting in the *Luton Post* stated that the unions were 'furious' with the Labour councillors for not consulting them adequately, and that fears about the works had been 'exaggerated out of all proportion' (11 June, 1980). While Labour councillors now recognised they could be in serious conflict with the trade unions on the issue, it did not initially alter their view.

The months of May and June had been busy with both sides clamouring for public attention. Each side had been powerfully reinforced, the NFU taking a strong anti-pollution line and the unions ranging themselves on the side of the company. In each case direct material interests — farming and jobs — had been threatened and provoked a response. There was one further influence that might persuade the uncommitted: the DoE report, which was published in June.

The Department of Environment report

The DoE report (1980) when it finally came, was, as had been anticipated, disappointing — a review of the current state of knowledge providing little new information.[70] In content it fell short of the deeper analysis provided by Cremer and Warner, though the slant of its interpretation was different. There was a degree of mystification in the presentation in that it was difficult to relate the various measurements used (e.g. average, peak, over different time periods) for each of the pollutants sulphur dioxide (SO_2) and fluoride (F) to the different threshold values regarded as possibly harmful from various researches that had been undertaken. Perhaps this was inevitable, but the report nonetheless felt able to conclude on the basis of dispersion modelling that 'contributions to maximum annual, daily and one to three hour concentrations are predicted to fall by up to 90 per cent of current values . . . Although the Cremer and Warner report predicts smaller differences between the current and proposed cases, their estimates for concentrations in the proposed case are also smaller than the current one.' (page 33) Despite the lack of consensus about threshold values and the lack of accurate measurement of peak concentration, the report confidently stated that 'there is thus no evidence that concentrations of SO_2 in the area are ever high enough to produce any detectable effects on healthy people (using available studies), and none of the values, whether considered as annual or daily means, or as peaks within the day, are as extreme as those seen in past years in London.' (page 12) It was equally definitive about the effect of fluorides on human health, arguing that the small contributions to human intake levels arising from brickfields emissions were of 'no concern to human health' (page 14). A survey of the literature and of local health patterns led the report to conclude that 'no effects on human health in the locality have come to our attention which are attributable to the fluoride emissions from the brickworks. It is concluded that these emissions make, at worst, a very small contribution to the total intake and that they will have no effect on respiratory tract disease, skeletal disease or on the general health of the local residents' (page 19). This assertion went beyond the more cautious findings of the Cremer and Warner report (see Chapter 3, page 99), though the DoE agreed that odours were the 'most intractable problem' and should be the subject of a pilot study into methods of removal.

The report also minimised the effects of pollution on animals and crops, emphasising the decline in cattle fluorosis resulting from better husbandry and reductions in brickmaking, and arguing that effects on crops could not be attributed 'solely to the emissions from brickworks' (page 36). The report confirmed the view of London Brick that no single abatement technique was feasible; described a series of control processes and their problems (App. 2); quoted the company's estimate of a 42 per cent price increase, necessary if tunnel kilns were used to remove odour; and reproduced a diagram (see Figure 4.4) purporting to demonstrate the decline in ground level concentrations that would arise once new works were in operation. Although the report considered measurement of SO_2 levels was satisfactory and information was 'sufficient effectively to discount the effects of atmospheric fluorides on human health' (page 39) it felt that some further measurement of fluoride on a 'before' and 'after' the new works basis might be helpful if there was felt to be a local need to remove fears about effects on animals, crops and materials. Routine inspection of children's teeth for dental mottling would discover if there was any build up of fluoride in the environment. It recommended that 'an integrated monitoring and measurement programme be formulated, with clearly defined and specified objectives which will give the maximum return in terms of information and resource allocation, so that the situation can be regularly reviewed and problems (if any) identified quickly' (page 41). This recommendation was taken up in the course of the subsequent debate.

The DoE report, though highly qualified and tentative, did appear to provide further official endorsement of the company's approach, as supported by the Alkali Inspector and the county planning officers. Not surprisingly, London Brick and its supporters were pleased with the findings. The Press claimed that the report provided 'shocks for

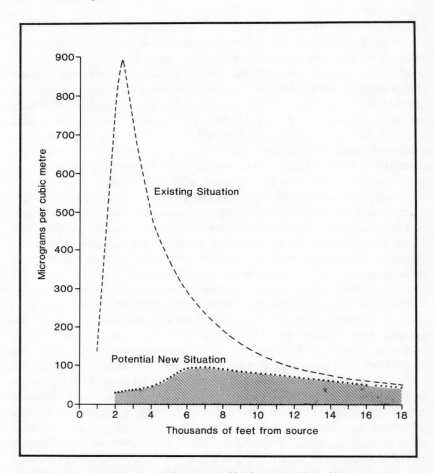

Figure 4.4: Diagram of existing and future ground level concentrations of SO_2
Estimates based on calculations by the Alkali Inspectorate comparing the ground level concentration (daily peak) from existing works producing 10 million bricks per week with twenty five 180′ chimneys with the anticipated concentrations from a new works of similar capacity with 400 feet chimneys
Source: Department of the Environment (1980) *Air Pollution in the Bedfordshire Brickfields,* Directorate of Noise, Clean Air and Waste, 6/80, figure 6

conservationists'[71] and 'deals a major blow to campaigners fighting to halt the brickworks plan'.[72] London Brick's spokesman said: 'The report clears up several issues and the most important one is the question of dangers to human health. The report bears out what we have been saying all along'. The Chairman of ESC, Keith White, felt the report provided a basis for approving the new works. Philip Hendry preferred another interpretation: 'I don't agree with their findings on human health, but they do say there are grounds for concern here.' In his view the concern for better monitoring in the report 'makes out the case for a public inquiry'.

When the DoE report came to the ESC on 19 June, with 30 councillors present, the debate was notable not for the new light it shed but on the rifts it exposed among members of the Conservative Group as they prepared for the major battle at the July Council meeting. In his presentation of the report Tony Griffin, the planning officer, underlined the 'startling similarity' between the report and that of Cremer and Warner. Indeed, Cremer and Warner, suitably primed for the occasion, presented a letter in which they said the differences between the two reports were minor and that the recommendation being put forward to the Council was consistent with their views.[73] 'Our conclusion is that the DoE confirms the advice you have been given.' Some members of the committee argued strongly in support of the package proposal. Councillor Janice Lennon, for example, felt that with the report London Brick had yet more ammunition and, if an inquiry were held, the Minister was bound to lean on the evidence produced by his own department. But opponents of the company were also anxious to disparage the report. The three PROBE members argued along similar lines, Councillor Chapman calling it 'bland and anodyne', Councillor Blowers arguing it was 'sporadic' and 'impressionistic' and Councillor Hendry suggesting the evidence could be interpreted either way, and insisting that certain things were being hidden. This led to an altercation between him and his Deputy Leader, Chairman of the Committee, Keith White, who said he would not allow undue bias to enter into the debate, and would insist on a fair presentation of the case so long as he was Chairman. This incensed Councillor Hendry who also fell out with another of his group, Mrs Gershon. The spectacle of Conservatives arguing among themselves in public demonstrated the divisions within the group, but more significantly, other influential Conservatives announced a change of mind. Roy Sollars, the member for Houghton Conquest in the brickfields, who had long been wavering and had previously voted for the proposal, savaged the report. Evidence was missing, it was full of 'ifs', 'buts', 'maybes' and 'don't knows', the figures contradicted themselves, and they wouldn't know the evidence if they saw it, he claimed. Yet the report was still prepared to draw conclusions. 'Having seen this I'm delighted, and I'm going for a public inquiry.' If Sollars had been recruited to the opposition camp Councillor Dixon, who had ensured a delay in the decision, had come to 'a totally opposite conclusion'. 'I must be influenced by the content of the report — a relatively authoritative report — I will support the application.' The meeting concluded by endorsing its former recommendations with some marginal but important changes in the voting patterns. This time there were ten in favour of the phase 1 permission for Stewartby and five against (including three Labour members and Councillors Sollars and Wootton, whose vacillation had an important bearing on later events), while the phase 2 permission (incorporating the agreement for research on control processes) and the deferral of a decision on the southern works were passed unanimously.

The DoE report, coming at a time when many minds had been made up, served to fuel the doubts of the company's opponents and reinforce the case for those supporting the permission. It was unlikely to exert a decisive influence on the outcome of the Council meeting. Both advocates and opponents of the permission had fought hard during May and June, and it was now left to the members of the Council to try once again to reach a decision. The Labour Group, despite union pressure, remained united, and agreed to support Philip Hendry's motion to ensure controls were made a condition of the phase 1 permission. The Conservatives were split. The pressure brought on individual members as a result of the PROBE decisions had failed to win over either Councillor Dixon or Councillor Whitbread but Councillor Sollars had changed his mind. There were still members who had not yet reached a conclusion. The dismay felt among the opposition after the April meeting had been transformed to a guarded optimism, and Councillor Hendry felt he detected a change in the mood, though the outcome was still impossible to predict. As he said: 'It all depends what happens on the day'.

The climax — the County Council debate, July 1980

The atmosphere was tense and expectant when the debate of the County Council began on 3 July, the long awaited day of final decision. The outcome was still as uncertain as it had been all along.

The main protagonists presented contrasting moods. Keith White, opening the debate, appeared depressed, unconfident and uninspiring. He covered the grounds of the debate, stressing that the plans were for replacement, not new works with a phased permission guaranteeing research for the later phases. There was no danger to public health at the present time and the amount of pollution had been falling. 'I hope people have been able to understand what I have been saying — we are giving a quarter of what is being asked for and gaining a period of research.' There was no technology available for pollution control. 'The crux of the issue is whether you believe new technology is around the corner or whether it is five years away.' By contrast Philip Hendry was ebullient, and produced a careful, exciting and persuasive speech 'subsequently agreed to be the best speech he has made in the chamber'.[74] He considered the environmental gains already made should have been granted 20 years ago, were not at risk, and were no more than the county was entitled to expect. Pollution was the key issue. 'Is it not incredible that in 50 years of brickworks in this area London Brick cannot come up with any answer at all for diminishing pollution. We have put men on the moon and cured diseases, but London Brick has stood absolutely still. The fact of the matter is that the new chimneys will produce exactly the same amount of pollution as the old ones and the reason for that is that London Brick have had no real incentive for trying to find an answer to the problem.' He proposed an amendment which would provide such an incentive. The amendment would add another condition, condition 9, to the permission for the first phase of the new works at Stewartby in the following terms: 'Before construction commences on that part of the kilns and plant to be incorporated in phase 1 of the proposed brickworks there shall be submitted to, and approved by, the County Planning Authority plans, sections and drawings showing their layout and detailed engineering construction, the kilns being so designed as to be capable of incinerating the organic components of the gases given off in the brick firing processes'.[75]

After this powerful opening the opposition sustained the initiative throughout the two and a half hour debate, during which 15 speeches were made in favour of the amendment and 11 against. Among those supporting Councillor Hendry were those who had already figured in earlier debates. The newly converted Roy Sollars argued that it was crazy to believe that because there was no problem now there would be no problem in the future; Councillor Chapman was convinced that London Brick would make no commitment to control unless forced to. Other speakers made persuasive contributions to the opposition case. Councillor Mick Farley, a Labour councillor, in a reasoned argument pointed out that the Council, unlike

London Brick, had to consider non-economic factors such as amenity. The same point was put more emotionally by a right wing Conservative, Ted Humphreys, who told the Council: 'You will do yourselves and your children and your grandchildren a favour if you reject the application'.

The debate was not all one way. Councillor Janice Lennon, the Liberal member of ESC, emphasised that the amendment would bring about an appeal the Council was unlikely to win, and Councillor Whitbread (Conservative) posed the question: 'Will the DoE insist on abatement in the private sector when a nationalised industry, the CEGB, is a much bigger polluter?' Councillor Dixon, who had been responsible for the deferral of the decision in April, also came out strongly against the amendment, claiming that the DoE report provided sufficient evidence on which to base a firm opinion.

It was clear that speakers were aligning themselves either with the company or its opponents, and many were confused about the implications of the amendment. Opponents seemed to assume that if the amendment was passed the company would appeal, and there would then be a public inquiry. They also assumed that the amendment covered all phases of the permission and referred to all the pollutants. In fact it covered only the first phase at Stewartby and related only to odours. This latter point (though not the former) was perceived during the course of the debate by Councillor Andy Blowers who, to ensure the meaning was unequivocal, suggested a reworded amendment altering the last part to read: '. . . the kilns being so designed as to be capable of removing the pollutants (sulphur dioxide and fluoride) and odours given off in the brick firing processes.' He argued that all pollutants must be covered, and the arguments about controls fully tested by the technical evidence at an ensuing inquiry. If the permission was passed unamended there would be no going back. 'It is a step into the unknown and will affect the generations to come. If there is a scintilla of doubt you should vote for the amendment.'

The new amendment was accepted by Councillor Hendry, who, in summing up, stressed that evidence was inconclusive and that London Brick depended on local clay and was unlikely to pull out of the county. Keith White, in a more strident vein, concluded that if the amendment was carried it would be impossible to implement and would place control over the permissions with the DoE rather than the County Council. There was much that would be lost and the county would get Hoffman kilns on all stages of the permission. 'If we lose any material benefit then you will be answerable, not me.'

Voting for the amendment at Council Meeting of 3 July, 1980.

On Party Lines

	Lab	Con	Lib	Ind	Total
For	9	28	1	0	38
Against	0	26	1	1	28
Absent/Abstain	0	17	0	0	17
Total	9	71	2	1	83

By District Council

North Beds

For	10
Against	5
Absent	6
Total	21

Mid Beds

For	6
Against	6
Absent	4
Total	16

South Beds

For	8
Against	6
Absent	3
Total	17

Luton

For	14
Against	11
Absent	4
Total	29

Figure 4.5: Voting at Council meeting, 3 July, 1980

The debate had involved many members over many months, it had split parties and caused personal rivalries. As one newspaper said: 'On what other subject could you line up such characters as Philip Hendry (Tory leader), Andy Blowers (Labour leader), Ted Humphreys (hysterical Right), Mick Farley (bleak Left), Brian (Funky) Gibbons (Liberal), on the one side against Ken Ball (nasty Right), Janice Lennon (Liberal guru), and Charles Cook (Independent, but only, one suspects, because his views are a bit to the right of Genghis Khan) on the other?'[76]

Though the debate had gone in favour of the opponents of the company, it was still expected that the voting would confirm the application proposed by the ESC. A recorded vote in which each councillor answered a roll call produced a quite unanticipated result. By 38 votes to 28, with 17 absent or abstaining, the amendment was passed and, it appeared, the opposition had won a conclusive victory. In addition, a further amendment accepting the principle of further monitoring as proposed by the DoE report was passed, and when the substantive motion, incorporating the two amendments, was put, it was passed by 35 to 17.

Conclusion

Throughout the months of confrontation, from the autumn of 1979 to the summer of 1980, the conflict had become more intense, but it had also become more simplified. During the preceding period of negotiation the debate ranged over many issues and involved a whole array of groups and opinions. By the time of the great debate in July 1980, the issues had been narrowed down to one — whether or not pollution control could or should be installed in the first phase of one of the new works. The antagonists had become polarised into two equally matched camps focusing their attention on the county councillors, the arbiters of the conflict. The issue had been refined through the Section 52 Agreement, which reflected both the consensus that had been achieved on the environmental issues and the conflict over the pollution question. The Vale of Belvoir inquiry promised a solution to the problem of dereliction left by years of clay extraction. These developments removed some of the force of the localised opposition which had centred on the amenity losses incurred by the creation of large knott holes and the lack of landscaping and restoration. The pollution issue had been narrowed down to a position where conflict existed only over the first phase of one new works at Stewartby. The salience of the pollution issue required a coordinated, influential and informed opposition covering the whole area — and PROBE sought to provide this. With its contacts in government, the media and its local landed interest it proved a worthy adversary for London Brick. The contest fought locally also had national, even international, repercussions, and became part of a wider debate about corporate power and the environment. The company was portrayed by its opponents as bent on profit, extracting maximum commercial advantage for least possible cost, the external costs of its operations being borne by the local community. The company in its turn argued that it brought prosperity to the local area and that its plans were expressly designed to overcome the major environmental disadvantages of its operations.

The battle was waged to influence 83 councillors, with whom the decision ultimately appeared to rest. Its outcome, uncertain to the last, resulted in a victory for the company's opponents. A number of factors contributed to this. The decision to place the matter before the full Council ensured a more open, less predictable debate, since the Environmental Services Committee had declared firmly in favour of the company. The decision to delay in April at a time when London Brick would almost certainly have won, gave opponents time to regroup and recover lost ground. The debate, when it finally came, went in favour of the opposition who took and sustained an initiative sufficient to convince enough undecided members. The recorded vote which initially went heavily in favour of the amendment may have convinced any remaining waverers. The decision hung on those who were undecided, though some crucial changes of opinion were influential.

At the March ESC the voting had been 12 to three in favour of the company. Of those ESC members voting at the July meeting three Conservatives (including Sollars and Wootton) had changed their vote and supported the amendment, and two were absent. Altogether the ESC vote in July split seven in favour of the amendment, ten against, four absent — a considerable weakening of support for the company. Overall the voting pattern showed Conservatives split (28 for the amendment, 26 against), and even the two Liberals divided (see Figure 4.4). Only the 9 Labour councillors voted together; had they voted the other way the result would have been different, but the result was different to that anticipated by the opinion poll in March (see page 137). There is little doubt that opinion, sufficient to be decisive, was swayed during the course of the debate. But the amendment still commanded less than half the Council's votes and the 17 abstaining or absent suggested that uncertainty had not, even yet, been overcome, though it was much less than that recorded in the opinion poll.

The issue had become thoroughly politicised, not in the sense of party since voting had crossed party lines, not in the sense that it was not a matter of technical or expert resolution, but one for political judgement and decision. Indeed, the influence of expertise had waned during the months leading up to the July debate. The planning officers, having secured early initiatives and influence with the ESC, had come to recognise that the issue was governed by forces outside their control. The experts, Cremer and Warner, and expert medical opinion, had produced their findings and recommendations, but increasingly these had been used to confirm or deny positions already reached. This is well illustrated by the DoE report, which, coming so late in the debate, scarcely impinged on its outcome. Had it done so the result might have been different, for, despite its qualifications, it provided a more solid case for the company than had Cremer and Warner. The fact was the issue had irretrievably entered the political arena and would be determined by the complex and intangible processes through which information is filtered and evaluated and emerges in a single, unambiguous answer — for or against.

Up to this point the external economic environment had provided a neutral influence on the debate. All along it had been assumed that the new works would be built, though the exact location was uncertain. The company's forecasts for future production were optimistic and the investment proposals remained firm. In the coming months a shifting economic climate and its specific influence on the market for bricks would add a new dimension to the issue. In July the opposition to the company was at its height. It would be sustained for a few months more and then the story would take on new twists which few, in the immediate aftermath of the July Council meeting, could have foretold.

Notes

1 Environmental Services Committee, Minute 78/11/163, 27 September, 1979.
2 Report of Environmental Services Committee, 27 September, 1979, item 14.
3 The Committee on *Planning Control over Mineral Workings* (The Stevens Committee) HMSO, 1976. See note 12, Chapter 3.
4 Draft Agreement, Mark VIII, clause 4(g), 8 February, 1980.
5 Ibid, clause 4(h).
6 The schemes included the working of pits in five year phases; temporary restoration; a master scheme for the restoration of the whole Vale subject to five year review; detailed landscaping of the Vale and noise control. Report to consultative sub-committee, 19 February, 1980, p.17.
7 Draft Condition 3, 4 February, 1980.

8 Indicated in letters from London Brick Company's Estates Manager to County Planning Officer, 6 and 11 February, 1980.
9 County Planning Officer, Proof of Evidence, Vale of Belvoir Inquiry, p.2.
10 Report to Environmental Services Committee, 22 February and 1 November, 1979.
11 See note 9.
12 London Brick Landfill Ltd., North East Leicestershire Prospect, Public Inquiry. Proof of Evidence, January 1980.
13 Forestry Commission, Mr D.F. Fourt, Proof of Evidence, Vale of Belvoir Inquiry.
14 Vale of Belvoir Inquiry, Transcript of the Proceedings, 27 February, 1980, p.51.
15 Ibid p.81.
16 Transcript of Proceedings, 28 February, 1980, p.25.
17 The Department of the Environment had sounded out the planning officers to see what grounds there might be for an inquiry and had indicated their doubts about the need for an inquiry.
18 *Bedfordshire Times*, 14 March, 1982.
19 Ibid.
20 Letter from Peter Goode to G. Wedd, DoE. 26 November, 1979, PROBE Press release, 21 November, 1979.
21 *Bedfordshire Times*, 11 January, 1980.
22 Blowers, A.T. (1982) 'The perils of being hung', *Local Government Studies*, Vol. 8, No.4, July/August, pp.13-20.
23 Report to the Consultative sub-committee, 19 February, 1980.
24 Report to Environmental Services Committee, 27 March, 1980, p.40.
25 North Bedfordshire Borough Council, 11 December, 1979.
26 The revised statement from North Bedfordshire was as follows: 'That the County Council be informed that the Borough Council re-affirms its view that the proposals represent a significant improvement to the environment of the Marston Vale and are pleased to note that the objections in respect of the landscaping and design are likely to be met. The Council is, however, still concerned about the atmospheric pollution and supports the County Council in their current investigations into improved kilning techniques involving the incineration of fumes.' (County Council Report, 24 April, 1980 80/k/44).
27 Cremer and Warner, 'Comments on the London Brick Company Research Laboratories' Memorandum (No. RM 564) on the Assessment and Implications of the Cremer and Warner Report prepared for Bedfordshire County Council', March 1980, p.1.
28 Letter from Cremer and Warner to County Planning Officer, 3 April, 1980.
29 Report to Environmental Services Committee, 27 March, 1980, p.49.
30 Ibid p.54.
31 Ibid p.59.
32 Ibid p.61.
33 The grounds for deferral were spelled out later. 'It was questionable whether the site for the new brickworks . . . would be physically suitable for the tunnel kilns which Messrs. Cremer and Warner hoped to see developed, and, in the circumstances the Committee considered that it would be advantageous for

further discussions to be entered into with London Brick Company Limited in view of the uncertainty about the actual site which might ultimately be required.' (Report of County Council, 24 April, 1980, 80/k/44).

34 Turnover £124.8 million (1978, £111.3 million). Profits £7.1 million (£6.7 million).
35 *Bedfordshire on Sunday*, 30 March, 1980.
36 Private conversation, 11 April.
37 Letter from James Aldridge, Chairman of Bedfordshire Preservation Society to councillors, 22 April, 1980.
38 *Bedford Record*, 22 April, 1980.
39 Letter from Marcus Fox to Stephen Hastings MP, 19 February, 1980.
40 Letter from Marcus Fox to William Benyon, MP, 22 April, 1980.
41 Ibid.
42 *Bedfordshire on Sunday*, 27 April, 1980.
43 Ibid.
44 *Luton Post-Echo*, 25 April, 1980.
45 *Bedfordshire Journal*, 1 May, 1980.
46 Ibid.
47 Although the invitation to the Minister to call the matter in was no longer a real option, it was, of course, still possible that an inquiry would result if the proposals were rejected, or conditions unacceptable to the company were required, and an appeal was made.
48 Letter from Councillor Blowers to Peter Goode, 10 May, 1980.
49 Letter from Peter Goode to Marcus Fox, Minister for the Environment, 20 April, 1980.
50 Letter from Peter Goode to Marcus Fox, 28 April, 1980.
51 The meeting was attended by the Marquis of Tavistock, Peter Goode, councillors Chapman and Blowers, Anthony Stanbury, and Roger Tagg.
52 Letter from Anthony Stanbury to Michael Heseltine, Secretary of State for the Environment, 27 June, 1980.
53 On this occasion Peter Goode, Anthony Stanbury and councillors Hendry, Chapman and Blowers were present.
54 *Milton Keynes Express*, 27 June, 1980.
55 *Bedfordshire Times*, 27 June, 1980.
56 *Luton News*, 22 May 1980, *Dunstable Gazette*, 12 June, 1980.
57 *Bedfordshire Journal*, 12 June, 1980, *Bedfordshire Times*, 13 June, 1980.
58 *Bedfordshire Times*, 20 June, 1980.
59 Letter from Beds. and Hunts. County Branch of the NFU to councillors, 3 July, 1980.
60 *LBC Review*, May/June, 1980, p.10.
61 *Bedfordshire Times*, 27 June, 1980.
62 *Private Eye*, 9 May, 1980. The four issues of 'Bricks and Slaughter' were published on 9 May, 20 June, 18 July and 19 December, 1980.
63 *Private Eye*, 18 July, 1980.
64 *Private Eye*, 20 June, 1980.
65 *Bedfordshire Times, Bedfordshire Businessman Supplement*, May 1980. It was during this period that Stuart Meier became External Relations Manager of

London Brick. He established good relations with the local Press, and his genial, critical attitude was a factor in the improved image the company was able to portray.

66 *Bedfordshire Journal*, 29 May, 1980.
67 *Bedfordshire Times*, 23 May, 1980.
68 *Bedfordshire Times*, 6 June, 1980.
69 *Bedfordshire Times*, 13 June, 1980.
70 Department of the Environment (1980), *Air Pollution in the Bedfordshire Brickfields*, Directorate of Noise, Clean Air and Waste, 6/80.
71 *Luton News*, 19 June, 1980.
72 *Bedfordshire Times*, 20 June, 1980.
73 Letter from Cremer and Warner to County Planning Officer, 18 June, 1980.
74 *Bedfordshire on Sunday*, 6 July, 1980.
75 County Council, 3 July, 1980, Minute 80/73.
76 *Bedfordshire on Sunday*, 6 July, 1980.

CHAPTER 5
THE CONFLICT RESOLVED

The stalemate continues

The triumph of the opposition was not, as was thought at the time, a conclusive victory. Over the next six months London Brick engaged in a battle of attrition and manoeuvre in an attempt to implement its plans and undermine the Council's decision, while making no concessions on pollution control. In this it failed, as the opposition was able to confirm its victory. But it turned out to be a pyrrhic victory, as external factors brought about a rapid transformation of the balance of power in the opening months of 1981. These changing circumstances were seized on by those favouring London Brick, who engineered an extraordinary and sudden breakthrough for the company. Thus the closing months of the conflict can be conceived in two phases — a period when the opposition maintained and consolidated its position, followed by a period when external forces shifted the political balance and fatally undermined the victory achieved. Although London Brick ultimately, whether by design or accident, secured its objective, the aftermath showed that no one had in fact gained much, after three years of the most intense conflict.

London Brick procrasinates

Once the Council had taken its decision, the next moves lay with London Brick. The company's immediate reaction was to argue that the condition imposed by the Council was impracticable. James Bristow said after the meeting 'What they are asking for would appear to be impossible. Existing methods might cut out 50 to 90 per cent of the present emissions of sulphur dioxide and so on, at the price of setting back the brickmaking industry, but we know of no methods that would get rid of everything, as the Council seems to be demanding'.[1] The company's position was, therefore, not deflected by the decision, but he hinted that it would take a considered look at the new situation. 'It is too early to say exactly what we will do next.

When we receive the Council's decision in writing we will have to study it carefully. On the face of it, however, we simply cannot build a brickworks capable of removing all pollutants.'[2] Although there were several options available to the company, it was clear the first move would be to explore the implications of the Council's decision.

This strategy led the company to take advice from Counsel. In a letter to the County Planning Officer the company produced the results of its legal advice.[3] This turned on the interpretation of two phrases of the new condition. One was the meaning of 'plant', and the company claimed that it was under no obligation to incorporate plant in the phase 1 permission, merely kilns. The gas treatment plant was only to be incorporated when it was practicable. More importantly London Brick's advice placed a subtle but significant construction on the words 'capable of removing the pollutants', which had been added during the Council debate. The company argued that 'whereas at the present state of knowledge there is no practicable mechanism whereby pollutants and odours given off in the brickfiring process can be eliminated within the works, future development may make this possible'. Consequently the company's Counsel had concluded 'that before London Brick Company construct the kilns they must submit to the County plans, sections and drawings showing their layout and detailed engineering construction and that the kilns must be so designed as to be capable of removing the pollutants and odours to the gas treatment plant *if and when an appropriate plant can be constructed*' (author's emphasis).[4]

This view was based on the belief that, since no such plant existed and given that permission for the new works had been granted, it must have been the Council's intention that the permission was capable of being implemented. The condition must have been intended to comply with government circulars and Common Law 'so as to be both reasonable and not repugnant to the permission'. To one observer this 'only proved that a Counsel could be found who would say that black was white if the fee was right'.[5]

The company announced its intention to go ahead on this basis at a Press Conference on 30 September. 'We will not appeal against the County Council's conditions — we will just get on with the job. Now the jigsaw is coming together. At last we are starting to move forward.'[6] The reaction of the opposition was one of disbelief. Councillor Hendry said: 'There is no way they can build these chimneys unless they can install equipment to remove all pollutants. There is no doubt about what the Council intended that day and there can be no doubt in the minds of LBC.[7] Later he indicated his fears that the company's ploy might succeed in converting officers and some members of the Council, and declared: 'I would expect that no member of the Council or staff would recommend acceptance of anything from LBC which did not match up to the removal of pollutants. If they did I would raise merry hell. I would go to the limit over it'.[8]

When the Planning Advisory Group met on 31 October to consider the plans submitted by London Brick under the terms of the permission they were presented with a clear recommendation to discount London Brick's interpretation of condition 9. The Deputy County Secretary, John Dawson, advised that the Secretary of State, or the Courts interpreting the language of a planning permission would assume 'that the language used is to be read in the normal everyday sense of the words'.[9] Only if such an interpretation could lead to absurd or inconsistent results would they be likely to apply special or unusual meaning to the words. Thus in the case of the phrase 'removing the pollutants' two different meanings were possible. 'To "remove" can mean simply to take away, withdraw or extract, and this may well have been the sense in which the word was intended. It can also mean "to remove or convey from one place to another", which is the sense in which LBC choose to read it. It is the first sense which we believe to be the natural and normal meaning of the words in the context'.[10]

London Brick's argument was both bland and ingenious. It was saying that since the condition was technically impossible and the Council must be reasonable people, they could not wish to impose a void condition. On the question of 'plant' John Dawson considered that the plans submitted by London Brick were deficient in failing to provide details of plant they intended to install. But he foresaw little difficulty in rectifying the point. In conclusion he argued that the plans should show the plant and that 'removing the pollutants' should be rendered in its natural meaning, and therefore recommended that London Brick be informed that its plans did not meet condition 9 since 'they do not show kilns so designed as to be capable of removing the pollutants (sulphur dioxide and fluoride) and odours given off in the brick-firing processes'.[11]

It appeared at the meeting that there was little doubt in anyone's mind as to the Council's meaning. Assuming this position was sustained the company had a number of options open. It might appeal against the conditions, but this was unlikely because the whole permission might fall if it won, since the Courts might hold that it would be wrong to leave the permission short of the crucial condition. It might invite the Secretary of State to arbitrate, though it was unlikely that he would accept jurisdiction.

It might have recourse to the Courts but, given rights of appeal, this would involve a protracted delay. Or it might decide to make a fresh application stating that the terms of the previous permission were unaccept-able. All the advantages of the Section 52 Agreement would be lost in such an event, and the Council would presumably want to reject the application leaving it up to the company to appeal. There was, of course, a fifth possibility that the company would simply do nothing. But, for the present, it was likely to persist with its reinterpretation of condition 9 in the hope of persuading councillors to accept it.

The Planning Advisory Group, though unhappy about the situation, appeared willing to accept the recommendation. But the Chairman, Keith White, was ambiguous and impenetrable. He pondered on possible changes in circumstances that might cause a change of mind, though no such changes were identified. Publicly his stance appeared clear. 'I know what the wording of the condition means. I know what the Council's intention was — to force a public inquiry. I shall go by what the Council intended, not on what the wording says.'[12]

When the Environmental Services Committee met on 6 November, his real intentions became plain. Once more the issue drew a large audience of 24 councillors and a packed public gallery. Again John Dawson gave his interpretation of the meaning of the condition, though he confessed in his measured, meticulous but disarming way that he could only guess 'what was in the minds of 90 or so members'. At this Philip Hendry scoffed that no one was in any doubt. Andy Blowers emphasised there had been no change in circumstances to warrant any change of mind by the Council, and Allan Chapman said that London Brick's interpretation was tantamount to saying: 'Nice of you to discuss it but owing to a legal or semantic technicality we are going to overturn your decision'. The vacillation of Keith White was the most interesting aspect of the meeting. He betrayed his resentment when attacking his fellow Conservative Councillor Humphreys, and sug-gested that the Council's decision had been unconsidered, taken in the heat of emotional debate. It was now clear that an impossible condition had been imposed — a change of circumstances sufficient for the Council to be given an opportunity to rethink its position. The committee decided by 8 to 7 votes not to stand by the obvious interpretation of the condition, but instead, by 9 votes to 5, to recommend that subject to the plant being shown the plans be approved.[13] This was a complete *volte-face* brough about by the doubts implanted in the minds of members by John Dawson and the strong advocacy of Keith White and his allies on the committee. Despite general agreement as to the Council's real meaning the committee had decided to prefer London Brick's interpretation and therefore cause a rerun of the debate at the December Council meeting. Thus far London Brick's tactics had proved successful, but it was not yet confident of success. 'This decision has taken us a little further along the road but no one is getting excited about it. We will have to wait and see what the County Council make of it.'[14]

London Brick's direct appeal

Throughout the months leading up to the July meeting London Brick had adopted a more aggressive posture, relying less on informal negotiation with officers and members and more on direct public appeal. From time to time it had sought publicity which might improve its image. On 18 October it launched, in conjunction with an unlikely bedfellow, the *Bedfordshire Times*, a competition, the winner of which would have the pleasure of demolishing the 18 chimneys of the redundant Coronation works, thereby creating a new world record and some favourable publicity for London Brick's clean–up of the environment.[15] On 30 November the winner, who had guessed that the largest chimney contained 149,649 bricks and had christened the enterprise 'Operation Oberon', blew up the chimneys to the accompaniment of a brass band, TV cameras, Miss London Brick Beautiful Eyes and media stars.[16] A little later, in a final calculated effort to win the Council's approval for their plans, the Chairman of the company appeared before members of the ESC to answer questions and to persuade them to reverse the previous decision.

The decision to invite the Chairman of a company seeking planning permission appeared to create an unsavoury and awkward precedent. The same day as they were promoting 'Operation Oberon' the *Bedfordshire Times* pronounced itself astonished at such a meeting, and the decision to hold it in secret. 'If this is the way the chairman (Councillor Keith White) wants to run matters, it will need a 400 foot chimney on top of County Hall to take the stink away. Why is he trying so hard to reverse a decision taken this summer by the council?' Philip Hendry was so incensed that he urged members to boycott the meeting. His advice was conspicuously successful since, despite an invitation to all members of the Council, only 12 members of the ESC were present with four other members. But the meeting was important in eliciting some clues as to the thinking of the company and hints as to what its future moves might be.

The meeting was preceded on 9 December by a smaller meeting to discuss progress with research made by the company, which was to become part of the Section 52 Agreement. In their report they stressed that the research focused on 'the reduction of pollutants including odorous compounds'.[17] The research had taken three directions. One was into processes which would give external treatment to gases removed from the kilns, and here catalytic systems were being investigated. Among the problems were destruction of the catalysts and the need for large quantities of lime to be imported and for sludge to be disposed. But the systems could be applied retrospectively using a gas treatment works. A second possibility was the recirculation or reverse flow of gases in conventional Hoffman kilns, which would produce considerable engineering problems and a five times increase in fuel input. The third alternative was to experiment with tunnel kilns, which might involve problems of pressure and produce poor quality bricks. All these proposals were in line with the findings of the Cremer and Warner report. Only the first could be applied to reduce all three pollutants and conform to the phase 1 planning permission. The other two approaches were directed at odour removal and were relevant to the phase 2 permission, which envisaged the possibility of alternative kiln design. But none of these had reached a stage which offered an immediate prospect of implementation. It was also clear that London Brick was putting its emphasis on odour removal. 'We feel we are singled out by odour. It is to the Alkali Inspectorate that we are answerable and they are stressing odours.'

The lack of immediately available technology had become the main plank in London Brick's platform, and was stressed several times when the company Chairman, Jeremy Rowe, met the members. He was bland, confident and knowledgeable. Clearly there were different impressions of the meeting, one newspaper describing him as 'at his happiest with platitudes and generalisations'.[18] There is some evidence for this view in the following comments he made.

> Overall there will be a dramatic improvement in atmospheric pollution and I would like to say that there is no question of the company being forced to do this. The company quite genuinely wishes to improve the present environmental position in the Marston Vale and I personally believe that this total package is one that provides the County . . . with a very good deal indeed.[19]

But he was also keen to stress that advantages were being offered which the Council would be foolish to reject in the absence of feasible alternatives:

> In our view half or 90 per cent of the loaf is better than no loaf at all. You are talking about total elimination which is not possible at this stage . . . it really is for you to decide . . . whether to go to the moon if you like, and possibly wait ten

years before that is achieved, or whether you want to make a start earlier, bearing in mind the improvement that can be achieved at this stage of technology.

There was also more than one hint of the iron fist within the velvet glove. By asking for unknown technology the Council was 'effectively blocking' the consent and by waiting for research 'you will have lost that and you will be taking to my mind a great risk because this opportunity may not re-occur'. External factors might not be propitious in the near future. 'All I can say to you is that at this point in time I do not envisage that our programme would be interrupted . . . by the effects of the recession.' In three crucial passages Mr Rowe indicated the consequences if the Council persisted in applying the pollution condition:

> I cannot believe that that will happen. If it does happen, then so far as the company and my Board is concerned we will have to very carefully consider the position. I don't want at this meeting to cross any more bridges than I have to. I must, however, say that you must not consider that the company would automatically think in terms of an appeal. We have many other investment opportunities, we have existing permissions for new works outside the county and I am not saying that in any way as a threat.
>
> I really cannot commit my Board at this stage to where it starts. The last thing I would like to suggest to you is that our position would be in any way influenced by the fact that we have now permissions both in Buckinghamshire and of course in Cambridgeshire . . . I would personally like to see a start in Bedfordshire.
>
> If they do not want us to proceed with modernisation, the existing works are profitable, they have been successfully operating for many years, and they can go on operating for many years, but what we are looking to is a breakthrough in environmental terms that improves working conditions and in terms of greater productivity.

Whatever his claims, some of the members clearly read the message as a threat. It was clear that the investment programme would depend on market conditions and was not certain to start immediately. Furthermore, it was also clear that the company would consider transferring its investment elsewhere, to where it had gained planning permissions, in both Buckinghamshire, and more recently in Cambridgeshire (see page 177).[20] For the moment the threat appeared partly a bluff to concentrate the minds of councillors, but very shortly it was to become a reality sufficient to transform the whole basis of the conflict.

The immediate impact of the meeting did not favour London Brick. It had been thinly attended and members felt that little new had been said. The precedent set by such a meeting had angered many councillors, and from the company's viewpoint had been counterproductive. Overall, during the six months since July, the company had tried by tactics of procrastination and direct appeal to drive a wedge among councillors which, it hoped, would secure a reversal of the decision. It had at least achieved one more opportunity for the County Council to decide.

The opposition keeps up the pressure

While London Brick was attempting to find a way around the July Council decision, its opponents were determined to make sure that their victory was not to be eroded and, if necessary, to put it beyond any doubt. Immediately after the July decision PROBE issued a Press release purporting to support the statement made by James Bristow, which claimed that filtration could remove up to 90 per cent of the emissions. Although his statement referred to the reduction in pollution that would arise from 'existing methods' (i.e. tall chimneys) PROBE chose a different interpretation. Lord Tavistock, PROBE's chairman, said:

> We welcome the recent statements made to the Press by LBC spokesmen, that filtration processes could remove up to 90 per cent of pollutants from the emissions. We feel that the speedy completion of these new works incorporating these processes will be not only of great benefit to the people of Bedfordshire, but will show major advantages to both workforce and shareholders of LBC.[21]

But any euphoria felt by PROBE and its supporters quickly diminished. It was clear that even if London Brick decided to appeal there would be little sympathy from the Minister for the environmentalists' position. In a letter to Stephen Hastings, MP for mid-Bedfordshire, written after the July decision, the Minister for Local Government, Marcus Fox, maintained his earlier view on an inquiry (see Chapter 4, page 136). 'I do not think that a public inquiry would provide any useful additional information and we remain of the view that the decision on these applications should properly be left to the local Council.'[22]

In any event it soon became obvious that London Brick had no intention of appealing but would seek to implement the permission on the terms devised by its legal advice. Protests about this tactic were made by the PROBE members of the Council but, once the ESC had decided to get the Council decision reversed, PROBE realised it would once more need to defend the position it had won.

A meeting was held at Peter Goode's farm at Brogborough on 24 November, attended by the three county councillors (Hendry, Chapman and Blowers), Lord Tavistock, Trevor Skeet, MP for Bedford, Peter Goode, two other members and Richard Payne, County Secretary of the NFU. It was agreed that the attack should focus on the fact that an attempt was being made to overturn a clear decision of the Council, and that this was based on a legal technicality, not on any new evidence or change in circumstances. At the Council meeting the debate should concentrate on the moral commitment to the previous decision and not enable the whole issue to be reopened. But it was recognised that there were problems. There was some resentment at the role played by PROBE, some members of the Council were becoming bored with the issue and there had been 17 members absent on the previous occasion. To overcome these problems it was agreed that PROBE should adopt a lower profile and let the NFU spearhead the attack. Richard Payne indicated that farmers would be visiting councillors before the meeting to impress on them the dangers to cattle, and would be lobbying outside County Hall on the day of the meeting. The Bedfordshire Preservation Society would be invited to write to all councillors. Finally pressure would be exerted on those members of the Council who might change their minds or who would resent the attempt being made to reopen the issue (a list of such members was drawn up).

The role of the NFU is intriguing. Throughout the years before the conflict the NFU had negotiated out of court settlements on behalf of its members, claiming damage inflicted by the brickworks (see Chapter 2, page 42 and Chapter 3, page 106). As the conflict intensified the local NFU adopted an increasingly aggressive posture. This shift from a position of cooperation to one of confrontation with the company poses questions about the role of the NFU. Whose interests did it serve? What was the nature of its relationship with the company, with local interests, with the leading decision makers? Why did it shift its strategy? What did it hope to achieve? The answers to such questions may give clues to the changing relationships during the course of the conflict.

Before the July decision the NFU had held a meeting with London Brick and issued a joint Press release in which the NFU maintained 'there could still be problems' from fluorine fall–out despite London Brick's assurances about the drop in pollution levels arising from the new works.[23] As the December meeting of the Council approached, the NFU set up a sub-committee to coordinate their lobby, and underlined their hostility to the plans. 'In all my years of NFU work I have never seen farmers so angry about one particular issue' said David Witherick, the Branch's vice-chairman.[24] The Branch requested a meeting with ESC similar to the one granted to London Brick, but only secured an interview with the committee's chairman and vice-chairman.[25] The lobby of individual councillors took place and a survey of voting intentions was compiled (Figure 5.1).

Figure 5.1: NFU Survey of Councillors.
Councillors were asked: 'Are you prepared to support a requirement that a condition be attached to the planning consent requiring filters on the new works?'

By Party

	Con	Lab	Lib	Ind	Total
YES	26	0	1	1	28
NO	28	9	1	0	38
Unknown	17	0	0	0	17
Total	71	9	2	1	83

By District Council

North Beds	
YES	6
NO	9
Unknown	6
Total	21

Mid Beds	
YES	6
NO	6
Unknown	4
Total	16

South Beds	
YES	7
NO	7
Unknown	3
Total	17

Luton	
YES	11
NO	14
Unknown	4
Total	29

Source: National Farmers' Union, Bedfordshire and Huntingdonshire Branch
National Farmers' Union survey of councillors voting intentions, December 1980

Before the Council meeting the NFU circulated every councillor with a letter arguing for an inquiry, and for an agreement between the NFU and the company, providing for monitoring and compensation where liability could be established. The letter closed with the appeal:

> We do not wish to be cynical, but it would appear that LBC are prepared to offer the County Council filtration at an undefined time after their permission has been granted. Equally they have indicated to the NFU that an agreement might be forthcoming. We request that positive steps need to be taken in both these sectors by the company before the final approval is given.[26]

The NFU had thus taken over the leading public role in the fight against London Brick, but PROBE was still orchestrating the campaign. James Aldridge, Chairman of the Bedfordshire Preservation Society, had been invited to send a letter to all councillors, in which he cast doubt on the legitimacy of the attempt to overturn the Council's previous decision:

> The clarity of that decision was indisputable and there is substantial public concern that the London Brick Company were . . . permitted to present their case to the Environmental Services Committee thereby, in effect, securing a rehearing of their planning application . . . The argument for filtration has been fought and won and the real issue now is the maintaining of the authority and integrity of the County Council.[27]

Finally, a third letter in similar vein reached all councillors from Lord Tavistock. He said that the meeting between Jeremy Rowe and the councillors 'must have created a precedent the County Council will come to regret' and that nothing had emerged since July to alter the Council's decision.[28]

On the day of the meeting, 18 December, farmers outside County Hall distributed a leaflet graphically showing the deterioration through fluorosis of one cow pastured at Ridgmont. For the third time the County Council was faced with the decision on the new brickworks and for the third time the company and its opponents had worked hard to gain an outcome favourable to their cause. The first Council meeting in April had agreed not to decide, the second in July had, contrary to most expectations, backed the opponents. If PROBE's strategy to confine the debate to the principle of upholding the previous decision worked then it was widely felt the Council would reaffirm its decision. But, as on the two previous occasions, there was no certainty about the outcome.

The County Council decides a third time

The debate on 18 December was once again opened by Keith White, this time in a more impassioned, well argued and convincing performance than he had managed the previous July. He posed the question 'Do you want to permit LBC to redevelop in Bedfordshire over the next three years while research goes on, or do you want stagnation until research catches up with us in the hope money is still available?' If the latter path was chosen it could be up to nine years before anything was achieved, he felt. He speculated on why councillors had voted for the pollution condition in July. Was it because they believed equipment was available? It was not available. Was it because they didn't want brickworks until control was available? If so they would lose immediate improvements to air quality. Or did they want to force a public inquiry? If so it should be clear that such an inquiry would not serve local interests. By supporting the pollution condition the Council would lose all the gains it had won. The environmental lobby was a disservice to the environment, causing delays and throwing away the chance to get a research programme vital to the future. Finally, he echoed the threat that had been implied by Jeremy Rowe. 'I urge you to vote for it — the investment question is important — Cambridgeshire has voted for it. The company can divert to Cambridgeshire. Further delay will bring us no benefits.'

As in July the main attack on White's position came from the three PROBE members on the Council. Philip Hendry moved an amendment designed to make the Council's decision clear beyond a peradventure:

> That the applicants be further informed that the reference to 'removing the pollutants' in the Council's previous decision meant extracting them from the effluent before discharge and, therefore, in the view of the County Council the plans, sections and drawings submitted do not meet the requirements of the said condition 9 because they do not show kilns so designed as to be capable of removing the pollutants (sulphur dioxide and fluoride) and odours given off in the brickfiring processes.[29]

His speech, though aggressive, lacked the oratory of his July speech, but was nonetheless effective. He argued the issue was already determined and that it was an insult, a disgrace to democracy and to the County Council that it should be resurrected in such an offhand and backdoor way. The Council had made its decision in July and 'LBC knew then and knows now exactly what the decision meant'. Andy Blowers was disturbed by four aspects of the proposal. First, there was the question of its legitimacy. Then there was the question of interpretation. Despite acknowledging the Council's real meaning the ESC had still chosen to prefer London Brick's. Thirdly, there was the issue of practicability, and here he believed that by focusing on fluoride removal progress could be made before new works were commissioned. Fourthly, there was the matter of timing and the possibility that the company might invest elsewhere. Blowers saw this threat as a way of placing the blame for poor working conditions and high pollution levels on the County Council. The job of the County Council was not to decide London Brick's investment strategy but to secure the best environment while maintaining a viable industry. 'We should not be haunted by hints or veiled suggestions made by LBC.' Alan Chapman insisted that the debate was not whether or not we should approve the permission but 'whether we should have our wishes flouted and flaunted on a legal technicality.'

During the course of the debate, however, Councillor White received considerable support. Councillor Hillier had found White's speech 'entirely persuasive'. Councillor Miss Wickson, a member of ESC, declaring that Councillor White was not her Svengali, felt London Brick had been frustrated at every turn. 'The meeting with London Brick was at least as honourable as the champagne before the last meeting.' The debate was, on the whole, of lower quality than the July debate, as if members, having experienced one climax, could not summon the energy for another. But there were two notable conversions since July, one for each side. Councillor Janice Lennon, a Liberal, who had strongly supported the ESC line previously, was disturbed by the tactics used to reopen the debate. 'I am beginning to feel that LBC, like a leopard, has not changed its spots. We cannot trust LBC any longer.' Conversely, Councillor Roy Sollars, who had already changed his mind twice, proposed to do so yet again, this time in favour of London Brick. He had had another look at the evidence and was now convinced that pollution would not spread further. The previous decision had been wrong. 'We have given a permission and have put in a dubious condition that is unenforceable.' His public conversions showed how complex the issues were and how difficult it was to arrive at a decision for those members who had not committed themselves to one side or the other.

In summing up, Keith White tried to broaden the issue, criticising his opponents for failing to answer the debate because they had got a victory on slender evidence. In his peroration he emphasised again the benefits of the package and urged 'Don't follow Hendry on the high road but ESC on the low road'. The appeal was in vain. For the second time in six months Councillor Hendry and his supporters gained a victory, this time by 42 votes to 33, with one abstention. The numbers were higher, the margin the same, and there had been some switches in opinion, but these were self cancelling.[30] On this occasion Labour and Liberal councillors all supported the amendment and the Conservatives were again split down the middle, with 32 for the amendment and 32 against (see Figure 5.2).

Voting for or against the amendment

By Party

	Lab	Con	Lib	Ind	Total
For	8	32	2	0	42
Against	0	32	0	1	33
Abstain	0	1	0	0	1
Absent	1	6	0	0	7
Total	9	71	2	1	83

By District Council

North Beds

For	15
Against	5
Absent	1
Total	21

Mid Beds

For	8
Against	8
Absent	0
Total	16

South Beds

For	9
Against	7
Abstain	1
Absent	0
Total	17

Luton

For	10
Against	13
Absent	6
Total	29

Changes in Voting from 3 July meeting

Previous Amendment Supporters

Voting Against	7
Absent	2
Total	9

Previous Absent Members

For the Amendment	6
Against	7
Absent	4
Total	17

Previous Amendment Opponents

Voting for the Amendment	8
Abstaining	1
Total	9

Figure 5.2: Voting at Council meeting, 18 December, 1980

On the face of it, despite London Brick's efforts to get the issue reopened, little had changed since July. Although in July the debate had been won by the performance of the company's opponents, a good performance by White and his supporters was not enough to reverse a decision which a majority of the members considered had already been taken. For the second time the opposition seemed to have cause to celebrate, but for the second time they were to discover their victory was short-lived, and on this occasion there would follow a defeat. Imperceptibly at first, but with increasing clarity, circumstances were changing, and as a new year opened external factors adverse to the commercial fortunes of the company paradoxically provided it with its opportunity to overcome the opposition to its redevelopment plans.

Transformation in changing circumstances

'What though the field be lost? All is not lost'

Milton, *Paradise Lost*, 1.105

Even before the County Council reaffirmed its decision in December 1980 there were signs that events were beginning to change the political environment within the county. Although these had apparently little effect on the December decision, which was really an endorsement of what had already been decided, shortly afterwards the climate of decision making shifted dramatically. Pollution was deposed as the major issue of concern and replaced by economic issues, involving the company's investment strategy and consequent employment prospects. The two factors which thrust the economic issues forward can be traced back over the preceding months, though it was not until early 1981 that their full force made its impact on the political process. The first was the availability of alternative locations for new works in other counties, the second was the deepening recession. Each of these unleashed new forces favourable to the company's plans in Bedfordshire, and in the space of three months, effectively overturned the Council's decision. From being a series of complex, though interrelated issues, the brickworks debate had narrowed down to a conflict over pollution; in this last phase its focus was employment. During the course of the debate many interests had been involved, eventually combining into two powerful groups. During the final months the labour interests were able to supplant the environmentalists from their leading role. And, as the County Council elections in May 1981 got closer, the brickworks featured in the calculations of individual councillors. The opponents of London Brick became more anxious, its supporters more inspired, as each side weighed the potential outcome of the conflict and its potential effect on the result of the election. The prospect of losing investment and therefore jobs concentrated the minds of councillors in the pre-election period when they felt most vulnerable.

It is possible to interpret the events of early 1981 as if they were part of some predestined manipulation by London Brick, exploiting the circumstances and playing on the raw nerves of sensitive politicians. Conversely, it is plausible to conclude that London Brick did not perceive the fortuitous outcome of its action (or inaction) in this period. A conclusion on this depends on how the evidence is viewed, but first it is necessary to reconstruct the events leading to the *dénouement*.

Cambridgeshire approves new works at Whittlesey

Although fletton brickmaking is confined to a localised resource (Oxford Clay), London Brick's activities span several local authority areas, each with different social, political, and economic characteristics. This provides the company with various investment options while weakening the ability of an individual local authority, such as Bedfordshire, to impose its terms on the company unilaterally. This feature invites the questions 'What is the impact of the spatial characteristics of the company on its investment strategy and what effect does the political geography of local authorities have on the outcome of a conflict between industry and environment?'

London Brick had applied simultaneously for two new works in Bedfordshire and one in Cambridgeshire, the Kings Dyke 2 works at Whittlesey (see Chapter 3, page 91). The local District Council, Fenland, as we saw, had recommended no decision be taken until the DoE report was published, and that full consultations should be carried out with Bedfordshire. A year later in the autumn of 1980, Fenland District Council reaffirmed their position and took an even stronger line, recommending:

> That despite the advantages both in employment and environmental terms to be gained by approving the present application, the atmospheric pollution is a problem of international significance and should therefore be determined at national level. Cambridgeshire County Council should therefore be requested to ask the Secretary of State to call in the application, failing that, to impose stringent conditions with a view to precipitating a public inquiry.[31]

This position was consistent with that which had been adopted by Bedfordshire when the stringent pollution condition was applied in July 1980. If Cambridgeshire maintained the common front then London Brick would be unable to bargain one site against another.

Cambridgeshire's Planning Comittee met to consider the King's Dyke application on 1 October, 1980. The contrast between the highly publicised debate and extensive reports that had already taken two years dominating the County Council in Bedfordshire, and the low key, almost perfunctory way the matter was treated in the neighbouring county was extreme. Instead of a packed public gallery there were three representatives from London Brick and two others from Bedfordshire with no member of the public from Cambridgeshire at all.[32] The brickworks was the 13th of 14 development proposals taken at the end of the meeting, by which time only 11 of the original 18 members of the committee were left to debate it. The debate took just half an hour. The report was only five pages, together with the conclusions of the DoE report. Apart from Fenland District Council, an objection had been received from Peterborough Community Health Council, and the local NFU expressed concern. Only five other consultees had responded and none of them objected, and a petition with 58 signatures (from 30 addresses) had been received objecting on grounds of pollution, traffic and noise. The planning officers' comments were cursory, emphasising the 'same broad conclusions' reached by the DoE and Cremer and Warner reports and concluding that the evidence suggested tall chimneys were the 'best current practical method' to deal with pollution and would significantly reduce local concentrations. On this basis the officers recommended that 'permission be granted . . . subject to appropriate landscaping conditions together with conditions requiring the demolition of Central 1 and 2 works and LB1 works within a period of 12 months after the coming into operation of the new works'.[33]

In opening the discussion the Planning Officer said he understood from a telephone conversation with Bedfordshire officials that Bedfordshire had imposed a condition on kiln designs to ensure removal of the pollutants, but he understood London Brick intended to submit plans which would introduce pollution controls when they became available not prior to commissioning. The new works at Whittlesey would provide 140 new jobs. Although there was a 'confusion of information' the DoE report and Cremer and Warner had concluded there was no danger to public health. He concluded they were unlikely to gather further information and that there were no reasons for opposing the development. His view was opposed by the Environmental Health Officer for Fenland, arguing that this was a major development with a 40 per cent increase in total pollution. A Whittlesey councillor spoke of the intolerable effects of pollution on local farmers and if action was not taken a chance might be lost for 100 years. Another member argued that Cambridgeshire should apply precisely the same conditions as

Bedfordshire. The Chairman of the Committee, Mrs Margaret Shaw, had reached a similar conclusion: 'If we deviate from Bedfordshire, if we go it alone, there is the possibility that LBC might say we'll put all our investment in Buckinghamshire and Bedfordshire'. This was a strange remark since, if Cambridgeshire went ahead on the terms proposed by its planning officer, it would provide a permission without strings likely to prove very attractive to London Brick. But it was clear there was a feeling that the two Councils should act in unison, and it was agreed that the Chairman should meet with her opposite number in Bedfordshire since she was not prepared to take any action that did not conform to that proposed by her neighbours.

When the Cambridgeshire Planning Committee next met on 3 December they were presented with the same report as the October meeting. However by that time London Brick had made clear its interpretation of Bedfordshire's pollution condition (see page 163) and the ESC had recommended that this interpretation be supported. Although the meeting between the two chairmen did not take place, a telephone call conveyed the views of the ESC, views which did not correspond to those of the County Council and which were to be rejected only a few weeks later. Thus at Cambridgeshire's Planning Committee it was reported that 'The Bedfordshire Committee had recommended the County Council to approve the detailed application which made provision to install emission control equipment *at some future date when it became available;* the Chairman indicated her view that this application should be approved in similar terms'[34] (author's emphasis). The Committee also resolved to negotiate a Section 52 Agreement similar to that adopted by Bedfordshire. Once this was completed 'the County Planning Officer [would] be authorised to exercise delegated powers to determine the application in the terms of the recommendation now before the Committee'.[35]

When the Section 52 Agreement was agreed on 11 March, 1981 the differences with Bedfordshire became clear. Its terms included research into pollution before works began and annual reviews of progress; the installation of four monitoring stations; and demolition of existing but abandoned works. But the crucial paragraph concerned the installation of equipment for the reduction of pollutants when it became available. If there was no agreement then the Alkali Inspector would insist on the installation if he thought it 'reasonable and practicable'. Although the terms of the agreement were broadly similar to those which Bedfordshire had applied to the later phases on the new works, it was highly permissive when compared to the Bedfordshire condition on the first phase at Stewartby. There it was clear (and in December it was made unambiguously clear) that pollution control should be installed *before* the works were built and not when it became available.

It is evident that Cambridgeshire were labouring under the delusion that their position was similar to that of Bedfordshire. In fact they were adopting the line of the ESC as promulgated by Keith White, and not the strict line of the County Council. It is interesting to speculate how Cambridgeshire could have been misled. Part of the explanation lies in the contrast between the perceived significance of the issue. In Cambridgeshire it was a marginal issue dealt with by the Planning Committee; in Bedfordshire it was the biggest single issue influencing the whole County Council. A number of reasons account for this. Cambridgeshire is a large county, nearly three times the area of Bedfordshire. Its brickfields occupy a small area in the north of a predominantly rural county, whereas in Bedfordshire the Marston Vale is extensive, and affects a substantial part of the county. The landscape and dereliction problems are more prominent in Bedfordshire where areas of high landscape quality overlook the Vale. These areas contain the more affluent villages in Bedfordshire, populated by middle class residents able to mobilise vocal opinion on questions of amenity. By contrast the Whittlesey area is flat, featureless, and noticeably working class, unlikely to generate environmental concern and more likely to respond to industrial and labour interests. In any case Whittlesey already had two new works and the third could be seen as a natural development and one to be welcomed since it would provide a net increase in jobs. Finally, Bedfordshire had taken up the issue first and so Cambridgeshire could adopt the role of following the lead of its neighbour. In fact, Cambridgeshire's officers and members remained uninformed and largely oblivious of events in Bedfordshire. What they did not suspect, but which soon became obvious, was that the permission granted for Whittlesey would become an Achilles Heel sufficient to destroy all the carefully orchestrated plans of the company's opponents in Bedfordshire.

The recession deepens

Throughout the last half of 1980 there were signs that the economic clouds for London Brick were darkening. Although the pre-tax profits for the first half of the year, at £7.2 million, were favourable the outlook appeared gloomy. The decline in construction of 11 per cent had already brought about a production cut back of three million bricks a week and a suspension of overtime; and by August brick stocks were running at seven weeks' supply. In September the company consulted the unions over further cut backs to achieve a 20 per cent drop in production, and in October a four day week was brought in. The second half of the year saw a ten per cent decline in volume, and brick stocks mounting to nearly 500 million, about four months' supply. Overall pre-tax profits were down on the previous year at £10.7 million (£12.8 million) but retained profit was slightly higher owing to tax adjustments and the performance of subsidiaries rather than trading results. In the first six months of 1981 the situation deteriorated further, with brick deliveries declining another 16 per cent and a 30 per cent fall in pre-tax profit. This decline in the industry and its consequences for the brickworks cast a shadow over the debate in the early months of 1981.

Before the July Council decision the trade unions had become anxious about future prospects in the industry and had applied pressure on the Labour Group of councillors (see Chapter 4). After the decision and as the recession began to make its impact the unions intensified their pressure. Their prime target was still the Labour Group who had voted for the pollution condition which the company said was impractical. Jack Skelton who had led the deputation to see the Labour Group before the meeting said 'I can only assume that the concession of meeting us was one of conscience and nothing more'.[36] Another union leader singled out Councillor Andy Blowers as the antagonist: 'I was appalled to read that not one of the Labour councillors supported the application. Did Councillor Blowers turn the screws?' These accusations were echoed by Stan Clarry, District Officer of the Transport and General Workers Union who called for Councillor Blowers' resignation: 'The vast majority of Labour voters in the county would not find his resignation difficult to accept. On the contrary it would, in my opinion, be one of the best things he has done for the Labour party'.[37]

Councillor Blowers retorted that his opinion had been backed by most Labour members he had met. 'What's being developed through this kind of debate is a degree of antagonism which had not existed before.' He underlined his support for new works and better working conditions and denied he had put any pressure on his colleagues in the Labour Group. This fraternal altercation prompted the *Bedfordshire Times* in one of its many leaders on the brickworks debate to ask 'Isn't it a trade union-versus-employer tactic to demand everything for a start and wait for the opposition to make the next move?'[38]

The trade unions had committed themselves firmly and publicly on the side of the company in its dispute with the County Council. It was naturally in the company's interest to cement this alliance, especially at a time when jobs were being threatened as a result of the recession. The day after the Council reaffirmed its decision in December the company made the following announcement to all its workers:

> Bedfordshire County Council yesterday decided to reject the detailed kiln designs put forward for the company's new Stewartby works. In doing so, they have further delayed the introduction of better working conditions and the improved environment we all want. The Directors are considering the implications of the decision, but our objectives in pursuing modernisation remain unaltered.[39]

The County Council were thus identified as the enemy of improved working conditions and a better environment, points which were thrust home in an article in the house journal by James Bristow. He was particularly aggressive about the 'few protestors', 'one or two councillors, one or two farmers, one or two academics and one or two landed gentlemen' who were intent on attacking a successful enterprise. PROBE should really be renamed 'Preservation of Rural Brickworks in this Environment' since the likelihood was now that the old works would have to carry on. He conveyed the ludicrous nature of the opposition from the NFU and imputed more sinister motives:

> Is the work of thousands of people to be prejudiced for the sake of one cow — a cow which was slaughtered in 1976? Where are all the others? Thirty thousand cows grazing near the chimneys should be affected, but they are not. Why? Interesting isn't it? Perhaps it is because the claims are baseless and the real motive is far removed from the quality of the air we breathe and concern for the wildlife, crops and countryside.[40]

Such sentiments might ensure goodwill between management and labour, but rhetoric had to be supported by action. After its second defeat at the hands of the County Council, London Brick's Estates Manager expressed again the hints given by his chairman at the meeting with councillors a few weeks before. 'There is no doubt that we shall now have to examine our entire policy of investment.'[41] Both supporters and opponents of the company did not have long to wait.

London Brick — first moves and first responses

Throughout the debate it had always been assumed that the company was firm in its intention to invest in new works. The conflict had focused on the siting of the works and what conditions would be imposed. Once the impact of the recession became clear it became a question of whether new works would be built when the recession eased. The recession emphasises the dynamic economic context against which the relative importance of the political conflict within Bedfordshire must be assessed. It raises the follow-ing questions: How far were the decisions in Bedfordshire shaped by external economic factors? Would the decisions taken have been different in different economic circumstances? The underlying theoretical question is: Are political outcomes in conflicts over environmental issues determined by economic forces?

Before the County Council meeting in December, Jeremy Rowe, the Company Chairman, had hinted at what might follow if their plans were defeated. The company now proceeded to make the hints a reality. On 30 December the company informed the County Council that it had aban-doned its intention to construct new brickworks in the county. Later the Deputy Chairman, Michael Wright, elaborated: 'The situation is that the planning application has been stopped. It is not possible at the present time to remove all the pollutants, because the technology required is not avail-able. It is going too far to say that the company's investment programme in Bedfordshire has been totally abandoned. We are reconsidering the position, and what the future holds must be a matter for conjecture'.[42] In *The Times* on 15 January there was the suggestion that the company might apply to build new works elsewhere.

That day the ESC met to review the situation. In his report to the committee John Dawson made it clear the company had no intention of appealing against the condition and understood the company 'would be prepared to continue on a voluntary basis to consult the Council from time to time on their researches into gas treatment processes, which they indicate will continue unabated'.[43] The County Planning Officer, Tony Griffin, pointed out that the new works in Cambridgeshire could go ahead once the Section 52 Agreement was concluded. The Vice-Chairman ruefully re-marked 'We've done the work, they get the advantage'. Roy Sollars felt the legacy of the decision would be a disaster, a mood that seemed pervasive. But there were also indications that the two most prominent supporters of the company were already thinking ahead. Keith White hinted that some options were left open as the Ridgmont application had been deferred. This was taken up by Michael Kemp, the councillor for Cranfield, Lidlington and Marston Moreteine, who pondered what the County Council's attitude might be now that it was clear that the company had withdrawn its investment. He asked, significantly, 'Don't we now have an opportunity to pursue those applications that have been deferred?' The committee agreed that a positive move was now required and agreed to seek the cooperation of the company on those matters which were embodied in the (now defunct) planning agreement. They also agreed to discuss the deferred applications for Ridgmont with the company in order 'to ascertain their present intentions'.[44] It was evident the company's supporters had not given up hope. Fired by the potential loss of investment and aware that Cambridgeshire was now well placed to attract it, they had rediscovered the applications for new works in the southern part of the Vale which had been twice deferred by the County Council on grounds of prematurity. With Stewartby no longer on the horizon, they reasoned, a decision on Ridgmont would no longer be premature.

London Brick — next moves and reaction

If the threat of investment withdrawal had begun to concentrate minds and weaken resistance the reality was likely to prove decisive. The recession had already resulted in short time working, but still the company was failing to match production to demand and building up brick stocks at an alarming rate. As was shown in Chapter 2, page 19, there comes a point when stockpiling and short time working can no longer be justified and the more dramatic alternative, the shut down of complete works, becomes necessary. That point had been reached in February 1981. On 19 February the company announced that it would shut down the Ridgmont works at the end of May with the loss of 1100 jobs. The company's position had worsened dramatically during 1980 and the prospects were gloomy, with government estimates pointing to a drop of 42 per cent in the public housing sector and 24 per cent in the private market. James Bristow commented 'We have taken this step with the greatest possible reluctance'.[45]

A number of reasons were responsible for the choice of Ridgmont for closure. The most obvious was that Ridgmont was a high cost plant of the size needed to reduce capacity. The Monopolies Commission report had revealed Ridgmont as among the high cost works (though not the highest), producing 1000 bricks at about 1½ times the cost of the new Kings Dyke and Saxon works in the early 1970s.[46] By 1981 Ridgmont 'was singled out because it is the least efficient works in the group'.[47] The works had a high level of wastage and could not compete for quality with the new works at Peterborough in a buyer's market. With stockpiles at 420 million bricks covering 50 acres — enough for 50,000 houses — the company decided to eliminate a complete unit.[48] Ridgmont was the second largest plant, producing about 14 per cent of the company's total brick output and was the appropriate size to reduce supply. Closure of one plant would enable the company to restore full time working at other plants, thus avoiding the inefficiency of short time working. The company steadfastly maintained that the recession and the need to eliminate the least efficient plant was the sole reason for the closure of Ridgmont.

Others were not convinced and searched for the 'real reasons' for the closure. One explanation was that Ridgmont had been picked to minimise union reaction. It was an isolated works relatively recently acquired by London Brick. 'We are ex-Marston Valley Brick Company here. The firm was taken over by LBC and we have always been the outsiders. I suspect that it why we have been picked off. The company thought there would be less trouble here.'[49] The workers at Ridgmont were bitter, believing that the reduction should have been spread across the company by voluntary redundancies, early retirement and further cuts in working hours. The Ridgmont workers had been isolated and could expect little support from workers in other plants. 'Our talks with the shop stewards in other plants have not given us any hope that they are prepared to take united action on the basis of converting the redundancies to last in, first out, in all the LBC plants. They are only too glad it is not their works that has been closed.'[50]

Despite the denials by the company, the trade unions and some councillors saw a close connection between the closure of Ridgmont and the County Council's blocking of the new works at Stewartby. 'No matter how we try to get around it the Council's bloody-mindedness is the reason LBC decided not to build the new works. Ridgmont is a lost cause but if the Council withdrew the conditions we believe LBC might still build the new works.'[51] The independent member on ESC, Charles Cook, was quite certain about the connection. 'No matter how we try to squirm out of it the truth is we have made a terrible mistake.'[52] Some workers even went so far as to suggest that Ridgmont had been deliberately shut to force the Council's hand on the new works. 'I have always believed the company wanted Ridgmont closed to make way for the Superworks. But we couldn't prove it.'[53] Whether the decision to close Ridgmont was a commercial necessity or a calculated strategy to overturn the Council's decision, its effect was the same. Coming shortly after the announcement of the withdrawal of investment plans in Bedfordshire it acted as a catalyst, weakening the opposition and irresistibly strengthening the hand of the company and its supporters on the County Council.

Intervention by the unions

The emergence of the trade unions as a major factor in the conflict after a long period of quiescence is another interesting aspect of this case. When they entered the debate it was in defence of jobs but in support of a company whose long term proposals would result in the loss of jobs through increasing productivity. They were in conflict with their natural allies in the Labour Group, though both claimed to favour improved working conditions, a cleaner environment and the security of employment. What accounts for this apparent division of working class interests? Another surprising feature is the unions' failure to support the Ridgmont workers. Was there a division between unions, between plants, or between leadership and membership? The questions about the unions' role suggest a broader question: Whose interests were the trade unions really representing?

In the latter part of 1980 the NFU had taken on the leading role for the opposition. In the altered circumstances of early 1981, with the threat to jobs a reality, the trade unions became the mainspring of the resurgence in favour of the company. They continued their attack on the councillors, accusing them of not paying heed to their constituents and arguing 'We feel very shaky about our jobs. The Council seem to be slinging jobs out of the window.'[54] The letter pages in the local newspapers were supportive of the need for investment in new works. The union leaders took a new initiative, seeking meetings with both the Conservative and Labour groups of councillors to see if any progress could be made.

The meeting with the Labour Group (three Labour councillors, six trade unionists) took place on 18 February. Just as at the previous meeting (see Chapter 4, pp147-8) the trade unions accused Labour members of being against new works, of opposing better working conditions, of failing to appreciate the benefits of new works for the work force, and of basing their opposition on flimsy evidence. In response Labour members Mick Farley and Andy Blowers stressed they favoured new works, that better working conditions were a matter for negotiation between management and labour, and that they had to recognise a wider consituency of interests including those affected by pollution. It was in the interests of the Labour party and the unions to avoid confrontation. The meeting appeared to be constructive and promoted the idea of tripartite talks between management, unions and councillors to explore possible solutions.

The dispute between the Labour councillors and the trade unions had been referred to a higher level, and a week later Councillor Blowers was invited to discuss the issue with Stan Clarry, the District Officer of the Transport and

The Conflict Resolved 187

General Workers Union (TGWU), three other union officials and two representatives of the County Labour Party to whom Labour county councillors were accountable. Stan Clarry repeated his attacks of the previous summer, asking: 'Who the hell are Hendry and Blowers to tell us our jobs?' Unless new works were permitted other plant would go the way of Ridgmont and London Brick's operations in Bedfordshire would cease. It was noticeable that there were no redundancies at Peterborough where the Council had given the go-ahead. Bryan Keens from the Stewartby works accused Blowers of completely misunderstanding the situation. It was clear that the Labour Group were being blamed by the unions for the closure. The County Labour Party representatives argued that it was typical of a company to seek a scapegoat and shift the blame from themselves by getting the party and the unions at each others' throats. Andy Blowers insisted that the permission and the closure were not linked, though he admitted the circumstances were now different and the protection of jobs was the key issue. Despite attempts at reconciliation the meeting was acrimonious and Stan Clarry said he was writing to all shop stewards asking them to ask all candidates in the forthcoming council elections 'Are you in favour of LBC works with no strings attached — yes or no?' There was also the threat that alternative candidates would be put up against those councillors who did not support the trade union line. At the meeting Councillor Blowers was put under severe pressure, and his stance on the issue in the coming weeks became more ambiguous as a result.

At the meeting between the trade unions and the Conservative Group on 24 February, the other adversary of London Brick, Philip Hendry, appeared to get off lightly. Although Keith White was able to lay the blame on Hendry and Blowers, it appeared that Hendry modified his position, claiming that he would be happy for a reduction of pollution not necessarily its total elimination, a line of thinking being promoted by PROBE supporters. He successfully turned the meeting into a publicity stunt, and the *Bedfordshire Times* produced a feature showing that Hendry had been exonerated from blame. It quoted one union official as saying 'As far as Ridgmont is concerned I now accept Councillor Hendry and the County Council had nothing to do with the closure. We have patched things up.' Hendry replied: 'The brickworkers delegation and I cut out all the flannel and spoke frankly. They now realise the closure of the Ridgmont works has nothing at all to do with me or the County Council's decision on the planning application for new works'. The meeting ended optimistically with one official claiming 'We believe there is still a chance LBC and the

County Council can get together and reach an agreement for building a new works'.[55] During February the unions had met the major opponents of the company's scheme in an effort to impress them with the urgency of the employment issue.

The tide turns

Against this background of increasing concern about employment the ESC met at the end of February. The agenda contained three separate, but apparently innocuous, items on the brickfields, but they were sufficient to evoke an extraordinary and quite unexpected response to the pressures being felt by members. The first item, concerning London Brick's working scheme for the Quest pit which had been the reason for the switch to Stewartby, raised little comment. The second item, a letter from Stewartby Parish Council (part of Councillor Hendry's constituency) expressed 'the dismay felt in Stewartby, and the neighbourhood, by the people most vitally concerned, the workforce and the ratepayers'.[56] This caused some mutual recrimination among members about the effects of the Council's decision on employment. But it was the third item, a report on future discussions with London Brick on its research programme which unleashed the emotions felt by members. The report indicated that London Brick would be happy to discuss its research programme, though progress on tunnel kilns would be less urgent now that its investment plans had been abandoned for the time being. The company would also be carrying out some of the improve-ment and landscaping work under the planning conditions. The company had also indicated that a decision on the deferred appplications for the southern works was 'no longer a matter of urgency. They are quite willing for these to remain in abeyance for the time being'.[57] But, since the company had not withdrawn these applications, John Dawson, County Secretary, confirmed they could still be determined by the committee.

This was the cue for Councillor Michael Kemp, representing villages in the south of the Vale, to make a major intervention. He pointed to the decision to defer consideration of the southern works, and to the need for an efficient works in the area now that Ridgmont was being closed. 'We can't guarantee a permission would be implemented, but we can urge that a barrier be removed. Isn't it time we took the initiative on our side and go to the County Council to recommend that permission be granted? I know that many are fearful the company will do what it likes.' To overcome this fear the company should be asked to accept an additional condition on monitoring. He ended by saying: 'I urge you to look at this very seriously. Let's avoid a situation which none of us want or desire.'

There seemed to be a general mood in favour of trying to salvage something. Even Councillor Blowers, while denying any link between the Ridgmont closure and the Council decision, accepted the committee should be prepared to take an initiative, to ensure that jobs were kept in Bedfordshire. Supporters of London Brick were more enthusiastic and even made moves to determine the matter there and then, although the item was not even on the agenda. John Dawson, recognising the issues such a move would raise, said 'It would be improper to grant it off the cuff'. But Michael Kemp was satisfied with the response to his suggestion, as it appeared that members were taking the view that they must help. There were signs that some people (a hint at Councillor Blowers' reaction) were changing their minds. It was fortuitous both that the Ridgmont applications were adjourned, and that Ridgmont's closure presented the committee with such an opportunity. There was now almost overwhelming pressure on London Brick to respond. Councillor Kemp felt permission should be granted on the terms originally proposed (i.e. without the pollution condition added by the Council). The Chairman, Keith White, felt there was still time before the May election for the matter to be debated at the next ESC meeting in March and, if necessary, by the last County Council meeting in April. It was agreed that the item should be placed on the agenda of the next meeting and it could be decided then whether the committee should decide itself or refer it once again to the Council. Meanwhile the Chairman and Vice-Chairman should meet the Chairman of London Brick.

This dramatic turn round in the debate can be explained at three levels. First, there was the change in the political environment brought about by the company's withdrawal of its redevelopment plans and possible switch elsewhere, and more importantly by the closure of Ridgmont and the consequent unemployment being created. Second, there was the opportunity which presented itself by virtue of the undetermined planning applications for the southern works. This enabled the ESC, always a firm supporter of the company, to continue its battle with the Council, on similar terms if on different territory. These two circumstances presented the supporters of London Brick, notably the trade unions and councillors like Michael Kemp, with the ammunition necessary to weaken the resistance of the opposition and the procedure to overturn the Council's decision. And third, with an election imminent, they could promote the idea of redeveloping

Ridgmont as a positive job creation proposal to counteract the impact of the closure.

The rhetoric of the campaign obscured the reality. Michael Kemp and his supporters were proposing a permission for Ridgmont on terms different from those accepted for Stewartby by the County Council. Despite his pleas of urgency the company had indicated it was quite willing to leave the plans in abeyance and had no intention of building any new works until the economic climate improved. The company was 'mildly interested' — any show of enthusiasm would have confirmed the suspicion that it had deliberately manipulated matters to apply pressure on the Council. Its statements about future prospects were vague and ambiguous. 'There is a glimmer of hope in the building market at the moment, and if we are climbing out of a recession [by the autumn of 1981] then I hope we will start building immediately. But if the economy does a further nose dive it is impossible to say when work would start.'[58] What it amounted to was an attempt by a defeated committee, inspired by a councillor for the brick-fields, to outmanoeuvre the Council. If it succeeded the company would have the unencumbered permission it had sought without providing any guarantees of investment. With the tide now running firmly in favour of the company, Councillor Kemp and the trade unions spent the month of March consolidating the position.

Preparing the way for victory

'I believe also that he will be successful who directs his actions according to the spirit of the times, and that he whose actions do not accord with the times will not be successful'

(Machiavelli, *The Prince*, Everyman Edition, p.140)

The unions' attack on the County Council masked their internal divisions, both between different plants and between different unions. The TGWU, with about 80 per cent of the union membership in the brickfields, appeared to be totally wedded to London Brick's position. They were not making noticeable efforts to resist the Ridgmont closure nor to argue the case for work-sharing for those made redundant. When Ridgmont closed, the *Bedfordshire Times* remarked 'how little reaction the announcement caused'.[59] There was a feeling that the Council, and specifically the Labour Group, were convenient scapegoats to mask the union's inactivity. Other unions, notably the Association of Professional and Executive Staff

(APEX), were concerned that the Council might be steamrollered into granting a permission which created no jobs, while giving the company a liberal permission with no guarantee of implementation. It was evident that all sides in the dispute should be brought together, and, accordingly, on the initiative of the joint unions from Stewartby works a tripartite meeting of management, labour and councillors was held in secret at County Hall on 17 March.

This was the only occasion during the whole dispute when most of the major protagonists were brought together face to face at the same time. Those present included James Bristow, John Wright and Stuart Meier (External Relations Manager) from London Brick; six trade unionists led by shop steward Wally Causer; and nine councillors including Philip Hendry, Keith White and Andy Blowers. The divergence of views quickly became apparent. Hendry believed the company, abetted by the ESC, were guilty of machination. 'LBC are acting as a very shrewd company. They have not got a fortunate track history — it is a question of trust and I think many councillors were concerned about secrecy, about promises not fulfilled and the lack of positive indications of the future. Councillors find it inexplicable that ESC are going out with a welcome mat.' Blowers supported him, inviting the company to state why they had never considered an appeal. James Bristow was at his most engaging. He accepted that a permission for Ridgmont would not affect the closure. But 'our intention would be to get working and start demolition as soon as the market picks up'. Already restoration was impressive and the new works would bring further improvements — 'the biggest clean up and the chance to get it right'. They had not gone to appeal because of the time involved and the need to open up the Quest pit. Keith White felt an appeal would solve nothing. 'If we can't sort out what's best, how can an inquiry do better?' If we had to wait for research to be completed nothing at all would be done. The trade union representatives suggested that a committee composed of all interested parties be constituted. On the face of it the meeting rehearsed entrenched positions, but the company and the unions were able to impress some of the members less involved in the conflict and left everyone with the clear impression that the application would succeed at the ESC.

Meanwhile, Councillor Kemp had been busy stirring up feelings in favour of the permission among his constituents. He issued a leaflet entitled 'New Brickworks — the Facts' in which he claimed 'The Council subjected the permission for Stewartby to impossible conditions relating to pollution'. He displayed the voting of the Council by party and noted: 'Having been satisfied with the improvements to our area under the planning agreement I voted for the new brickworks and spoke in support'. When Ridgmont's closure was announced 'I begged and implored the committee responsible to make a recommendation at their next meeting and then the matter will be debated by the full Council. I now appeal for the support of every person who cares about the matters in the planning agreement made with the company, who cares about improved working conditions and who wants to see brick production continue'. He ended with the comment 'There can be no guarantee that the closure will be withdrawn but we can give the company every opportunity to withdraw by securing planning permission'. The leaflet was intended to lay the blame for the problem on the County Council but was careful to note that a change of mind might not bring about immediate benefits.

Councillor Kemp elaborated his position at a public meeting attended by over 150 people at Marston Moretaine on 16 March. He said 'I have never felt so bitter about a single issue in all my life.' Bryan Keens, one of the Stewartby trade unionists who had attacked the Labour Group, now blamed the Conservatives for failing to permit the new works which he felt would have avoided the closure of Ridgmont. But London Brick's spokesman denied this: 'The Ridgmont closure was nothing to do with County Council matters — it was due to the depression. However, if the Council gave the go-ahead for new works it could lead to an early start on demolishing and clearance work at Ridgmont'.

Kemp's role in the resurrection of the Ridgmont planning application was attacked from three quarters. Predictably Labour councillors saw it as a smart piece of publicity which drew attention from the real cause of the closure, the recession, which they attributed to Conservative government policies. 'LBC have made it clear that the cause of the closure of Ridgmont is the economic situation brought about by the party Councillor Kemp supports. There is a nauseating whiff of hypocrisy here . . . He is just electioneering' said Councillor Blowers.[60] Kemp's seat had previously been held by Labour, and was thought to be marginal in the coming election. There were also suggestions that Kemp had other motives for promoting the issue. The previous December *Private Eye* had noted 'One of LBC's strongest supporters is Councillor Michael Kemp. One piece of information which, no doubt quite by chance, he has never given the Council is that Powage Press of Aspley Guise, of whose directors he is chairman, has a lucrative contract for printing LBC's magazine, *LBC Review*'.[61] The question of Kemp's interest and impartiality was a theme of the final stages of the debate. A third criticism concerned the legitimacy of the attempt to reinstate a planning permission twice denied by the County Council when the company was not pressing for a decision, and when circumstances had not materially altered. Although employment had become an issue there was absolutely no guarantee that the granting of the permission would make any difference to immediate jobs prospects. The question of changing circumstances and the credibility of the ESC's position was also to loom large and to become the subject of a complaint to the local ombudsman. For the moment, Councillor Kemp stuck to his claims: 'I don't think I am building up false hopes. If we gave planning permission the possibility of using people for demolition is there. I shall be broaching it to LBC as soon as planning permission is granted. I will not do it before because I would not want it said that LBC used closures as a weapon nor do I want it said I am a mouthpiece for LBC.'[62]

Opposition on the run

During 1980 the opposition, orchestrated by PROBE, had twice pulled off major victories in the County Council. But in 1981, with pollution taking second place to employment as the main issue, its recuperative powers were much diminished. PROBE had virtually ceased to exist, and Peter Goode had already conceded defeat and was looking further ahead, possibly to the courts via the NFU. He accepted that the ESC would grant the Ridgmont permission; the only hope lay in taking the matter to the County Council the fourth time. The committee had delegated powers to pass the planning permission but on the previous two occasions it had chosen (under considerable pressure) to refer the matter to the Council for decision. If the Committee chose not to refer it then, under para. 4(3) of the General Instructions to Committees, once permission had been granted, a quorum of members (in this case six) could 'require that the resolution then passed shall be submitted as a recommendation at the next available meeting of the Council'. The opposition therefore needed to ensure that at least six members could be found to 'stand' at the committee to make sure it was referred to the Council. Even this was beginning to look unlikely, so powerful was the surge in favour of granting permission at the committee level.

With PROBE inactive, the opposition was left to long standing opponents of the company's plans on the Council, but even here there were signs of weakening resistance. Councillor Blowers, who had been under considerable pressure from the trade unions, was thought to be contemplating a change of mind. 'One of the most startling "converts" is Labour Group leader Councillor Andy Blowers, who fought for months to see that the pollution conditions were attached to the planning permission. Now Councillor Blowers is not so sure. "The priorities have changed. Now we are in a position where fears about unemployment have overtaken fears about pollution . . . If I could have some guarantees from LBC about pollution abatement and the amount of control the Council would have over it together with a promise of new jobs I would vote to drop the pollution-free condition".'[63] Such posturing provoked an abusive leader in the *Bedfordshire Times:* 'But the crown of humbug must surely be awarded to Councillor Andy Blowers, supreme local politician . . . He is already savouring the warmer climes of siding with the vociferous minority . . . Such a change of heart of course stems from the date of the County Council elections — brilliant timing by LBC which could well now get its own way by trading on ambitious politicians desperate for votes.'[64]

Councillor Philip Hendry was 'sticking to his guns', but his position was weakened by the fact that he was not a member of ESC where the decision would be made. He too, like Blowers and Kemp, had felt the pressures of the coming election. The local Conservatives felt that if he stood again for his seat, which included Stewartby, 'defeat by brickworkers organised to vote against him would be a near certainty'. At first he seemed unwilling to move elsewhere: 'I have served the people of my district well for the past eight years and I would be prepared to stand or fall on my record. If I lost, well, that's what politics are all about after all. But there has been pressure from my colleagues to stand in a safer area to try to ensure that I get back.'[65] A few weeks later Hendry decided to fight an impregnable Conservative seat in north Bedfordshire. Although he was still opposed to the company, he stated publicly that he 'would not be surprised if the committee went against the two full Council decisions',[66] and privately bet five pounds that the matter would not be referred to the Council.

All three councillors, Kemp, Blowers and Hendry, were, in their different ways, making political calculations according to the 'law of anticipated reactions'.[67] Each believed the forthcoming election result might turn on public reaction to the brickfields issue. Kemp, representing several brick-fields villages, sought to capitalise on the fear of unemployment; Blowers was anxious about the damaging effects on Labour's chances if they were seen to be fighting workers' interests; and Hendry, vulnerable to a backlash in his own constituency, had sought safer pastures. Keith White, representing a Luton seat far away from the brickfields, was in no electoral danger, but he faced a hostile reaction from some members of his group who believed he was trying to cheat the Council of its victory. He firmly believed the Council had made a mistake and indicated that he would be happy for the committee to take the decision this time. He felt the committee had the expertise, though his actions were regarded with suspicion. When Frank Branston, reporting for *Bedfordshire on Sunday*, discovered White and his Vice-Chairman talking to John Wright of London Brick over lunch he claimed: 'When they spotted me Councillor White's face froze and Mr Wright seemed to be choking on a sandwich'.[68] But the meeting had been authorised by the ESC and White could legitimately claim that there was nothing untoward about it.

In the weeks before the ESC meeting in March the proponents of London Brick had successfully shifted opinion from concern over pollution to fears about employment. For the first time the ESC felt it had the public support it had lacked previously. As the election loomed the political debate became acrimonious and personalised. The battle was no longer between environmentalists and a major company, but an internal struggle between factions within the County Council, a battle between a committee and the Council. There was no doubt the committee would once again support the company, the only question was whether they would allow their decision to be ratified by the County Council.

London Brick triumphant

The ESC meeting of 26 March opened with a discussion of Kemp's interests. He declared that he had taken advice and he was able to assure the committee that his interest was not such as to preclude his participation in the debate. He also gave a categoric assurance that he had no interest other than his involvement with *LBC Review*.

The next issue was the future of London Brick's investment plans. Councillor White outlined the results of his discussions with the company. These had revealed the following points:

1. The company had no intention of appealing against the Council's condition on the Stewartby works since this might prevent them excavating the Quest pit, which was part of the application. In any case Stewartby was no longer their first priority.

2. The closure and demolition of Ridgmont works made it easier to

redevelop there and it would be possible to accommodate tunnel kilns in phase 2 within 4-5 years, which would be required if research proved their feasibility.

3. The company was prepared to set up a liaison committee with the NFU to exchange information about research and monitoring.

4. The company had planning permissions at Bletchley in Buckingham-shire, which must be started within ten years, and at Whittlesey to start within five years.

5. Once the brick stocks at Ridgmont were cleared, demolition could begin, providing up to 75 jobs. When the economy improved construction could commence with 200 jobs.

6. Given acceptable planning permissions at all the sites applied for, London Brick's priorities would be first Ridgmont, second Whittlesey, third Stewartby or Bletchley. Without an acceptable permission in Bedford-shire the order would be first Whittlesey, second Bletchley and third Ridgmont or Stewartby. Thus, with the permission there would be re-employment, better working conditions and a reduction in pollution — without it there would be stagnation.

Since the December meeting circumstances had changed, with the granting of permission in Cambridgeshire and the closure of Ridgmont. Councillor White declared: 'In approving today everybody wins. The Council are saved the embarrassment of changing their stance. I am concerned that we do the best thing for Bedfordshire. I don't mind being a bad guy.'

Two issues dominated the ensuing debate. One, pressed by the wavering Councillor Blowers, concerned the reality of the employment prospects. His attempt to get a binding agreement on job creation from LBC was described as blackmail, to which he replied — 'We're all blackmailing each other'. Councillor Kemp commented 'If we don't give planning permission there will certainly be no extra jobs at Ridgmont. If we do, there might be'. The other issue was whether the matter should be referred to the Council, and here the Council's Chief Executive, John Elven, intervened. 'I think it would present a strange image if the Council adopted one view and the committee adopted another.' A Labour member, Martin Thornley, noted: 'It will be said that this committee twice tried to get its way in council, failed twice and then did not have the courage to go to council again'.

Predictably the committee passed the permission for the works at Ridgmont without any stringent pollution condition on phase 1, but with the agreement that research should determine whether controls should be implemented in phase 2. The voting was 10 to 1 (Conservatives for and one Liberal against) with Blowers and his two Labour colleagues abstaining. All rested on whether six members would 'stand' in order to refer it to the Council. Until the last it was thought there would be enough, but in the event only five stood (three Labour members, the Liberal, Janice Lennon, and one Conservative, the Chairman of the Council, Marion Shepherd). The sixth member expected to stand, Conservative Ted Wootton, had quietly left the chamber shortly before the vote because, it was claimed, he had a train to catch to keep a vital appointment in London. Later it was rumoured that he remained in Bedford that day and he denied that he would have 'stood' had he remained at the meeting. But the incident enabled one newspaper to declare: 'After two years of debate the brickworks issue was decided by a man who had a train to catch'.[69]

The last rites

Although the Council had been denied the final say there was no certainty that they would have rejected the committee's recommendation. The whole political climate had altered and the decision had about it an air of inevitability. All that was left to the opposition was accusation and recrimination. Peter Goode commented 'If that is what this committee calls democracy I give up. I still cannot believe ten people could have blatantly overturned a Council decision'.[70] Philip Hendry accused the committee of 'cheating and manipulating the system for their own ends'.[71] For all the sound and fury the decision had been taken and was irrevocable and all that remained was an inquest at the County Council meeting on 23 April.

In defence of his committee's decision Keith White rested his case on the change in circumstances since the Council's December decision, and the need to secure potential investment for Bedfordshire along with the environmental benefits of the Section 52 Agreement. Philip Hendry wondered why, if the case was so changed, the committee had not got the courage to bring it before the Council. In reply to two questions from Hendry, White said that his committee had acted correctly and that its decision was final. It was left to other members of the Council, most of them relatively uninvolved in the saga, to pick over the remains of the issue. Labour's Councillor Tom Andrews said 'Many members of this Council regret the backdoor manner in which the Environmental Services took this decision'. Liberal leader Brian Gibbons regarded it as a 'stab in the back'. Andy Blowers asserted that it was no defence to suggest that the case for Ridgmont was any different from that which the Council had debated for Stewartby. 'We all know that although the sites were different the issues were the same'. These were the comments of a defeated group. In summing up Keith White was at pains to justify what he clearly felt was a good decision — the Council was not the right forum for deciding planning applications; its procedures denied officers from speaking, speeches were cut short, and much depended on emotional appeal; and the landowning and farming lobby had caused a two year delay. 'The committee didn't take a decision to spite the Council but in spite of the Council decision'.

At a personal level the councillors involved in the conflict had been affected in different ways. Among the opponents of the company Philip Hendry had changed his seat, though he was easily elected the following May (and his old seat was retained by the Conservative against trade unionist and brickworker, Bryan Keens standing for Labour). Andy Blowers, too, won his seat convincingly and the putative opposition from the brickworkers failed to materialise. Among prominent supporters of the company Michael Kemp was subject to an investigation into his interests, including not only Powage Press but as consultant for a company based in the Isle of Man which held shares in LBC. It was not until the following September that he was cleared by the Director of Public Prosecutions saying 'I still believe that someone passed on misleading information about me out of malicious mischief. It is no coincidence that they did so just before the County Council elections'.[72] In those elections he, too, held his seat, but during the campaign announced he was leaving the Conservative party and standing as an Independent. Keith White did not escape unscathed. After the election he was deposed as Deputy Leader of the Conservative Group, partly it was thought, as retribution for the part he had played in the conflict, though he had lost much of his support in Luton as Labour took over most of the seats there.

The new Council was elected in May 1981, with the Conservatives losing many seats mainly to Labour in Luton. There was no overall control, with 39 Conservatives, 34 Labour, 8 Liberals and 2 Independents. It became absorbed in conflicts over cuts in spending programmes initiated by central government and the problems of school closures in a situation of falling school rolls. The brickfields issue at last dropped out of the headlines. The closure of Kempston Hardwick at the beginning of 1982 brought a loss of 330 jobs and a further reduction of pollution levels. It made little impact on the Council, and the brickfields issue was relegated to the Environmental

Services Committee to oversee the various agreements that had been forged by the previous Council.[73]

The *dénouement* had been sudden. After a long period of negotiation in which the issues were narrowed down there ensued a confrontation between two equally poised antagonists. The battle had been uncomprising and the result uncertain until, at last, the company's opponents secured what seemed to be a conclusive victory. Almost as soon as it had been won their position crumbled. As recession brought about the threat of investment withdrawal to Cambridgeshire, and Ridgmont was closed, the economic issue assumed an urgency that pollution could not match. Within three months the Council's position had been overturned. What was eventually conceded was greater than the opponents wished but less than the company had originally sought. In the months that followed the implications of the political settlement became clear.

Implications

The dereliction issue
Improvement in the landscape of the Marston Vale had been the planners' main objective from the outset. The Oxford Clay Subject Plan, presented in 1982, summarised policies already agreed and put forward some new ones. These included provision for a 'consultation area' covering the brickfields but extending eastwards, in which the brick industry would be consulted so that development which might sterilise potential clay resources could be avoided. The plan emphasised the need to restore old workings to ground level but, failing that, would prefer schemes for the restoration of pits for agriculture at low level. The flooding of pits would only be acceptable if other forms of restoration proved impossible or if there was a justified need for water-based recreation or wildlife conservation.[74] In a tart letter to the County Planning Officer, the company argued that the Oxford Clay Subject Plan was unclear, subjective, factually incorrect and exhibited 'a lack of understanding of the needs of the industry and of basic commercial practice'.[75] In particular the plan treated the concept of low level restoration 'as though the feasibility is proved and well tried although the authors know that there are strongly held opposing views'.[76] Thus, at a time when political sympathies for the company were improving, there was a noticeable souring of relationships between the company and the planning officials.

There were, however, signs of improvement in the apppearance of the

Vale. The old works at Marston and Coronation had been demolished, and during 1982 the works at Ridgmont, with its parallel sets of 24 chimneys, was dismantled. Various planting schemes were started, an ecological study area created, and plans were submitted for the working of new pits, the regrading and screening of old pits and the block planting of trees in the 'stand-off' areas. The restoration of 'L' field with refuse from London continued, and disposal of Hertfordshire waste in Brogborough No.2 was begun.

In March 1982 the Secretary of State's decision on the Vale of Belvoir coal mining proposal was announced. Although he refused the application, he made it clear that a future application might prove acceptable if the environmental problems could be overcome. Of particular importance to Bedfordshire was this statement: 'He is of the opinion that before local tipping at any of the three sites could be contemplated the possibility of remote disposal of spoil, for example in Bedfordshire, should be explored in greater detail'.[77] A working party was established to investigate remote tipping but cost was likely to prove a sticking point. The Coal Board feared that 'it would be delivered into the hands of a monopoly whose charges are unknown and who would be in a bargaining position which any commercial organisation would love to have'.[78] In October, Leicestershire's planning committee granted permission for coal mining at one of the sites, subject to a later decision on its waste disposal.

The working party reported in October 1983 confirming that remote tipping of colliery spoil from Leicestershire in the brickfields of Peterborough and the Marston Vale 'have sufficient advantages to be worthy, at the appropriate time, of serious consideration for a remote disposal operation'.[79] The problem was one of cost since remote disposal would put between £1·05 and £1·52 on the price of a ton of coal. Although the coal industry might be expected to pay, the '"polluter pays" principle would seem to equally apply to the creators of the void spaces into which colliery spoil may be tipped'.[80] The prospect of large amounts of colliery spoil coming to Bedfordshire was tantalising but, both in terms of time and cost was, like the distance, a remote one.

The pollution issue

The two major reports on pollution produced during the conflict had stressed the need for adequate monitoring of the pollutants. Cremer and Warner had concluded that future control of fluoride emissions must depend on the problem being quantified and its severity assessed, and the

DoE report had urged the creation of 'an integrated monitoring and measurement programme'.[81] The Fletton Brickworks Liaison Committee took up the problem. After a series of meetings the reluctance of member authorities to contribute to a monitoring project was overcome and it was agreed to set up ten sampling stations in the Marston Vale to assess the levels of airborne fluorides emitted by the Stewartby works over a period of three years.[82]

The monitoring could only apply to existing works and focused on fluoride. By contrast, the research into pollution control measures only related to new works with provision for a third flue. In addition it quickly became clear that London Brick was primarily concerned with the odour problem, whereas the County Council had identified fluoride as the major concern. The company, backed by the reports and the Alkali Inspector, was also able to rely on the terms of the planning permission for phase 2 of Ridgmont. In their anxiety to secure tight control over phase 1, by applying a condition covering all pollutants, the Council had overlooked the conditions which applied on later phases. These stated that 'The kilns shall be tunnel kilns so designed as to be capable of incinerating the organic components of the gases given off in the firing processes' unless research demonstrated that this was not the 'best practicable means of eliminating or minimising the odours which derive from the said organic components'. Thus, one of the unintended consequences of the conflict was that there was monitoring into the effects of fluoride from existing works and a research programme into the control of odours from the non existent new works.

The meetings of the research committee did little to resolve the different attitudes of the two sides. London Brick described its work on a range of processes for odour control, none of which promised a breakthrough. Internal incineration in Hoffman kilns gave rise to various technical problems and would raise the fuel costs by five times. Early work on tunnel kilns had predicted damage to the bricks under the high temperatures involved. Any chance of success would depend on the development of heat recovery systems. There had been some work on the possibility of removing the acid gases but the processes required large inputs of lime and created obnoxious by-products. In any case, the company argued, tall stacks would eliminate the problem but would not fully counteract the problem of odour. Evidence produced by Cremer and Warner confirmed the much lower levels of pollution already experienced in the Vale as a result of works closure at Ridgmont and, later, at Kempston Hardwick. Using dispersion modelling to predict the levels of SO_2 and fluoride, projections revealed that the highest average concentration of fluoride had been reduced to three-fifths of 1979 levels and that average annual levels had been reduced by more than half over a substantial part of the Vale.[83] The introduction of a new works would produce only a marginal increase. If the older parts of Stewartby were closed 'there would be a further improvement in air quality'.[84] The projections revealed the surprising conclusion that pollution levels from the more modern parts of Stewartby plus one new works would be little different from those projected from two new works. This underlined the fact that pollution was created by the existing works, particularly from the smaller chimneys of the oldest plant. Furthermore the location of the new works, whether at Ridgmont or Stewartby, made little overall difference to pollution levels, although there were marginal differences in its spatial distribution. Although the odour problem would be reduced it would persist 'until some practicable means for elimination of odours at source can be developed and implemented'.[85]

The monitoring programme was intended to allay any lingering doubts about future pollution levels. The research into pollution control appeared likely to reveal processes other than tall stacks which could attack the problem. But the evidence was strongly pointing to the marked improvement brought about by the elimination of old works with short chimneys, and suggested that the improvement could be sustained even if a substantial part of the existing works at Stewartby were retained. This opened the way for the company to put forward proposals which would achieve production levels of 20 million bricks per week by combining one new works with the output of the newer parts of the existing Stewartby works. In 1983 London Brick launched a new initiative.

Stewartby reborn?

One of the features of the conflict had been London Brick's ability to switch between sites in the Marston Vale, and between locations in Cambridgeshire and Bedfordshire. Its initial preference had been for Ridgmont, then it switched to Stewartby, and later accepted a permission without the pollution control at Ridgmont, clearly stating it was its first priority for investment. Were these changes in locational strategy a reaction to changing circumstances or were they part of a reasonably coherent strategy designed to exert leverage on the County Council? The idea that the company was opportunist receives some support from events in 1982 and 1983.

The year 1981 saw the nadir of the recession. A quarter of the company's employees (2,100) left and five works, 30 per cent of its brickmaking capacity, were closed. Despite this, pre-tax profit was up on the previous year at £11.154 million (1980: £10.742 million). This was achieved by rationalising production, increasing productivity at the remaining more efficient works and by increasing brick prices by 10 per cent. Even so, profits on bricks were down but were compensated by increased profits from other activities. By 1982 the benefits from rationalisation had led to a revival, in which bricks made the running and profits overall were up 37 per cent at £15.328 million, a record for the company. During this period the company had been reorganised,[86] had invested a 20 per cent share in an Australian brick company and had made a £28 million bid for Ibstock Johnsen, one of the major non-fletton producers of bricks in the UK (7 per cent of brick production, 21 per cent of the non-fletton market) and with interests in Holland, Belgium and the USA.[87] The chairman stressed that the company was not trying to become a conglomerate but 'we remain primarily brickmakers'.[88] By the autumn of 1983 London Brick was itself facing the possibility of a takeover by the Hanson Trust, owners of Butterley, the second largest non-fletton brick producer, the outcome of which is described at the end of the book.

Bedfordshire had suffered disproportionately during the recession. In 1981 two works had closed, Ridgmont and later Kempston Hardwick, leaving only the Stewartby works with 1500 workers still operating in the Marston Vale. In October 1982 the company announced that it had abandoned plans to build the new works at Ridgmont. One of the reasons cited was that the design imposed by the County Council for the new works was too expensive. James Bristow argued 'The works would not be viable. I could not see them ever showing a profit'.[89]

This proved merely a prelude to the next move made by the company. In January 1983, James Bristow unveiled a new strategy to a meeting of the Brickworks sub-committee. He confirmed that the company had no intention of building at Ridgmont. The demolition of the old works 'had resulted in a great improvement in the landscape of that area which . . . it would be a pity to disfigure by rebuilding a replacement brickworks on such a prominent site'.[90] Instead the company favoured building in the Coronation pit at Stewartby, where it already had permission but with the unacceptable pollution condition. A works there would be less conspicuous and could be constructed in 'a more utilitarian and less costly style'. The cost of such works would be about £25 million for the first phase and £42 million for both phases; as against costs of £25 million and £55-60 million at

Ridgmont. It would create 100 jobs during construction and 250 when the first phase was built, rising to 350 with both phases in operation. The Coronation works would replace the permission for Ridgmont. Instead of two new works, the company now only envisaged one and had 'no intention of running down the existing Stewartby works'. Kempston Hardwick would be mothballed, retained only as reserve capacity. The new works plus Stewartby would give a capacity of about 20 million bricks per week, the same as would have been provided in the original plan for two new works at Ridgmont and Stewartby.

In return for a permission at Coronation on the same terms as that given for Ridgmont (i.e. without the pollution condition), the company was prepared to relinquish the consent at Ridgmont by a revocation order without payment of compensation. However, it saw Ridgmont 'as a valuable commercial site and alternative uses would be sought for it'. The value of the site for industrial purposes was £5-10 million and could provide a subsidy for the construction of new works. Further, the company wanted to use sites of all its demolished works for commercial or industrial purposes. It had ingeniously coupled a transfer from Ridgmont to Stewartby with a plan to use redundant sites as commercial assets, a philosophy quite consistent with its attitude to worked out pits. Later in 1983 the company switched the site of the new Stewartby works from Coronation to nearby Rookery pit.

On the specific question of transferring the Ridgmont permission to Coronation or Rookery there was little dispute. Environmentally it was a better proposition (the planners had never supported the Ridgmont site), would enable the Section 52 Agreement for the northern area to be implemented, and there was no discernible difference in potential pollution levels. But the environmental gains, a fundamental aim of the various agreements, would be sacrificed if Ridgmont was used for another industry. Indeed, the use of old brickworks for new industries contravened the Section 52 Agreement which regarded agriculture or forestry as the appropriate uses, and contradicted the Structure Plan which foresaw a concentration of industry around the urban areas and opposed such development in rural areas. There was adequate industrial land available and the use of scattered rural sites would create industries distant from labour markets as well as intruding on the rural landscape. The whole concept of a gradually improving landscape in the Marston Vale as old works were demolished and returned to agricultural uses would be threatened by the proposal. While the plan offered considerable advantages to London Brick there was no guarantee that new brickworks would actually be built. Not surprisingly, the planning officers, while prepared to recommend the transfer of permissions, were clear also that the idea of developing the old brickworks for industry should be resisted.

Conclusions

A great deal had happened in the six years from 1978 to 1983. Instead of three works only one was still operating in the Marston Vale, reclamation had begun, pollution had declined, and the amenity of the area was improving. The company's plans had changed from complete redevelopment to a more modest but still substantial investment in new works in the centre of the Vale. In some ways those affected by the conflict had gained something but all had also lost. There was less pollution but there was less production and the prospect of pollution controls was dim. The company possessed permissions in three counties but so far no investment had occurred. The Council's control over the landscape had been increased, but the prospect of sufficient landfill for major restoration was uncertain. Above all the workers had lost, since plants had been shut and there was little likelihood of new work being created in the immediate future.

Throughout this study questions have been posed. The intriguing questions concern the role played by the company and its opponents. Was the company a master of its own fate always able to secure its desired outcomes with only the details to be settled by local debate? Or, was the company all along uncertain, a prisoner of changing and unforeseen circumstances, unable to control the political and economic forces which would settle the matter? Were there numerous interests involved, each with potentially equal access to decision makers, or was it a conflict between élites exercising a disproportionate amount of influence? Was the conflict which absorbed so much time, dominating the life of a County Council for almost three years, ultimately important, or was it a marginal issue unlikely to affect the long term environmental and economic prospects of the area? The answers to these questions will now be explored in the theoretical analysis which occupies the next part of this book.

Notes

1 *The Guardian*, 4 July, 1980.
2 *Bedford Record*, 8 July, 1980.
3 Letter from Estates Manager, London Brick to County Planning Officer, 29 September, 1980.

4 Ibid.
5 *Bedfordshire on Sunday*, 6 November, 1980.
6 *Bedfordshire Journal*, 2 October, 1980.
7 *Bedfordshire Times*, 3 October, 1980.
8 *Bedfordshire on Sunday*, 26 September, 1980.
9 Report Planning Advisory Group, 13 October, p.1 para.4.
10 Ibid p.3 para. 10.
11 Ibid p.4.
12 *Bedfordshire Times*, 7 November, 1980.
13 Environmental Services Committee, 6 November, 1980, Minute 80/K/136.
14 *Bedfordshire Times*, 7 November, 1980.
15 *Bedfordshire Times*, 24 October, 1980.
16 *Bedfordshire Times*, 5 December, 1980.
17 London Brick Company Ltd., Section 52 Plannning Agreement, clause 4(g), Outline Research Programme.
18 *Bedfordshire on Sunday*, 14 December, 1980.
19 Environmental Services Committee, 9 December, 1980. Transcription of proceedings, p.5 + ibid 8, 9, 12, 14, 19, 20.
20 Permission at Newton Longville, Bletchley, granted in 1975; a Section 52 Agreement to be negotiated later.
21 PROBE, Press release, 10 July, 1980.
22 Letter from Marcus Fox, Minister for the Environment, and Stephen Hastings, MP, 7 July, 1980.
23 London Brick Company Ltd. and National Farmers Union (Beds. and Hunts. County Branch) Joint Statement, 26 June, 1980.
24 *Bedfordshire Times*, 5 December, 1980.
25 Letter from Richard Payne, County Secretary, NFU to Keith White, Chairman, Environmental Services Committee, 8 December, 1980.
26 Letter from County Branch, NFU to councillors, 8 December, 1980.
27 Letter from James Aldridge, Chairman of the Bedfordshire Preservation Society to councillors, 15 December, 1980.
28 Letter from Lord Tavistock to councillors, 15 December, 1980.
29 County Council, 18 December, 1980, Minute 80/162.
30 Seven councillors who had supported Hendry in July had switched their votes against his amendment, while 6 (and 1 who abstained) had changed in the other direction.
31 Cambridgeshire County Council, Planning Committee, 1 October, 1980, item 13(x).
32 There were four members of the Press present. The two observers for Bedfordshire were the author and his assistant.
33 See note 31.
34 Cambridgeshire County Council, Planning Committee, 3 December, 1980, Minute 295.
35 Ibid.
36 *Bedfordshire Times*, 18 July, 1980.
37 *Bedfordshire Times*, 22 August, 1980.
38 *Bedfordshire Times*, 22 August, 1980.

39 Notice posted on all London Brick Company notice boards, 19 December, 1980.
40 *LBC Review*, Vol.11, No.1 January/February 1981, p.1.
41 *Bedfordshire Times*, 24 December, 1980.
42 *Bedfordshire Times*, 16 January, 1981.
43 Environmental Services Committee, 15 January, 1981, Agenda item 2(b).
44 Environmental Services Committee, 15 January, 1981, Minute 81/K/4.
45 *The Guardian*, 20 February, 1981.
46 The report shows the costs per 1000 bricks, indexed from Kings Dyke as 100:

	1973	1974
Kings Dyke	100	100
Saxon	104	95
Stewartby	128.4	141.0
Ridgmont	150.2	141.0
Kempston	165.5	171.3

Source: The Monopolies and Mergers Commission, *Building Bricks: A Report on the Supply of Building Bricks*, London HMSO, 1976, Table 17, p.37.
47 *Bedfordshire Times*, 6 March, 1981.
48 *Sunday Times*, 12 July, 1981.
49 *Bedfordshire on Sunday*, 22 February, 1981.
50 Ibid.
51 *Bedfordshire Times*, 6 March, 1981.
52 *Bedford Record*, 3 March, 1981.
53 *Bedfordshire Times*, 2 June, 1981.
54 *Bedfordshire Times*, 23 January, 1981.
55 *Bedfordshire Times*, 27 February, 1981.
56 Environmental Services Committee, 26 February, 1981, Agenda item 5, A.10.
57 Environmental Services Committee, 20 February, 1981, Agenda item 6.
58 *Bedfordshire on Sunday*, 22 March, 1981.
59 *Bedfordshire Times*, 31 May, 1981.
60 *Bedfordshire on Sunday*, 15 March, 1981.
61 *Private Eye*, 19 December, 1980.
62 *Bedfordshire on Sunday*, 15 March, 1984.
63 *Bedfordshire Times*, 20 March, 1981.
64 Ibid.
65 *Bedfordshire on Sunday*, 22 February, 1981.
66 *Bedfordshire Times*, 20 March, 1981.
67 R. Gregory (1969) Local elections and the 'rule' of anticipated reactions: *Political Studies*, 17, pp.31-47.
68 *Bedfordshire on Sunday*, 22 March, 1981.
69 *Bedfordshire on Sunday*, 29 March, 1981.
70 *Bedford Record*, 31 March, 1981.
71 Ibid.
72 *Bedfordshire Times*, 17 September, 1981.

73 The ESC established a Brickfields sub-committee to deal with the issues, and two of its members, councillors Sollars and Blowers, represented the Council on the group overseeing the research programme into pollution control.
74 Bedfordshire County Council, *Oxford Clay Subject Plan*, Consultation draft, May, 1982, especially policies 1, 11 and 12.
75 Letter from Estates Manager, London Brick to County Planning Officer, also reprinted in *Oxford Clay Subject Plan*, results of public consultation, June/July 1982, pp.39-41.
76 Ibid. The County Council, with London Brick, was supporting a research project into the agricultural potential of the callow which overlay the Oxford Clay. As a result of the altercation with London Brick it was agreed to appoint consultants to investigate the feasibility of low-level agriculture in the old clay pits.
77 Vale of Belvoir decision letter from Department of Environment to National Coal Board, 25 March, 1982.
78 Quoted in *Bedfordshire on Sunday*, 4 April, 1982.
79 North East Leicestershire Coalfield Remote Disposal Working Party, Final Report, Department of the Environment, October 1983, p.133.
80 Ibid p.130.
81 See Chapter 4.
82 The project was to be undertaken by Aston University and assessed by Warren Springs Laboratory. The Liaison Committee were also funding a herbage sampling programme.
83 Cremer and Warner, 'LBC emissions — predictions of current dispersion pattern and resultant concentration at ground level', Report No. 82066, 18 June, 1982.
84 Cremer and Warner, 'The January 1983 proposals by London Brick Company for developments in the Marston Vale and their effect on improvements in air quality in the area', Report No. 83039, p.12. By reducing the output of Stewartby to ten million bricks per week, the emission from short stacks on the older plant would be eliminated.
85 Ibid p.13.
86 Under the restructuring, London Brick PLC became the parent company, and, in addition to its existing subsidiaries, three new operating companies were formed — London Brick Engineering, London Brick Property and London Brick Products (the brick making company). See Chapter 2, note 14, p.51.
87 There was a counter-bid from Redlands, and both bids were referred to the Monopolies Commission which, later, cleared the proposed takeover. Ironically, this also opened the way for a possible reverse takeover of London Brick by a company with interests in non-fletton brick production.
88 London Brick PLC, *Report and Accounts*, 1982, p.5.
89 *Bedfordshire on Sunday*, 3 October, 1982.
90 Brickfields sub-committee. Minutes of meeting on 31 January, 1983.

CHAPTER 6
CORPORATE POWER AND LOCAL POLITICS

'A plague o' both your houses'
(*Romeo and Juliet* Act 3 Sc. 1)

Theoretical Perspectives

Until recently theoretical debates about power have been developed from apparently opposing perspectives. The *pluralist* view, defined by exponents such as Dahl and Polsby[1] and supported by empirical studies of community power,[2] reflect an ideology that is optimistic and consensual, and indicates a polity that is supposedly open, responsive and representative. Conflict occurs between competing interests and is resolved through cooperation, concession and compromise. Participation is widespread and power dispersed. Business is one of a number of interests pursuing its objectives but reacting to pressures exerted by other interests such as consumers, labour and environmentalists. Pluralist accounts are devoted to studies of visible decision making.

By contrast, *élitist* theory points to two features of the exercise of power which, they claim, pluralists fail to take into account.[3] One is that the interests involved in a specific conflict do not necessarily compete on equal terms — some interests possess resources and access to decision makers that confer upon them superior power. This disparity in power resources may be explained by a second feature, the ability to exercise power in ways unavailable to less powerful interests in ways that are not visible. Thus much of the more recent élitist literature, often described as neo-élitist, is concerned with the concept of non-decision making, the exercise of power either consciously through suppression, manipulation and control of information, or consciously through reputation, inaction and the mobilisation of bias.

Whereas pluralist and élitist approaches have focused attention on competing interests and the groups which are denied influence, marxist *structuralist* accounts emphasise the fusion of political and economic power which ensures the domination of capital, and the fundamental conflict between class interests. The state apparatus is regarded as functioning in support of capital. There is vigorous debate within marxism, for example over whether such changes as the introduction of the welfare state should be interpreted as a major challenge to capital or rather a means of accommodating and defusing potential challenge. Whatever interpretations are made, marxist explanations focus on class. For them, therefore, business is not simply an interest but 'its role is akin to that of a ruling class or dominant élite'.[4]

Each theoretical perspective — pluralist, élitist and marxist — is preferred by its adherents as a comprehensive basis for the analysis of power. There is a tendency for each to reflect particular ideological traditions. Pluralism is regarded by its proponents as an affirmation of liberal democratic theory, and by its detractors as a celebration of the status quo. Lukes observes that pluralism 'inevitably takes over the bias of the political system under observation and is blind to the ways in which its political agenda is controlled'.[5] Élitist approaches appear to be ideologically ambiguous. On the one hand their emphasis on the role of interests and focus on political activity or inactivity place them within liberal political analysis. The early élitist theories attacked marxist concepts such as the withering away of the state as absurdities and defended, if even in the guise of a new realism, the values of hierarchy, order and excellence.[6] On the other hand, neo-élitists, with their emphasis on the hidden dimensions of power, have sought to undermine the conservative assumptions of pluralism and to provide explanations which have much in common with marxist approaches. Marxist theory is not merely concerned with explanations of the sources of power but urges *praxis*, the merging of theory and practice. 'Social life is essentially practical. All mysteries which mislead theory to mysticism find their rational solution in human practice and in the comprehension of this practice.'[7] For the marxist the world is not merely to be understood but to be changed.

It is however possible, indeed desirable, to be theoretically agnostic at the outset. In attempting to evaluate alternative perspectives two problems must be recognised. One is the role of values and ideologies. Clearly they have an influence on different theories, but this does not imply that everything is open to purely ideological interpretation. The kind of values and ideologies that are held are constrained by the knowledge we hold of the world, and there is therefore an interaction between values and ideologies on the one hand and explanations and evidence on the other. My intention is to put forward a theoretical integration which provides a more adequate constraint upon value propositions and a more adequate expression of them.

The second problem concerns the comparability and compatibility of different perspectives, an issue already raised in Chapter 1. Prior commitment to this or that view forestalls disinterested appraisal, however impossible that may be in the ultimate. The vision of the researcher should not be clouded by presuppositions which lead to a failure to weigh up the evidence, to ignore points inconvenient to the support of an argument or to urge conclusions that rely on insubstantial (or conflicting) evidence. Some would argue that opposing perspectives are 'largely irreconcilable, and neither is capable of absolute proof'.[8] In a strict sense this is true since they are perspectives conceived as modes of explanation rather than sets of propositions. There is a hiatus between such grand scale theory and detailed empirical evidence. The facts underdetermine the theories and hence the theories appear inadequate. The solution to this problem, which I shall attempt in the next chapter, is to introduce mediating concepts which provide a reconciliation of theory and evidence.

The broad perspectives examined here, while not directly comparable, are complementary in the sense that each focuses on different aspects of the case. Saunders argues that 'No single body of theory and no one paradigm can be expected to provide all the answers to questions . . . a degree of theoretical pluralism and epistemological tolerance is thus an essential precondition'.[9] The notion of 'theoretical pluralism' suggests integration can be performed merely by adding together those parts of different perspectives which shed light on the case. This may be an alternative to using empirical material to evaluate and eventually to justify a preferred perspective. Neither seems, in my view, satisfactory. It seems to make better sense to use empirical material as a vehicle for exploring the contribution to explanation of alternative perspectives. In doing so we must recognise that these perspectives tend to be 'ideal types', 'a syndrome of interrelated assertions, arguments and beliefs, taken to their logical conclusions'.[10] Though their ideological premises distinguish them as explanations, there are certain points at which they appear to be compatible, as we shall see. In other words, evidence which seems to underpin one perspective can equally well be used to justify (rather than refute) another. Thus, a close analysis of apparently competing approaches can, as Dunleavy argues, 'show the extent of interaction and common ground between different perspectives'.[11]

This is the method adopted in this chapter. It seems likely that each perspective will provide insights, but that each will prove inadequate for the whole course of the process and its outcomes. The case of London Brick presents an opportunity to analyse the relationship of business to local politics when economic and environmental objectives are in conflict. In particular it can be used to pursue questions which are at the heart of the theoretical debate and which were posed in Chapter 1, and raised at different points throughout the case study. The various questions relate to three central issues: Was it a conflict between competing interests or classes? Was the exercise of power concentrated or dispersed? Was the conflict and its outcome determined by the agencies involved or by structural forces? Behind these questions lie different interpretations of causes, and the answers provide some further intriguing questions which can lead to generalisations, which will be pursued in the following chapter.

In this chapter the case of London Brick will be analysed against each of the major theoretical perspectives — pluralist, élitist and the structuralist perspective which embodies neo-marxist approaches in urban studies. Each will be treated as an ideal type, a perspective, since at the present level of theoretical development, there are various versions of each providing different emphases. The major components of each approach will be described and their contrasts and similarities explained. In one sense the flexibility of each perspective aids empirical analysis but it also offends notions of rigour and precision. The problems encountered in attempting to relate each theory to the evidence will suggest that the provision of conceptual linkages offers a more promising way forward.

The pluralist interpretation

'This proverb flashes thro' his head,
The many fail: the one succeeds',

(Tennyson, *The Day-Dream*)

One of the criticisms of pluralist studies is that researchers have got by 'with virtually no discussion either of power generally or of power studies, non–decisions, mobilisation of bias, and the other conceptual contributions of the neo-élitists'.[12] Wolfinger, himself a pluralist, goes on to say that little seems lost by this omission. 'In this complex and imperfect world, this does not seem to be deplorable, particularly if one thinks that the value of theory is measured by its utility in facilitating empirical research'.[13] Pluralists see their strength as being an ability to test their ideas through empirical observation. Whether or not made explicit, they possess a conception of power defined as a capacity to do something. This has been formulated by Dahl as follows: 'A has the power over B to the extent that he can get B to do something that B would not otherwise do'.[14] This has led pluralists to explore the empirically self evident, to 'concentrate on power exercise itself'[15] through, as Dahl puts it, 'the careful examination of a series of concrete decisions'.[16]

It implies power to do something and is difficult to distinguish from influence or control. Indeed this is freely admitted by Polsby: 'one can conceive of "power" — "influence" and "control" are serviceable synonyms — as the capacity of one actor to do something affecting another actor which changes the probable pattern of specified future events'.[17] The salient role of action, and the ability of individuals or groups to determine events is paramount. Added to the pluralists' belief in the visibility of action and access to participation it becomes a persuasive, if limited, means of analysing a decision making process such as that surrounding the London Brick case.

Pluralist theory envisages 'a socio-political system in which the power of the state is shared with a large number of private groups, interest organisations, and individuals represented by such organisations'.[18] Pluralist theory has its origins in the United States, reflecting the liberal democratic traditions of that country: 'a congeries of hundreds of small special interest groups, with incompletely overlapping memberships, widely differing power bases, and a multitude of techniques for exercising influence on decisions salient to them'.[19] A similar pattern is said to apply to Britain where 'there is likely to be a multiplicity of decision makers, representing a multiplicity of interests, with a variety of definitions of the situation, of assessments of priorities, and of proposed courses of action'.[20] In this situation power is fragmented, shifting and tentative and pressure is applied on a weak polity.

The form of government is representative and accountable, and expected to respond to pressure exerted through public opinion and the electoral system. The issues which are debated are those which concern people. Key political issues are those which 'require as a necessary although possibly not a sufficient condition that the issue should involve actual disagreement in preferences among two or more groups'.[21] This underlines another principle of pluralism, that interests are expressed as preferences. In summary pluralism involves 'a focus on *behaviour* in the making of *decisions* on *issues* over which there is an observable *conflict* of (subjective) *interests*, seen as express policy preferences revealed by political participation'.[22] The political strategies of pluralism are those associated with responsive government, involving negotiation, bargaining, conciliation, compromise and resolution through established, visible and democratic political machinery.

Given this characterisation of pluralism the research strategy necessary to defend it is, indeed, self evident. It will be based on 'a careful examination of concrete decisions'.[23] Since key decisions will be those which arouse conflict they will be on the public agenda, and study of the decision process will provide insights into the balance of power and the outcomes in terms of who wins or loses. This is an obvious method of study and one that apparently provides few obstacles for the empirical researcher. 'For is not this what politics is all about? Political power is a matter of making key decisions'.[24] In a pluralist study there will be uncertainty, the outcome will not be predictable since changing circumstances can influence the twists of fortunes in the conflict. Actors will use circumstances to advance their cause. They are at the centre of the stage deploying the various skills of persuasion, brokerage, and salesmanship necessary to mobilise the resources necessary to achieve victory.

Although pluralism has been criticised on empirical and theoretical grounds it remains a perspective worthy of careful, if sceptical, examination. The London Brick case has the ingredients necessary to apply a pluralist interpretation, to sift out its strengths and weaknesses. There are aspects of the case for which pluralism provides a satisfactory explanation. But there are other aspects which pluralism fails to answer adequately and these stem from theoretical weaknesses. The elements of a pluralist perspective may be defined as follows: *Power is dispersed in the community among interests, including business interests, in competition. These interests have different objectives expressed as preferences. Each interest is able to participate through visible conflict in a responsive and accountable decision making process, employing strategies of negotiation, concession and compromise. The outcome of conflict is uncertain, depending on changes in circumstances which favour certain interests against others.*

Analysis

A pluralist approach suggests that London Brick was an interest prepared to engage in negotiation and to make concessions in order to achieve its objectives. In Chapter 2 we saw how technological innovation (notably the introduction of the fletton process), the control of a large and cheap source of raw material, and the development of transportation and handling transformed a scattered and localised industry into one of large scale production units serving a national market. A combination of economic circumstances and entrepreneurial opportunism brought about a concentration of the industry, resulting eventually in a monopoly of fletton brickmaking in the hands of London Brick. Through a combination of diversification, increasing productivity, pricing policy and flexibility in matching supply to demand the company sustained its profitability despite the vicissitudes of the business cycle — at least until the major recession beginning at the end of the 1970s.

Business as an interest
London Brick was, in its local context, a successful and powerful industry, but was its power so great that it had a privileged position? Was it an interest with strength and resources placing it in a favourable and superior position to other interests? Pluralists emphasise the existence of a diversity of significant interests. They would point to the potential vulnerability and weakness of London Brick in the face of challenge from other interests.

Its commercial position was weakening at the time of conflict. Despite its monopoly in the fletton industry, the company's share of the brick market was less than half the total, and the market was shrinking in the face of competition from other materials. The company had little control over its market, since the demand for bricks is a derived demand and depends on decisions in both the public and private sectors. Furthermore demand fluctuates and business cycles expose the company to short term disruption (short time, stockpiling, shutdown) which can affect long term investment plans. The company is tied also to one product and a specific resource which limit its room for manoeuvre and make it dependent on the local community for support. This dependence lays it open to challenge.

From a pluralist viewpoint the company's strengths lie in its control of a local asset and its importance as an employer and generator of wealth. These are the cards with which it negotiates. But its weakness, which was becoming more evident and which coincided with the growing strength of environmental opposition, renders it an interest in competition with other interests in the community.

While this may be a plausible interpretation of the period of conflict which began at the end of the 1970s, when the forces appeared to be evenly matched, it is inadequate for the passive phase which preceded it. Pluralists might contend that the lack of action on either dereliction or pollution through these years reflected the lack of a problem. This is hardly convincing, however, since both issues were recognised, and were the subject of reports and research, and were a source of public complaint and debate (as at the Brickfields Conference for example). The company, too, appeared to recognise the problems as is evidenced by its actions either to mitigate the dereliction or to suppress the conflict over pollution. Pluralists would have to rely on the absence of any countervailing interest sufficiently aroused to pursue the company as an explanation for the long period of quiescence over the issue.

An obvious explanation is that during this long period there was a general recognition of the national interest in the supply of bricks. Over the long term there was a shift in values, and an apparent increasing awareness of environmental problems. The emergence of 'environmentalism' provided a background for growing local protest. Industries like London Brick were open to attack and to the call for regulations designed to ensure that industry pays at least part of the cost of the externalities it imposes. London Brick found itself entangled in a conflict of values. Bartlett, recounting the history of Reserve Mining Company's conflict with environmental interests over pollution in Lake Superior, sees this feature as 'a classic case of the politics of values in transition'.[25] 'Thus the Reserve Mining Company with no change whatever in its policies or behaviour, found itself being transformed from a benefactor of economic progress to a malefactor of environmental degradation'.[26] Similarly, London Brick found itself persecuted. Its past evasiveness, its secrecy, its denial of a problem helped to create a climate of suspicion and hostility which, matched with growing evidence and public disquiet, brought it face to face with a conflict it could no longer avoid. A problem which had apparently not existed became a key issue in the pluralist sense of a disagreement over preferences between competing interests.

A number of difficulties remain. Is a shift in values over a considerable period sufficient explanation for the relatively rapid transition of pollution and dereliction from unimportant to key issues? Why was there no relationship between the severity of the pollution problem and the intensity of opposition? It is paradoxical that the conflict was at its height at a time of reduced production, and that at the times of highest pollution (up to the early 1970s) there was little opposition. A pluralist answer might be that as the dereliction became more visible, and the hazards of pollution more certain, so the issue became more important. Once it had emerged it irresistibly entered the decision making arena. But the issue was entering the arena not so much because of public protest but because the company needed a new site for toxic waste disposal (the 'L' field issue) and, on a large scale, permission to rebuild its ageing works in the Marston Vale.

Again pluralists would contend that only when it became necessary for a decision to be made would the conflict of interests become apparent. Circumstances which made it imperative for the company to seek permissions were also propitious for its opponents.

Pluralism does not provide a completely convincing explanation for the period before the conflict. It does not satisfactorily explain why a matter of public concern was not a matter of visible and public decision making. Its assumption that business is simply an interest in competition with others is not a convincing argument for the period in which the company faced no effective opposition, while dereliction increased and pollution continued unabated. As we shall see, neo–élitist arguments prove far more compelling explanations for this passive phase in the conflict. But, once the issue did become a matter for public debate and decision, pluralist approaches appear to provide a satisfactory interpretation of the conflict. The idea that interests once aroused are able to participate within an accountable decision making framework, using strategies of negotiation, concession and compromise is certainly one way of assessing the evidence. The pluralist case here will rest on two related propositions being upheld. One is that the company, faced with opposition, was prepared to make significant concessions in a process of political bargaining. The other is that its strategy was altered in ways that it did not initially foresee in response to political challenges. In short, the company, acting within a pluralist framework, sought compromises with other interests in order to secure a mutually acceptable package.

Interests in competition
Once the applications for development were announced the issue entered a legal and governmental framework ostensibly open to all participants. The opportunity for regulating the company's activities was presented to its opponents. David Vogel draws a theoretical conclusion about the power of environmental interests, drawing on American experience which is applicable to this case. 'Ironically, while those who challenged corporate prerogatives during the late 1960s and early 1970s were highly critical of the pluralist paradigm, their success in increasing public controls over business does, in part, confirm the pluralist vision: the political system did, in fact, prove highly responsive to antibusiness forces.'[27] But, in this case, it was not

so much the intensity of the opposition but the needs of the industry that brought about the change.

The early negotiations over the site of the southern works demonstrate the openness of the system to participation. The company declared its indifference to the siting question, claiming that any of four alternatives would be acceptable; though it became clear that the real choice lay between a site in Marston Thrift preferred by the planners and a site on or near the existing Ridgmont works. The planners' preference was opposed by the Cranfield Action Committee, who campaigned through meetings and the media, provided its own expert evidence and eventually induced the company to apply for permission at mutually exclusive sites: a fifth site at Marston Thrift (site 5) and one at Ridgmont (site 2) (see Figure 3.4). This satisfies the pluralist case in so far as the company was prepared to accept the planners' advice and present options for debate and resolution after a full and open debate. It also demonstrated the ability of a group interested in the issue to participate and to influence the eventual outcome. A quite different interpretation is also possible which contradicts the pluralist case as we shall see.

On the dereliction issue, too, the company was prepared to negotiate and to give ground. All sides seemed reasonably satisfied with the negotiations. At the outset London Brick indicated a willingness to demolish old works, to preserve topsoil, to create 'stand-off zones', and to incorporate a whole range of environmental matters in a Section 52 Agreement. Negotiations over details proceeded were portrayed by one campaigner, Ray Young, as a case of mutual bargaining: 'We can do a deal on two different things. You enter a Section 52 Agreement on this particular pit and we'll let you have the brickworks'. Ray Young's pressure group, GASP, were keen to create at least a stand-off zone for Houghton Conquest village, and this was readily conceded. Later the company presented a comprehensive list of environmental proposals with its applications, and signed an Agreement covering issues not in the planning application — including the revocation of the original permissions. All this could be interpreted as a response to the pressures exerted by environmental interests and a willingness to reach compromise through negotiation. Several questions remain to be answered. Did the company concede more than it was prepared to at the outset? Were the concessions more than would normally be expected of a company whose operations have a major impact on the landscape? Did the proposals amount to a significant improvement in the environmental quality of the Marston Vale? If the concessions are regarded as significant rather than cosmetic then the idea of interests participating in a public debate to achieve an acceptable compromise is upheld. If not, then we need to look elsewhere for explanation.

Although the company's stance on the air pollution issue appears more resolute and intractable, there is evidence here, too, to support a pluralist view of concession brought about by participation. The company, supported by the Alkali Inspector, proposed tall chimneys to disperse the pollutants, and made provision for a third flue which could be used for future abatement. It argued that abatement technology was unproven, impracticable and too costly. Opponents claimed that pollutants were harmful and that abatement must be a condition of an acceptable planning permission. A fierce and public debate on the issue made each side more implacable. The impasse was eventually broken with the publication of the Cremer and Warner report. Its conclusions were somewhat equivocal, offering support to the case presented by each side, but it did lead to further negotiations and concessions over the issue. The company accepted a clause in the Section 52 Agreement committing it to a research programme on kiln design involving the County Council. And it accepted the concept of a part permission in which only the first phase of one of the new works would be approved in detail, incorporating Hoffman kilns. The subsequent three phases would be approved in outline, the eventual kiln designs depending on the outcome of the research programme.

These negotiations may be regarded either as gestures unlikely to impede the company's plans, or as genuine concessions involving the company in some costs it might not otherwise have incurred. In either case it would be consistent with a pluralist notion of an interest responding to opposition and initiatives from other interests in reaching a negotiated settlement. On the other hand, if the company had little intention of pursuing research, other than that on which it was already embarked, it can be argued that there was merely the appearance of participation in negotiation while the company pursued its premeditated path.

On each of the three issues of debate — siting of works, dereliction and pollution — there is evidence to support a pluralist case, though it is not wholly convincing. Other interpretations are possible and, in certain respects, more convincing, as we shall see. So far we have focused on the idea of business as an interest pursuing its objectives through strategies of negotiation and compromise. That it possessed the resources needed to promote its objectives is obvious, but whether these gave it disproportionate power when pitted against other interests able to draw on different resources is not yet clear. To investigate this we need to investigate the decision making process, to see if the system in Bedfordshire corresponds broadly to that delineated by Dahl: 'A system dominated by many different sets of leaders, each having access to a different combination of political resources'.[28] This notion of different interests, competing for access to decision making in a particular arena of conflict is the cornerstone of the pluralist thesis.

Power and participation
The brickfields case motivated a large number of interests. At the most passive level there were the respondents to the various participation exercises. At the Brickfields Conference, for instance, there were representatives of industry, farming, conservation, and local authorities, though trade unions and local communities were notable absentees. When the major conflict arose it inspired opposition not only from traditional objectors but encouraged the formation of *ad hoc* groups specifically established to fight the proposals. Among these were the three locality–based groups concentrating on single environmental issues prominent during the early part of the campaign. They adopted legitimate forms of protest, and each secured its objectives — BACAP secured the removal of toxic dumping from Elstow; GASP ensured a stand-off zone for Houghton Conquest; and CAC eventually succeeded in removing the threat of new works from Marston Thrift. This success appears to bear out Allison's contention that 'the argument for intensity justifies the political victory of an intense minority over a majority whose preference is more marginal'.[29]

There are, however, aspects of the case which suggest these groups were less influential than at first appears. They were ephemeral, with a marginal impact on the major issue of pollution. They were divided rather than united in a common cause. CAC was prepared to treat with London Brick, and regarded as treacherous by the other groups. GASP fell out with its local parish council. They were pushing at a door already half open. It was in the mutual interest of London Brick and the County Council to do a deal over Elstow and 'L' field whatever BACAP's views on the matter; stand-off zones had been agreed at the outset, and GASP failed to remove the permission for pit 81 next to Houghton Conquest; even CAC were arguing the case for a site at Ridgmont which was the preferred alternative of London Brick. Their success may then be more apparent than real, and though the system seemed open, participative and responsive it is possible, as I shall show in a moment, to put forward a different interpretation.

A similar point may be made about the local parishes involved. They were automatically consulted, held public meetings and put pressure on their local councillors. Such pressure was a factor in Michael Kemp's stand in favour of the company and, though Philip Hendry did not deviate from his opposition to the plans, fears that he would be deserted by his local electorate caused him to seek a seat elsewhere. But, on the whole, the parishes were in the background of the debate, contributing to the constituency of concern that was being mobilised for and against the proposals. Their voice was heard but only by those who wished to hear it, and the divergence of views among the parishes, some supporting the company for the jobs it would ensure, others opposing it because of its environmental effects, gave ammunition to both camps. Although a large number of groups took part, this does not by itself indicate a pluralist system of participation with involvement in, and influence on, decision making. These groups seemed to form part of what Winkler describes as 'the institutionalisation of participation', whereby participants are used to legitimate decision making rather than to influence it.[30]

There were three interest groups who had a major influence on the course of the decision. PROBE for a long time appeared to be a powerful rival to the company. It built on the hostility to the company fostered by the media and local pressure groups. It was able to penetrate the political system through contacts with councillors, the most prominent of whom were its members. It could command expertise, select information and capitalise on incidents such as the claims made by Elizabeth Keyes and Farmer Goode about the dangers to health and cattle. By choosing its own ground, air pollution and fluoride in particular, PROBE struck at the most vulnerable point in the company's case, the area where least was known and the greatest anxiety could be established. But the group's élitist composition, its privileged position relative to the decision making process and its links with landed interests hardly made it an exemplar of a pluralist pressure group.

The second of these groups, the local NFU, had, over the years, been content to negotiate with the company on out of court settlements. By the end of the conflict it had become its most prominent opponent. It was the NFU which threatened an injunction, the NFU, too, represented a farming and landed interest and possessed resources and access that ensured paramount influence.

The third group which exerted major influence was the trade unions. Their interest was closely identified with the company's redevelopment proposals which would bring improved working conditions and greater job security. The unions sought their access to decision makers initially through the small but influential Labour Group, resulting in a much publicised fraternal confrontation. When the prospect of job loss became a reality the unions precipitated a decisive change in the political environment. They met members of both Conservative and Labour groups and initiated the first, and only, tripartite meeting between company, unions and council. The unions had been able to raise employment as the key issue, exert leverage on the Labour Group, and put pressure on other councillors as the elections drew near. They were a decisive influence in making certain that the closure of Ridgmont and the threat of investment elsewhere were used to ensure the passage of an acceptable permission for the new Ridgmont works. The unions, too were an example of an interest with privileged access and greater influence than the majority participating in the conflict.

The pluralist idea of a multiplicity of interests, overlapping and using different resources is only superficially borne out. It is the case that many different interests participated but they did not participate on an equal basis. The interests which had the most profound impact were those of capital, land and labour in the form of London Brick, PROBE and the NFU, and the unions. Each had access to decision makers, each used public and covert methods of influence, each was able to exploit changing circumstances and each defended a material interest in profit, jobs or land. This is hardly unequivocal confirmation of the pluralist case for a dispersal of power among many competing interests.

Against this, modern pluralists would argue that the idea of privileged access and concentration of power is not consistent with the evidence in this case. Rather, the existence of several groups engaged in a specific area of conflict is compatible with the pluralist thesis.

Responsive decision making

A final aspect of the pluralist case is that decision making occurs within a responsive and accountable democratic system. The influence of interests depends not merely on the resources they can mobilise but upon the opportunity to deploy them. The essence of a pluralist political system is that it offers, in principle, access to all wishing to participate. It is a responsive system, with elected politicians receiving signals, influences and pressures from a variety of sources, and acting in a democratic and accountable framework to arbitrate conflicts. In such a system we should expect politicians to reflect the pressures transmitted to them directly from groups and party political sources, and indirectly through the media. They will act in the hope of public approbation or the fear of electoral reprisal.

Orthodox theories which tended to stress the electoral chain of command or the doctrine of responsible party government have been reassessed by some recent detailed studies of local politics, and have been abandoned in their cruder forms.[31] In particular, the importance of national calculations in local politics have been stressed. Dearlove suggests this can lead to a denial of local politics. 'In many ways this theory is one which eliminates politics from policy-making and makes government merely a matter of administering what is largely agreed by all who have regard for the national interest, over and above narrow sectional advantage'.[32] The apparent reality of local politics merely becoming a mirror of national political calculations can lead to pessimistic conclusions about the role of local politicians. 'If this is the case, then local politicians are free within very broad limits to do what they want, knowing that the most unpopular policies are unlikely to have much impact on their fate at the polling stations.'[33] But most authors seem to be agreed that this, like the old orthodoxy which it replaced, tends towards an extreme view, since vestigial elements of local responsiveness remain. Local politicians do appear to act, however irrationally, in the belief that their actions are noted by the local electorate and that they will be accountable for their actions.[34] 'There is no compelling reason for the law of anticipated reactions to operate in local elections, and most councillors know this, but, nevertheless, powerful forces push them to try to anticipate electoral reaction, even though in their calmest and most logical moments they know their efforts have only a marginal effect.'[35] In conflicts such as London Brick where the issue crossed party frontiers and, in its later stages, was enacted in the highly charged atmosphere of an imminent election, electoral calculations played a part in determining outcomes. And even in the early stages, long before the council's electoral mandate was waning, politicians showed considerable anxiety to respond in various ways to pressures which they believed were being exerted by the local communities.

The London Brick case provides some endorsement of the pluralist concept of responsiveness. The politicians were acting within a political environment, informed and influenced by conflicting information and pressures, which was reflected in conflicting and, ultimately, polarised political positions. What this view does not take into account is the influence exerted by the politicians themselves. Far from being a passive element, absorbing and responding to a variety of signals and seeking to translate them into decisions, the political organisation itself participated and helped to create the environment of decision making to which it was responding.[36] This circular process, of politicians both creating and responding to the political environment, is an aspect which I shall develop further in the next chapter.

For the present we may briefly consider the evidence for the pluralist ideal of a responsive polity. As the conflict developed, so it became more open, and the contestants made increasingly energetic appeals to public opinion. The privileged access to officials, and covert methods of pursuing objectives were no longer enough to ensure success for London Brick. A political environment hostile to its cause was being created. The role of the media was crucial in this. Throughout the conflict the local and national Press and TV took an anti-company line. A similar tendency was observed by Crenson, and he explained it thus: 'Newspapers like to think of themselves as public crusaders or guardians of the public welfare, and the fact that a newspaper claims the public in general as its constituency, and things in general as its field of competence, reinforces these self-conceptions'.[37] The Press regarded the issue as a campaign with London Brick as a powerful company able to despoil and pollute almost at will. The campaign was fed by activists in PROBE especially, but conducted by journalists like Frank Branston of *Bedfordshire on Sunday*, who took a cynical view of all the company's pronouncements and actions. The company recognised that its credibility was at stake, and attempted to create a more favourable image. At crucial points it launched Press releases, and sought coverage that suggested a company providing wealth and prosperity and prepared to create a better physical environment. These efforts preceded major events in the conflict. Thus 'Operation Landfill' was promoted just before the planning applications were made. A publicity feature in the *Bedfordshire Times* appeared a little before the crucial July 1980 Council meeting, and 'Operation Oberon', the spectacular demolition of an old works, coincided with the critical negotiations led by the chairman of the company during the autumn of that year. The coincidences may, of course, be merely that, but the anxiety they reflect is clear.

The company, though unable to overcome the hostility of the Press, was able to use the media. Throughout the conflict it rebutted criticisms, and in the last phase of the conflict Press coverage of the unions' stance, and the fears of unemployment were major influences on responsive politicians.

The company was increasingly forced into the open. Injured by poor publicity, James Bristow recognised that a higher public profile was needed.

Although company officials had attended public meetings early on in the debate, such as those at Marston Moretaine in December 1978, and at Whittlesey in August 1979, these were simply to present proposals and listen to public reaction. The officials at these meetings were people like John Wright, the Estates Manager. Once the company apppreciated the dangers of its position it appealed from the highest level, with first James Bristow appearing in a public debate with his major opponents at Ampthill in February 1980, just before the first of the critical decisions were taken, and later, the Chairman himself, Jeremy Rowe, made his unprecedented direct appeal to the politicians in December in a last ditch effort to rescue the planning permission. All this suggests that, once the issue was in public and decisions had to be taken, the field was wide open to those wishing to persuade the public and, through them, the decision makers.

Open decision making
London Brick appears to have belatedly recognised the openness of the decision making framework. Its opponents, drawing on a highly successful propaganda campaign, had already perceived that by invoking the whole Council in the decision, the success of the company would no longer be inevitable. It was evident that so long as the decision rested with the Environmental Services Committee it would favour London Brick — a view confirmed by the 12 to 3 majority in favour of the negotiated proposals in March 1980, the reaffirmation of the position by the committee in December 1980, and the eventual passing of the unencumbered permission in March 1981. The committee was strongly influenced by the officials, had detailed knowledge of the negotiations, and was led by a chairman who strongly favoured the company. Only one of its members, Andy Blowers, was a member of PROBE, and Philip Hendry, the most prominent and influential opponent in the Council, was not on the committee. The committee was deeply immersed in the issue, had gathered expertise and had reached conclusions from which it would not be dislodged.

The Council was an altogether different matter. Most of its members were uninvolved in the issue and would respond to selective reasoning, emotional appeals and political leadership. Councillors would be susceptible to 'the processes of bargaining, negotiation, salesmanship and brokerage, and of leadership in mobilising resources of all kinds'.[38] The issue could be decided in full Council by appeal to general principles and latent anxieties. Furthermore, given the procedures of a Council meeting, the burden of persuasion would rest with the politicians, since officials would not be allowed to speak.

Many commentators regard Council meetings as pure theatre, a ritualistic legitimation of decisions already taken. Thus Sharpe describes Council meetings as 'largely a hollow ritual';[39] Heclo comments: 'they are not as important as they seem and are not taken very seriously by many councillors themselves';[40] and Saunders is even more cynical: 'no decision is ever changed at a Council meeting — it is the climax of the whole democratic "performance" '.[41] Such views are too dismissive. In 'hung' Councils, an increasingly common phenomenon nowadays, the Council is *the* forum to which all crucial decisions are referred for resolution.[42] Even in Councils with majority party control, there are not infrequently decisions which may be amended by the Council, or those which are left to a free vote of members. Council meetings are increasingly recognised as the point of final decision. Lobbying, demonstrations, marches, petitions, and intense media coverage are an increasing feature of Council meetings where cuts in services, closure of schools or other major issues are debated. Environmental issues do not always lend themselves to clear party political alignment. Such was the London Brick case. With the majority party split, and the votes of the minority parties important, the issue was uncertain and the committee's decision not conclusive. A decision by the whole elected assembly represented, in this case, the apotheosis of pluralism.

Uncertainty was compounded by circumstances. The delayed DoE report provided a breathing space, during which opponents of the company could use both general appeal and specific persuasion by key councillors. The issue was narrowed down to a simple question of whether or not to impose a pollution condition. The July debate was dramatic, and there is little doubt the outcome hinged on the comparative performances of the major protagonists. The preparatory work had ensured the support of a substantial number of councillors in both camps, but surveys prior to the meeting indicated a depth of indecision which could be converted into support on the day. Whether the result depended on the relative strength of the interests involved (pluralist thesis) or was more a matter of the events and personalities involved in the struggle and superimposed on the interests is a matter for debate. What is clear is that an open political system had offered opportunities to the opponents of the company which they had fully exploited: a lesson not lost on London Brick.

For a while the company hoped that it might recover its ground through its interpretation of the pollution condition. Secure in the support of ESC, it hoped this could be pressed on the Council. It even tried direct persuasion through its chairman, which proved counterproductive. The Council recognised in this an attempt to subvert a democratic decision and reaffirmed its position. The pluralist case offers a tenable explanation for the political events of 1979–80. In 1981 external circumstances — the abandonment of the investment programme and the closure of Ridgmont — intervened to fatally weaken the opposition. Urged on by the unions, and with an election imminent, councillors reacted to the changing prospects. Leading opponents lost ground. Philip Hendry shifted seats and Andy Blowers took an increasingly equivocal stance. By contrast, Michael Kemp grew increasingly bold, and Keith White, smarting from defeat at the hands of the Council, found an opportunity to overturn its decision. The application for Ridgmont was still on the table, and it could be passed by the ESC without reference to the Council. The opposition, already on the run, could not even muster sufficient support to enable a further tilt at the issue at a full meeting of the Council. The Council, the embodiment of liberal democratic pluralism, was, at the last, simply circumvented.

The decision making framework ostensibly supports a pluralist interpretation of the conflict. All the interests involved were able to participate, first through consultation, later through the representative institutions of the committee system and the Council. The decision was taken on a free vote by all the members able to arbitrate the various aspects of the case. This only applies, however, to the phase of confrontation. In the early stages London Brick enjoyed privileged access and was able to discuss its plans in secret with officials. Through the officials the planning committee could be socialised into accepting the plans.

Finally, the committee was able to defy the Council, though it is by no means clear what the Council would have done at that stage. There is, in this case, some evidence of the importance of individual actors, of widespread participation and of a responsive polity which suggests a dispersal of power. The interaction of participants in changing circumstances suggests a high degree of uncertainty as the conflict developed. A pluralist interpretation sheds light on aspects of the conflict, but it is a partial perspective. Despite its emphasis on actors, it neglects the impact of the polity on the political environment. Its conclusions are questionable. Faced with the same evidence it is possible to conclude that an ostensibly pluralist system was manipulated in the pursuit of élitist ends — a possibility I shall now seek to demonstrate.

The élitist interpretation

> 'For when men were in low water, they came to him, Snaith, and he helped them; and when he helped them, he had power over them, and, he told himself sardonically, he had taken to secret power as another man will take to secret drink . . . He did not bully; he did not use the power necessarily for his own profit. He was, in a queer kind of way, disinterested'.
>
> (Winifred Holtby, *South Riding*.)

The neo-élitist critique has focused on two aspects of the exercise of power. One, inherited from the earlier élitist studies, is that power is concentrated, not diffused, and that certain groups — élites — possess disproportionate power derived from superior resources. A power élite is unrepresentative of the community. 'It will be largely made up of middle and upper class people who possess more of the skills and qualities required for leadership.'[43] Overall an élitist system will have the following characteristics: 'limited numbers, limited consultation with affected groups, disproportionate control of scarce resources of money, skills and information, and a certain continuity and communality of interest'.[44] If the existence of an élite controlling affairs is to be confirmed we should expect evidence of 'consciousness, conspiracy or coherence', and success in achieving policy outcomes.[45]

A second feature of the neo-élitist critique is that key issues are not necessarily the visible issues. For pluralists the key issues were those which had emerged. This poses two problems. 'One is that the model takes little account of the fact that power may be, and often is, exercised by confining the scope of the decision-making process to relatively "safe" issues. The other is that the model provides no *objective* criteria for distinguishing between "important" and "unimportant" issues arising in the political arena.'[46] Neo-élitists argue that the key issues are not necessarily the visible issues. 'A key issue, in our terms, is one that involves a genuine challenge to the resources of power or authority of those who currently dominate the process by which policy outputs in the system are determined.'[47] Pluralist decisional studies are conditioned by the inbuilt bias and values of the system under scrutiny. They inevitably ignore indirect influences which 'can equally operate to prevent politicians, officials or others from raising issues or proposals known to be unacceptable to some group or institution in the community.'[48] In an élitist system those holding power will seek to prevent or suppress issues devoting 'energies to creating or reinforcing social and political values and institutional practices that limit the scope of the political process to public consideration of only those issues which are comparatively innocuous'.[49]

The decision making strategies favoured by élites are likely to be corporatist in nature. The concept of corporatism, which is discussed more fully in the next chapter, implies institutionalised arrangements which provide particular interests with privileged access to decision making. Such arrangements are exclusive, and usually removed from public scrutiny. Through a process of bargaining, mutually acceptable compromises emerge. At local level the bargaining between business and local government officials may be regarded as evidence of corporatism. If it prevents issues emerging, or circumvents representative decision making once an issue has emerged, it may be regarded as successful. Even if the issue cannot be contained within corporatist strategies, it may be the case that effective power lies outside the local democratic arena and is settled at regional or national level. In order to reveal an élitist system it must be established that issues are prevented from arising, and confined once aroused so that the success of an élite can be assured.

The two features of power identified by the neo-élitists, its concentration and its hidden nature, have led them to emphasise the concept of *non-decision making*. To understand this we need to consider both those affecting decisions and those affected by them. In the first group are those with an interest in preventing or suppressing an issue by engaging in *negative decision making*. They do this by a capacity to coopt, to defer or simply not to act. Inaction poses an interesting theoretical problem. People may not act for purely cynical reasons, recognising that by doing nothing they will achieve their objectives. They are favoured by the rules of the game, and no intervention is necessary.[50] 'Put simply, the rules (both formal and informal) governing differential access to political power generate a bias in favour of some sections of the population and against others, and the causal responsibility for this bias can be traced to those who operate the rules'.[51] Alternatively, it may be that élites are simply unaware of these biases, and neither action nor inaction is therefore contemplated. In the first case there may be a deliberate decision not to act, in the second no decision is necessary. This latter construction is dismissed as sophistry by Bradshaw: 'The passivity of an individual with recognised power in a known issue area is, in fact, a *decision*, albeit an unobservable or informal one, not to act.'[52] He illustrates the point by reference to Crenson's study of the inaction of US Steel in Gary, and suggests the company managers must have been aware that they were polluting the air, that techniques existed to reduce pollution and that action to prevent such pollution had been taken in nearby East Chicago. 'If the managers *were* aware of some or all of these points then, I submit, the inactivity of US Steel was the result of a *decision* or *decisions* not to act, even if not taken formally in the boardroom.'[53] Applying this argument in the case of London Brick it would seem that inaction was conscious because action was unnecessary.

The second group of actors, those affected by non-decisions, do have an interest in raising an issue, but for various reasons do not do so. There are three possible explanations for this advanced by neo-élitists. The first is the case of *anticipated reactions*: 'people may be inactive because they perceive themselves to be powerless and without influence'.[54] They recognise no good will come of action, or that the consequences of action may be undesirable. Such inaction is very difficult to establish. It seems just as plausible to suggest that people may protest or make their feelings felt even if they anticipate no results will be forthcoming. In the case of London Brick there was a history of such protest and public debate during the long period when the company was unwilling or unable to redress their grievances. It was this combination of public hostility and company inertia which gave such impetus to the opposition when the issue did eventually reach the agenda. The second explanation put forward is *abstention*. But, as Polsby suggests, there may be two reasons why people might abstain on an issue: 'either it is being suppressed or there is a genuine consensus that it is not an issue'.[55] Thus although abstention could be a result of the issue being kept off the agenda, it could also stem from acceptance or indifference. This should occasion no surprise. 'How does abstention differ from apathy, laziness, pessimism, or lack of interest in politics? These are all widespread; indeed they are the common condition. Most people prefer spending their time, money, and skill for purposes other than shaping public policy.'[56]

A third explanation for non-participation relies on the concept of *mobilisation of bias*, first coined by Schattschneider to describe the function of organisations in the suppression of conflict.[57] This is the other side of the coin of negative decision making. The inbuilt biases and values of the political system face us with 'the problem of distinguishing the complacency which stems from a position of strength from the fatalism which stems from a position of weakness'.[58] In the words of Bachrach and Baratz, the mobilisation of bias is 'a set of predominant values, beliefs, rituals, and institutional procedures ("rules of the game") that operate systematically and consistently to the benefit of certain persons and groups at the expense of others'.[59] Whereas in the case of anticipated reactions non-participants are conscious of their interests, but do nothing to promote them, and in the case of abstention they may lack consciousness and so are not motivated to act, in the case of mobilisation of bias they are suffering from false consciousness, and so are unaware of the possibility of action.

There is a considerable lack of conceptual clarity in neo-élitist thinking on the question of interests. On the one hand, neo-élitists tend, like pluralists, to apply a subjective concept of interests as revealed by preference. On the other, the idea of false consciousness brings them close to a marxist formulation relying on an objective conception of interests; a point to which I shall return.

This conceptual confusion renders a rigorous definition of alternative positions exceedingly difficult. It lays neo-élitists open to the pluralist attack that it is impossible to know what interests exist when individuals themselves do not recognise them. Pluralists would suggest there is quite a plausible and relatively straightforward explanation for non-decisions. This would hold that values for long remain uncontested and interests unaroused. Once a problem has been identified, hitherto latent interests become mobilised; leading to a conflict which is arbitrated through an open and responsive decision making process.

The theoretical problems posed by the neo-élitist perspective make the criticisms made of it on empirical grounds readily understandable. Crenson claims that 'Inaction is just as much a fact, just as susceptible to empirical verification, as is action'.[60] Critics would argue that it is impossible to study non-decisions since 'non-decisions are non-events, and since non-events cannot be empirically studied, any discussion of them moves into the realms of the non-falsifiable and empty speculation'.[61] Jones reaches a similar conclusion from his empirical study of clean air policies in Pittsburgh.[62] Such a judgement may be harsh, since non-decision making does not necessarily imply that no interest is evinced or that no decisions are taken. It rather urges researchers to peer behind the scenes to see if they can discover instances where issues have been deferred or suppressed. Élitist theory does pose severe methodological problems. It is difficult to relate theory to evidence. But its insistence that 'there is more to local politics than meets the eye' does urge us to widen the scope of an investigation into power, and to view the process in terms of its informal and more hidden aspects.[63]

A major empirical problem is how to discover a non-issue. Two criteria appear to be necessary. '1. They would have to rely on *ex post facto* detection based on an increase in political action subsequent to the period under study. 2. Some threshold for the passage from non–decision to a place on the agenda would have to be established.'[64] In the major studies of non-decision making published so far the accounts rely on retrospective analysis of issues that have subsequently become a source of public comment or concern.[65] In the brickfields case, too, the analysis looks back at the period when pollution was not on the agenda but was recognised as a problem. It is clearly impossible to identify issues which really are non-events but which will be the source of future conflict. One can obviously speculate that, for example, the dangers of certain toxic substances as yet unknown will be major issues in the future. The problem of asbestos has already reached the agenda, and fluorides, as this study shows, have emerged as a source of concern.[66] At least an élitist perspective creates uneasiness, by encouraging us to question potential problems. This is preferable to the unwitting complacency which may be induced by a purely pluralist focus on visible issues and conflicts.

Non-decisions pass through several stages, from apparent invisibility to becoming matters of conflict. 'At what point along the continuum of visibility from the pole of unconscious but "real" interests to the pole of daily front page coverage does an issue area stop being a non-decision?'[67] In the brickfields case three phases were charted, from dormant through passive to active, and the active phase was divided into phases of negotiation, conflict, confrontation and resolution. The issues of dereliction and pollution emerged at different times, and though dereliction caused most of the early controversy, it was pollution that dominated its final stages. For a long period nothing was done, and here we should expect élitist explanations of non-decision making to offer insights. But even when the issue had become active, the élitist stress on the concentration of power, and the informal means by which it was exercised should enrich our understanding of the later phases of the conflict.

Power is concentrated among élites who possess the resources and information to secure their objectives. This power is exercised on decisions through privileged access to the formal and informal processes of a political system, with in–built biases in favour of élite interests. Élites also engage in strategies of non-decision making which involve the suppression of issues and the non-participation of groups affected by them.

Analysis

Matthew Crenson's book, *The Un-politics of Air Pollution*, offers a sustained theoretical and empirical attack on the pluralist position.[68] The issue he tackles parallels, in certain respects, the London Brick case. He asks why Gary (Indiana USA), with an air pollution problem similar to that of East Chicago, adopted a pollution control ordinance some 13 years after its neighbour. He details the complicated process by which the clean air issue in Gary reached the public agenda and the evasion, procrastination and bureaucratic procedures which delayed the measure. He suggests the delay rested in the inaction of the company which possessed a reputation for power. 'To the extent that it has an identifiable effect on local politics, the reputation for power is itself a form of power.'[69] US Steel was the dominant industry in Gary, able to invest in new plant or to shut down existing works. Public opinion was not aroused and the company could stand on the sidelines like a 'benign, pliable and passive giant'.[70] This was a case of negative–decision making through inaction on the part of the company, complemented by anticipated reactions and abstention on the part of the authorities and the public. Is there any evidence to suggest a similar situation in the case of London Brick?

Non-decision making

For some years after the Second World War public opinion on dereliction and pollution in the Marston Vale was quiescent, and the companies, defended by formal and legal institutions, appeared unassailable. Until the late 1940s the brick companies did not even require planning permissions, and those granted later by the Minister were exceedingly porous as far as safeguarding the environment was concerned. The industry chose to interpret the restoration conditions in a way which would promote profit rather than accept the costs of the externalities imposed. The local authorities were unable or unwilling to seek enforcement action over dereliction, and regarded air pollution as outside their competence. The lack of public debate and the craven attitudes of the local authorities seem to support Crenson's view that the reputation for power was enough to keep the companies immune from challenge.

This is only a partial view of the evidence. At no stage was the problem a non-issue and the decision process a non-event. Even the early permissions gave cursory acknowledgement to the problems, and applied conditions, however vague and feeble, to cope with dereliction. As dereliction grew, the company's neglect, its lack of persistence in seeking to secure landfill, and its determination to use the pits as commercial assets fuelled public hostility. Although air pollution was the province of the Alkali Inspector and he denied any danger, it could not be dismissed as a non-problem.

Sulphur oxides were already the subject of an extensive national survey, and in Bedfordshire the Brothwood report, for all its statistical uncertainty, had not exonerated the brickworks.[71] Evidence on fluorides was more elusive, but the probable damage to cattle was well established[72] and the damage to crops and vegetation, though not conclusively proved, was strongly inferred.[73] Despite the tendentious nature of many of the arguments, they could hardly be said not to exist, and were matters of public concern.

The non-decision was not, therefore, a matter for reputation alone, if at all. The evidence strongly suggests that not only was London Brick fully aware of the problems it was creating, but that it was active in its efforts to suppress them. It controlled most of the information on pollution levels and abatement processes. It took steps to secure itself from legal challenge and to defuse opposition by buying–up potentially dissident farmers and by imposing a restrictive clause on its tenants. Compensation claims were dealt with by out of court settlements. At no stage could dereliction, or even pollution, be regarded as a non-issue. But they were non-decisions for which neo-élitist concepts of negative–decision making, abstention and anticipated reactions offer a plausible explanation. The alternative, pluralist position would imply that the problem was not regarded as sufficiently important at that time to become a matter for political conflict.

The transformation of the issue into a matter for public decision making requires a further explanation. The neo-élitist approach here is rather unconvincing. According to Crenson there comes a point in the course of decision making when an issue can no longer be contained and must take its place on the agenda. It is not enough for the matter to be discussed, it must be advocated by the community's leaders. 'Only when advocacy or opposition has made an appearance will we say that a topic has taken its place on the local political agenda.'[74] This point apparently arrived in the 1970s when London Brick first mooted its plans for redevelopment, thus giving focus to political protest. The concept of mobilisation of bias might be recruited to explain the change. Over time, as controversial evidence was produced and the national need for bricks declined, there was a shift in the climate of opinion distinctly unfavourable to the company. This shift in values prepared the ground for a conflict which the need for new permissions precipitated. There is little evidence to suggest a condition of false consciousness, a population failing to recognise its interest in pollution control or landscape improvement. It is more plausible to argue that, with changing values, the problem of the environment was likely to become prominent, and displace economic arguments assuming conditions of economic growth.

The rise of opposition would be a natural corollary of changing perceptions. This corresponds more closely to a pluralist version than convoluted and untestable assumptions of false consciousness and mobilisation of bias. Crenson concludes that 'industrial influence does inhibit the growth of the air pollution issue, but the nature of this inhibitory effect depends upon the actual level of pollution'.[75] Yet, as we have seen, the issue became prominent at a time when, though dereliction was increasing, air pollution was at lower levels than in the early 1970s. Moreover, the development proposals were promising much lower levels in the future.

As a set of explanations for the period before the conflict, neo-élitist arguments are helpful, despite their flaws. There is evidence of suppression, there does appear to have been abstention and anticipated reactions on the part of the authorities and the public. The company was able, by various means, to prevent the emergence of the issue. But the idea that its reputation for power was sufficient or that there was a mobilisation of bias in its favour seem both unlikely as well as untestable, at least as far as the issues of dereliction and pollution are concerned. What is clear is that the political environment changed in response to changing values, and London Brick found its privileged position at risk as other interests were able, at length, to participate in the decision making process on equal terms. The other aspect of the élitist case is that, once the issue is a matter for decision, certain interests possess both informal and formal means of ensuring preferential access and privileged status. The polity is neither so open nor so penetrable as the pluralists would maintain. How far does the evidence support this élitist version?

Privileged access
In the early part of the active phase of the conflict London Brick's position appeared strong. It had ready and private access to planning officials, and was able to negotiate the deal with 'L' field, propose comprehensive environmental improvements and appeared flexible as to the siting of new works. The planners recognised the company's resistance to pollution controls and did not wish to put the environmental gains in jeopardy. London Brick had clearly sensed their influence with the officials. Lindblom describes this relationship. 'Yet ordinarily as new conditions or problems arise — for example, public demands for restriction on air pollution — businessmen know that government officials will understand their wishes — in this case their unwillingness or incapacity to bear without help the costs of stopping industrial discharges into the air.'[76] The idea of

preferential treatment was denied by the County Planning Officer: 'There has been no more secrecy in our discussions with the company than there would be in any possible application for a new house, a factory or whatever.'[77] The point is that applicants do have prior and privileged access to the bureaucratic machine, and are able to persuade the officers and to strike bargains in secret as part of a routine process of decision making.[78] This supports an élitist interpretation of corporatist decision making. The point was put cryptically by Ray Young, chairman of the local pressure group GASP: 'There's an awful lot of dealing goes on, behind closed doors.' The difference in this case was that the doors were, to an extent at least, left ajar, and the process was revealed.

London Brick were not alone in enjoying privileged accesss to decision makers. It faced an opposition able to make 'a genuine challenge to the resources of power' hitherto concentrated in the hands of the company. The PROBE organisation also possessed privileged access. Its tactics, such as the champagne party at Woburn Abbey, the use of the NFU and the Bedfordshire Preservation Society as fronts for its operations, and its contacts at local and national levels and in the media showed a sophistication and level of resource quite beyond the scope of other participating organisations. It also showed an intelligent understanding of the political system superior for a while to that of London Brick. PROBE first argued for an inquiry, then perceived its best hope lay in circumventing the committee and persuading the Council to adopt a tight pollution condition. Overall its campaign was beautifully modulated both to stimulate and reflect changes in the political environment.

PROBE can be seen as an example of an élitist organisation representing business, farming, landed and political interests. Its role and influence raises some interesting theoretical problems. Was it a contest between powerful élites? Although PROBE and London Brick were the most prominent, other interests were involved and not simply as adjuncts to the main contestants.

The local pressure groups were not directly aligned with PROBE and their objectives were somewhat different. It is possible to question their influence as we have seen, but they were largely middle class. Later, although the NFU and the Bedfordshire Preservation Society were closely allied to PROBE, each pursued an independent line and the NFU continued its opposition long after PROBE had disappeared. Once again we encounter conceptual problems in trying to distinguish different perspectives. The existence of several interests with overlapping memberships is redolent of pluralism. The fact that certain groups played a more prominent and influential role might be explained in terms of more *powerful interests*. The communality between the various groups is not necessarily evidence of élitism. The major groups might be regarded as *powerful élites*, but strictly only if there is evidence of 'consciousness, conspiracy and coherence' in achieving policy outcomes.

How do we explain the role of the unions, so decisive in the later phases of the conflict? Not normally regarded as an élitist group, the unions also possessed, and were able to use, their privileged access on behalf of a capitalist company. The cross–cutting alignments do not suggest a simple élitist model. The situation was more complex and perplexing than either a pluralist idea of participation or an élitist model of power concentration would suggest. These accounts provide a descriptive basis for diagnosing the relative concentration or dispersal of power, but do little to enlighten us as to why these particular divisions and allegiances existed. These questions are important theoretically, and I shall return to them in the next chapter.

Élitist theories explain the role of politics in terms of the political culture. Thus Crenson argues that US Steel's success in delaying pollution control in Gary was aided by the tightly knit partisan political culture of the city which was able to resist initiatives. The more open (pluralistic?) city of East Chicago was more penetrable. His diagnosis concentrates on the indirect influence on decision makers. An élitist approach would ascribe too much influence to the pressures applied by PROBE, by the company and by the trade unions on the politicians. Politicians were exposed to a multiplicity of influences including those from the media, from their party organisations, and from their own electoral calculations. Nor was it a case of simply absorbing and weighing up these various influences. The politicians themselves helped to create the political environment. There were, of course, those politicians deeply involved in the issue closely identified with the major protagonists, but even these showed a sensitivity to changing political circumstances. But there were also many more with less interest in the debate, lacking knowledge of the issues, and, as the various surveys revealed, uncertain as to how they would vote. As has already been argued, this situation, with its air of uncertainty and unpredictability, comes closer to a pluralist explanation than the idea of competing élites, each able to command and marshall a block of committed votes.

The élitist interpretation is, in certain respects, complementary to the pluralist one. It is particularly suggestive for the period prior to the conflict, when there is evidence of non-decision making, even if the notion of inaction through reputation may be discounted. The notion that certain interests, notably PROBE, the company and the unions, had greater resources and better access to the decision making process does have relevance in this case. However, élitist theories are insufficiently developed to provide a fully satisfactory account of the active phase of the conflict, and offer no explanation of the motivations behind the various positions adopted. Both pluralist and élitist accounts focus on descriptions of the distribution of power rather than on underlying reasons for the conflict and a concern with the outcomes. These are the subject of structuralist approaches, to which I now turn.

The structuralist interpretation

'Man lives consciously for himself but unconsciously he serves as an instrument for the accomplishment of historical and social ends. A deed done is irrevocable, and that action of his coinciding in time with the actions of millions of other men assumes an historical significance. The higher a man stands in the social scale, the more connections he has with others and the more power he has over them, the more conspicuous is the predestination and inevitability of every act he commits.'

(Tolstoy, *War and Peace*, B. 3 pt. 1)

Structuralist approaches provide quite different emphases to those considered so far. They derive from classical marxism a view that the class interests of capital possess the power necessary to achieve their ends — the realisation of profit. Power, from this angle, represents 'the ability of a class or group to realise its own specific objectives'.[79] In this case London Brick must be seen as representative of the capitalist class. A second feature of structuralism, important in this context, is that production processes cannot be studied in isolation, but need to be linked up to regional and national levels. Thus, we must examine London Brick's overall investment strategy which, as we have seen, despite its dependence on a spatially limited resource, certainly involved decisions outside Bedfordshire, and influence at national level. This introduces a third element of structuralism, the role of the state. Although neo-marxists recognise the separation of the economic and political spheres, the state is perceived as relatively autonomous, functioning in support of capital. Lastly, structuralism, as its name implies, emphasises the underlying economic determinants of social change.

There is a debate within marxism as to the political implications of these underlying determinants. The more functionalist, mechanical versions of structuralism argue that everything serves the interests of capital, which is therefore able to ensure outcomes favourable to itself. In order to realise their objectives capitalists may need to make concessions either in response to pressure or to preempt opposition. Such concessions are seen as tactical, providing a means to an end which is guaranteed by superior power, and supported by the way the state mechanism operates. The problem with this is that outcomes are inevitable. If this is so then what is the purpose of political action? There is little point in fighting if the end result is somehow predetermined. Other, more flexible versions of structuralism argue that outcomes depend on the balance of class forces prevailing at a point in time.

In this version it is conceivable that a challenge to capitalist interests may be sustained by the non-capitalist class. This flexibility enables the marxist position to maintain the salience of economic forces while trimming explanations to take into account political conflicts which would otherwise appear to be pointless and irrational.

The structuralist approach may be directed towards answering questions which focus on the class interests involved in the conflict. What contradictory class interests were expressed and how were they exposed or concealed? Were the outcomes determined by economic factors which enabled the class interests of capital to succeed? To pursue a structuralist interpretation we need to consider three conceptual problems — the resources available to the company, the nature of interests and the outcomes of the conflict.

Business power

If the idea that London Brick possessed superior power is tenable then it must be translated in empirical terms. Vogel offers an empirical definition of business power: 'its ability to define the political agenda, to win political victories, and to benefit disproportionately from outcomes'.[80] Among the strategies employed by industry are the use of advance intelligence, privileged access to officials and decision makers and the raising of public consciousness by rational argument on the merits of the case.[81] We have seen how London Brick employed such strategies but, in these respects, it was no better off than its opponents, who were at least as skilful in using similar tactics. In the early years there is evidence that the company controlled information sources, but in the heat of the conflict information became freely available, independent sources of information were commissioned and the company's opponents were not lacking resources to supply their own. Other strategies, such as exploiting divisions among opponents or building powerful coalitions with other interests, are also not the exclusive prerogative of industry, although London Brick was apparently adept at using them. If business superiority over other interests lies anywhere at all it is in the sanctions at its disposal. 'The most powerful weapon of business is commonly thought to be its ability to withhold additional capital investment if its demands are not met.'[82] Since business decisions determine the size of plants and firms, the location of industry, and the organisation of markets and transport, they can exert leverage on local as well as national decision makers.[83] Even this power has been contested, with the growth of environmental interests seeking to impose regulations on industry. But this power has its limits. 'Only under very extraordinary circumstances will government be willing to invoke the ultimate sanction of closing down plant, or making demands that would knowingly result in permanent shutdown.'[84]

It seems possible to argue the case both ways. On the one hand, business can be portrayed as holding reserves of power to be used either as a threat, or deployed if necessary to realise objectives. Business will make concessions up to the point of — but not beyond — what it deems acceptable. If the demands made are intolerable then business still has options available to take its investment elsewhere. On the other hand, business can be regarded as faced by opposing forces which also hold powerful cards, and which are able to force concessions which business would not otherwise make, and which may be contrary to its interests. This brings us face to face with the empirical question — whether London Brick is part of a dominant class or group or whether it is simply an interest in competition with other interests.

Interests

Pluralist and élitist approaches regard interests as subjective. For pluralists, the empirical focus becomes one of studying interests once they have been converted into policy preferences. In a sense this is unproblematic, since it becomes a contest between interests who prefer clean air or restored landscapes against interests preferring profit and jobs. But, even empirically, it is not as simple as that for two reasons. First, as pluralists recognise, part of the population may have an interest in both sides of the conflict. Second, the intensity of the preference varies among social groups, geographical locations and over time. It is very difficult in fact (if not in principle) to measure subjective preferences, and policy makers rely on assumption and assertion.

Marxists do not deny the existence of subjective preference as interest.

But they go on to argue that 'it is certainly possible, indeed, likely, that political issues or decisions implicate individuals, in the sense of altering dramatically their life-chances, even if they express or hold no preferences with respect to them'.[85] For marxists 'The assumption has been that, in one sense or another, interests are susceptible to objective identification, quite independently of the "actual" or empirical wants of those to whom interests are attributed'.[86] Balbus makes a similar point: ' "Interest" in this sense, then, is objective because it refers to an effect by something on the individual which can be observed and measured by standards external to the individual's consciousness.'[87] Thus objective interests exist whether or not individuals recognise them. If individuals are unaware, then they are unlikely to act, and even if they are aware they are unlikely to engage in a battle they are likely to lose. The marxist case is that class position determines the realisation of interests or their denial; and they deplore a system which denies objective interests from becoming political issues.

Not surprisingly this esoteric conception has been attacked. 'To say that the interests of a class are determined by their position in society . . . is to give us no clue at all as to what these interests are.'[88] Interests can only be realised when people recognise them and begin to struggle for them. The idea of objective interests is difficult to put in operational terms, though Connolly has made the attempt. 'Policy x is more in A's interest than policy y if A, were he to experience the *results* of both x and y, would choose x as the result he would rather have for himself.'[89] This is both convoluted and unfalsifiable. To this charge marxists would reply that since interests are determined by class positions they are deduced and not testable. The debate on interests is a classic case of a dialogue of the deaf.

The debate does have some bearing on this conflict however. It urges that we do not simply accept an expression of preference through visible conflict, but attempt to recognise those real interests being promoted in a decision and those being ignored. In a contest between business and environmental groups there are material interests at stake. There are material interests in production and profit and material interests in defending land and amenity. Over many other areas of policy these interests may coincide as a class interest, and be against the material interests of those who do not feature prominently in the conflict. 'In the power struggle for scarce resources some publics are amply supplied with the political resources necessary to press their case, while others have few resources, some have powerful sanctions, others have weak ones, some are organised into cohesive and influential power blocks, others are isolated and atomised.'[90]

Again we are faced with the problem of distinguishing between alternative perspectives. Was it a conflict between competing interests, contending élites or opposing classes? In the brickfields conflict there were at least two sets of interest, each representative of capital, each able to command resources and apply sanctions. It appears as a struggle between different fractions of the same class interest. Even so it was hardly the case that the interests of those working in the brickfields or those living in the area breathing in the fumes or living in derelict landscapes were ignored. Neither can it be said that they were unaware of their interests. It might be held that the support of such groups was solicited: the workers by the company, the community by the environmentalists. Such an argument has to contend with the apparently independent role played by other pressure groups early on in the conflict and by the trade unions in its final phase. If the domination of capitalist class interests is to be upheld then their relationship with these other groups has to be one of subordination in which the fundamental interests of workers and community are realised incidentally if at all. There will also be material interests outside the conflict, but standing to gain or lose by it, such as workers and communities in Cambridgeshire.

Outcomes

A structuralist perspective urges a focus on outcomes which, unlike interests, appear to be empirically testable: 'costs and benefits do exist objectively and may be analysed empirically in any specified context of action'.[91] This is the acid test of power. 'Power is visible only through its consequences, they are the first and final proof of the existence of power.'[92] This takes us beyond the question of who wins and who loses, the fulcrum of pluralist and élitist concerns, to an evaluation of who benefits and who loses. Unfortunately we are faced with similar problems to those affecting the discussion of interests. Consequences are not confined to the population immediately under observation. In this case there were consequences for neighbouring counties, even, it was argued, for neighbouring countries. Consequences are difficult to measure, since the benefits of employment to a small population must be weighed against the costs of environmental damage to a larger population and vice-versa. The problem of consequences is as much a case for speculation as for empirical measurement. The best we can do, even with a case as detailed as this one, is to speculate on the outcome and its likely costs and benefits.

The case does lend itself to analysis of whether the outcome (as measured by the eventual decision and its presumed consequences) was inevitable (a foregone conclusion), or whether it was unpredictable, a result of chance and changing circumstances. The idea of inevitability supports a functionalist position — a dominant class interest will be able to realise its objectives. The problem here is that the capitalist class was represented on both sides of the conflict, and one or other side was bound to succceed. We could attempt to finesse the problem by simply posing the question in terms of London Brick as representative of productive capital, but even this presents insurmountable difficulties. If a functionalist assessment of the power of productive capital is correct then we should expect London Brick to have displayed an ability to manipulate the political system, to exploit circumstances and to coopt or subvert the opposition. The idea that London Brick was all-seeing, somehow able to engineer the economic circumstances propitious to its ends seems ingenuous. The alternative, flexible view would presume a conflict in which productive capital does not possess overwhelming power, is forced to make unpremeditated concessions and to adopt strategies which attempt to wrest the initiative from opponents. In this instance London Brick will appear pliable and conciliatory, but still able to achieve a victory determined by economic factors. The problem here is that, had not the recession supervened, the straightforward economic explanation might have been undermined. The distinction between a marxist and a pluralist explanation becomes in the end a matter of assertion rather then unequivocal fact.

Another interesting feature of the case, the cross-cutting alignments between class interests which it illustrates, will be taken up in the next chapter. For the present, the main features of the structuralist interpretation to be applied to the case are as follows: Power, defined in terms of the ability of a class (or fraction) of capital to realise its objectives (production for profit), is exercised through strategies which best exploit the circumstances and which transcend the framework of local decision making. The material interests of other groups may incidentally be realized where they can be coopted to promote the capitalist interest. The state apparatus functions in support of capital. Outcomes are unpredictable and can only be arrived at through social conflict.

Analysis

The important advances made by neo-marxist theory have yet to be confirmed at an empirical level.[93] This is especially true at the level of local politics. It is difficult to transpose deductively derived propositions relating to national political systems to a context of localised conflict between environmental and productive interests. Despite these reservations, the London Brick case, when viewed from a structuralist perspective, offers insights which are not brought out in other approaches. Inevitably it also raises a host of further questions.

The passivity of London Brick during the period before the conflict is, from a structuralist viewpoint, largely unproblematic. The company had achieved a local monopoly; its permissions gave it freedom to pollute and create dereliction; and the state (both local and national) lacked enforcement powers. Indeed, the local planners were supportive, perhaps deserving the charge that they were 'totally pusillanimous' which was levelled at the county planning authority many years later.[94] But once the company applied for new works the legal and governmental framework provided an entry for opponents to try to enforce regulation. (The fact that these opponents were, in part at least, also capitalist is a major problem for a class conflict analysis, to which I shall return in the next chapter). A structuralist perspective suggests explanations for the conflict and its outcomes in three areas — the siting of new works, dereliction and air pollution.

Siting of new works

The company's indifference to the site for the southern works masked a preference for a replacement at Ridgmont. By offering alternative sites the company could accept the site attracting least opposition, knowing that Ridgmont would be chosen. The company could sit back while the planners carried the can for their choice of Marston Thrift. This was a neat example of a non-decision, a decision not to decide. London Brick, without any overt action, gained the backing of the Cranfield Action Committee and several local villages. Eventually the planners were forced to concede, and to recommend (in March 1980) the Ridgmont site. Ridgmont ultimately became the site, you will recall, for which planning permission was eventually granted in March 1981. All this fits neatly with the view that the company, by a combination of masterly inaction and subtle manipulation, was eventually able to secure its preferred site. It would also seem strange, to say the least, that a major company whose locational requirements are fairly fixed and therefore cost sensitive, would really be indifferent to the precise location of a major new development.[95] But if the company was so sensitive as to site, how can its apparent flexibility, with regard to overall location strategy, be explained? At crucial points in the conflict London

Brick switched its priorities from Ridgmont to Stewartby, and seemed ready to invest in Cambridgeshire in preference to Bedfordshire.

The most obvious explanation for the switch to Stewartby was that delays at Ridgmont made it sensible to build first at Stewartby to take advantage of the new Quest pit there which was an integral part of the planning application. It is possible, however, to see in this a deliberate exploitation of the political situation. The company had applied for two new works in Bedfordshire and, though the precise siting of the southern works had commercial implications, either of the two locations at Stewartby or at Ridgmont could be open first, depending on the progress of negotiations. While the site of the southern works was in some doubt, that at Stewartby was never at issue. The company could be seen as indifferent as to location (if not to actual site), and by switching to Stewartby it avoided siting problems and pursued what appeared to be the least contentious option. It appears to be a case of exploiting the circumstances to fit its objectives.

By the time London Brick had decided on Stewartby as first priority it had run into trouble over the pollution condition on the first phase. But the company not only possessed options between two sites for the southern works and between Stewartby and Ridgmont, it also had options in other locations. It was simultaneously applying for three new works — Stewartby, Ridgmont and Kings Dyke — and already had a permission in Buckinghamshire. This enabled it to pose a threat to the local decision makers. A structuralist interpretation would see the investment strategy as deliberately designed to seek out the weakest points in the local decision making framework. It was a strategy which appeared to work. The threat that investment might be diverted to Cambridgeshire was a major factor in weakening the opposition and preparing the way for a permission in Bedfordshire acceptable to the company. But, by that time, the company was back to Ridgmont as its priority.

The fact that the company appeared willing to switch sites in Bedfordshire and change its investment priorities between counties suggests that its real purpose was to build wherever it could get permission without tight pollution controls. Indeed, it suggests that the company was determined to gain acceptable permissions at every location. This would explain the move back to Ridgmont, where it was again able to manipulate the circumstances in its favour. By closing the old Ridgmont works the threats became real. London Brick had never withdrawn its application for Ridgmont, and it could appear passive in the knowledge that local pressure, inspired by its own workers fighting for jobs, would do the rest. Throughout the conflict

London Brick, by carefully manipulating its options and keeping in the background while other interests (workers and local groups) fought its cause, was able to ensure its objectives. It had at its disposal all the resources and strategies available to business discussed earlier.

At certain points this neat argument stretches the bounds of credulity. It wholly rejects the possibility that the company was indifferent to the siting of the southern works, and that it was also agnostic as to its overall investment priorities. It suggests that, even without the recession and the closure of Ridgmont, it would eventually have achieved its objectives. It argues that the simultaneous application for three works, the alternatives offered for the southern works, and the keeping-on of the Ridgmont application were all part of a deliberately constructed strategy of divide and rule. It neglects the possibility that, although London Brick was likely to get permissions for new works, there was no guarantee that it would get them in Bedfordshire. The structuralist case presupposes that the company was, throughout, fully aware of the options open to it and the flexibility conferred on it by sheer investment power. Despite its problems the structuralist argument does have a neat symmetry and a plausible logic, and its emphasis on underlying economic determinants is persuasive, even if the outcomes were not predictable in detail.

Dereliction

This emphasis on economic factors also provides a coherent explanation for the company's success in resisting environmental and pollution controls. The various environmental improvements offered by the company, and embodied in the Section 52 Agreement, can be construed as purely cosmetic. The demolition of disused works was hardly a concession, and the landscaping, stand-off zones, topsoil conservation and master plans for restoration were a small price to pay for goodwill created. As Councillor Hendry remarked, it was no more than would normally be required of a company seeking a major planning permission. Even Councillor Kemp, a supporter of the company, recognised this: 'We are not making LBC pay nearly enough for the privilege of avoiding a public inquiry'. The company had, however, managed to persuade the planners that major concessions had been made and that the Council ran the risk of losing them. The planners' tone was conciliatory: 'Be nice to London Brick. You need good relations for waste disposal.' Yet on this issue, the reclamation of the exhausted pits, the company's position had long been clear. As the Deputy Chairman had argued at the Brickfields Conference: 'We regard these pits as one of our assets, and as such we have always made a charge, a very reasonable one, for their commercial use in any shape or form.' Despite protestations it was clear that reclamation would depend on terms acceptable to London Brick Landfill. Thus, 'L' Field was restored, but the more substantial reclamation possible from the Vale of Belvoir spoil would require payment by the National Coal Board for the privilege of tipping. London Brick would supply the space but not the finance to remove an externality it had created.

Pollution

Similarly, in the case of air pollution the company made it clear it would do no more than was required by the Alkali Inspector. The relationship between the industry and the Inspectorate was 'like that of the doctor getting the patient's cooperation in treating a disease'.[96] Abatement techniques were either inapplicable, or harmful to the product, or caused offensive by-products, or were too costly — a view endorsed by the DoE report. Although the company accepted the County Council's participation in a research programme on kiln design, it was soon evident that this would not promote new initiatives. The Council had been concerned with fluoride removal, despite the insistence of the company, the Alkali Inspector and their own consultants that odour was the major problem. The Council had imposed a tight condition on the first phase of the new works applying to all the pollutants. When that was overturned they imagined that the same condition applied to the later phases which were dependent on the outcome of the research programme. But, in the heat of debate, the Council had failed to amend the conditions applying to the later phases. It required the works to have tunnel kilns 'so designed as to be capable of incinerating the organic compounds of the gases given off in the firing processes'.[97] It applied to odours and not to fluorides. As a result London Brick could claim that they 'were surprised that the County Council had referred to research into fluoride removal'.[98]

Moreover the Council involvement in the research programme was weak in other respects. There were significant loopholes in the agreement with the company. The company was only obliged to install 'as and when they become available at an economic cost such further practicable refinements for the reduction of pollutants as may be agreed' between the company and the Council, or if they did not agree, by the Alkali Inspector.[99] The requirement for tunnel kilns would not be binding if the Alkali Inspector 'certified in writing that after the conduct of a research programme by the applicants . . . the use of such kilns would not . . . constitute the best practicable means of eliminating or minimising the odours'.[100] Not only was the company effectively freed from fluoride removal, its research work was dependent on the relationship with the Alkali Inspector, as it always had been. Knowing this, London Brick could quite happily agree to a conditional approval on the later phases of the works in the confident expectation that when the second phase was needed it would, in all probability, get the go ahead using conventional Hoffman technology, since alternatives were impracticable. As Councillor Blowers remarked at the March 1980 meeting of the ESC: 'If we grant phase 1 are we, in effect, granting all four?'

The company had not deviated in any way from its major objectives. It enjoyed the support of the Alkali Inspector and of the Fletton Brickworks Liaison Committee which, instead of proving a watchdog on pollution matters, was a mouthpiece for London Brick, issuing Press releases of fulsome complacency. London Brick's power was tacitly accepted by the county planners. In Cambridgeshire it secured a planning permission without tight pollution controls which could be used to defeat opposition in Bedfordshire. In Bedfordshire the tight condition was eventually dropped, and the condition on the later phases was revealed as a paper tiger. From the company's viewpoint all the activities of its opponents might be construed as a wearying but marginal irritant, able to delay, but not deflect it from its predestined course.

It might be felt that the delay was decisive. If matters had proceeded as smoothly in Bedfordshire as in Cambridgeshire the company might have got its permission a year earlier. By the time it had won, the recession prevented an investment that might have been implemented. Here again there must be doubts. The company, even if it had begun construction, could have halted it again, and it showed no great concern over the delays it encountered. It was content to await the outcome of the DoE report, and, when the Council imposed its pollution condition, was prepared to procrastinate. In any case it had extant permissions elsewhere which it showed no signs of implementing. If all else failed it still had recourse to an appeal which most observers expected it to win. There is, in all this, evidence that London Brick, far from being affected by the intense debate in Bedfordshire, was biding its time and playing its options. The structuralist argument suggests the building of the new works depended solely on market factors, not on the outcome of a localised and, to the company, marginal conflict.

Conclusion

The structuralist perspective stresses the superior power of business, the predominance of economic factors, an ability to exploit circumstances and the relevance of regional and national influence on local decision making. It argues that the support of the central authorities and the compliance of local bureaucracies demonstrate the state apparatus functioning to support productive capital. In this view the issue is never in real doubt, though its detailed progress will reveal a response to local factors. But while structuralism offers an explanation of outcomes, it studiously ignores the role of local actors, and the intensity of a local conflict which involved a council for three years. This caused divisions among groups normally united, and promoted alliances between strange bedfellows. It remains a matter for debate as to whether the issue was significant, whether the conflict did markedly influence the company or affect its objectives and whether the outcome was predictable. Although structuralism provides an answer to these questions it does not say anything about the significance of participation of the various groups in the conflict. Insofar as these played a significant role in altering perceptions, changing the relationship between company and community and securing greater control over environmental development, they cannot be totally ignored. If they are, and the whole issue is reducible to a kind of crude economic determination, there would be no point in studying such conflicts, indeed little point in actors participating since action would have little effect. People act in the belief that they can influence events, and both beliefs and actions help to explain the shifting balance of power upon which environmental outcomes rest. While structuralist explanations provide an explanation of underlying causes they do not explain the tantalising complexity of events, or answer the perplexing problem of why this issue appeared at the time to be so important to a particular local community.

Competing or complementary theories?

The theoretical perspectives which have been applied to the London Brick case offer ways of interpreting the material and answering certain questions. It is clear that each perspective is a combination of ideas, concepts, and hypotheses developed over a long period. They are ideal types, with ideological connotations, and ways of looking at the world which makes a precise relationship between theory and evidence difficult to construct. They also focus on different levels of analysis. For instance, neo-élitist approaches owe their origins to a critique of pluralist approaches, and are limited to an analysis of the distribution of power and the means used in exercising it. Structuralist theories, by contrast, are derived from marxist theories which are comprehensive, seeking both to explain the nature of social relations and to urge the fusion of theory and practice.

Comparison between approaches is further complicated by the different applicability of theories to local politics. Whereas pluralist and neo-élitist studies of community power emerged from empirical work conducted in specific localities, structuralist theory has been more concerned hitherto with grand deductions and an empirical focus (where it exists) on national and productive processes: though this emphasis has been counteracted more recently.[101] As Saunders remarks: 'It should be clear that a one-sided theoreticism is likely to prove as sterile as a one-sided empiricism, and that structuralist perspectives in particular are often characterised by the development of elaborate theories whose complexity varies in inverse proportion to their empirical applicability.'[102] A further problem exists in the lack of conceptual clarity of some of the propositions of the different theories. For instance, it is sometimes difficult to perceive what characteristics precisely differentiate an élite from a class interest when viewed in the local context.

Such differences are inevitable in an area of theory which is both controversial and developing, and where problems of its relationship to empirical evidence in a variety of contexts have been relatively neglected. There are signs that the need to relate theory and evidence is not merely acknowledged by lip service but is recognised as genuine academic commitment. The problems facing those who attempt to specify and study the relationship are all too apparent in this study, but the attempt needs to be made to ascertain the utility and applicability of theory in particular contexts.

On the basis of the analysis so far it is clear that different perspectives illuminate different aspects of power conflict, and that each is flawed. Pluralist theories are particularly strong in the analysis of the active phase of conflict, and there is some evidence to support the idea of widespread participation, responsiveness and the role of actors. The neo-élitist critique is to an extent complementary, with its emphasis on the prior phase of non-decision making when issues are prevented in various ways from emerging for public debate and decision. The élitist stress on inequalities of power between competing groups contrasts with the pluralist thesis, and offers certain parallels with the structuralist focus on the domination of powerful interests. But structuralism takes the analysis further with its emphasis on the class nature of interests, the stress on underlying economic forces and its denial of the importance of individual action to the outcomes of the conflict. In the broadest sense both contrasts and convergences among these perspectives may be recognised, perhaps justifying Dunleavy's claim that 'it does not seem utopian to detect signs of empirically supported common ground, underlying the fundamental theoretical disputes which separate the two halves of the debate'.[103]

Having analysed the strengths and weaknesses of these perspectives against the evidence, we are in a position to establish more clearly the grounds of the debate between them. We are in a position to provide answers to the questions posed at the outset which, though they still leave room for debate and disagreement, are based on a dialogue between empirical material and theoretical perspective. From these answers we can derive further questions to be addressed in the next chapter.

Was the conflict between interests or classes?
This revolves around what constitutes an interest. To pluralists (and-élitists) interests are subjective and expressed as policy preferences for, say, amentity or jobs. Pluralists argue that those groups who wish to express their interest in an issue are able to do so, and there is, therefore, competition between opposing interests. Élitists take the view that certain interests possess greater resources of power and are able to pursue their interest with greater expectation of success. In the London Brick case there were, apparently, several élite interests: the company, the environmentalists led by PROBE, and the NFU and (more doubtfully) the trade unions. This comes close to an idea of élite pluralism. Structuralists would argue that it is impossible to distinguish these élites from classes. 'This "élite pluralism" does not, however, prevent the separate élites in capitalist society from constituting a dominant economic class, possessed of a high degree of cohesion and solidarity, with common interests and common purposes which far transcend their specific differences and disagreements.'[104] The powerful, in a structuralist analysis, are permanent, defined by class position, not simply an interest group whose membership may change and whose interests may differ according to issues.

The problem with this case is that none of the positions provides a satisfactory explanation. Pluralist accounts do not really allow for differential power and access, and élitist accounts cannot explain the role of the trade unions, which, though not élitist in the sense of communality of interest, did enjoy privileged access and a decisive influence on events. Structuralist accounts, derived from analysis of productive capital and the class conflict it provokes, insist that interests are objective, and are deduced from class position and need not be expressed as preferences. But in this case representatives of the capitalist class are found to be in conflict, and capital and labour in collusion. It is probably fruitless to try to disentangle the conceptual knots in the debate over interests, but this much is clear. The interests which possessed power in this conflict were materially based, and able to apply leverage on the decision makers. The company with its interest in capital formation possessed the power of investment withdrawal; the environmentalists, some of whom had a base in landed interests, could motivate opposition to protect amenity; and the trade unions, with an interest in employment, were able to evoke fears that played on the minds of sensitive politicians. It was, in short, a case of the triumph of material interests.[105] This seems to uphold a structuralist position of class interests based on material foundations in land, labour and capital. But these are conclusions from a specific occurrence. What remains is to explain the nature of the objective interests at stake, and the reasons for the paradox of allegiance between opposing class interests and the division between normally congruent interests.

Was the experience of power concentrated or dispersed?

In some respects this is a similar question, and the answer is, in part, already clear. But it raises another issue: the question of the relationship between interests and the decision making process. The pluralist claim that the polity is open, enabling all with an interest to participate, is, as we have seen, partly fulfilled. Decision makers were responsive to signals from their constituents, as transmitted through the media, at public meetings, and through pressure groups. The fear of electoral reprisal also played a part in their calculations. Their task was to transform these signals into policies through negotiation in open debate in the full Council. Neo-élitists contrast this with a view of a political system that encourages differential access through which élitist groups achieve privileged positions by the use of non-decision making. Power is therefore concentrated and exercised through informal processes hidden from public view.

From a structuralist viewpoint, the political process at local level is largely irrelevant since the system can be exploited in the interests of the dominant class anyway. From an analysis of this case we can, I think, conclude that the formal and informal structures of an ostensibly open, pluralist polity were manipulated and exploited to serve élitist ends. Power was at one level dispersed but, at the level which mattered, the level at which conclusive decisions were taken, it was concentrated. None of the theoretical positions pay much attention to the relationship between the political environment and the political organisation. Each provides a view of how the political environment was developed, but regards the relationship as a responsive one in which decisions were conditioned on the receipt of signals (pluralist) or underlying structures (structuralist). In practise the relationship is iterative, with the political organisation composed of elected representatives and officials both responding to, and helping to create, the political environment. The politicians either, in the case of the company's opponents, sought to promote changes in the political environment in order to strengthen their cause, or, in the case of the company's advocates, sought to resist such changes in the expectation that events would take a favourable course. The relationship between organisation and political environment leads into a discussion of the role of the state, and whether that role is autonomous or functionally dependent on capitalist interests.

Was the conflict and its outcomes determined by the agencies involved or by structural forces?

The problem here is posed by Hindess: 'How do we analyse outcomes and the conditions in which some outcomes are reached rather than others?'[106] There is a stark contrast between the more extreme versions of pluralism and structuralism on this question. Pluralists assert the intrinsic importance of agents: 'Decisions, after all, are made by individuals, or by small groups of men, and not by impersonal entities called firms or organisations'.[107] It is possible, looking at this case, to ascribe the crucial role to individuals and groups acting on the course of events. If this is so then we should expect the unanticipated, the unpredictable and the fortuitous to be significant in determining outcomes. But it would be foolish, a descent into pure empiricism, simply to describe the actions of agents divorced from a social and political context, which provides stimuli and constraint on their actions. By contrast a functional structuralist position would be most contemptuously dismissive of the part played by agencies. 'For who are these "actors"? Can they be defined in themselves, without any reference to the social content that they express?'[108] In this view, whatever the exertions of individuals or groups, the end result would be preordained, inevitable and predictable. Such a view would deny that social structures are sustained and reproduced by actors who have reasons for acting, and a belief that action can be effective. It would be presumptuous to imply that individuals act mindlessly and are unable to influence the course of events. Both positions require a willing suspension of disbelief.

What is necessary for the evaluation of theory is to consider the relationship between individual action and outcomes. It means recognising that 'struggles over divergent objectives really are struggles, not the playing out of some preordained script'.[109] At the same time agents involved in such struggles are not operating in a social vacuum, free from constraints imposed by economic circumstances. Modern pluralists recognise the role of constraints on action, and the more flexible versions of structuralism accord a role to agents which is not wholly predetermined. This apparent convergence may appear like fudging the issue. It does enable both sets of theories to subscribe to the plausible, if somewhat feeble, claim that 'although the agents operate within structurally determined limits, they nonetheless have a certain relative autonomy and could have acted differently'.[110] It also enables different explanations to be applied in different circumstances. Although a structuralist explanation appears appropriate for the outcomes in this particular case, it is conceivable that, had not the recession altered the political environment in 1981, the pluralist claims would have been upheld.

This, of course, ignores the wider spatial and political context in which the conflict occurred. When the context is widened to include the other counties involved, and when other similar cases are identified, it may be possible to discover whether the different case histories relate to specific local circumstances or whether underlying similarities are revealed. The study of an environmental issue in a specific local context has suggested that certain theoretical assumptions derived from other issues on a national basis may be challenged. To see if the conclusions reached so far have any more general validity we need to investigate the relationship between the state and capital at local and national levels.

So far some answers, not all of them conclusive, have been provided to some of the descriptive questions about the distribution and the exercise of power which have fascinated theorists following established perspectives. But, inevitably, the analysis has generated a series of further questions.

Among these questions are the following: Why was there conflict between those normally in agreement, and agreement between those normally in conflict? Why are there differences between local governments and between local and central government in their relationship to industry on environmental issues? Why was this issue important, or more provocatively, was it important? These questions need further refinement, but they provide a starting point for a closer examination of the role of the state in environmental planning. They require a fresh look at the evidence to see if the processes and causes revealed in Bedfordshire are capable of a more general application which contributes to theoretical insight and speculation.

Notes

1 See, for example, Dahl, R. A. (1958) 'A critique of the Ruling Élite model, *American Political Science Review*, 52; Polsby N.W. (1963) *Community Power and Political Theory*, New Haven, Yale University Press and 2nd Edition, 1980.

2 The most wellknown example of an explicitly pluralist account of power structure is Dahl, R. A. (1961) *Who Governs? Democracy and Power in an American City*, Chicago University Press.

3 More general élitist theory derives from Mosca, Pareto and Michels. Élite theory was first placed in an empirical local context by Floyd Hunter (1953) in *Community Power Structure* set in Atlanta. The neo-élitist critique of pluralism begins with Bachrach, P. and Baratz, M. S. (1962) 'Two faces of power' *American Political Science Review*, vol. 56 and (1970) *Power and Poverty*, New York, Oxford University Press. Among the empirical neo-élitist accounts are Crenson (1971) referred to below (note 37) and Domhoff, G. W. (1978) *Who Really Rules?* New Brunswick, N.J., Transaction Books, which is a critique of Dahl's New Haven study.

4 Vogel, (1981) 'How business responds to opposition. Corporate political strategies during the 1970s', unpublished draft, pp.1-2.

5 Lukes, S. (1974) *Power: a Radical View*, London, Macmillan, p.57.

6 Jack, M. (1974) 'Élite theory: ideological, tautological or scientific?', Ch. 9 in *Élites in Western Democracy*, edited by Ivor Crewe, British Political Sociology Yearbook, Vol. 1, London, Croom Helm, p.34.

7 Karl Marx, 'Theses on Feuerbach' in Marx, K. and Engels, F. (1969) *Selected Works*, London, Lawrence and Wishart, p.30.

8 Goldsmith, M. (1980) *Politics, Planning and the City*, London, Hutchinson, p.21.

9 Saunders, P. (1980) *Urban Politics: a Sociological Interpretation*, Harmondsworth, Penguin, p.14.

10 Reade, E. J. (1982) 'The British planning system', Unit 19 of *Urban Change and Conflict*, Open University, p.38.

11 Dunleavy, P. (1980) *Urban Political Analysis*, London, Macmillan, p.21.

12 Wolfinger, R. E. (1972) 'Non decisions and the study of local politics'. *American Political Science Review*, vol. 65, pp.1063-1080.

13 Ibid, p.1080.

14 Dahl, R. A. (1957) 'The concept of power', *Behavioural Science*, 2.

15 Polsby, N. W. (1963) op. cit. p.119.

16 Dahl, R.A. (1958) op. cit. p.358.

17 Polsby, N. W. (1963) op. cit. p.3.

18   Presthus, R. (1971) 'Pluralism and élitism', in Castles, F. et. al. (eds.) *Decisions, Organisations and Society*, Harmondsworth, Penguin, p.331.
19   Polsby, N. W. (1963) op. cit. p.118.
20   Muchnik, D. N. (1970) *Urban Renewal in Liverpool: A Study of the Politics of Redevelopment*, Occ. Papers on Soc. Admin. No.33, G. Bell, p.22.
21   Dahl, R. A. (1958) op. cit. p.360.
22   Lukes, S. (1974) op. cit. p.15.
23   Dahl, R. A. (1958) op. cit. p.358.
24   Parry, G. and Morriss, P. (1974) 'When is a decision not a decision?' In Crewe, I. op. cit. Ch. 11. p.319.
25   Bartlett, R. V. (1980) *The Reserve Mining Controversy*, Bloomington, Indiana University Press, p.6.
26   Ibid, p.4. Introduction written by Lynton F. Caldwell.
27   Vogel, D. (1981) op. cit. p.35.
28   Dahl, R. A. (1961) op. cit. p.86.
29   Allison, L. (1975) *Environmental Planning*, London, Allen and Unwin, p.103.
30   Winkler, J. (1977) 'The corporate economy: theory and administration'. In Scase, R. *Industrial Society: class, cleavage and control*, London, Allen and Unwin.
31   See Dearlove, J. (1973) *The Politics of Policy in Local Government*, London, Cambridge University Press; Dearlove, J. (1979) *The Reorganisation of British Local Government*, London, Cambridge University Press; Newton, K. (1976) *Second City Politics*, Oxford, Clarendon Press; Dunleavy, P. (1981) *The Politics of Mass Housing in Britain 1945-1975*, Oxford, Clarendon Press.
32   Dearlove, J. (1973) op. cit. p.28.
33   Newton, K. (1976) op. cit. p.14.
34   Gregory, R. (1969) 'Local elections and the "Rule of Anticipated Reactions"', *Political Studies*, vol.17, pp.31-47.
35   Newton, K. (1976) op. cit. p.19.
36   The interaction of the political organisation with the political environment is discussed in Chapter 1.
37   Crenson, M. A. (1971) *The Un-Politics of Air Pollution: A Study of Non-Decisionmaking in the Cities*, Baltimore, The Johns Hopkins Press, p.152. On the role of the Press in local politics, see Murphy, D. (1976) *The Silent Watchdog*, London, Constable.
38   Polsby, N. W. (1963) op. cit. p.120.
39   Sharpe, L. J. (1960) 'The politics of local government in Greater London', *Public Administration*, vol. 38, pp.157-72, p.120.
40   Heclo, H. H. (1969) 'The councillor's job', *Public Administration*, vol. 47, p.195.
41   Saunders, P. (1980) op. cit. p.227.
42   On the politics of 'hung' councils see Blowers, A. T. (1977) 'Checks and balances: the politics of minority government in Bedfordshire', *Public Administration*, Autumn, pp.305-316; (1982) 'The perils of being hung', *Local Government Studies*, vol. 8, No.4, July/August, pp.13-20.
43   Presthus, R. (1971) op. cit. p.338.
44   Ibid, p.338.

45 Crewe, L. (1974) (ed.) *Élites in Western Democracy*, London, Croom Helm, p.15.
46 Bachrach, P. and Baratz, M. S. (1971) 'Two faces of power', In Castles, F. et. al. (eds.) *Decisions, Organisations and Society*, Harmondsworth, Penguin, p.378.
47 Bachrach, P. and Baratz, M. S. (1970) op. cit. pp.47-48.
48 Lukes, S. (1974) op. cit. p.37.
49 Bachrach, P. and Baratz, M. S. quoted in Lukes, R. S. (1974) op. cit. p.16.
50 See Saunders, P. (1980) op. cit. and (1974) 'They make the rules: political routines and the generation of political bias', *Policy and Politics*, 4, pp.31-58; Parry, G. and Morriss, P. (1974) op. cit.
51 Saunders, P. (1980) op. cit. p.80.
52 Bradshaw, A. (1976) 'A critique of Steven Lukes' "Power: A Radical View"', *Sociology*, vol. 10, pp.121-7, p.125.
53 Ibid, p.123.
54 Kirk, Gwyneth (1980) *Urban Planning in a Capitalist Society*, London, Croom Helm, p.63.
55 Polsby, N. W. (1980) op. cit. p.216.
56 Wolfinger, R. E. (1972) op. cit. p.1071.
57 Schattschneider, E. E. (1960) *The Semi-Sovereign People: A Realist's View of Democracy in America*, New York, Holt, Rinehart and Winston.
58 Saunders, P. (1980) op. cit. p.22.
59 Bachrach, P. and Baratz, M. S. (1970) op. cit. p.43.
60 Crenson, M. A. (1971) op. cit. p.36.
61 Newton, K. (1976) op. cit. p.485.
62 Jones, C. O. (1975) *Clean Air: The Policies and Politics of Pollution Control*, Pittsburgh, University of Pittsburgh Press.
63 Crenson, M. A. (1971) op. cit. p.178.
64 Wolfinger, R. E. (1972) op. cit. p.1078.
65 The major empirical studies of non-decisions embracing alternative theoretical perspectives are: Crenson, M. A. (1971) op. cit. on air pollution in Gary; Saunders, P. (1980) op cit. on urban redevelopment in Croydon; and Dunleavy, P. (1981) op. cit. on high rise housing, using case studies of Newham, Birmingham, and Bristol.
66 On asbestos see Sandbach, F. (1982) *Principles of Pollution Control*, Harlow, Longman and (1982) 'Pollution control; in whose interest?', Paper presented to conference on *Environmental Pollution and Planning*, Institute of British Geographers, Southampton.
67 Wolfinger, R. E. (1972) op. cit. p.1078.
68 Crenson, M. A. (1971) op. cit.
69 Ibid, p.80.
70 Ibid, p.60.
71 Bedfordshire County Council (1960) *Report on Atmospheric Pollution in the Brickworks Valley*, The Brothwood Report, Health Dept. See Chapter 2, p.36, for commentary on the report.
72 Burns, K. N. and Allcroft, Ruth (1964) 'Fluorosis in cattle: occurrence and effects in industrial areas in England and Wales', *Animal Disease Service Report*

No.2, Min. of Agriculture, Fisheries and Food, London, HMSO. The evidence on fluorosis in cattle is reviewed in Chapter 2.

73 Brough, A., Parry, M. A. and Whittingham, C. P. (1978) 'The influence of aerial pollution on crop growth', *Chemistry and Industry*, January, pp.51-3. The experiments undertaken in Bedfordshire on crop damage are also discussed in Chapter 2, pp.38-9.

74 Crenson, M. A. (1971) op. cit. p.30.

75 Ibid, p.120.

76 Lindblom, C. E. (1977) *Politics and Markets: the World's Political-Economic Systems*, New York, Basic Books, p.184.

77 Comments of County Planning Officer to Ray Young, Chairman of GASP. See Chapter 3.

78 See note 50.

79 Sandbach, F. (1980) *Environment, Ideology and Policy*, Oxford, Blackwell, p.135.

80 Vogel, D. (1982) op. cit. p.4.

81 Kimber, R. and Richardson, J. J. (1974) *Campaigning for the Environment*, London, Routledge and Kegan Paul.

82 Vogel, D. (1982) op. cit. p.9.

83 Lindblom, C. E. (1977) op. cit. p.188.

84 Bartlett, R. V. (1980) op. cit. p.215.

85 Balbus, I. D. (1971) 'The concept of interest in pluralist and marxian analysis', *Politics and Society*, 1:2 pp.151-78, p.164.

86 Benton, T. (1981) '"Objective" interests and the sociology of power', *Sociology*, 15, pp.163-84, p.170.

87 Balbus, I. D. (1971) op. cit. p.152.

88 Plamanetz, J. (1954) 'Interests', *Political Studies*, vol. 2, pp.3-17, p.4.

89 Connolly, W. E. (1972) 'On "interests" in politics', *Politics and Society*, vol. 2, pp.459-79, p.472.

90 Newton, K. (1976) op. cit. p.236.

91 Saunders, P. (1980) op. cit. p.48.

92 Westergaard, J. and Resler, H. (1975) *Class in a Capitalist Society*, London, Heinemann, p.141.

93 Gwyneth Kirk (1980) op. cit., an advocate of a marxist approach comments: 'Much of this work is very recent, explorative in nature and to some extent tentative, often at a very high level of generality, and acknowledged by the authors to be inadequately formulated or as yet incomplete' (p.79). In similar vein, Dunleavy states that marxist approaches 'have rarely been applied empirically and they are phrased in a much more general way than . . . other theoretical approaches . . .' (1981 op. cit. p.189).

94 See Chapter 4.

95 Although the Marston Thrift site was adjacent to clay extraction, its development would require construction of an access road including a tunnel. The hill top site near the existing works would also require infrastructure investment. The cheapest option was likely to be replacement on the existing site — which was the decision ultimately taken.

96 Ashby, E. and Anderson, Mary (1981) *The Politics of Clean Air*, Oxford, Clarendon Press, p.136.
97 The crucial difference was that the first phase of the first new works would have the new condition 9 covering all pollutants applied to it, but phase 2 retained the condition on tunnel kilns applying only to odour removal (County Council, 3 July, 1980 80/k/74 1. b. 3). For discussion of the conditions see Chapters 4 and 5.
98 Minutes of meeting to discuss the outline research programme into methods of reducing pollution from brickworks, 5 January, 1982.
99 Section 52 Agreement 4 h. For discussion see Chapter 4.
100 Section 52 Agreement condition 3. For discussion see Chapter 4.
101 This is especially true of French writings, which have investigated local political processes. For example, Castells, M. (1978) *City, Class and Power*, London, Macmillan, Ch. 4-6, Coing, H. (1966) *Renovation Urbaine et Changement Social*, Paris. Ed. Les Editions Ouvrières. Dunleavy, P. (1981) has examined the applicability of a neo-marxist perspective, among others, to the high rise housing phenomenon (op. cit.).
102 Saunders, P. (1980) op. cit. p.14.
103 Dunleavy, P. (1981) 'Alternative theories of liberal democratic politics: the pluralist-marxist debate in the 1980s', Paper for Open University Social Sciences Foundation course, p.16.
104 Miliband, R. (1969) *The State in Capitalist Society*, London, Quartet Books, p.45.
105 Blowers, A. T. (1983) 'The triumph of material interests: geography, pollution and the environment', *Political Geography Quarterly*, Vol. 3, No. 1, pp.49-68.
106 Hindess, B. (1982) 'Power, interests and the outcome of struggles', *Sociology*, vol. 16, No. 4. November, pp.498-511, p.498.
107 Gregory, R. (1971) *The Price of Amenity*, London, Macmillan, p.14.
108 Castells, M. (1977) *The Urban Question*, London, Arnold, p.251.
109 Hindess, B. (1982) op. cit. p.506.
110 Lukes, S. (1974) op. cit. p.54.

CHAPTER 7
POLITICS, ENVIRONMENT AND THE STATE

'It is a capital mistake to theorise before one has data'.
(Arthur Conan Doyle)

The limitations of theory
In recent years the study of local politics has been transformed by the emergence of what has come to be called 'urban studies'.[1] Indeed, it would be no exaggeration to say that urban studies has been lifted from a relative backwater to the centre of the stage in the development of theory, making major contributions to the understanding of the inequalities of power in society. The theoretical debate in urban studies draws its strength from a multi-disciplinary approach inspired by a vigorous challenge to 'orthodox' positions provided by both neo-weberian and neo-marxist critics.[2] 'While the value of these perspectives remains controversial and fiercely contested, there is little room for doubt that the interaction between new and old approaches has sparked a widespread reemergence of theoretical interest in "urban" issues. The central grounds of controversy and debate over cities and urban phenomena have been projected into sharper focus in all disciplines, and very different analytic approaches.'[3] Inevitably, in a rapidly developing area there is a danger of theory outrunning empirical application, of empirical accounts lacking an adequate conceptual basis for useful generalisation, of ideological assumptions masquerading as scientific premises and evidence being strained to support hypotheses which bear little relationship to the complex and confusing pictures presented by experience. In a new, innovative and somewhat innocent area such as urban studies there are bound to be methodological problems of falsifiability and conceptual precision. But, if the promise of new developments is to be fulfilled in substantial theoretical advance, then an immediate problem is to see how far the concepts of contemporary urban studies illuminate and complement long standing debates in a variety of empirical applications. In

260

this chapter I shall try to develop the theoretical perspectives already outlined, by introducing mediating concepts which may help to relate broad theoretical perspectives to specific circumstances. The attempt is exploratory, and reveals the difficulties encountered in the effort to clarify and explain the complexities and contradictions encountered in empirical research. My justification is that the attempt must be made if theoretical advances are to be consolidated.

From the previous discussion we arrived at some tentative conclusions, each perspective contributing to explanation of the London Brick case. The pluralist approach, with its emphasis on open, responsive government arbitrating competing interests, expresses the active phase of the conflict. The élitist perspective both contradicts and complements the pluralist analysis. Its emphasis on the covert exercise of power during the non-decision making phase, and the inequalities of access and influence during the active phase suggests that power was concentrated; effectively excluding non-élite groups who nonetheless had a real interest in the outcomes. Both these approaches focus on interests and the role of actors in a local context. The structuralist approach, on the other hand, emphasises the underlying determinants of social conflict and the influence of a broader regional and national dimension on local politics. In the most simplistic terms we can say that, in the case of London Brick, a pluralist polity was exploited by élitist interests, and the outcome depended on underlying structural forces. In short, each perspective provides a partial explanation, though each is flawed.

It does have to be recognised, however, that any attempt to reconcile pluralism with structuralism must confront the fact that they are theories which are constituted at different levels. Pluralism (and élitism) have empiricist foundations, and seek to test out hypotheses through a detailed investigation of what are taken to be the facts, in order to develop generalisations about the distribution and exercise of power. Critics have frequently charged empiricism with being unable to deliver its promise of the objective investigation of neutral facts, and have pointed to the theoretical and ideological load carried by such investigations. Nevertheless, pluralists and élitists are to be distinguished from structuralists in so far as they have concentrated on detailed empirical investigation, and have taken such work to be the key to exploring the reality of social and political life.

Structuralists, by contrast, have placed greater explanatory weight on broad theoretical concepts. Their work has been pitched primarily at the theoretical level. This has led critics to describe marxist based approaches as a 'breathtaking intellectual imperialism' intent on explaining everything.[4] They point to the functionalism of certain marxist accounts, the denial of individuality, and the reduction of everything in terms of an (outmoded) version of class conflict. 'The battle lines are clearly drawn: here the bourgeoisie, there the proletariat' in which 'the gap between theory and observable reality has widened to the point where attempts to press the diversities of contemporary social structure into the old mould stretch our credulity'.[5] We have already seen that the London Brick case does not fit precisely into a simple class conflict model in so far as intra-class conflict was a prevailing feature. A closer examination of the relationships involved in the case will further underline the applicability of different perspectives to different aspects of the conflict.

This examination can be achieved by focusing on what I call *mediating concepts*. Four pairs of related and interacting concepts can be identified. The first pair identify the issues in conflict, which are *environment* and *economy*; the second relate to the interaction of *politics* and *expertise*. The third and fourth pair provide a broader context for the evaluation of the specific case. The third concerns the role of the state — both *local* and *national* — and the fourth introduces the dimensions of *time* and *place*. Each pair will be examined in turn, successively building a series of conclusions which lead from the particular case towards more general propositions. This method is, to a degree, artificial since all these concepts ultimately interrelate in a complex fashion. But conceptual disaggregation is essential if we are to be able to explore some of the more puzzling features and fascinating questions which have been raised in this case. It will also assist in our evaluation of the explanatory power of the broad theoretical perspectives outlined in the previous chapter. At the end I shall attempt to show how the analysis of mediating concepts assists the reconciliation of empirical evidence with broad theoretical perspectives.

Environmental issues

'Ill fares the land, to hast'ning ills a prey,
Where wealth accumulates, and men decay;'
(Oliver Goldsmith, *The Deserted Village*)

Some recent neo-marxist work has focused on so-called 'urban protest movements', the potential for mobilising working class protest around issues of collective consumption.[6] This has extended the concept of class conflict from a conflict over production to conflict over the consumption of goods provided by the state. The argument is that the state functions to support capitalist interests through the provision of social capital.[7] This is of two kinds. First, there is the state's *social investment* into physical capital such as roads, sewerage systems and energy supply which relieves industry of costs, and into human capital through the provision of education and other services which increases the productivity of labour. Second, there is the provision of collective services — *social consumption* — such as housing, public transport and health which ensure that the social wage is externalised by industry, thus lowering its labour costs. It is this social consumption which supposedly becomes the source of protest against state institutions acting for capital.

The idea that the state functions to support capital has been challenged by critics who point out the difficulties of defining collective consumption, and argue that state provision goes far beyond what is necessary simply to ensure the health of capitalist enterprise.[8] Pahl argues that 'there does seem to be a large gap between the complex analysis of urban contradictions by the intellectuals and the perceptions by the workers of repression experienced in the sphere of consumption.[9] The relatively pusillanimous nature of urban working class protest over such issues as housing is thus seen as evidence, on the one hand, of the repressive power of the state acting on behalf of capital or, on the other, as demonstrating the fragmented nature of social consumption, and the inability of the working class to organise sustained protest.[10] Quiescence is the prevailing condition. 'There may be dissatisfaction which they do not bother to voice, either because they do not know how to do so or because they feel that government, or whatever organisation is the likely target, would take no notice.'[11] A third possibility, that they are relatively satisfied and therefore not moved to protest, would presumably be discounted in a marxist explanation.

This focus on working class protest or quiescence on issues of collective consumption has diverted attention from other, perhaps more significant features of urban conflict. First, it has neglected the fact that environmental issues provide vehicles for organised protest and participation. Second, this protest is not confined to the working class but rather finds its voice among more privileged groups able to appeal across the divides of class. Thirdly, environmental protest provokes reaction from business able to build coalitions with working class interests to resist control over production. With such emphasis laid on the role of capital, it is curious that 'despite a growing literature on the power of the multi-national corporations, particularly as they affect national decision making, there has been very little study of their impact upon sub-national political entities.[12] The London Brick case forces attention on these hitherto neglected features, showing that the conflict between economic power and environmental forces transcends the class divides which have obsessed marxist approaches. It provides some evidence for the view that in advanced industrial societies there are newly emerging patterns of class conflict. Lipset for example, argues that in such societies it is the middle class who are the real agents of change, with the working class acting as the bulwark of stability.[13] In the context of specific social issues, such as the environment, this argument deserves to be taken seriously. However, radical protest often has conservative motives.

'Environment' is an ambiguous term combining a number of issues.[14] Among these is *amenity*, which arouses conservationist sentiments but which is confronted by producer and consumer interests willing to sacrifice some environmental benefits in order to reap the material advantages of production. Another is *public health*, which embraces a wide constituency of protest. Both are relevant to the London Brick case. The desirability of better amenity — the reclamation of the derelict environment — was not seriously challenged, though there were considerable differences on the question of how much could be achieved and who should pay.

Amenity is a relative concept, prized most by those who have already secured most of the goods needed for survival and affluent living. Not surprisingly it has been a vehicle for middle class protest groups. Such groups have the time and resources to defend their interests, as, for example, Jones noted in his study of pollution in Pittsburgh: 'The environmental issue area is a prime candidate for massive public concern . . . for it was among the middle- and upper-income groups that environmental interests found support for their cause'.[15] Since amenity is a cause around which all can unite, these groups are able to make common cause with other groups in society, a point that arouses the utmost cynicism in Castells: 'The ideology of environment, "apolitical", humanitarian, universalist and scientific, transforms social inequality into mere physical inconveniences and blends social classes into one army of Boy Scouts'.[16]

Where concerns about public health can also be aroused the appeal of environmentalist causes is greatly strengthened. The main thrust of public concern in Bedfordshire was the hazard from pollution, not the improvement of amenity. A broad alliance, based on consensus, provides substantial power to groups whose primary concern is the protection of their *positional goods*: goods that are 'fixed in supply and whose consumption is dependent upon one's position in society'.[17] This fundamental inequality inherent in the espousal of environmentalism has been alluded to by several authors.[18] It is an assertion of the status quo, the maintenance of privilege by affluent groups or affluent countries who, by attempting to control economic development, may deny the opportunity of incomes, jobs and consumption of goods to less privileged groups. As Gregory observes: 'It is not difficult to see what many cynics have in mind when they suggest that many conservationists can afford to concern themselves with intangibles because they already have enough of everything else and are appalled at the consequences of extending their own standard of living to the rest of the community'.[19] A rather more generous construction is offered by Crosland who calls them 'kindly and dedicated people. But they are affluent, and fundamentally, though of course not consciously, they want to kick the ladder down behind them'.[20]

In the brickfields case the environmentalist cause, as we have already seen, was predominantly led by landed, farming and middle class elements. It was able to mobilise public opinion on a broad front and to penetrate the decision making system. But we should be careful not to read too much into the presumed motives of the environmentalists. It is true that the pressure groups protected their own amenity through stand-off zones and the siting of new works, and that farmers stood to profit from a drop in pollution levels. But their adoption of the anti-pollution cause in a wider public interest was, no doubt, perfectly genuine — an example of paternalistic élitism. What is patently clear is that the environmental issues of dereliction and pollution were able to arouse sustained protest because they appealed to a privileged section of the community with the power and resources needed to fight a major company. Our first conclusion therefore can be stated in the following form: Environmental issues which embrace amenity and public health become the focus of protest by groups anxious to defend their positional interests, but able to mobilise widespread support which transcends class barriers.

Economic issues

Economic interests, when threatened by environmentalist pressures, likewise transcend traditional class barriers and produce apparently unholy alliances between labour and capital. Class conflict over production is dissolved when that very production seems threatened, but the power of labour and capital is imbalanced. The weakness of trade unions, especially in times of recession, is clear. The union movement, we are told, is fragmented, incorporated, unaware of its real interests and suffering from a false consciousness rendering it incapable of transforming social relationships and realising its true power.[21] Certainly in the case of London Brick the unions had signally failed to gain improvements in working conditions over a long period, wage levels were depressed as a result of the recruitment of immigrant labour, and jobs were insecure as successive recessions brought short time working and redundancies. The unions were scarcely consulted over the Ridgmont closure and were unwilling to mount any effective protest. Despite these inequalities the company enjoyed good relations with its workforce. A compromise was forged whereby lower manning levels resulting from the development of new works were accepted in return for better working conditions and job security for the remaining work force.

The company management had a long tradition in brickmaking, and was involved in the local community, providing facilities, including housing, for its workforce. Management attitudes had changed from the benign paternalism of the Stewarts to the more progressive, open image fostered by Jeremy Rowe and James Bristow. This identification of company, workers, and community had brought dividends for the company in terms of union support. The promise of better working conditions and greater job security was enough to ensure union support for a company primarily concerned with improving profitability through increased productivity.

The alliance between unions and company was strengthened by the weakness of both in the face of the combined threat posed by environmental opposition and the recession. The company's apparent inability to allay the environmental opposition brought the unions to its side, and the prospect of job loss cemented the coalition. But there is evidence of ambivalence in the unions' stance, and they were partly aware of their own weakness in relationship to the company. As one union leader admitted: 'if the economy had been more buoyant it's likely we'd have caused the company more bother'.[22] They were anxious to lay the blame on the Council or the Government rather than the company. Occasionally an awareness of the realities of the situation was evident: 'I suspect that Mrs. Thatcher's new spirit of freedom is allowing many companies to take advantage of the recession. Workers are too afraid to speak out for fear of losing their jobs. Is the company doing an unpopular thing and trying to blame the Council? What guarantees are there that even with a permission they will actually build the works?[23]

The unions suffered no so much from being aware of the realities as from an unwillingness to accept them, for to do so would reveal their own weakness. Unable to prevent the closure of Ridgmont, and unwilling to defend the workers there they found themselves with nowhere to go but to support the company in the illusory hope that a planning permission would secure future jobs. The Council decision proved a timely and fortunate scapegoat, offering a target which concealed the impotence of the unions' position. Thus the unions' support for the company and their attack on Labour and Conservative councillors can be read as a defensive gesture, a confession of weakness, not a principled assertion of union power and influence. It is also possible to see in it support for a company which was acting in the union's best interests. Whatever the interpretation, in a situation where redundancies were taking place, and further job losses in prospect, the union's position is perfectly understandable. At the very least the unions focused attention on those who were suffering most as a result of the recession, and for whom a debate about environmental issues was a luxurious irrelevance.

Paradoxically, the recession which weakened the prospects of the company and its workers strengthened their relative bargaining position in the local community. The alliance between company and union suggests a further proposition:

The influence of business power in a community is strengthened in times of recession when the prospect of investment withdrawal ensures the support of labour in defence of jobs.

A conflict between environment and economy, therefore, cuts across class frontiers, suggesting that a simple class conflict model needs modification. For marxists there is a supreme irony here in the fact that, in order to protect their own survival, the workers have to give aid and comfort to capitalist interests. And, as we shall now see, capitalist interests can also successfully pursue their goals through the political process.

Political conflict

'It is in vain to say human beings ought to be satisfied with tranquillity: they must have action; and they will make it if they cannot find it.'

(Charlotte Bronte, *Jane Eyre*)

The environmentalist and corporate interests in the conflict took divergent paths through the political process. Whereas the company enjoyed a close relationship with the officials and the committee, its opponents secured their influence through the more pluralist forum of the Council. Here, the influence of officials was weak, and success depended on the exercise of political skills — 'passion and manipulation . . . the projection either by eloquence or other means of successful "public image" '.[24] The transformation of the issue into a pluralistic conflict provoked tensions within the Conservative Group and between Labour members and the trade unions. The emergence of the Council in a dominant role suggests the ability of elected representatives to take up an issue. 'Politics is like lightning, in that it may suddenly strike into any corner of the administrative system, but only rarely does so. The great bulk of administrative operations continue in political obscurity.'[25] For a time, it appeared that the exercise of power through pluralist politics would give the environmental interests the upper hand.

Environmental interests were able to exploit the divisions within a dominant Conservative Group on questions of environment and economy. Normally, the association of Conservatives and business interests is expected to be close. But, as Westergaard and Resler note: 'Business and Conservative Party interests are likely to be divided on a variety of issues, and on lines that differ from one issue to the next'.[26] In Bedfordshire, a county which combines an urban industrial base in Luton and Bedford with a surrounding area of wealthy farming, such a division was, perhaps, inevitable. The analysis of voting intentions and voting patterns (see Figures 4.3 and 4.4 and Figures 5.1 and 5.2) provides some confirmation of this, with the southern areas, being more industrialised and further from the brickfields, tending more to favour the applications, and the northern area leaning in the other direction. But, up to half the Conservative Group remained uncertain or indifferent right up to the decisive vote, reflecting a lack of involvement in the issue or instinctive preference. Indeed, the pattern of identification between constituents and voting patterns was not at all clear. Anomalies were embodied in the leading protagonists. Philip Hendry, representing the workers of Stewartby, took a leading anti-company role, whereas Michael Kemp, also representing the workers from the southern part of the Vale, was a prominent supporter of the company's cause. Samuel Whitbread, a prominent landowner whose constituency embraced Elstow, a village hostile to the company, spoke strongly in favour of the application as did Rex Upchurch, a farmer. Thus the split in Conservative ranks is not easily explained in simple terms of electoral politics or occupational affinities.

In a more general sense, the economy–environment tension is evident in

Conservative attitudes, a cleavage expressed cogently by the two Conservative leaders. Philip Hendry emphasised the interests of Bedfordshire. 'I'm not anti-party, but I don't believe in writing blank cheques for anyone — especially London Brick. Bedfordshire comes first. I wasn't stopping building, I just wanted to get additional safeguards with more construction work not less.'[27] Keith White, too, believed he was serving local interests, but he stressed the economic prospects secured by supporting investment in private enterprise. 'Do you want better conditions for the work force? . . . Don't follow Hendry on the high road but ESC on the low road . . . The environmental gains are such a wonderful package. If you can't see it then ESC has done its best.'[28] The conflict within the Conservative Group can be interpreted as representing the divergent economic interests supported by the party. On the one hand there is the support for landed and farming interests, on the other support for private industry. It was also a conflict of leadership and charisma designed to attract the agnostic and malleable members of a group whose votes remained uncertain. Indifference was as common as commitment and provided the political potential for the environmentalist cause.

The split in Conservative ranks was paralleled by divisions among labour interests. Although the small Labour Group were united in support of the environmentalist position, they found themselves hopelessly at odds with the trade unions representing the brickworkers. It is easy to see this in terms of a divorce of leadership from grass roots, a tendency highlighted by several writers.[29] The link between the leadership of the political parties, cemented by PROBE, was potentially embarassing for Labour, suggesting, as Hindess observes, that Labour politicians 'have more in common with their opposite numbers than the people they supposedly represent'.[30] But, Labour councillors asserted their position was consistent, not contradictory. They favoured new works, but they recognised widespread anxieties about pollution. If the company could not implement the Council's condition then it could always appeal. The defensiveness of Labour members was evident in the following statement by Councillor Farley:

> It wasn't and isn't our wish to be at loggerheads with trade unions of any description. It has been blown up into confrontation. But we do have a wider constituency. I want to emphasise that we went out of our way to state our belief in the importance of the clay fields. The poor working conditions have existed for many years and I do find it distasteful that the company should now say we've not improved conditions since we've been waiting for new works.[31]

For a time the rift between the Labour Group and the unions, and the attack on private enterprise by a substantial section of the Conservative Group, were the major political anomalies providing support for the environmentalists. But, as the job threat increased so the Labour Group's stance weakened to the point where Labour members abstained during the decisive vote on the Ridgmont permission, and Conservatives, too, showed little stomach for continuing the battle. The environmental cause had constructed a brittle alliance which collapsed once the issues of jobs and investment withdrawal became paramount. The environmental position, apparently strong, was, in fact, constructed on the basis of political support which was both shifting and vulnerable.

Administrative politics

While the environmentalists sought to exploit the possibilities of pluralist politics, as embodied in the County Council, the company pursued its course through its influence on the planning officials, and through them, the members of the Environmental Services Committee. The power of bureaucracy over politicians has been emphasised by many writers from Weber and Michels[32] down to the present.[33] Bureaucracy is said to imply a convergence of rationality, expertise, and disinterested judgement. 'Bureaucracy is itself a method of bringing scientific judgements to bear on policy decisions; the growth of bureaucracy in modern government is itself partly an index of the increasing capacity of modern government to make use of expert knowledge.'[34] By contrast, the part time amateur politician in local government is regarded as little match for the full-time bureaucrat whose 'control of information is a powerful base of his influence'.[35]

Neo-pluralist approaches have addressed the role of administrators in the modern industrial state. They argue that the risk of responding to public opinion can no longer be adequately fulfilled by the representative political process. Instead, this role is undertaken by bureaucrats with a strong and conscientious conception of the public interest. This process is facilitated by the professionalisation of administration. Thus, for example, planners are able, using their expertise and professional judgement, to weigh up the public interest in applications for development. At the same time the decentralisation of administration expressed in the various democratic and semi-autonomous institutions disaggregates issues into separate decision making arenas, preventing a concentration of power. The state thus develops what Dunleavy calls a 'technostructure' which is seen as 'meeting the needs of ordinary citizens and as overwhelmingly orientated to those needs'.[36] The questions for examination in this case are whether the professional administrators (the planners) exercised power which affected outcomes, and if so what interests they were responding to. The answer depends on a prior set of questions about the relationship between the planners and the politicians. Was it a dominant, dependent or interactive relationship?

There is certainly some evidence that the planners exerted the power of expertise and bureaucratic influence in the London Brick case. 'So all-embracing are the planners' concerns, and so "complete" is their ideology . . . that planners seem to pose a real threat to the politicians, to be well prepared to replace politics by technocracy.'[37] In a succession of planning documents and agenda reports they urged the case for environmental improvements as a condition of the acceptance of the planning permission. They were at the interface between the company, local politicians and central government. They conducted the negotiations and were the clearing point for information coming in from the company, the consultants, other authorities, official agencies and pressure groups. They could act as brokers and mediators, sifting, selecting and evaluating the evidence. They made judgements on the siting and design of new works, the desirability and feasibility of environmental improvements, and on the limits of pollution control.

Their power lay in access to a wider range of information than was available to any other participant in the conflict. They emphasised the environmental issues, arguing that the Minister would allow the issue to be determined locally. Conversely, they played down the pollution issue, recognising the limitations of the Council's powers. From the outset they urged a 'package' of proposals based on negotiation, cooperation and compromise with the company. When the Council decided to reject this advice, the officers pointed out the fallibility of the Council's position, and the prospect of the package being sacrificed either in the courts, through ministerial intervention or as a result of the company taking its investment elsewhere. The permission ultimately granted at Ridgmont was substantially the same as that which the planners had advocated for Stewartby a year before.

Were the planners really so successful, their power and expertise vindicated by eventual success? There are grounds for arguing that their influence waned during the course of the debate, that positions they had adopted were weakened and proposals they favoured defeated. They favoured a site at Marston Thrift but bowed to public pressure. They saw landscape and restoration as the prime issues but were forced to concede that 'pollution is the main consideration'. They favoured a part permission, but saw this turned down twice by the County Council. Their influence was greatest where consensus prevailed. All parties subscribed to the package of environmental improvements. But air pollution was a different matter forcing the planners away from their role of experts to a role in which they had to bargain, to advocate and to persuade. In doing so they adopted political roles, and became dependent on politicians to achieve their objectives. It was only in combination with political power that the planners were able to exert influence, and only when they acted politically that they could cultivate success.

In a sense, this meshing of bureaucratic and political roles can be seen as a vindication both of the pluralist notion of democratic politics and the neo-pluralist refinement of administrative experts influencing the course of events in the public interest. But, critics have exploded the idea that planning has claims to expertise. Experts, according to Reade, are aware of the fact–value distinction and are able to make this clear in the advice they tender to politicians. Town planners, by contrast, 'are characterised by their unawareness of the fact–value distinction, and by their inability, even privately, to distinguish the points on which they need empirical evidence or tested theory on the one hand, and opinion on the other, in order to formulate their recommendations'.[38] Planners tend to insist that planning is not political, although they recognise that planning policies must be legitimated by politicians. They accept, too, that policies may involve choices, choices which must be taken by politicians.[39] But they rarely assert (though some may accept) that 'planning is power. Planning is politics'.[40] But, if the claims to expertise are unfounded and planning requires judgements to be made which rest on evaluation and preferences, then planners inevitably must combine the roles of bureaucrat and politician. Even if planners are unable to make fact–value distinctions, their claims to expertise are unjustified and they fail to understand the political nature of decisions, it could still be argued that they are qualified in terms of experience and information to make sensible means–ends judgements. This neo-pluralist position is tenable, but it neglects the interactive relationship between bureaucrats and politicians.

The role of politicians also reveals certain ambiguities. Mere association with bureaucratic procedures and information creates an environment of socialisation in which fact–value, rationality–evaluation and politics–expertise become fused. Indeed, some have argued that political and administrative roles have been reversed, with officials shaping policy and politicians involved in routine administration. This is going too far, but there is ample evidence to support Lee's observations on Cheshire County Council: 'Everyone knows that the orthodox doctrine of elected representatives deciding policy and paid officials executing orders no longer fits the facts of local government'.[41] According to Self, councillors need to acquire a wide range of administrative and political skills: 'a fair understanding of the complex processes of technical management, of relations with central government departments, and of the views and assumptions of principal officers; they need to be tolerably numerate, literate and industrious'.[42]

This admixture of politics and expertise is found in the committee system of local government, where separate roles are less distinguishable than in the full Council. Although officials prepare reports and make recommendations and councillors debate and make decisions, this formal process is overlain by discussion of procedures and policy by both councillors and officials on a broadly equal basis. The critical relationship is that between committee chairman and chief officer, for they will discuss proposals and tactics prior to meetings and, usually, enjoy a close working relationship.[43] They possess the information and draw together the external influences — developers, party politics, interest groups, government advice etc. — which propitiate particular courses of action. Dunleavy's observations on the salience of the chairman-chief officer relationship are typical: 'Overwhelmingly the chief officer-chairman nexus dominated interviewees' accounts of decision making, and back-benchers seem to have accepted or occasionally criticised but rarely directly opposed their proposals.'[44] This dependence of committee members on the leadership of the chairman is the key to committee decision taking. 'The chairman seems to be a crucial figure in so far as many committee members rely on him to keep a close watch over committee business and to take firm action if necessary.'[45]

The committee system may be characterised by the term, 'administrative politics'.[46] The sifting of information, the rejection of certain alternatives and critical negotiations are conducted within the bureaucratic machine, and between chairman and officials prior to public debate in committee. This system represents a concentration of information and power that subverts, to a degree, the concept of open and democratic decision making. Hill notes the tendency: 'Administrative politics is a paternalistic style of government in which much crucial decision making occurs without any scrutiny by the electorate. It involves a system in which élite influence may be very significant, and yet be unnoticed'.[47] In the London Brick case meetings were held between the chairman, vice-chairman and the company at crucial points. London Brick even made a direct appeal to the committee.

A group of committee members negotiated the Section 52 Agreement. Keith White's influence over his fellow Conservatives on the committee was substantial, to the extent that one of his adherents felt it necessary to proclaim, 'Councillor White is not my Svengali'.

It was an influence clearly recognised by opponents. Philip Hendry sensed the inequality of power and influence he faced. 'Initially, the strength against us was a David and Goliath situation. LBC, the officers, and the committee were all against us. We were asking "Is anyone for us?" '

Although he managed to bring the issue into the open, the triumph of pluralistic politics was short-lived and administrative politics was able to reassert its influence. Philip Hendry clearly understood:

> ESC used the back door method. One thing that held firm all the way along was the committee support — Keith [White] commands a lot of support; and the structure of the ESC, the monthly meetings, the working groups, mean that members are working together, meeting regularly and therefore get a tight bond to the committee. When they were overridden twice by the Council their pride was at stake and they used a process of the Council to get their way.[48]

Not surprisingly, Keith White made a spirited defence of the committee's role:

> I believe that an issue of this complexity would be better not dealt with by the Council. ESC is geared to deal with such an issue, in depth and over a period of time. The members understood the issue. Not all the 83 members of the Council had sufficient information to make the decision.

He considered the committee's decision to grant a permission at Ridgmont without reference to the Council was fully justified.

> I emphasise it was the committee and not I that had taken the Ridgmont decision — it was an expression of loyalty to me I believe, and a belief that the Council had come to the wrong decision, based entirely on personality, and not based on the facts that the committee knew and understood so well.[49]

In these statements by the major adversaries on the Council, opposing views of administrative politics are encapsulated. It is regarded by the one as a somewhat sinister denial of pluralist politics, by the other as the desirable means for ensuring fully informed decision making. What, in effect, both are acknowledging is the existence of separate decision making arenas to which different interests have access.

The idea of administrative politics recognises that the formal separation of functions is suffused by interchangeability of roles. Politicians are seen not as mere ciphers, administering bureaucratic ends, but as actors in partnership with officials. The model explains much of what goes on in local government. The fact that, for a while, power seemed to be wrested from the confines of administrative politics and vested in the more open, politically uncertain, realm of the full Council, is a significant feature of this case. There is a duality here between environmental influence dependent on outside pressures operating through Council members, and the company exerting its influence from the inside on the committee. It suggests a further proposition:

Environmental influences draw their strength from external pressures exerted on pluralist forms of decision making. Business influence exploits the system of 'administrative politics' in which privileged access is legitimated by the interaction of politics and expertise.

It may be argued that the forces were evenly matched, that the eventual outcome was determined by unpredictable changes in political and economic circumstances. The company was supported on the outside by the unions and on the inside by the officials and the ESC acting within the framework of administrative politics. The environmentalists, orchestrated by pressure groups outside the Council and with considerable support within the Council, appealed over the heads of the committee. So far we have only focused on the conflict between environment and economy in the context of the specific situation in local politics. If we widen our attention and bring in the local–national and time–space dimensions we are forced, however unwillingly, to acknowledge the imbalance of power that existed. Placed in this broader context the complex, intangible and idiosyncratic history of new brickworks in Bedfordshire takes on a more intelligible and inevitable appearance.

Local versus national

Central government exercises considerable influence, even control, over local government, and the acceleration of this trend has been a theme of recent research.[50] Some see the trend as decisive, the loss of local autonomy and the denial of the concept of representative local government. The trend is particularly evident in those areas which are affected by spending controls such as education and social services. In the case of planning, which influences the location of investment in development, central power is exercised by the Minister, through his endorsement of development plans, and his quasi-judicial role in deciding appeals. Recognition of the powers of central government is an important component in business strategies since it provides companies with a second line of defence if they fail to secure agreement at local level.

A trend, noted by several commentators, has been for big business to vacate its political role in local government, leaving its place to be filled by small businesses and commerce who swell the ranks of local Conservative politicians.[51] The surrender of influence may, however, be more apparent than real. As Bealey comments: 'They may decide to influence local politics "behind the scenes" for example, by withdrawing their local investments: or they may decide there is much more to be gained by trying to alter local conditions by operating at national level.'[52]

London Brick certainly nurtured its local influence but its local support was not pervasive. The rupture in Conservative ranks expressed not only the environment–economy cleavage, but also differing attitudes on the relation of national to local policies. Whereas environmentalists urged pollution control in the local interest, supporters of the company linked the issues of employment and environment together, and recognised the power of central government to impose a solution if local agreement could not be found. That solution was likely to be less sensitive to local environmental needs, and at a public inquiry the Minister would be bound to give full support to the tall chimneys advocated by the Alkali Inspector. The lack of proven alternative technologies was also clear. The environmentalists failed to acknowledge that, faced with a public inquiry, their position would become indefensible.

Although environmentalists might be unwilling to recognise it, the support of central government for the company was clear. This support might initially be explained in terms of the national interest for cheap bricks, so clearly identified in the early planning permissions. By the time of the conflict support was expressed in more general terms, with the need to facilitate investment by a significant private enterprise. Central government officials and ministers neither saw the need, nor possessed the desire, to intervene in a local political conflict. They may have assumed that the issue would ultimately be resolved in the company's favour, but, in any case, they were aware that the company had investment options and the Minister could, at any time, use his power to 'call in' the application, or if required, determine it on appeal. The Minister, backed by advice from the Alkali Inspector, research opinion and a report prepared by his own department (all of which endorsed the planning permission), could afford to adopt a passive stance, content in the knowledge that if agreement could not be found at first, then ultimately the investment could not be thwarted. His general support for the proposals was quite clear. 'Certainly I do not consider there is at present sufficient evidence of damage to justify more stringent — and potentially very costly — measures by industry.'[53] From his viewpoint the local conflict seemed to have marginal significance.

There is an apparent dualism in the contrasting attitudes of central and local governments. On the one hand there is a community of interest between business and central government, on the other hand intense conflict between business and environmental interests at local level. This has led Saunders to propose the 'dual state' thesis.[54] In essence this thesis argues that the central state's primary function is social investment in support of capital accumulation. It performs this through corporatist strategies, the exclusive bargaining between major interests, such as business and labour, which focus on production issues using quasi-representative agencies at regional and national level. As a result 'crucial economic policies not only are increasingly determined outside the competitive sector of politics, but they are also increasingly removed from local control'.[55]

The primary function of local government is social consumption. At this level interests are mediated through competitive politics. This suggests the hypothesis that 'local political processes can to a large extent be explained . . . by a pluralist theoretical perspective which recognises that political outcomes are likely to reflect the relative weight of effective preferences, as articulated through shifting political alliances between different consumption sectors in the population'.[56] Conceived in this way the state's ability to cope with conflicting pressures becomes explicable:

> Thus, it may be suggested that the reason why the state (viewed as a whole) appears both to act in the long term interests of capital and to respond to the demands of other groups in the population is that social investment policies are typically developed at national level in close consultation with capitalist interests within corporate state agencies, while social consumption policies are relatively responsive to local popular pressures exerted on and through representative state agencies.[57]

At national level corporatism is 'a politico-economic system in which the state directs the activities of predominantly privately-owned industry in partnership with the representatives of a limited number of singular, compulsory, noncompetitive, hierarchically ordered and functionally differentiated interest groups'.[58] This notion of corporatism is ambiguous in that it 'is variously used to refer to an ideology, a process, or a strategy'.[59] It appeals to élitists with its idea of exclusive participation and to marxists with its suggestions of collusion between state and capital. What is clear is that corporatism is seen as a burgeoning, pervasive mode of government threatening pluralistic institutions: 'The competitive role of interest groups — which is held to safeguard the democratic nature of pluralism — will be replaced by an orderly, cooperative and stable relationship'.[60] Neo-pluralists might claim that corporatism is merely another way of expressing interest representation in the modern administrative state.

The dual state is presented as an ideal type, it is not a simple dichotomy. It is possible to recognise elements of corporatism which have percolated into environmental policy making at local level. Local planning authorities are dependent on the initiatives of developers for the implementation of plans. They may refuse permission (though they may lose on appeal, or the development may go elsewhere) but they cannot ensure it takes place. This lack of positive power has encouraged planners to collaborate with developers. There is growing evidence that planners have entered into a corporatist relationship with the private sector. There is close consultation in the creation of structure plans, strategic planning proposals for counties, and a tendency, noted by Flynn,[61] for industrial interests to gain greater influence, resulting in plans for economic expansion as against the more conservationist policies that typified the initial structure plans.[62] More directly planners enter into legal agreements with industry in which certain planning gains are secured in return for the grant of planning permission. These bargains are forged in secret, suggesting a corporatist approach in which 'developers and planners are likely to develop shared perspectives as to which things are in "the public interest" and which are not'.[63]

There is considerable evidence of corporatism in London Brick's relationship with local planners and politicians. The company was consulted in the preparation of the Structure Plan and the Minerals Subject Plan. Although the company was criticised, its interests were safeguarded in these plans, and there was even a policy protecting potential clay deposits within an area extending well beyond the existing brickfields. The development of the Section 52 Agreement is a clear example of the bargaining process between business and government which is the characteristic of corporatism. These corporatist elements represent an extension of the informal process of administrative politics which confers and legitimates the privileged access of business interests in local government. Backed by the support of corporatist agencies of central government, such as the Alkali Inspectorate, and the tacit endorsement of its plans by ministers the company was in a relatively secure position. Whereas environmental interests had limited appeal beyond the boundaries of Bedfordshire, London

Brick could command the support of state agencies at central and local level. The example suggests a modified version of the dual state thesis. Whereas social consumption policies are developed at local level through competitive politics, social investment policies are elaborated through corporatist strategies which penetrate both national *and* local levels.

There is a further feature of the case which emphasises the relative power of business. This is the influence of information. Although the relevance and direction of research was contestable, the major official agencies were prepared to give unequivocal backing to the company's position. The Alkali Inspector was convinced there was no health hazard from the pollutants, and insisted there was no practicable alternative to tall chimneys as a means of pollution abatement. Official medical research opinion, provided by Professor Lawther of the Medical Research Council's Toxicology Unit, dismissed the pollution hazards and was backed up by the local Area Health Authority's Dr. Lobban. Warren Springs, the government research establishment responsible for monitoring pollution, was also satisfied there was no problem. The much awaited Department of the Environment report was substantially a reworking of existing evidence. An official admitted that 'information just isn't available. The quality of the data varies enormously'. Nonetheless the report felt able to conclude, without much qualification, that fears about human health were unfounded. Its views on crop and animal damage were more circumspect, indeed it could hardly contradict the evidence gleaned by another government agency, the Rothamsted Experimental Station, which revealed by experiment considerable yield losses in vulnerable crops. The DoE report, hardly surprisingly, was taken as a vindication of the company's application. It was clear that the company would receive overwhelming support from the agencies of government should it ever have to defend its application at a public inquiry. The notion, fostered by the environmental lobby, that a public inquiry held by a DoE appointed Inspector advising a Minister of the Environment could take a different view requires a heroic leap of imagination.

Information was not, however, just a government and industry monopoly, nor did it all point in quite the same direction. Although much of the information culled and broadcast by the environmentalists was circumstantial, or inapplicable to the particular case, they could point to the local anxieties aroused much earlier by the Ministry of Agriculture report on cattle fluorosis and the Brothwood report, on the health effects of brickmaking in the Marston Vale. More relevantly, the compendious Cremer and

Warner report undertaken by independent consultants, though guarded, acknowledged potential health hazards and, initially, urged deferral of the applications.

What is striking is the way in which such information was used. The various government agencies, despite an admittedly fragile scientific assessment, were prepared to offer the weight of scientific judgement in favour of the company. It was tantamount to asserting that absence of evidence to the contrary was confirmation that there was no danger. The Cremer and Warner report could not easily be gainsaid. But, the Alkali Inspectorate maintained that its findings were similar to the DoE's, and London Brick published a Press release purporting to show that Cremer and Warner substantiated its case that there was no health hazard. They then proceeded to demolish the report's claims that pollution control measures were available. The planning officials used the Cremer and Warner report to negotiate a part permission and then persuaded its authors to back their recommendation, despite the report's argument that permission should be deferred or refused. By contrast, the environmentalists saw the Cremer and Warner report as a substantial endorsement of their concerns, ignoring the fact that the report emphasised odours rather than fluorides as the main problem.

It is quite impossible to make an objective assessment of the research evidence on pollution. The dangers of sulphur dioxide were well researched. Although levels in Bedfordshire were abnormally high for a rural area, the hazard was thought to be reduced by the lack of particulates in the atmosphere. There was general acceptance that the hazards had been reduced in urban areas by the Clean Air Act, and it was also acknowledged that local levels would be generally reduced as a result of tall chimneys. But much less was known about the dangers of short term peaks occurring in the brickfields. There was also concern that tall chimneys would increase the possibility of pollution being exported, to be precipitated as 'acid rain' in Scandinavia. The risks from fluoride were less well researched and, for that reason, increased monitoring of fluoride emissions was proposed and eventually undertaken. Even more problematic were the synergistic effects of pollutants acting in combination. In a situation where the 'problem' was defined or denied on the basis of inadequate and inconclusive research, the dangers were a matter for speculation, and the case against the company remained unproven. While such speculation might impress local environmentalists and their political sympathisers it carried much less weight at national level where opinion, advice and attitudes favoured the industry. An issue that was, whether justified or not, important in the local context was singularly unimportant in those theatres which would have a decisive effect on the outcome in the long run.

Three points are evident concerning the role of information in the conflict. One is that scientific evidence is heavily concentrated in the hands of government agencies and industry. Information on pollution levels is often undertaken, as in this case, by industry. The government, through the Alkali Inspectorate, is thus engaged in a process whereby evidence provided by industry is circulated through its agencies, who, not surprisingly, find in favour of the industry. It is a circular and closed process, hidden from public view, and depends on an unhealthily close relationship between government and industry, in which industry provides the evidence used in its defence. The second point is that scientific evidence is controversial and inconclusive. Science, as Bartlett observes, 'at best, provides not proof but merely strong inference'.[64] The third point is that, even in those cases where effort is made to gather disinterested expertise, the findings are used selectively to support this or that position. Hence the carefully qualified conclusions of the Cremer and Warner report were transformed by the Alkali Inspector, London Brick and the environmental lobby from matters of opinion to statements of political fact.

The local–national dimension, applied to this case study, suggests an imbalance of power between economic and environmental influences. It points to a further development of conclusions already reached:

Whereas environmental interests tend to exploit competitive politics, business interests are transmitted through corporatist strategies at both central and local government levels. A feature of this corporatism is the concentration, control and selection of information which further enhances business power.

The evidence of this case cannot be taken as conclusive. There are examples of environmental interests acting on a broader national front, able to apply influence at national level. This is particularly the case with proposals for nuclear power stations, though, even here, the planning inquiry system tends to be confined to specific site discussions. What I think we can say is that the power of business, promoted by the privileged access provided by administrative politics, confirmed by the support of corporatist strategies at local and national level, buttressed by the weight of scientific opinion, is consummated when placed in the broader context of time and space.

Time and Place

One of the problems with current theories is that they tend to neglect temporal and spatial factors, or, at best, assume that change is continuous over time. The London Brick case demonstrates that the balance between economic and environmental interests shifted over time. Viewed over time it is clear there were periods when the company was on the defensive, followed by periods when it was aggressive. There was, it is true, a gradually developing opposition, promoted by increasing awareness of environmental values. It was not a continuous process, however, since economic forces were able to retaliate. There appears, as we have seen, to have been an inverse correlation between the commercial environmental challenges. This iterative process whereby first one, then the other, of the opposing forces gains acendancy has led Vogel to make the following general observation from his study of trends in environmental politics in the United States. 'Instead of endlessly debating the power of business in the abstract or focusing on the outcomes of particular policy disputes, political scientists need to pay more attention to the processes by which the power of business as a whole varies over time.'[65]

Similarly, the relative power of environmental and economic forces varies from place to place. Indeed, where a company is not tied to a specific resource or other locational need it is highly likely that it will enjoy considerable freedom. If it fails to succeed in one location it can shift elsewhere. This locational flexibility places enormous bargaining power at the disposal of major companies, and multinational corporations have been adept at manipulating varying political circumstances in their favour. But, even in a case such as London Brick, a medium sized company, dominated by a single product, predominantly based in the United Kingdom and tied to a specific resource, certain locations offered a more propitious political environment for investment than others. The changes in the balance of power in Bedfordshire over time and the contrast between the situation in Bedfordshire and neighbouring counties requires explanation. In particular it raises the question why there was so much conflict in one area at a particular time and an absence of conflict in another.

The conflict did not suddenly explode in Bedfordshire in 1978. The grounds for conflict had been evident on a number of occasions, notably the Brickfields Conference, the Woburn Sands Inquiry and the debate on the Structure Plan. These debates indicated a gradually developing shift in values with both general and local components. In general the growth of environmental concern reflected a growing belief that, in a more affluent society, cheap production should not be achieved at the expense of amenity and public health. Locally, the shift in values partly represented a changing population structure. The importance of brickmaking in the county's economy had declined, fewer people were directly dependent on the industry, and the rapid growth in the county's population included a substantial adventitious and environmentally sensitive component. Areas such as Aspley Guise and Woburn Sands at the southern end of Marston Vale, and Cranfield in the centre, had grown rapidly, and their middle class residents could be quickly mobilised in support of environmental issues.[66] The contrast between planning permissions granted at a time of national concern about brick production just after the Second World War, and the more sophisticated controls demanded of industry in the more affluent, environmentally conscious circumstances of 30 years later was stark. The discordance was potentially explosive, it wanted but an opportunity which was presented at the end of the 1970s by the redevelopment plan.

It was not simply a clash between different value systems representing different epochs. The company fully recognised the shift in public attitudes and attempted to accommodate them in the various environmental improvements it offered in its package deal. Nor was the shift in one direction. The company's ability to resist controls, and its eventual success in gaining a permission largely on its own terms illustrates the resilience of economic forces in fighting off environmental pressures, especially during a recession. However, the fierce contest in Bedfordshire was not paralleled elsewhere. In Cambridgeshire the issue was low key for all the reasons advanced in Chapter 5. The explanation for the scale and significance of the conflict in Bedfordshire lies in the conjunction of political and economic circumstances at a particular point in time. The potential for conflict was inherent; it was released when environmental interests succeeded in promoting the issue and encouraged local political leaders to take it up. It became, as we have seen, as much a test of political virility and a contest of power, in which victory was as important for itself as for the fruits it had won.

Looked at in specific terms, the Bedfordshire case, as we have seen, is open to alternative interpretations which reflect different ideological viewpoints. Pluralists would stress the role of local circumstances and individual leadership in articulating and accommodating conflicting interests. The environmental interests urge the merits of conservation and freedom from pollution against business interests, which promote economic growth and improved working conditions. An alternative view is that it was a contest between élites. The environmentalists were not challenging industry primarily on behalf of consumers (though there was a convenient alliance with a wider constituency of protest), but seeking to avoid those undesirable aspects of industrial activity which affected farming and the environment of affluent communities. They could protest on behalf of a national public interest in order to safeguard their specific material interests. London Brick was more concerned to protect its investment than to improve the position of its workers.

This protection of specific interests suggests a wider interpretation based on concepts of class interest. There appears to be a systematic suppression of those issues which affect the real interests of the less privileged. In Bedfordshire, throughout the period 1978-81, the London Brick case dominated the local political stage. The time devoted to it absorbed energies that could not be spent on other issues of more direct relevance to underprivileged groups such as education, public transport and social services. These were policy areas over which the County Council had more control, and which were more important in terms of real interests to more people than an esoteric debate over pollution whose outcome would be largely determined elsewhere. There are a limited number of issues that can command attention, and the agenda tends to be fixed by those with most political clout. Pollution and amenity are issues of collective consumption which appeal to the already privileged who know how to make their presence felt. Other issues of collective consumption which appeal largely to underprivileged groups, such as council house rents, or bus services, or nursery education, may give rise to protest but it is protest which, as Saunders has shown in his Croydon case study, can be diverted, coopted or simply excluded. The idea that urban protest movements can cohere around issues of collective consumption and become effective weapons in the class war, as inferred by Castells, seems exceedingly unlikely in the British context. Far more likely is a condition of acceptance, of fatalism and a belief in the futility of action. It is a question of power. 'Power seems to create power. Powerlessness serves to reinforce powerlessness. Power relations, once established, are self-sustaining.'[67] With Balbus we may feel that 'there is something fundamentally wrong with a polity in which events of major social importance, i.e. events which dramatically affect the life chances of millions of individuals, do not become "political affairs" and hence the subject of collective decision making'.[68]

That the pollution issue was important to environmentalists who fomented the conflict can scarcely be doubted. But the company, looking at it over a wider time and space horizon, was not unduly discomfited by the opposition it had provoked over its Bedfordshire plans. The conflict was no doubt irritating, but London Brick had always hinted that it was relatively insignificant when taken in the context of the options open to it. At one point James Bristow claimed: 'Frankly, we are getting bored with the issue. It's getting to the stage when we shall say we won't do anything. We are seriously considering withdrawing the application'.[69] The company toyed with the idea of an appeal but its attitude remained ambiguous. After his company's defeat at the July 1980 Council meeting, Bristow commented 'We have no course but to appeal; but it's too early to say'. Veiled hints about appeal or investment withdrawal suggested the company was well aware of its potential leverage. It fully recognised the opportunity to divide and rule, using its strong position in Cambridgeshire as a bargaining counter in Bedfordshire. Government support, investment options and the desperation of the unions in time brought the desired result. At worst, from the company's viewpoint, the conflict was frustrating and might cause it to review its investment priorities. But at no stage can it be said the company stood in any danger of defeat on its overall investment strategy even if, as a result of the actions of local politicians and pressure groups, it might have lost a specific battle in Bedfordshire.

Once we place the Bedfordshire conflict in a broader context the idea of the dual state reinforcing corporate power is compelling. Throughout, the environmentalist cause, despite efforts to involve local MPs, government ministers and the Scandinavian countries, was substantially confined to the level of local politics. London Brick had a much broader base of support, with extant permissions in two other counties and central government backing. The central authorities could afford to let the local debate take its course, resulting in some amelioration of dereliction, so long as the company's investment plans were not, ultimately, thwarted. It is an illustration of the operation of the dual state as described by Clegg:

> Through a division of powers and functions between levels of government, social investment decisions and corporate mechanisms tend to be located within regional or national agencies removed from the influence of electoral politics. Social consumption will continue to be treated at the local level, which usually means that the extent and quality of social provisions can be indirectly controlled by the financial and administrative restrictions imposed by higher levels.[70]

London Brick's power at both national and local levels was formidable. At central level, support for industry was a basic tenet of economic strategy. At local level, the need for jobs and wealth creation was a practical and tangible counter to emotional and intangible appeals for cleaner air and a more attractive environment. London Brick could argue its case in both local and national interests, and rely on a powerful coalition of interests deeply committed to its progress. For a time the fundamental weakness in the environmentalist's case was hidden by the belief that new works and pollution control at source were compatible goals. Once the problem of jobs became paramount the case collapsed.

In one sense, both sides had won and lost. The company had won its permission, and this was an asset that could be cashed or traded at a later date when economic conditions improved. The environmentalists had achieved modified permissions beyond what the company had initially offered, bringing the prospect of some improvement in the appearance of the Marston Vale. The company had forfeited its investment and the workers their jobs, though as a result of recession rather than opposition. The environmentalists had failed to achieve pollution control at source, their major objective. The intensity of their opposition may have been counterproductive in preventing an earlier start on investment either at Stewartby or Ridgmont. A conflict which had forced itself from the confines of administrative politics into the public and pluralistic arena of the County Council had achieved remarkably little, and may quite possibly have harmed the long term economic interests of the county in which it was fought. This was certainly the view expressed by Keith White:

> For LBC some may say the outcome was not unreasonable. LBC needed more. Every commercial concern then and now needed to open up options. LBC decided to process applications in all areas, to be in a position to consider what was available to them. They declared the conditions imposed were too stringent. History will show we were too hard on LBC and were overtaken by time. If it hadn't been protest led there would have been a decision sooner and the planning permission given could have been put into effect by LBC. We lost time . . . the delay could certainly have altered their plans.[71]

It appears that environmental and economic interests vary over time according to changing values and economic circumstances. Variations in political circumstances from place to place provide business with investment options which strengthens its power to resist and defeat local environmental opposition.

Conclusions

In the previous chapter the pluralist, élitist and structuralist perspectives were each examined against the case of London Brick. It was tentatively concluded that each contributed something to an explanation of the course of the conflict and its outcomes. At that point any definitive conclusions on their validity was suspended. In this chapter the evidence was once again examined, this time by introducing mediating concepts to try to gain a more detailed fit between the empirical evidence and theoretical constructs. Recent theoretical developments, such as the identification of corporatist tendencies in the relationship of capital to the state and the idea of the dual state, were introduced. What remains is to see whether these conceptual developments help to enhance our understanding of the case and whether they enable any firmer conclusions to be made about the applicability of the theoretical perspectives previously outlined. The problems encountered in attempting to fit an empirical case to theoretical perspectives are severe, and amply demonstrate the conceptual inadequacies and contradictions facing social science research at the present time. Nonetheless it is possible to draw from this case a number of features which confirm existing work and which suggest some modifications of existing assumptions.

One way of summarising our findings is to relate the various concepts discussed in this chapter in the form of a matrix (Figure 7.1). The matrix is constructed so that the economy–environment issue is expressed in terms of the other three pairs of concepts. From the diagram it is evident that environmental and economic issues possess different trajectories as they pass through the political and decision making processes, and are transformed into policy outcomes. The first column expresses the political processes encountered. Environmental issues tend to attract a diversity of interests, which set up pressures imposed on decision makers. These interests are consulted and participate in the development of land use planning strategies. Indeed, in many cases they may affect the political tone of development plans, many of which have a conservationist, low growth philosophy. In a sense, environmental issues are exposed in a version of politics characterised by a participative, open and representative polity. In the London Brick case this was represented in the debate, which eventually involved a wide range of participants and was arbitrated by the whole County Council. But, as we have seen, environmental interests are motivated by groups who enjoy the access necessary to press their case on decision makers. In the competition for attention they are likely to succeed. Thus pluralist politics becomes a vehicle at the disposal of groups anxious, in part, to protect vested interests. The constitution of these groups into an élite, in the strict sense of the term, bound together by consciousness, coherence and conspiracy may be doubted. It is clear, for example, that the

Figure 7.1

Issues	[1] Politics/Expertise *Political Process*	[2] Local/National *Decision making strategies*	[3] Time/Space *Outcomes*
Environment	Exploitation of pluralist polity to secure positional values	Social consumption issues the focus of local protest and conflict	Outcomes reflect local circumstances
Economy	Administrative politics – interaction of politics and expertise promotes business interests	Social investment issues developed by corporatist strategies at local and national levels	Temporal and spatial variations ensure outcomes favourable to business

political process was not impenetrable, as the ability of the trade unions to make their case with the politicians makes clear.

The economic interests of developers such as London Brick are usually channelled through the process of administrative politics. They naturally possess access to officials, with whom they may discuss their application in secret and indulge in a mutual bargaining process. Planning officials become mediators between popular pressures for environmental controls or benefits and the insistence of developers that such controls are either not feasible or too costly. Planners profess expertise when in fact they are making assessments, often subjective, as to where acceptable compromises might lie. Political pressures are brought to bear through the chairman and committee members, who also come to recognise and accept the limitations imposed by the developer. There emerges a collaborative, cooperative relationship between developer, officials and politicians which provides outputs in the form of recommendations and agreements for endorsement. Although the relationship precludes direct participation by other interests it does not deny the influence of workers through the company, or of environmentalists through the political participants. Thus, although the combatants use different political processes, they cannot be regarded as mutually exclusive.

This tendency for different, but interconnected, political channels to be employed by the different interests is further expressed in the decision making process (col.2.). Here the distinction is made between social consumption and social investment–decision making processes put forward in the dual state thesis. Environmental issues comprise amenity and public health. Unlike other collective consumption goods, these are not directly provided by the state, but state intervention through land use planning and pollution control policies is essential if amenity is to be conserved and health improved. And, unlike some issues of collective consumption, an attractive and healthy environment is not restricted to certain classes of consumers, but is of general benefit. Any deterioration in the environment through dereliction or dirty air elicits protest. The very depth of appeal of environmental causes ensures that protest can be mobilised, particularly by those, usually more privileged, who, having already secured the necessities of life, have most to lose by any deterioration in environmental conditions.

Economic issues, particularly the creation of better working conditions or security of employment, appeal more strongly to the working class. Although workers are in conflict with employers over the distribution of the wealth created by industry, they have little choice but to make common cause with business interests against environmental pressures in defence of their livelihood. Economic issues are issues of social investment, and at national level the corporatist strategies pursued by government, industry and trade unions have been identified by several writers.

Corporatist tendencies exist at local level too, particularly where industry confronts environmental opposition. The idea of the dual state is useful in identifying contrasts between strategies for determining issues of social investment from those of consumption. It must be seen in a context of increasing centralisation, however, in which national and local decision making interact. Social investment policies are developed at local as well as national level and show vestiges of corporatism in local government. Certainly it would appear that the corporatist tendencies inherent in administrative politics are pervasive at local level, where economic and environmental issues are in conflict. Conversely, environmental issues are not simply confined at local level but are able (though not in this case) to impinge on national policy making. Otherwise it would be difficult to see how any general environmental improvements, such as those achieved by the national Clean Air Act for example, could ever take effect.

Turning to column 3 in Figure 7.1 we see that the dimensions of time and place need to be included to provide an adequate explanation of the outcomes of a conflict between environment and economy. If the focus is on the specific case, such as London Brick's applications in Bedfordshire, then the conflict played out — between environmentalists employing pluralist politics, and business pursuing economic goals through the administrative politics of local corporatism — may indeed be uncertain in outcome. As was suggested in the previous chapter, circumstances may favour first one interest then the other. So long as the company's investment priorities remained firm the opposition could maintain its attack with impunity. In this case it was probably unlikely that the environmentalists could have persisted in denying the company the permission it sought. At any time the company could appeal, or it could bide its time, withdraw its application and try a new one. Causes swept on by emotional waves can as easily evaporate. There were signs during the conflict of shifting allegiances, and the election in 1981 in any case caused a massive turnover of membership of the County Council.[72] A strong Labour Group was unlikely to be able to ignore union pressure, as their predecessors had done, and Conservatives were increasingly conscious of the plight of industry in the recession.

In this case when we look further afield it becomes clear that the environmental cause, building on shifting political and economic sands, was doomed. In other counties London Brick already had permissions, and government support was waiting in the wings. The excitement, the theatre and the expectation built up in Bedfordshire was in reality a sideshow, and even marginal to the course of London Brick's progress. For, over and above the conflict, forces were at work which rendered the ambitions of the environmentalists futile and the eventual triumph of London Brick (pyrrhic though it might have been) seemingly inevitable.

This conclusion is one that tends to support a structuralist position. It is a conclusion that admits the possibility of alternative explanations, and acknowledges pluralist and élitist elements. Without the pluralist politics available to the environmentalists the issue would probably never have been stirred, as indeed it was not stirred in neighbouring counties. Pluralist politics are important as a safeguard, a safety valve, from time to time exposing issues and overturning the process of non-decision making by which issues remain hidden. Elements of élitist explanations are also evident in this case. Elitism suggests exclusiveness, the ability of the powerful to dominate the agenda of decision making, the denial of other, less privileged interests. Both élitism and pluralism emphasise the importance of actors, and focus on the locality as 'the key focus of influence and decision making'.[73] This is a strength in that it forces us to recognise that individual and group action is important and cannot simply be discounted. But it is also a weakness in that it neglects the wider context which prescribes the constraints and the opportunities available to local decision makers.

Structuralism offers a more general and, perhaps more satisfactory explanation of the events in Bedfordshire and surrounding counties between 1978-81. It exposes the real interests at stake, the dependence of the workers on the company, and the ability of the company to achieve its goals despite an apparently powerful and implacable opposition. Structuralism provides an explanation which, ranging over time and space, relates the individual event to the scheme of underlying processes. However, the play was not yet over. The belief of politicians and pressure groups that their actions could affect the course of history ensured that the outcome, in Bedfordshire at least, was not a foregone conclusion.

Notes

1 See Dunleavy, P. (1982) 'Perspectives on urban studies' in Blowers, A. et al (1982) (eds) *Urban Change and Conflict*, London, Harper and Row.

2 Among the important contributions to the debate are the following, which have been cited at various points:
Castells, M. (1977) *The Urban Question*, London, Arnold; (1978) *City, Class and Power*, London, Macmillan; Saunders, P. (1979) *Urban Politics*, Harmondsworth, Penguin; Dunleavy, P. (1980) *Urban Political Analysis*, London, Macmillan.

3 Dunleavy, P. (1982) op. cit. p.1.

4 Elliott, B. and McCrone, D. (1982) *The City; Patterns of domination and conflict*, London, Macmillan.

5 Ibid, p.16.

6 The concept of urban protest movements (or urban social movements, or, simply, urban movements), was introduced by Castells (see note 2) and has been a consistent theme of neo-marxist accounts of urban processes.

7 O'Connor, J. (1973) *The Fiscal Crisis of the State*, New York, St. Martin's Press.

8 Clegg for example, points out that public transport functions to support both production and consumption processes. Clegg, T. (1982) 'Social consumption, social investment and the dual state: the case of transport policy in the Paris region', paper for the Political Studies Association, Canterbury.

9 Pahl, R. (1977) '"Collective consumption" and the state in capitalist and state socialist societies', in Scase, R. (ed) *Industrial Society: aspects of class, cleavage and control*, London, Allen and Unwin, Chapter 9, p.160.

10 Examples of protest over housing issues will be found in Castells, M. (1978) op. cit. Chapter 5. Coing, H. (1966) *Renovation urbaine et changement social*, Paris, (ed) Ouvrières; Olives, J. (1976) 'The struggle against urban renewal in the Cité d'Aliarte (Paris), in Pickvance (ed) *Urban Sociology; critical essays*, London, Tavistock, pp.174-97.

11 Kirk, G. (1980) *Urban Planning in a Capitalist Society*, London, Croom Helm, p.63.

12 Gaventa, J. (1980) *Power and Powerlessness: quiescence and rebellion in an Appalachian valley*, Urbana, University of Illinois Press, pp.238-9.

13 Lipset, S. M. (1981) 'Whatever happened to the proletariat?' *Encounter*, June, pp. 18-34.

14 Goodin, R. (1975) *The Politics of Rational Man*, London, Wiley.

15 Jones, C. (1975) *Clean Air: the policies and politics of pollution control*, Pittsburgh, University of Pittsburgh Press, p.140.

16 Castells, M. (1978) op. cit. p.159.

17 Newby, H. (1980) *Green and Pleasant Land?*, Harmondsworth, Penguin.

18 See, for example, Sandbach, F. (1980) *Environment, Ideology and Policy*, Oxford, Blackwells; Stretton, H. (1976) *Capitalism, Socialism and the Environment*, Cambridge University Press; Schnaiberg, A. (1980) *The Environment: from surplus to scarcity*, Oxford University Press; O'Riordan, T. (1976) *Environmentalism*, London, Pion Press.

19 Gregory, R. (1971) *The Price of Amenity*, London, Macmillan, p.103.

20 Crosland, A. (1974) *Socialism Now*, pp.77-8.

21 Miliband, R. (1973) *The State in Capitalist Society*, London, Quartet Books, Chapter 6.

22 Interview with Bryan Keens of the Transport and General Workers Union, 16 June, 1981.
23 Speaker at meeting at Marston Moretaine, 16 March, 1981.
24 Self, P. (1972) *Administrative Theories and Politics*, London, George Allen and Unwin, p.186.
25 Ibid, p.151.
26 Westergaard, J. and Resler, H. (1975), *Class in a Capitalist Society*, London, Heinemann, p.248.
27 Interview with Philip Hendry, 27 October, 1982.
28 Keith White's speech to meeting of County Council, 18 December, 1980, see Chapter 5, pp.73-74.
29 For example, Michels, R. (1915) *Political Parties*, New York, Free Press 1959; Hindess, B. (1971) *The Decline of Working Class Politics*, London, MacGibbon and Kee.
30 Hindess, B. (1971) op. cit. p.130.
31 Councillor Farley at meeting with trade unions, 18 February, 1981.
32 Michels, R. (1915) op. cit.; Weber, M. (1947) *The Theory of Social and Economic Organisations*, New York, Free Press.
33 Miliband, R. (1969) op. cit.; Self, P. (1972) op. cit.; Hill, M. J. (1972) *The Sociology of Public Administration*, London, Weidenfeld and Nicholson; Hill, D. M. (1974) *Democratic Theory and Local Government*, London, Allen and Unwin.
34 Braybrooke, D. and Lindblom, C. E. (1963) *A Strategy of Decision*, New York, Free Press, p.79.
35 Hill, D. M. (1974) op. cit. p.88.
36 Dunleavy, P. (1981) *The Politics of Mass Housing in Britain*, Oxford, Clarendon Press, pp.187-88.
37 Reade, E. (1982) 'Officers and councillors, "facts" and "values"', paper presented to Urban and Regional Studies Unit, University of Kent, Canterbury, p.12.
38 Reade, E. (1976) 'An attempt to distinguish planning from other modes of decision making', Seminar paper, University of Manchester, 24 November, pp.8-9.
39 Davidoff, P. and Reiner, A. (1962) 'A choice theory of planning', *Journal of the American Institute of Planners*, vol.28, May.
40 Wildavsky, A. (1973) 'If planning is everything, maybe it's nothing', *Journal of Policy Sciences*, vol.4, No.2, pp.127-153, p.132.
41 Lee, J. M. (1963) *Social Leaders and Public Persons*, Oxford, Clarendon, p.10.
42 Self, P. (1971) 'Elected representatives and management in local government: an alternative analysis', *Public Administration*, vol.49, Autumn, p.275.
43 Among those who have commented on this relationship are: Bulpitt, J.G. (1967) *Party Politics in English Local Government*, London, Longmans; Buxton, R. (1973) *Local Government*, Penguin, Harmondsworth; Dearlove, J. (1973) *The Politics of Policy in Local Government*, Cambridge University Press; Friend, J. K. and Jessop, W. N. (1969) *Local Government and Strategic Choice*, Tavistock, London; Heclo, H. H. (1969) 'The councillor's job', *Public Administration*, vol.47, pp.185-202; Richards, P. (1973) *The Reformed Local Government System*,

London, George Allen and Unwin; Blowers, A. (1980) *The Limits of Power*, Oxford, Pergamon; Alexander, A. (1982) *Local Government in Britain Since Reorganisation*, London, Allen and Unwin; Elcock, H. (1982) *Local Government*, London, Methuen.

44 Dunleavy, P. (1981) op. cit. pp.340-1.

45 Newton, K. (1976) *Second City Politics*, Oxford, Clarendon, p.157.

46 See Hill, M. J. (1972) op. cit. Chapter 11; Self, P. (1972) op. cit.; Blowers, A. (1981) 'The Administrative Politics of Planning', *Policies, People and Administration*, Open University course D336, paper 14.

47 Hill, M. J. (1972) op. cit. p.234.

48 Interview with Philip Hendry, 27 October, 1982.

49 Interview with Keith White, 25 November, 1982.

50 For example, Jones, G. (ed) *New Approaches to the Study of Central-Local Birmingham Relationships*, SSRC, Gower; Raine, J. (ed) *In Defence of Local Government;* Alexander, A. (1982) *The Politics of Local Government in the United Kingdom*, London, Longman.

51 Dearlove, J. (1973) op. cit.; Buxton, R. (1973) op. cit.; Saunders, P. (1980) *Urban Politics*, Harmondsworth, Penguin, discusses political and business relationships in Croydon.

52 Bealey, F. (1982) 'Changing patterns of business leadership in local parties in Britain and the USA', Paper for the Political Studies Association, Canterbury, p.3.

53 Letter from Marcus Fox, Minister for the Environment to Stephen Hastings MP, 19 February, 1981.

54 The dual state thesis is outlined in Chapter 8 of Saunders, P. (1981) *Social Theory and the Urban Question*, London, Hutchinson and developed in 'Why study central-local relations?', *Local Government Studies*, May/June, 1982, pp.55-66.

55 Saunders, P. (1981) op. cit. p.265.

56 Saunders, P. (1982) op. cit. p.64.

57 Saunders, P. (1981) p.270.

58 Cawson, A. (1978) 'Pluralism, corporatism and the role of the state', *Government and Opposition*, Vol. 13, No. 2, pp.178-98.

59 Flynn, R. (1983) 'Cooption and strategic planning' In King, R. (ed.) *Capital and Politics*, Routledge and Kegan Paul.

60 Cawson, A. (1978) op. cit. p.184.

61 Flynn, R. (1982) op. cit.

62 For a discussion of the development of specific structure plans see, Sarah Buchanan, 'Power and planning in rural areas: preparation of the Suffolk Structure Plan,' in Moseley, M. (1982) (ed) *Power, Planning and People in East Anglia*, Centre for East Anglian Studies, Norwich; and Blowers, A. 'The politics of consensus — the Bedfordshire Structure Plan', Chapter 7 of *The Limits of Power*, Oxford, Pergamon.

63 Reade, E. (1982) 'Section 52 and corporatism in planning' *Journal of Planning and Environmental Law*, January, pp.8-16, p.13.

64 Bartlett, R. (1980) *The Reserve Mining Controversy*, Bloomington, Indiana University Press, p.157.

65 Vogel, D. (1981) 'How business responds to opposition: corporate political strategies during the 1970s', draft paper p.3.
66 Evidence of earlier protest from residents in these areas is given in, Porteous, A. et al (eds) *Pollution: the Professionals and the Public*, Milton Keynes, The Open University Press, in a chapter on the inquiry into brickworks at Woburn Sands; and in Blowers, A. (1980) op. cit., Chapter 4 dealing with the mining of fuller's earth at Aspley Heath.
67 Gaventa, J. (1980) op. cit. p.256, see note 12.
68 Balbus, I. D. (1971) 'The concept of interest in pluralist and Marxian analysis', *Politics and Society*, 1:2, pp.151-78, p.175.
69 Interview with James Bristow, 2 January, 1980.
70 Clegg, T. (1982) op. cit. p.2.
71 Interview with Keith White, 25 November, 1982.
72 After the elections of May 1981 the party balance was as follows: Conservatives 39, Labour 34, Liberal 8 and Independents 2.
73 Dunleavy, P. (1981) op. cit. p.346.

CHAPTER 8
POLLUTION, THEORY AND POLICY

The politics of control

There do appear to be some broad conclusions about the conflict of corporate power and the environment which emerge from this case, which may well be confirmed by other cases in different circumstances. Each case has its own history, its own political and institutional context, and its own personalities affecting the course of action. But we might expect, for instance, that the alliance between company and unions, the ability of the company to deploy investment options, and the willingness of privileged landed interests to espouse conservationist causes will be repeated elsewhere. In this chapter cases will be discussed which offer some confirmation of the processes described for London Brick.

The outcome of environmental and economic conflicts, whether an individual case or taken at a more general level, is not just of theoretical interest. Outcomes affect the quality of life of communities, amenity, health, jobs and wealth — issues fought for by both sets of contestants. The balance between competing and conflicting goals which is struck in one place or one society at a particular time reflects the interaction of values and interests, and is expressed in specific policies. Theories explain the nature of the conflict and its outcomes, policies provide a representation of the state of conflict. Theory enables us to state propositions about potential outcomes, policy provides the parameters for the achievement of specific outcomes. The links between process and outcome, and theory and policy need to be exposed and understood if we are to comprehend the contrasts and similarities encountered in examples of conflicts between environmental and economic interests. For example, if a theoretical explanation of a conflict suggests an élitist process of decision making, we might expect the institutional and policy processes to reflect this. As we shall see in a moment, there does appear to be some correlation between the nature of the decision making process and the policy framework adopted in different societies. But the relationship is not a tight fit since, at the present time in all advanced societies there are broad similarities in the outcomes of the conflict whatever the institutional arrangements for policy making.

There is undeniably greater concern for environmental values in advanced industrialised countries than was the case two decades ago. Although the early enthusiasm for environmental causes which erupted in the 1960s and early 1970s has waned in the face of increasing economic difficulty, environmental issues have moved up the list of social priorities.[1] 'As competing social problems such as poverty, housing and racial tension became less serious in the affluent post Second World War period, then pollution problems (as low-order social problems) were able to capture public attention.'[2]

The evidence of public opinion polls provides further confirmation.[3] Society has responded to these pressures by increasing the range and capacity of control policies. Industry has met the challenge by a combination of resistance, compliance and evasion, seeking to protect its profitability while, at the same time, acknowledging changing values. The problem facing societies in this area is 'how to strike a balance between the benefits of a rising standard of living, and its costs in terms of deterioration of the physical environment and the quality of life'.[4] In this chapter I shall trace the growth of environmental concern as an international issue, and the policies for control which have been adopted. These policies will be seen to be rooted in the political institutions of different societies. The consequences of policies, intended and unintended, will be related to theoretical explanations of the outcomes of conflicts between environmental and corporate interests.

The analysis of the relationships between theory and policy in the case of environmental pollution raises a number of questions. Some of these can be answered in substantially abstract terms. The first addresses the necessity for intervention to reduce pollution. Does pollution tend to increase? Pollution is a social product and therefore its distribution is likely to be systematically distributed, reflecting differing social evaluations of costs and benefits. This possibility leads to a second question: What are, in theory, the social distributional effects of pollution? Different evaluations of costs and benefits also lead to different views of the necessity for control, posing a third question: What are the reasons for and against pollution control? Related to questions of the justification for control and its distributional effects is the question of the means adopted to arbitrate the conflicts involved. This can be formulated as a fourth question: What policy alternatives are available to control pollution?

This question leads us towards issues which need to be answered through empirical evidence on the consequences, in practice, of effecting controls. What are the social and spatial consequences — intended and unintended — of pollution control? The answer to this enables us to relate the theoretical social distribution of pollution to what occurs in practice. This broad question will be explored through an examination of policies and their implications at a general level, and by the use of detailed case studies which may be compared to London Brick. I shall try to answer a fundamental question relating theory and policy, namely: How far can alternative theoretical perspectives explain the policies and outcomes of environmental conflicts in the contemporary world? Each of these questions, moving from the theoretical to the empirical, and from the local to the international scale, will be explored in turn in the sections which follow.

The need for control

The need for control of pollution arises out of the answer to the first question posed (does pollution tend to increase?). As we shall see, there are different views on this issue. Pollution may be defined as a physical, social and legal problem. Physically, it occurs 'when, as a result of man's activities, enough of a substance is present in the environment to have harmful effects'.[5] This suggests its origins are social. 'Pollution cannot be defined with any scientific or mathematical finality. The definition hinges on the concept of human use, and thus, while we may be able scientifically to define what level of environmental quality is necessary for particular uses, the definition of what constitutes pollution is dependent on the public's decision as to what uses it wants to make of its environment.'[6] The notion of harmful effects socially produced is central to questions of control for, although some forms of pollution may have natural origins (e.g. dust from volcanoes), they are not susceptible to control by human action. A legal definition of pollution brings us closer to the problem of control — 'A polluting activity has been seen as one which imposes uncompensated harm (costs) on third parties'.[7] This introduces the notion of pollution as an externality, a cost which is not internalised by the producer but imposed on others. There is a tendency to regard all pollution costs as externalities, but this is not strictly correct since 'they are only externalities so long as the firm can get away without paying for them'.[8] Thus the application of controls amounts to a means of imposing some of the costs of pollution on the polluters. The problem becomes one of assessing how much of the costs of control should be borne by the polluter and, conversely, how much of the costs of pollution should be borne by the community.

The problems of pollution increase, and the costs and benefits of pollution control have been a source of debate among economists. One view suggests that there is an inevitable tendency for pollution to increase. 'Since the polluter reaps all the gains and pays only part of the costs, he will pollute far beyond the point where total costs begin to outweigh gains.'[9] This view derives from the concept of 'the tragedy of the common' first put forward by William Foster Lloyd and revived by Garrett Hardin.[10] It demonstrates that the optimal solution for society may be quite different from the optimal solution for individuals. The social optimum will be the point at which a common can carry the maximum number of sheep without the loss of productive capacity. But an individual herdsman may add more sheep to his herd so long as he continues to increase his wealth, even if in so doing he contributes to overgrazing and the overall loss of output. This is because he enjoys all the incremental gain by adding to the herd while the costs of reduced output are spread among the herdsmen as a whole. Only at the point when the increase from adding one sheep is balanced by the loss to his herd from the reduced carrying capacity of the common will he cease to increase his herd. By that point the overall loss in production will be considerable.

This principle may be applied in certain cases where individual and social costs are different. Thus populations will continue to increase beyond the point where numbers are in an optimal relationship to resources, and so 'overpopulation' occurs; nations will continue to fish beyond the point where overfishing occurs; and governments will continue to stockpile armaments well beyond the point needed for the annihilation of the enemy. The principle also appears to hold true for pollution. 'The rational man finds that his share of the wastes he discharges into the common is less than the costs of purifying his wastes before he releases them. Since this is true for everyone, we are locked into a system of "fouling our own nest", so long as we behave as independent, rational free-enterprisers.'[11] There is thus a conflict of rationality, for what is rational for the individual herdsman, business or nation is not rational for the society. It poses a dilemma because 'rationality dictates the same conclusion to everyone, and the common thereby becomes rapidly destroyed'.[12]

An alternative view is that the tragedy of the common represents a special case. It assumes a set of behavioural assumptions in which individuals, companies and so on are self interested, independent profit maximisers, and a set of institutional assumptions such as free access to a common property resource (e.g. free air). In such circumstances it is likely that the resource will be overused and eventually depleted. A further assumption is made that the individual affects his own revenue as well as that of others, and will only desist from polluting activities when it becomes costly to do so. Under these assumptions pollution will continue to increase, and voluntary arrangements to limit it will not be possible. At a global level and for a long period this may hold true. Looked at more locally it is likely that a polluter affects only parties other than himself.

Producers are able to use resources such as free air at no cost to themselves while imposing costs on others. But, since others also have a right to use such resources this leads to conflict, and the possibility of voluntary agreements at limitation being reached, or, failing these, the imposition of controls. In such circumstances pollution levels may well diminish. In the case of London Brick the company had a right to use a public resource (free air) in order to dispose of unwanted waste products. In doing so it imposed offensive odours and potential pollution hazards on other users. As a result of the conflict the company was prepared to reduce the impact of pollution by voluntary agreement (Section 52) as well as by the controls (tall stacks) required by the Alkali Inspector. All parties agreed that these measures would considerably reduce the local levels of pollution.

These different viewpoints provide an explanation for the tendency for pollution to be increasing on a global scale while it may be reducing within certain regions. The discussion leads on to the second question, of what the social distributional effects of pollution are. Following the tragedy of the common argument, Dawes et al show that where wealth is unequally distributed, the richer individuals, businesses and nations will bear the heaviest costs of pollution and therefore have the greatest incentive for its reduction.[13] The same does not apply to the poorer nations who may still continue to reap a marginal return from an incremental increase in their herds. This tendency has some fascinating implications. It suggests that with fewer large polluters there is both a better incentive for control, and its achievement is easier since there are fewer cases involved. But it also suggests that the wealthier nations will encounter the need for control earlier than poorer nations who still have an incentive to achieve greater wealth. As a result the richer nations may try to alleviate their pollution both by exporting polluting activities and by exporting pollution. The same principle appears to apply on a more local and regional scale where wealthier, environmentally conscious groups are able to resist industrial development — thus pushing it elsewhere.

Rather than using the tragedy of the common argument, the explanation for the distributional effects of pollution can be explained as a simple case of the operation of social inequality. 'In so far as inequalities in income, property rights and political influence are interdependent and positively related, one would have *a priori* reasons for supposing that the less advantaged members of society suffer more from externalities, and benefit least from improvements.'[14] The rich prize environmental goods, and are prepared to spend more on them as their income becomes larger. They are quite content to reap the benefits of economic growth provided that the costs do not fall on them. In the highly integrated economy of an advanced industrial nation this may be possible, since the wealth created by polluters is spread more generally across the community. Production of coal, iron and steel, energy, chemicals, bricks and other commodities may create problems for areas in which plants are sited, but the goods they produce are distributed across the economy as a whole. As the economy becomes more international it becomes feasible for dirty industries to develop in areas anxious for economic development, with concomitantly less concern for the environment and less stringent controls. While the affluent are able to benefit from this distribution, the less privileged groups living in affluent areas may lose jobs in favour of a cleaner environment, while those in poorer areas may gain jobs but suffer increasing pollution.

It is actually more complex than this since the changing industrial pattern is a result of many factors, of which pollution is only one, and probably only a minor one at present. The geographical impacts of pollution are also more complex. The same groups may experience both costs and benefits but in different degrees. In our Bedfordshire case the community as a whole derived some benefit from the presence of London Brick in the form of rates and income generation, and also suffered generally from the dereliction and pollution created. The farmers claimed material loss as a result of pollution sufficient for them to oppose the redevelopment of the works unless pollution controls were imposed. Conversely, the workers in the industry stood to lose most if the investment was lost; and their preference for jobs far outweighed any concerns they may have had about pollution. Furthermore, loss of the investment in Bedfordshire would have provided the benefit of job creation elsewhere (e.g. in Cambridgeshire) and the potential increase of pollution in other communities.

The problem of pollution control poses conflicts of rationality. At the international level 'There is little reason for a nation to refrain unilaterally from polluting unless there is some reason to believe that others will respond to its initiative'.[15] This is the reverse case of the decision to pollute. If a nation decides to stop polluting it will bear the costs of doing so while the benefits will be enjoyed generally. Acting responsibly in this way becomes a case of cutting off one's nose to spite one's face. It would be irrational, not to say foolish, for a county to deny its own self-interest. Therefore appeals to responsibility amount to 'a verbal counterfeit for a substantial quid pro quo. It is an attempt to get something for nothing'.[16]

At the local level a similar problem of rationality exists whereby social goals do not coincide with individual actions. As we have seen, this may be solved by mutual agreement, or, failing that, by recourse to state intervention, requiring compliance by polluters to achieve a socially desirable outcome. The recognition of the need for control poses two problems. One is the need to justify intervention by making the reasons for control explicit, the other is the operational problem of applying the means of control which will prove effective. I shall now examine each of these in turn.

The reasons for control

The question 'What are the reasons for and against pollution control?' requires an investigation of the arguments put by both sides in the conflict between economy and environment. In general terms it is evident that growing worldwide concern about the environmental impact of industrialisation has resulted in a shift in values, which favour greater controls over industrial pollution. This is most pronounced in some more affluent countries.

Looked at more closely two features are evident. One is that environmental values are composed of different components with varying public appeal, the other is that the growth of concern is not consistent and progressive, but punctuated by advances and retreats as opposition from economic interests is encountered. The environmental cause is not uncontested, but, in several respects, deeply controversial. In terms of outcomes, environmental gains in some directions or in some geographical areas may result in other unpredicted or unintended economic and environmental losses. These features of the conflict and its outcomes have already been evident in the case of London Brick. Here, I shall indicate some of the more general consequences.

The upsurge of environmental concern which began in the 1960s seems to have been part of a more general political protest embracing campaigns against the Vietnam war, the student unrest and the race issues of that decade. Whatever the explanation for its origins, this environmental concern was signalled by the publication of several influential books which raised Malthusian fears about the capacity of the earth for survival.[17] Pollution incidents in a number of countries provided the evidence needed to generate and sustain public concern. Thus in Japan the mercury poisoning in the bay of the fishing village of Minamata, the cadmium pollution at Toyama producing the *itai-itai* disease and the deaths caused by air pollution at Yokkaichi were the most publicised of a series of incidents resulting in 4000 deaths and leading to over 70,000 people officially recognised as pollution victims by 1979.[18] In Italy the chemical pollution of the air at Seveso in 1976 'could probably be taken as the demarcation line' of changing attitudes in that country.[19] In the UK the disaster at the Flixborough chemical plant in 1974 had a similar effect. Major oil spills, such as that caused by the *Torrey Canyon* in the English Channel (1976, 117,000 tons) and the oil well blow out off the Californian coast at Santa Barbara in 1969, brought home the increasing risk to the environment.[20]

The dangers of possible nuclear accidents, as foreshadowed at Windscale in the UK in 1957, and at Three Mile Island, Pennsylvania in 1979, are of an even greater magnitude, leading Sandbach to claim that: 'It seems only a matter of time before a major nuclear disaster takes place elsewhere'.[21]

The widespread alarm generated by the environmental movement may have abated somewhat as a result of recession and concern about economic growth. Business has been able to defend itself with growing confidence. Nevertheless public awareness of the possible risks to the environment has been firmly established.

There is a distinction between the perceived and the objective measurement of risk which produces a problem for policy makers of what is an acceptable level of risk.[22] The case of London Brick illustrates the quandary. The perceived risk from the disposal of toxic wastes in 'L' field, although totally discounted by experts, was sufficient to alarm the local public and to spark off opposition to the company. During the course of the debate the risks from fluoride to animals, crops, and especially to people, perceived by the environmentalists was in sharp contrast to the absence of risk portrayed by the company. Expert opinion on the risks was divided and qualified, with Cremer and Warner taking a more cautious line than the Department of the Environment, who considered, on the basis of the evidence, that the pollution levels in the Marston Vale were not harmful to human health. The expert responsible for pollution control, the District Alkali Inspector, was unequivocal in his claims about the absence of dangers, especially with the installation of tall stacks. Thus an expert evaluation of risk suggested a form of control that was insufficient to allay fears based on the perceived risks involved. The Alkali Inspector was able to ignore local public protest in advocating tall stacks, but the County Council was likely to heed and to reflect local pressures insisting on stronger safeguards. 'As a general rule, the more directly accountable a decision maker is to the public, the more likely it is that public perception will receive consideration in priority setting.'[23]

In general terms then, the demand for pollution control may be seen as a product of growing environmental concern, reinforced by increasing apprehension of risks which are, from time to time, revealed in pollution incidents. But this general environmental concern consists of several components. It is necessary to disaggregate these components if we wish to understand the interests at stake in specific instances of conflict. The term 'environment' purveys an image of public interest when it may, in fact, be concealing the prosecution of specific interests.

Goodin has recognised four components or 'strands' of the environmental issue. The first is *amenity*, which arouses conservationist sentiments. It is a value judgement and tends to be more highly prized by affluent groups as we have seen. While conservationist sentiments may be sufficient to mobilise middle class support, it is not necessarily sufficient to provide successful opposition against pollution. Therefore, in order to broaden the environmental cause, another component, *public health*, may be invoked: 'Presumably, more people would object more violently to an unhealthy practice than to one which is only unsightly'.[24] This was precisely the approach adopted in Bedfordshire, where the environmentalists recognised that fears about public health, added to long standing concern about dereliction, were likely to rally maximum public support against the activities of the company. In this case, as no doubt in many others, a compromise position was not available. 'In many cases there is no technological solution to pollution problems, and there is no way to avoid a showdown between a healthy environment and all the countervailing advantages of an unhealthy environment.'[25] These advantages are tangible, while the virtues of a clean environment are more illusory — 'There are some people who it appears would prefer to breathe pure air in a state of industrial bankruptcy'.[26] While no one in the London Brick case was pressing the case that far, it was clear that the controls demanded by the environmentalists could not be yielded, leaving the loss of investment as the only option that would remove the pollution problem.

While amenity and public health are the components of the environmental case exploited in local conflicts over pollution, at a more global level environmentalists have deployed two other criteria. One is the argument that *survival* is at risk. Much of the impetus behind the environmental movement of the 1960s was based on fears that pollution burdens were rising to a degree when ecosystems were threatened. Fears were aroused about the 'greenhouse effect', caused by higher carbon dioxide levels, and other cataclysmic climatic effects through changing chemical balances in the atmosphere, while concern was also expressed about levels of toxic substances in rivers, lakes and the sea. While such fears are not without foundation, the present consensus of scientific opinion suggests that disaster is not imminent since present global levels are well below significant thresholds — although locally problems are already evident.

Coupled with the concern about survival has been anxiety about *resource depletion* though this, too, has been contested. It is argued that depletion is not exponential, that new resources are being discovered and that substitutes may be found.

These reassuring arguments seem, for the time being at least, to have dampened the idea of an inexorable drive towards disaster so widely canvassed by the environmental movement at its height in the 1960s and 1970s. Thus, for the present, the reasons for control are based largely on questions of amenity and public health. As a result the conflicts over control and the policy measures designed to arbitrate the conflicts are largely confined to local and national levels of government. But, as fears of transboundary pollution begin once more to emerge in the 1980s, so the call for international action gathers strength.

The challenge presented by environmental interests has been resisted. The nature and force of the challenge itself inevitably provoked a reaction when the most ominous claims were not immediately fulfilled. It is easy to portray the decline of environmentalism as a case of a movement which over-reached itself, and which waned once the doom predicted did not occur. But this is an oversimplification. In the first place, environmental concern has not disappeared. It manifests itself in many local conflicts, of which London Brick is an example. Secondly, the conflict has become institutionalised. Partly as a result of environmental pressure, the advanced countries in particular have adopted legislative programmes designed to safeguard environmental values. In the United States the Clean Air acts and amendments, the establishment of the Environmental Protection Agency, the state implementation programmes and a whole range of regulations have been enacted during the last two decades. In other countries, notably Japan and West Germany, there is evidence of legislation and procedures aimed at securing environmental protection.[27] The measures adopted have varied, reflecting the historical and political circumstances of different countries.

The means of control

'Sed quis custodiet ipsos custodes?'
(But who is to guard the guards themselves?)
(Juvenal, *Satires*, iii 347)

The fourth question posed at the outset ('What policy alternatives are available to control pollution?') relates to the different styles of legal and political institutions established to ensure the principles for control are translated into policies. Theoretically, the problem may be approached in three ways. One is through taxation. 'The basic logic of such solutions is that the incentives can be adjusted so as to make polluting prohibitively expensive or pollution abatement irresistibly profitable.'[28] In principle taxation is simple and sensitive and provides incentives for innovation. It could induce the biggest polluters to control emissions, thus having a marked effect on pollution levels. In practise, it is exceedingly difficult to apply a taxation strategy. It is difficult to establish a monetary cost to externalities, since the origins and quantities of emissions are difficult to assess. Taxation, according to Sandbach, raises problems of complexity, since complex technical processes with varying emission rates are difficult to monitor.[29] There are problems of uncertainty in that the impact of industrial technology is unknown, and might result in inappropriate technologies being applied. Changing tax rates would create great uncertainty for firms. There is the further problem of insensitivity, imposing large burdens on small firms unable to reap economies of scale from pollution control measures. Finally, a taxation system is liable to prove expensive to administer. These problems have been sufficient to preclude taxation as a means adopted for pollution control.

The method which has been adopted in advanced industrial societies is regulation. Within a regulatory system a third form of control, mutual enforcement, may also be present. This occurs when polluters find it in their interests to comply with controls, but to adopt a system of incentives and sanctions as a means of self-regulation. Although, in a sense voluntary, it is a system which appears to work as a complement to a regulatory framework, not as a self-contained system of control. It must therefore be regarded as a subsidiary approach. Regulation is the universally accepted method and takes two forms. One is based on standards, the adoption of legal limits both for air quality and emission levels which are enforced comprehensively. The other may be called the pragmatic approach, whereby cases are treated individually on their merits, and related to the circumstances applying at the time. The former method is the most common and may be illustrated by reference to the United States, the latter is the approach adopted in the UK.

The United States legislation covering air pollution control is exceedingly complex and only its essential features can be described here. The National Clean Air Act, first passed in 1955 and amended since (notably in 1967, 1970, 1977 and 1982), is the legislative basis, while the required standards are established through the Environmental Protection Agency (EPA). National Ambient Air Quality Standards (NAAQSs) have been set by the EPA for the seven 'criteria' pollutants — sulphur dioxide, total suspended particulate, carbon monoxide, nitrogen oxide, hydrocarbons, ozone and lead. The country is divided up into air basins each of which must attain the relevant standards, though the worst polluted areas are given longer deadlines for compliance. Pollution control at source is enforced through emission standards — new source performance standards (NSPS) using the best available control technology for major stationary sources, and specific standards for vehicle emissions (though the implementation of these has been delayed under pressure from the car industry). Strategies for the attainment of ambient air standards and the enforcement of emission controls are the responsibility of state governments through State Implementation Plans (SIPs). Further delegation operates through district air quality management districts, usually covering specific air basins, responsible for the implementation of programmes.

A careful system of checks and balances has been introduced to avoid the deterioration of air quality while not inhibiting economic growth. In those areas which are below the standards (non-attainment areas) a system of 'offsets' has been introduced whereby any new source of pollution must be able both to apply the lowest technically available emission rate and, at the same time, provide a net reduction in pollution by controlling an existing source of the same pollutant within the same area. This has led to considerable problems concerning the location of appropriate sources for trade-offs, problems of defining emission levels and problems of defining the appropriate reduction ratio.[30]

The problem of availability has led industrialists in some areas to develop systems of emissions banking, whereby credits for emission clean–ups can be banked against future emissions, or traded with companies seeking appropriate offsets.[31] While this stimulates technological innovation it infers a level of emissions higher than could be achieved. A further problem with offsets is that they can favour existing industries able to clean up their old plants in order to justify expansion. In principle, however, the system is intended to enable industrial expansion to take place in non-attainment areas, without vitiating the improvement of air quality.

In those areas already reaching the required air standards, the principle of Prevention of Significant Deterioration (PSD) is applied. 'Without a PSD programme that also requires the most effective available pollution control equipment for industry locating in clean air areas, industry would have an economic incentive to move to, and pollute, clean areas.'[32] Within these areas air quality is protected by allowing only small increments of pollution by industries which are using the best available control technology. The intention is to protect the pristine air covering the country's wilderness areas and to prevent the development of 'pollution havens' attractive to industries wishing to evade the tight controls applying in the non-attainment areas. The problem of geographical variation in pollution control programmes is an inherent one in a system of standards. Following the principles of the tragedy of the common it will be in the short run interest of individual states to apply lower standards in order to attract economic growth. This would, of course, be against the long term interests of clean air for the nation as a whole. In order to encourage compliance by the states, the federal government can impose construction bans and the withdrawal of federal funds.

It is very difficult to evaluate the effectiveness of the system of controls now applied in the United States. On the one hand it is argued that it has secured cleaner air and protected clean areas from worsening conditions. On the other it is argued that it has slowed economic growth, precluded the development of more effective control technologies, and focused on new sources while ensuring the maintenance of existing high pollution sources. It is a system characterised by increasing complexity, relying on the detailed development of a whole range of standards and procedures. 'Faced with complex and intractable problems, legislators created new agencies, commanded them to achieve specific results by specific dates, and armed them with a combination of regulatory, adjudicatory, and enforcement powers.'[33] Given the American predilection for litigation, the system has encouraged legal challenge and protracted judicial review as the demands made by environmentalists result in counterattacks by industrial interests. As a result the problem of rule making in the pollution field has become highly controversial, and encouraged adversarial attitudes to policy making.

By contrast the system of pollution control evolved in the United Kingdom relies on a cooperative and even collaborative relationship between government and industry. As we have seen in the case study, control powers are dispersed among a number of authorities. District councils (Environmental Health Departments), operating under the Clean Air Acts (1956 and 1968), are responsible for the control of smoke emissions from domestic and commercial premises; controls are also exercised over emissions of smoke from furnaces. District councils are also empowered (Public Health Act, 1936) to apply retrospective controls over industrial processes which cause a nuisance, and prospective controls over 'offensive trades' (e.g. fish meal, or manure manufacturing). But, as Wood observes, there are many thousands of manufacturing processes 'which are not subject to any prospective or anticipatory controls'.[34]

The major polluters, who, because of the quantity of emissions or the technical problems of control, cannot be dealt with locally, are registered under the Alkali Acts. They are subject to the control of the Alkali Inspectorate which has prospective powers over new works and retrospective powers over existing works. Alkali Inspectors (now called District Industrial Air Pollution Inspectors) employ the concept of 'best practicable means' for pollution abatement. 'The Chief Inspector . . . lays down the broad national policies and, provided they keep within their broad guidelines, inspectors in the field have plenty of flexibility to take into account local circumstances and make suitable decisions. They are given plenty of autonomy and are trained to be decision makers with as much responsibility and autonomy as possible.'[35] The essence of the system is a government inspectorate, using presumptive standards which can be changed according to technical advances or to reflect concern about pollution levels, applied to industry but varied according to local circumstances, such as age of plant and so on. Thus, in the case of London Brick, the Alkali Inspector, while not prepared to insist on the elimination of pollutants at source since the means were unavailable, did prescribe both tall stacks and the provision for a third flue which could be used if and when appropriate techniques were available. Although these features were to be applied to the new works, the existing works were not required to apply new methods of pollution abatement.

The advantages and disadvantages of the British approach to pollution control have been much debated.[36] There is the view that its flexibility ensures appropriate controls without placing unnecessary or impractical burdens on industry. The Royal Commission's Fifth Report regarded the system as 'consistent with the realities of pollution control'.[37] By contrast it found that 'The problem with a system of rigid standards is that their consequences in local and national terms are often not apparent until after they have been imposed, and it may then be clear that the benefits of reduced pollution are outweighed by the costs to society'.[38] The Alkali Inspectorate has also been criticised for being too secretive; for operating in a 'cosy' relationship with industry; for being insufficiently accountable to the public; for lacking adequate surveillance (few inspectors, few visits, few prosecutions) and for lacking relevant expertise on economic issues. This latter point had led Bennett to argue that lack of appropriate competence 'must cast doubt on the soundness of its decisions'.[39] The Inspectorate's relationship with industry, and its lack of public accountability has brought criticism of its 'élitist and technocratic stance'.[40] These various criticisms, amounting to public disquiet over the role assumed by the Inspectorate, were all present in the London Brick case and contributed to the force of the environmentalists' arguments about the need for greater public scrutiny of the operations of the company.

It is virtually impossible to evaluate the relative merits of the alternative systems of control. The American approach is comprehensive, available for scrutiny, and seeks to avoid inequalities between industries, states or geographical areas. But it is cumbersome, complex and costly. The British system operates flexibly, and according to local economic and environmental circumstances, but it relies heavily on administrative discretion and a close relationship between government and industry remote from effective public challenge. Vogel argues that:

> Neither approach is 'better'. Each stems from a particular set of historical circumstances and each has advantages and shortcomings. The contemporary British, or cooperative approach, is probably more efficient, since it significantly diminishes the likelihood that unnecessary environmental constraints will be imposed on business. It also dispenses with the considerable procedural costs inherent in the adversarial mode of regulation. On the other hand, the adversarial or contemporary American approach is probably more effective: it substantially enhances the likelihood that regulations that are needed will in fact be enforced. It can also bring about changes in corporate practices far more rapidly.[41]

The British system hinges on a tendency to trust officials — the outcome of a predominantly élitist system of government. The American system represents the more pluralist approach to public policy making, relying on detailed rule making, judicial review and agency enforcement. 'American culture has always contained a powerful strain of distrust of government officials, from the highest political appointee to the lowest bureaucrat.'[42]

The contrasts, however, are more apparent than real. As we saw in the case of London Brick, élitist forms of government may be challenged by environmentalists using pluralist local political frameworks. In Britain the land use planning system with its high degree of public debate and scrutiny, has been increasingly employed as a vehicle for applying greater public pressure in questions of pollution control. Land use planning policies can influence the source of emissions through their powers over the location of activities. They may use discretionary powers through the application of planning conditions on polluting activities, through agreements with industry and pollution conditions applied to planning permissions. The problem of duplication of powers has led the Department of the Environment to remind authorities that 'planning conditions should not be used to regulate pollution where appropriate specific powers can be used'.[43] Nevertheless, where pollution is a significant local issue, local planning authorities may use their powers to the point where there is inherent conflict with the powers of the Alkali Inspectorate. Environmentalists will use planning conditions and policies in an attempt to exert control over industry. Industry will resist such attempts, relying on the support of the Alkali Inspector. Both these tendencies were evident in the London Brick case.

Where the issue cannot be resolved a public inquiry may ensue. Asimow regards the public inquiry system as the British equivalent of the detailed public involvement already present in the American system. It may be that compromise can be effected in other ways, such as by agreement between the industry and the planning authority. The increasing use of Section 52 Agreements is evidence of the mutual interest both sides have in reaching a compromise which avoids the expense and uncertainty of a conflict which may result in an inquiry. They may be justified as a means of securing planning gains in return for planning permissions, but they are also instruments for gaining greater control over areas in which formal planning powers are relatively weak. Thus the use of an Agreement to introduce conditions covering pollution might be viewed, on the one hand, as an unwarranted intrusion of planning into an area under the jurisdiction of another agency (the Alkali Inspectorate) or, on the other, as an assertion of the local public interest in an area where it might otherwise be unrepresented. The British system has therefore adapted to the changing circumstances in which public interest in pollution control has emerged. The introduction of environmental impact assessments under the proposed directive of the EEC[44] amounts to a further development of the UK system in directions already evident in other advanced industrial societies. Such assessment, for instance, would provide for considerable public debate about the potential effects of a polluting activity.

The development of pollution control systems has responded to the increase in public concern for amenity and public health. Although the systems vary according to different historical and political traditions, they are designed to resolve the inherent conflicts between the demands for greater control and the requirements of economic growth. There is a tendency for industrial interests to represent their viewpoint through élitist methods of decision making, and for environmentalists to pursue their objectives through pluralist political processes.

Although a long term shift in values towards greater environmental concern is everywhere apparent, the trend is neither consistent nor continuous, but marked by fluctuations in the relative power of business to defend its position. Superimposed on the more general trends are wide variations in local circumstances, with success for industry in one area matched by apparent defeat elsewhere. It is therefore difficult to generalise about the effects of pollution control policies, whether at a national or local level. There is an absence of systematic research on this question, though assertions about consequences — intended and unintended — abound. There is, however, some empirical evidence both of individual cases and, in the case of the United States, of the national effects of policies which can yield some indications of the current state of the conflict over pollution control and its consequences. In the following section I shall review some of this evidence in an attempt to answer the fifth question posed earlier: What are the social and spatial consequences — intended and unintended — of pollution control?

The consequences of control

So far we have looked in detail at one case, that of London Brick. From this example a number of conclusions were drawn about the relative power of corporate and environmental interests. Although the events occurred in the context of the British control system certain features of it may be capable of more general application. In particular we might expect that the sources of power used by the company and its opponents find echoes in different circumstances elsewhere. By investigating other cases it may therefore be possible to reach conclusions which do seem to have support in empirical evidence on a wider basis than the individual case. Although detailed analyses of corporate power and environmental politics are rare, there are examples which complement the analysis provided here, and which help to reinforce its conclusions. These examples are drawn from American research. Although the circumstances of American politics and pollution control are, as we have seen, quite distinctive and different from those operating in the UK, there are broad parallels enabling us to make valid comparisons and to suggest tentative generalisations.

United States Steel in Gary and East Chicago

Although Matthew Crenson's book, *The Un-politics of Air Pollution*, relates to a relatively early stage in the contemporary concern with pollution, it provides some interesting conclusions about the nature and exercise of corporate power. Its theoretical concern with non-decision making has already been discussed in Chapter 6. Here I shall focus on Crenson's explanation of why United States Steel was able to evade pollution controls in Gary (Indiana) long after they had been imposed in neighbouring East Chicago.

Crenson identifies two critical factors in explaining the contrast between the two cities. One was the fact that US Steel was the dominant activity in Gary, and, by closing down plant or not investing in new activities, it could disrupt the economy of the whole community. Industrial power was less concentrated in East Chicago. Hence, in Gary, Crenson claims US Steel could prevent the issue of air pollution surfacing on the political agenda through its mere reputation for power. US Steel's interest was single-minded whereas opposition was dispersed. The idea that industrial power rests on reputation alone has been challenged as we have seen.[45] Whether or not the company was active behind the scenes, publicly it could adopt a stance of 'strategic neutrality', because it could rely on a sympathetic local polity.

The nature of the local political culture forms the second factor explaining the delay of pollution control in Gary. The city had a tightly-knit partisan political organisation, responsive to US Steel, conspiring to suppress public interest in the pollution issue. This close relationship succeeded for a while, but eventually, as public interest developed, the pollution issue could no longer be ignored and the control ordinance passed relatively easily. By contrast, in East Chicago, with a more fragmented and penetrable political system, the company's influence was less pervasive, public opinion was alerted at an early stage and thus control was adopted much earlier. Crenson goes on to investigate patterns of pollution control in several American cities to support his thesis that local political factors have a significant effect on the geography of pollution control.

Although the circumstances are different, there are some interesting parallels with the London Brick case. We have already seen how the pollution issue was kept off the public agenda in Bedfordshire for many years. In this case, while London Brick's influence was strong it was not entirely passive, applying various strategies of non-decision making to preclude effective challenge. Reputation for power alone was insufficient, so an exercise of power was necessary. London Brick was unable to rely on a sympathetic local polity, since public concern about dereliction and pollution was aroused from time to time. As in Gary, there came a point when the issue could no longer be contained by non-decision making and it became a major issue for debate and resolution.

Crenson's focus on differences in political culture is reflected in the contrasts between Bedfordshire and neighbouring Cambridgeshire. In Bedfordshire, where London Brick affected a large area of the county, the combination of public concern, political opposition, and an open decision making process ensured the pollution issue a high salience. In Cambridgeshire, the pollution issue was confined to a relatively small area, political attention was minimal and the issue was relatively insignificant. Crenson identifies the relationship between 'issue-ness' and political culture. In areas with apparently similar patterns public and political reactions may be quite different. There seems to be little correlation between the problem of pollution and the amount of public and political attention it generates. The effect of a new brickworks in Cambridgeshire is broadly similar to the effect in Bedfordshire, yet the local reaction was quite different. The London Brick case appears to confirm Crenson's thesis that political culture is the crucial variable in defining the salience of an issue. This may be put in terms of the following proposition: The importance of the issue depends on local circumstances rather than on the intrinsic nature of the issue itself.

Reserve Mining Company — Lake Superior

This conflict, described by Robert Bartlett in *The Reserve Mining Controversy* centres on the environmental damage done by iron ore processing on the shores of Lake Superior in the Arrowhead district of Minnesota.[46] The Reserve Mining Company (jointly owned by Armco and Republic Steel), had developed a technique for processing the low grade ores (taconite) of the

Mesabi area to the west of the lake, producing 15 per cent of the iron ore used in the US steel industry. When production began in 1956-7 it was regarded as a major economic development, extending the life of the ores in the area and saving imports of foreign ores. However, the process involved the dumping of 67,000 tons of taconite tailings each day into the lake. The water and air pollution caused by the company became the focus of a controversy extending over eight years (1969-77) of the most byzantine litigation. It was eventually resolved, and the company was forced to dispose of the tailings on land rather than in the lake.

The case has a number of similarities with London Brick. One is that the company was exposed to changing values. 'Thus the Reserve Mining Company, with no change whatever in its policies or behaviour, found itself being transformed from a benefactor of economic progress to a malefactor of environmental degradation'.[47] Increasing public concern about the environment was reflected in increasingly tough legislation, with the passing of the Water Pollution Control Act (1970) and the establishment of the Environmental Protection Agency. Standards of air and water quality were being set and enforced at state level. Environmental interests increasingly used the courts to challenge the activities of industry. All this provided the opportunity for shifting environmental values to be translated into the enforcement action. Likewise London Brick found that the dereliction and pollution it produced became increasingly unacceptable as environmental opposition developed. Its activities had not changed, but the public reaction to them had shifted over time.

A second common feature between the two cases was the change in the nature of the issue. At first it was largely an aesthetic problem, dereliction of the landscape, discoloration of Lake Superior, and possible harm to fishing and recreational interests. But, as Goodin observes, once concern for public health was aroused, the opposition was able to mobilise greater strength.[48] Revelations about a possible link between the asbestos-like amphibole mineral tailings, emitted both into the lake and into the air from the pelletising plant, added a new dimension to the dispute. The public health risks from contamination of the water supply and from breathing air from a known carcinogen were a much more formidable weapon to deploy against the company. In the case of London Brick, too, once fluoride had been identified as the key issue, public anxiety grew about the possible risks, although these were impossible to establish firmly.

This controversy over evidence is a third point of similarity in the two cases. The evidence used by both sides in the Reserve Mining case was inconclusive. 'Rather than playing an independent role in the controversy, science was being used by Reserve and its detractors to support positions taken for non-scientific reasons.'[49] It was as impossible for the environmentalists to prove their case as it was for the company to refute it, since 'science, at best, provides not proof but merely strong inference'.[50] All kinds of unanswerable questions were raised — were the fibres from Reserve akin to asbestos? Were they mainly emitted by Reserve? Was there a link with disease? What thresholds were significant? These questions have their echoes in the London Brick case. The evidence provided by Cremer and Warner and the Department of the Environment on health risks was qualified and tentative, providing support for both sides of the argument. As in the Reserve case, the problems of sources, thresholds and consequences of fluoride could not be identified unequivocally. These were questions that could only be resolved politically.

A fourth parallel between the cases is the ability of industry to avoid costs which it regards as unacceptable. Industry recognises its economic power. Although at one point Reserve was ordered to cease discharges into the lake, the threat this posed to over 3000 jobs enabled it to gain time, in order to find alternative methods of disposal. The company's initial claims that the pollution was harmless, and that there were no alternatives to disposal in the lake were insufficient, and so it resorted to the defence that alternative methods of disposal were uneconomic. A compromise was reached, and a site seven miles from the lake selected. By tactics of procrastination the company had gained eight years, during which the cost of litigation was much less than the cost of on-land disposal. The company eventually moved to a site that was cheaper than the possible alternative, and more environmentally acceptable sites. Although the environmentalists had apparently won their point, the company had retreated slowly, with its position largely intact. As one commentator observerd: 'Jobs have won out over the environment'.[51] Similarly, London Brick, when under pressure, had apparently made concessions and shifted its investment options around while ensuring its major objectives remained inviolate. Here, too, the issue finally focused on the choice between jobs and the environment.

The Reserve Mining case supports the following conclusions drawn from our earlier analysis of London Brick. Changing environmental values and, in particular, increasing anxiety about the risks to public health may force industry to accept pollution controls or make other environmental concessions. But, lack of incontrovertible evidence on the risks, combined with the economic costs of control, enable industry to avert what it regards as unacceptable costs.

Reserve Mining had to make significant concessions because it had no alternative investment options. It was dependent on a local taconite reserve and, if it was to remain in business, it had to remain in Minnesota. Where industry has greater locational freedom its ability to avoid control is greater, as the next examples demonstrate.

California — Dow Chemical and Sohio

In 1975 Dow Chemical proposed to build a chemical plant employing 1000 workers in the environmentally sensitive Delta area north of San Francisco. The plant posed a threat to water and wildlife, but the problem of air pollution was the major issue since state and federal air standards would not be met. It was a classic instance of economic development against environmental costs, and there were a number of other industries with an interest in investment in the area. The local political interests welcomed the company but, as one critic cynically remarked: 'your average county politician, when confronted by a big new factory coming into his territory, is about as critical as a cow in heat'.[52] The company attacked the pollution controls, insisting that it was using the best technology and was being penalised, while existing, older polluting industries were not suffering similar restrictions. 'Many of us believe it was not the intention of the authors of the Clean Air Act . . . to bring about an end to industrial and economic growth in this country.'[53] The state claimed that it was not preventing the industry, but Dow Chemical pulled out before it had secured the necessary permits. It was able to lay the blame on the pollution controls although it was clear that California was only one of several investment options being considered by the company.

The controversy over Dow Chemical led California to review its regulations on air trade–offs in non-attainment areas. The problem of trade-offs was at the heart of the arguments about Standard Oil of Ohio's plans in the late 1970s for an oil transfer terminal at Long Beach in southern California. The company wanted to bring its oil from Alaska, transfer it at Long Beach into existing gas pipelines and transport it overland to Texas. The proposal would add to air pollution (from tankers and storage tanks) in an area where air quality standards were already violated two out of three days a year. The authorities argued that 'the company could provide necessary pollution trade-offs in Long Beach and realise a substantial profit for the project'.[54] They calculated this would only add about 1½ per cent costs to the $10 billion project. There were in any case, alternative routes either over land or through Panama, though the latter would be more expensive. The company argued that 'a project like the pipeline, which has been endorsed by all levels of government, should experience such difficulty when the economy is facing its most serious threat in energy supply must be as astounding to the rest of the country, and the world, as it has been to Sohio'.[55] Despite efforts to arrange an adequate solution satisfying both parties the company withdrew. It later became clear that the pollution problem was being used as a smokescreen in order to enable the company to overcome the embargo on oil exports, and what it really wanted was to export oil to Japan. 'Had there still been something in it for Sohio, the company would have hung in there when all signs indicated final approval was close at hand.'[56]

These cases illustrate two further features of the exercise of corporate power already encountered in the study of London Brick. One is that certain industries are able to play off one area against another in their efforts to secure their objectives. London Brick was able to drive a wedge between Cambridgeshire and Bedfordshire in order to reduce opposition. The other point is that pollution controls may be used as the reason for investment withdrawal when it is really other considerations that are fundamental. Although it must be said that London Brick did not claim controls as the reason for the closure of Ridgmont, and its lack of investment there indicated a general belief that the actions of the County Council had precluded development in Bedfordshire. The Chairman of the company had made it clear that unless an acceptable permission was granted — 'We have many other investment opportunities, we have existing permissions for new works outside the County and I am not saying that in any way as a threat'.[57] The common features in these cases enable us to substantiate a further proposition: Where an industry possesses alternative investment opportunities it may use variations in environmental controls as a means of exploiting political circumstances in order to secure its economic objectives.

Further evidence of the ability of industry to manipulate political circumstances comes from the next example.

Coal-fired power plants in the United States

The ability of industry to exert political influence by building powerful alliances is well illustrated by the coal industry in the United States during the 1970s. During this period the industry had to face increasing regulations, reflecting the success of the environmental movement. There was an inherent conflict of interests between eastern and mid-western coal producers with high sulphur coal and the developing western coal producers whose coal was low in sulphur content. Eastern producers were liable to suffer if emission standards were set at a level which imposed costs on them, while western producers were unaffected. The 1967 Clean Air Act Amendments represented a victory for the traditional alliance of eastern coal, industry and trade unions, which resisted the imposition of emission controls in favour of ambient air quality standards. Vogel explains this in terms of the concentration of eastern coal interests able to mobilise influence, combined with dispersal of the electricity industry (the main market for coal), anxious to avoid the higher costs entailed if emission standards were imposed.[58] But by 1970 the environmental interest was sufficiently strong to achieve the imposition of a federal standard which would restrict sulphur dioxide emissions to 1.2 lbs per million British Thermal Units (MBTUs).[59] This was to be achieved by the installation of scrubbers on all new coal fired plant in order to remove 70 per cent of the sulphur content. This standard adversely affected eastern coal producers, whereas western states could achieve the standard without scrubbers.

It led to seven years of intense lobbying by eastern coal interests, described by Bruce Ackerman and William Hassler in *Clean Coal/Dirty Air*.[60] It brought about the unholy alliance between eastern coal producers and environmentalists favouring the imposition of both a common standard and universal scrubbing, though for different reasons. Eastern coal producers feared that without universal scrubbing, power plants might turn to low sulphur coal from the west as a cheaper alternative, thus eroding their market for coal. Environmentalists favoured universal scrubbing since, combined with low sulphur coal, it would achieve emission levels in the west as low as 0.1 lbs per million BTUs. This alliance was successful in achieving protection for local coal, thus helping the East, while the introduction of legislation that would prevent the deterioration of the high air quality in the West (Prevention of Significant Deterioration) would remove any incentive for industry to shift from the East to the West to avoid pollution controls. The split between eastern and western interests was clear. 'Frost Belt Senators were more than happy to gang up on PSD to screw the Sun Belt.'[61] Eastern coal interests, backed by the unions, won because 'they were fighting for the very survival of their industry'.[62]

This shift brought about a realignment of interests on more traditional lines. In the West business and car interests opposed the imposition of tough standards which would prevent industrial development. The various agencies and congressional bodies began to explore alternative combinations of emission standards and scrubbing levels. The proposal to improve the standard to 0.55 lbs per million BTUs threatened eastern coal once more, and would impose higher costs on the power plants. As events moved towards the prospect of tougher pollution controls the natural alliance of eastern coal, anxious about its market, and electricity utilities concerned to avoid high costs, was reasserted while environmentalists, the erstwhile allies of eastern coal, were in favour of the most stringent controls possible.

This example demonstrates the unintended consequences that ensue from attempts to introduce pollution controls. Ackerman and Hassler point out that by imposing a particular form of technology for new plants it ignored cheaper means, such as washing coal, which could have been applied to all plants. As a result, investment in new plants was likely to be delayed, and higher pollution levels continued as a result of the maintenance of old plants. By applying comprehensive regulations the possibility of improvement through flexible and sensitive decisions at local level was neglected. By its concern with overall pollution levels the relative impact of pollution on populations was ignored. The focus on sulphur dioxide (SO_2) diverted attention from the potentially more harmful emissions such as sulphates (SO_4), which was becoming a matter of serious concern in areas some distance from power plants. The debate focused on means rather than ends. At a broader level Navarro suggests that pollution controls on coal promote alternative fuels such as oil, which implies imports and the loss of oil reserves, or nuclear energy with its potential risks.[63] The use of scrubbers is expensive, uses up more energy, and increases other forms of pollution through sludge disposal and contamination of water. Overall the cost of control has been 'restricted energy development, increased oil-import dependence, inflation, and, ironically, in some cases not less but *more* pollution'.[64]

Although this example relates to the impact of regulations on industry at national level in a specific political context, it does substantiate some of the features of the London Brick case. There are three areas in particular where the broad similarities are striking. First is the ability of industry to construct alliances in order to achieve its objectives. The combination of environmental interests with eastern coal has no parallel in the London Brick case. On the other hand the alliance of Labour and Conservative politicians against unions and company cut across conventional barriers. And, when jobs were threatened, the traditional alliances reestablished themselves. Like eastern coal, London Brick could rely on the support of the trade unions. Vogel regards union support as a critical factor in promoting industrial interests. He cites other instances such as the support given by car workers to the car industry's resistance to pollution controls. These cases tend to confirm the structuralist thesis that underlying economic forces ensure the ultimate success of business.

A second, related feature in the two cases is the concentration of business power, both in terms of the size of the industry and its geographical location. Both eastern coal and London Brick are substantial, if not dominant, economic influences in their localities. The prospect of closure in such industries has profound implications for the workforce and the community as a whole. Empirical research on the ability of companies to evade income tax supports the idea that big companies are able to mobilise effective power.[65] The geographical concentration of eastern coal enabled it to focus its opposition on pollution controls which would devastate whole communities. At the same time the dispersal of coal consuming industries arguing for cheap coal gave it a broad constituency on which to consolidate its case. Similarly, London Brick as a major local industry could concentrate its power locally once the economic threat was evident, and could also rely on the support of government. Thus reflecting the geographically dispersed building industry with its interest in cheap brick production.

The third similarity in the cases is the tendency to focus on a specific problem, and on means rather than ends. The environmentalist opposition resulted in the United States in an emphasis on a technical solution and on a specific pollutant, and ignored the broader economic and environmental consequences. In the London Brick case the environmentalists concentrated on fluoride rather than odour, which was the most obvious problem. Their insistence on a technical solution was liable to result in other forms of pollution (such as sludge) and impose heavier costs on industry than the tall chimneys proposed by the company. The industry's unwillingness or inability to introduce controls was likely to have the effect of maintaining old plant and delaying investment in new works, resulting in higher rather than lower pollution levels.

The correspondence at a general level between the case of the United States coal industry and London Brick in their ability to resist onerous pollution controls is sufficient to suggest two further propositions.

1. The ability of an industry to resist the imposition of costs which threaten its survival is greatest when, as a result of its geographical concentration, it can draw on the support of the local workforce and community, and can build coalitions with more dispersed interests which depend on its products.

2. The tendency for environmental interests to seek technical solutions to

environmental problems, rather than evaluate overall costs and benefits, leads to a focus on means rather than ends and the production of unforeseen or unintended consequences.

Corporate power and the environment — policy and theory

In this final section I shall assess the relative influence of corporate and environmental interests on policy making. I shall draw on the evidence of London Brick and the cases reviewed in this chapter to relate theory and policy in answering the following question: How far can alternative theoretical perspectives explain the policies and outcomes of environmental conflicts in the contemporary world?

In certain respects greater environmental awareness has achieved considerable success. The freedom of industry to impose the external costs of dereliction and pollution on society has been checked. Restoration of landscape and control of emissions is a common feature of policy making in all the countries of the advanced industrial world. By raising public consciousness through developing contacts, expertise and access to decision makers, environmental groups, national and local, have secured detailed regulation of industry. It is a matter of debate whether comprehensive standards (as applied, for example in the US) are a more effective system than the more pragmatic and flexible approach adopted in the UK. It is clear that the consequences of control vary in detail, and may create economic and environmental problems that are not foreseen. Overall, however, it appears that environmentalists have succeeded in ensuring that pollution control is a factor in corporate decision making.

The success of environmentalists may be more apparent than real. A considerable amount of the reduction in pollution levels has been achieved as a result of technological and social change. Waller points out that much of the improvement in air quality in British cities would have occurred without the intervention of the Clean Air Act.[66] The redevelopment of the inner areas of cities reduced the concentration of population (and hence of pollution sources), and the introduction of high rise housing led to pollution being dispersed through its emission at greater velocity at higher levels. In any case, there was already a shift from coal to other fuels (notably natural gas), and the introduction of smokeless coal would probably have occurred anyway. The Act was a factor but by no means the only one. Sandbach (1981) points out that the change from heavy to light industry, increasing population dispersal, and changes in energy consumption have been the predominant factors. He argues that 'even when policy making and state intervention have appeared to play a part this merely acts to reinforce the economic interests of the polluter and the polluted'.[67] He demonstrates, using the example of the asbestos industry, how industry can successfully resist controls. He suggests that pollution controls only succeed where 'it is in the direct interests of the polluter to reduce waste'.[68] Although there remain pollution controls which impose costs on industry and which industrialists would wish to avoid, the costs may be only a marginal consideration in terms of the industry's overall economic objectives.[69]

The evidence from the cases surveyed tends to support the view that environmental controls are a factor affecting local decisions, but are rarely decisive. Reserve Mining was forced out of Lake Superior, and Dow Chemicals and Sohio were unable, so they claimed, to secure the permits which would enable them to develop in California. London Brick responded to environmental pressure by shifting its proposed site for a new works, accepted a package of environmental improvements and a part permission with a guarantee of research into pollution abatement. But there were other motives which played a part even in these local decisions, and the companies were able to secure tactical successes. Reserve Mining resisted on-land disposal for eight years, and eventually achieved a compromise site. London Brick's shift to Stewartby was largely based on its need to open up clay reserves nearby. Later, having secured a permission at Ridgmont, it reverted again to Stewartby as the cheapest location. Dow Chemical and Sohio clearly had broader objectives which were largely unaffected by their failure to secure permits in California. It appears that corporate interests may have to accept a degree of control over their activities, but there are few signs that pollution controls are forcing major changes in corporate strategies, which still respond mainly to other economic signals. The case of the coal fired power plants suggests that corporate interests are able to resist limitations that would fundamentally alter the economic geography of coal production. We are left with the conclusion that corporate interests possess greater effective power in the contest with environmentalists.

There seem to be several reasons why this is so, and they relate to the theoretical explanations put forward earlier. In brief, industry is able to exploit pluralist political frameworks, has an established position as an élite interest, and is able to rely on structuralist forces which favour its political dominance. Both business and environmentalists are, as we have seen, élitist groups using pluralist politics in pursuit of their ends. The very success of the environmental movement in the 1960s and 1970s provoked a reaction. The movement lost its appeal, its sense of direction and its unity. The appeal of its more extreme advocates for alternative technologies seemed both impracticable and inequitable.[70] The defence of positional values for an already privileged élite provoked the fears of consumers and labour who aspired to the material benefits of economic growth. The business community was able to benefit from the growing bankruptcy in the arguments of its opponents. 'The contemporary revival of the political influence of business is due less to the appeal of conservative social and economic policies than to the growing public awareness of the inadequacies of the political vision of the left-liberal tradition of American reform.'[71] The introduction of regulations exposed the problems of imposing technical solutions, which resulted in potentially undesirable outcomes and also failed to provide adequate solutions to environmental problems. It was not simply a matter of the opposition losing its appeal or running out of ideas or failing to find appropriate solutions. The business community was regrouping and re–arming to fight off the challenge. Like its opponents, business used the opportunities afforded by pluralist politics. It intensified its lobbying, improved its public relations and used similar tactics and strategies.

The revival in the political power of business coincided with a reversal in its economic fortunes. There appear to be 'political cycles' during which the power of business waxes and wanes.[72] The dynamics of such cycles are difficult to trace, and their relationship to political and economic trends are complex. It does appear that a combination of recession and sympathetic government halts the progress of environmental regulation. Eastern coal and London Brick were able to turn economic weakness into political strength. At such times politicians are responsive to the needs of business.

Pluralist politics enable business to press home its advantage by exploiting political circumstances. The examples chosen reflect this tendency. London Brick was aided by the internal political divisions within Bedfordshire and by differences of attitude between Bedfordshire and Cambridgeshire. Reserve Minning was able to exploit the various levels of decision making and legal process to delay the inevitable move to on-land disposal. Sohio used the obstacles encountered to their Long Beach project to induce the federal government to relax its oil export embargo. Eastern coal backed universal scrubbing to secure its position against western coal interests. The ability to take advantage of political divisions is enhanced by a willingness to build alliances with other interests. Eastern coal producers joined with environmentalists in supporting universal scrubbing and reverted to its traditional alliance with the power companies when tighter emission controls, and therefore increased energy costs, were in prospect. In all the cases considered here the support of organised labour and local communities were a major factor in business success.

Business also succeeds through corporatist forms of decision making. There is, as we have seen, a period before an issue becomes public during which an industry can exercise power through non-decision making. Knoepfel et al describe this as the 'pre-parliamentary' phase, during which 'cooperative relationships in the form of bargaining will develop. Since bargaining is the form of cooperative interaction, which as a rule presupposes mutual trust between the protagonists with regard to the exchange of confidential information, those affected by pollution are often excluded from mutual decisions made in this way.'[73] We saw how London Brick was able to use its relationship with officials to advance its case and US Steel's influence over decision makers in Gary was sufficient to preclude agitation of the pollution issue.

Even when the issue is made public industry's control over information may be decisive. As Schnaiberg points out, scientific and technological expertise is wedded to productive industry. Industry provides the funds for scientific research, and the output of the scientific community is biased towards productive enterprise. There develops 'an infallibility of expertise'. 'This aura of infallibility, of the technical nature of production decisions, reinforces the existing treadmill of production.'[74] London Brick was able to command research evidence, to refute the claims made by opponents and was supported by 'official' scientific evidence from the Department of the Environment and the Alkali Inspectorate. Similarly, Reserve Mining exhibited 'the modern tendency to value scientific evidence much more highly than other kinds of evidence'.[75] This argument must not be pushed too far. Industry has nowadays no monopoly of expertise. Cremer and Warner's evidence did not fully support London Brick, and a report produced by various federal agencies was largely responsible for fanning concern about the hazards of Reserve Mining.[76] Industry and environmentalists occupy élitist positions, able to command the expertise necessary to inform their case and urge decisions based on non-scientific reasons. These reasons are profit on the one side and the defence of amenity on the other. The needs of the non-élites, the workers in industry and the local community, are secondary considerations in the conflict.

It may be argued that pluralist politics offer business and environmental interests broadly equal opportunities to compete. Further, the inherent advantages possessed by industry as a privileged élite, in terms of its access to decision makers and possession of information, may have been eroded as environmentalist groups have penetrated the political process and gathered their own expertise. That may be so but structuralist forces tend to provide industry with an unassailable position. The economic sanctions at industry's disposal are sufficient to command the allegiance of labour and subvert the opposition. Large industries possess a number of investment options. They can delay new investment and thereby continue high levels of pollution. The costs or technical problems involved in applying pollution controls provide an incentive to keep old plants in operation, as happened with London Brick and in the case of the coal fired power plants. Alternatively, industry can often threaten to move elsewhere, as did London Brick or actually do so as was the case with Dow Chemicals.

As a last resort industry can shut down its operations. The closure of Ridgmont, though for economic reasons, was sufficient to mobilise support for London Brick and ensured the collapse of opposition. Occasionally government may consider closure of an offensive works, but the economic consequences are usually sufficient to prevent such action. Although a closure of Reserve Mining was ordered at one point, a stay of execution was quickly secured. The economic sanctions available to business may be used more widely to gain tax concessions, favourable locations and other benefits. Industry's power rests on the fact that 'the economic viability of particular communities, regions and the nation as a whole is largely dependent on the rate and location of corporate investment'.[77]

Much of the analysis of this book has been confined to local and national aspects of pollution. With such power at its disposal it is not surprising that industry retains the initiative in national conflicts over pollution. But there is, increasingly, an international dimension. Industry has been able to invest in regions or countries where economic growth is welcomed. Eventually the transfer of pollution to 'pollution havens' in newly developing countries may arouse hostility and place industry on the defensive. Of more immediate significance is the problem of trans-boundary pollution within the advanced industrial societies. The problem of 'acid-rain' caused by the long distance transfer of sulphur dioxide and nitrogen oxide over long distances is well known. The rapid increase in the acidity of rain over Scandinavia led to an OECD study in 1972 which, with all the necessary qualifications about the validity of the data, found that Britain during 1973-4 put 6 million tonnes of sulphur dioxide into the air, 60 per cent of which left the country.[78] It was further estimated that Britain contributed

16 per cent of the sulphur pollution in Sweden from known sources (11 per cent from all sources) and 47 per cent (26 per cent) of that in Norway. But the costs of desulphurising Britain's coal fired power plants would far exceed the costs imposed by the pollution on the Scandinavian economies. The problem of acid rain has intensified the pressure for the adoption of common standards of air quality throughout Europe, which poses a direct challenge to the methods of control adopted in Britain. 'British legislation must appear to our fellow Europeans to be pragmatic, piecemeal, *ad hoc,* the product of expedience, not principle: a policy to be described as a non-policy.' A shift towards a standards based policy would have severe economic implication for Britain.[79]

This example and others demonstrates that policies aimed at a national level may be in conflict with the demands for an international solution to pollution problems.[80] Problems solved in one area may lead to problems elsewhere. As pollution spreads across national frontiers and begins to threaten ecosystems, so the ability of industry to evade controls may weaken. However, the history of pollution control suggests that industry possesses the technical capability and the political power to avoid any fundamental challenge to its interests.

The Marston Vale, 1984

Five years have passed, and the Marston Vale presents quite a different scene from that of 1978 (Figure 8.1).[81] The traveller, passing south from Bedford, encounters first the signs of industrial decline and dereliction, and some evidence of restoration. The Kempston Hardwick works remain, but are mothballed and unlikely to ever open again. The Coronation works were demolished in 1980, and, like the nearby pit, will prove difficult to restore to agricultural use. Elsewhere, in this northern part of the Vale, the pit at Elstow is being gradually filled in with refuse from Bedford. There are signs of landscaping and tree planting to shield the empty pits from the roads, and the site of a former workers' hostel has been cleared and left as an ecological study area. Nearby is the Elstow storage site, the centre of a developing controversy over the prospect of nuclear waste disposal.

Towards the centre of the Vale, surrounding the village of Stewartby, the scene changes from the past to the present of the fletton industry. One exhausted pit has been converted into a lake and another, 'L' field, is in the course of a long period of restoration using domestic waste brought by rail from London. The only working pit is Rookery, south of the village,

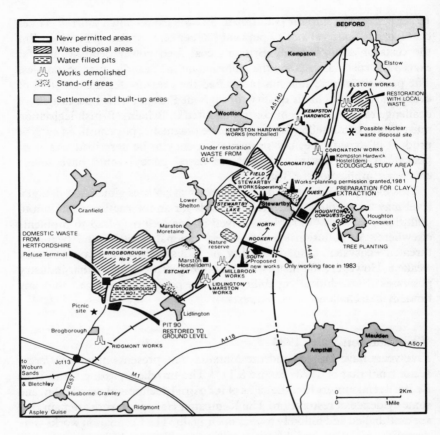

Figure 8.1: The Marston Vale 1983
Source: Bedfordshire County Council

feeding the Stewartby works — currently the sole producer of bricks in the Vale. To the east is the Quest pit, shortly to take over from Rookery, and currently being stripped of topsoil and callow to reveal the 15–metres–thick bed of clay beneath. Next to Houghton Conquest a stand-off zone is being established and planted as part of the agreement to safeguard the village from the impact of future clay working. By the time the pit at Houghton Conquest is used, there may be a new super-works in the bottom of the Rookery pit.

Continuing south down the Vale, the signs of past activity and future uncertainty emerge once again. Around Marston Moretaine are abandoned workings and large areas reserved for possible future extraction. The old Marston works at Lidlington has been demolished, but the site may be used as a rail transfer station if imported waste (such as that from the Vale of Belvoir) ever becomes available in sufficient quantities to reclaim the empty pits. Further south, the massive rubbish dump which was once such an eyesore when viewed from Brogborough Hill has been flooded, screened and landscaped. Refuse, brought in by road, is now dumped in the huge Brogborough No.2 pit, until recently supplying clay for the Ridgmont works. Most of this pit remains unexcavated. At the southern end of the Vale the decline of the industry is most evident. The once familiar rows of chimneys of the Ridgmont works, which dominated the skyline and whose emissions offended motorists on the motorway, have now gone. All that remains are the old pan sheds, some derelict buildings, and mountains of brick rubble being crushed to resurface the nearby motorway. Plans for a new brickworks here have been dropped and the future use of the site is a matter of speculation.

In the short span of five years the Vale has been transformed. Two works have closed, three have been demolished, excavations have ceased in two pits, and about 1500 jobs have been lost. Some restoration has begun, and there is the possibility of a new works when the industry revives. Behind the visible signs of decline and change lies the story of conflict which has been told in this book. It was a conflict of values, in which the issues were clean air, an attractive environment, jobs and investment. The outcome has satisfied no one, since the impact of economic and industrial decline could not have been foreseen. The voices that were raised, sometimes so passionately, in the brickworks debate, are now silent, echoing the silence and emptiness that pervades Ridgmont. The conflict had an impact on the course of events, and will yield benefits in the future appearance of the Vale. Whether it had a fundamental influence on the scale, location and development of the industry in Bedfordshire is a matter for theoretical debate, as this study has shown. Whatever the detailed explanations for changes within the Marston Vale, there were structural forces responsible for the decline of the industry during this period which profoundly affected the outcome of the debate. The Marston Vale today stands as a poignant testimony to the contemporary economic and political forces which, in a short space of time, have diminished much of our nation's traditional industry.

Epilogue — the takeover of London Brick

The story of this book has been that of a large national company with strong local roots in conflict with local interests. By the end of 1983 it was becoming clear that the independence of the company was threatened as it tried to defend itself against takeover. As the clouds of recession lifted, London Brick's fortunes and future prospects revived but, ironically, made it an attractive proposition. In December 1983, the Hanson Trust, an international conglomerate with substantial industrial holdings, made a bid for the company. The bid valued London Brick at £170M. and offered 120p. cash for shares. Hanson already owned Butterley, the second largest non-fletton brick producer and, together with London Brick's fletton and non-fletton production (40% and 8% of the total respectively) a successful bid would give Hanson about two-thirds of the total British brick production. London Brick rejected the bid and urged the Office of Fair Trading to refer it to the Monopolies Commission as being against the national interest. The ensuing contest proved to be one of the most fiercely contested takeover bids ever witnessed by the City.

In January 1984, Hanson made a second offer valuing the company at £212M. at 165p. cash per share. Again London Brick rejected the offer, claiming it underestimated the company's value. In its defence the company produced a profits forecast for 1983 of £26M., a rise of 70% on the previous year and a dividend increase of 30%, claiming that 'London Brick is a revitalised company whose profits have grown and whose prospects have never been better'.[82] At the same time the company's assets, notably in its Oxford Clay reserves, had been revalued at £300M. Profits for 1984 were forecast to be even higher at £36M. with a possible doubling of dividends. But the Hanson bid was not referred to the Monopolies Commission. London Brick's earlier attempt to increase its own share of brickmaking by purchasing Ibstock Johnsen (see Chapter 5, p.203) had been cleared by the Commission and this can be seen in retrospect as cutting the ground from under the company's feet. Jeremy Rowe, London Brick's chairman, commented, 'now that the uncertainty is out of the way we can devote all our energies to combating this unwelcome predator'.[83]

Hanson's response was to make a third and final offer at £267M. with 165p. cash per share. Share prices for London Brick had been rising from a low point of 62p. in 1983 to about the 160p. mark. Hanson had been increasing its stake in the company from 9.6% when it first bid to about 30%. The shareholders were being wooed by London Brick's claims of a strong financial position from which they would benefit and by Hanson

Trust's offer of an attractive price for their holdings. Much depended on the attitude of the institutional shareholders with about 60-65% of the total stock. Up to the last London Brick appeared confident of holding off the bid, declaring, 'The institutions are solidly behind London Brick'[84], and engineerig a substantial purchase of shares. But, at 3.20 p.m. on February 28th, 1984 Hanson announced that they had secured 58% of the holdings and the takeover had succeeded.

Although the takeover occurred long after the main events of this story, its impact was likely to add to the uncertainty already surrounding the future of the economy and the environment of the Marston Vale. The revival of the industry seemed to have brought nearer the development of the new works at Stewartby. A planning application for the new works at Rookery pit was received the day after the takeover but, if approved, its implementation would depend on commercial assessments made by the new owners of the company. Fears about jobs were discounted by Hanson who argued they were interested in a strong British brick industry, but here, too, there was uncertainty. Over the years of conflict, close relationships had been forged between London Brick and the County Council and were beginning to provide environmental benefits. The environmental attitudes of a new company, remote from the local community, were unknown.

By 1984 another environmental issue was overshadowing Bedfordshire. The possible use of the Central Electricity Board's site at Elstow for the disposal of radioactive nuclear waste had met with universal hostility from the local community and the united opposition of the County and District councils. Encouraged by the County Council, London Brick had applied for permission to extract clay from this site. This would help to increase the company's assets while the County Council would be able to demonstrate an alternative use for the site in its efforts to defeat the proposal for the burial of nuclear waste. Thus the Council and London Brick, for so long locked in battle, were now allies in defending the local environment, engaged in a conflict in which the adversary was, ultimately, the government itself.

Notes

1 Royal Commission on Environmental Pollution (1971) *First Report*, HMSO, London, Cmnd. 4585, p.4.
2 Sandbach, F. (1982) *Principles of Pollution Control*, London, Longman, p.104.
3 For example a Harris poll published in the US on 11 June, 1981 showed that at a time when politicians were contemplating relaxing environmental controls, only 12 per cent of Americans felt the provisions of the Clean Air Act should be less strict, and 40 per cent felt the existing standards were not protective enough.

4 Royal Commission on Environmental Pollution, op. cit. p.4.
5 Ibid, p.7.
6 Davies, J. C. and Davies, B. S. (1975) *The Politics of Pollution*, 2nd ed., Indianopolis, Pegasus, pp.18-19.
7 Ogus, A. I. and Richardson, G. M. (1977) 'Economics and the environment: a study of private nuisance', *Cambridge Law Journal*, 36 (2), pp.284-325, p.290.
8 Sandbach, F. (1982) 'Pollution control: in whose interest?' Paper given to Conference on Environmental Pollution and Planning, Institute of British Geographers, Southampton.
9 Goodin, R. E. (1976) *The Politics of Rational Man*, London, Wiley, p.165.
10 W. F. Lloyd first advanced the concept in 1833 in 'Two Lectures on the Checks to Population'. The idea is developed in Hardin, G. (1968) 'The tragedy of the commons', *Science*, 162, pp.1243-1248.
11 Hardin, G. (1968) op. cit. p.1245.
12 Dawes, R. M., Delay, J. and Chaplin, W. (1974) 'The decision to pollute', *Environment and Planning*, A. vol.6, pp.3-10, p.3.
13 Ibid.
14 Batten, P. (1974) 'Economics and the environment', Unit 16c in *Microeconomics*, Course D222, pp.59-69, p.68.
15 Goodin, R. E. (1976) op. cit. p.194.
16 Hardin, G. (1968) op. cit. p.1247.
17 Among the most influential publications were, Carson, R. (1965) *The Silent Spring*, published in Penguin, 1965; The Ecologist, (1972) *A Blueprint for Survival*, Vol.2, No.1, also published by Penguin; and Meadows, D. L. et al (1972) *The Limits to Growth*, London, Earth Island.
18 Foljanty-Jost, G. and Weidner, H. (1981) 'Environmental disruption: government policy and the anti-pollution movement in Japan', Paper presented at the European Consortium for Political Research, Lancaster; Hase, T. (1981) 'Japan's growing environmental movement', *Environment*, Vol.23, No.2, March, pp.14-36.
19 Lewanski, R. (1981) 'Environmentalism and new values in Italy: new skin for an old ceremony?', Paper presented at the European Consortium for Political Research, Lancaster.
20 A summary of oil spill and their effects is given in Royal Commission on Environmental Pollution (1974) *Fourth Report, Pollution Control: Progress and Problems*, London, HMSO, Cmnd. 5780, pp.46-7.
21 Sandbach, F. (1982) op. cit. p.30.
22 Slovic, P. and Fischoff, B. (1979) 'How safe is safe enough?' In Pollitt, C. et al *Public Policy in Theory and Practice*, Hodder and Stoughton, pp.42-64.
23 Kasper, R. G. (1980) 'Perceptions of risk and their effects on decision making', In *Societal Risk Assessment*, Plenum Press, pp.71-84, p.79.
24 Goodin, R. E. (1976) op. cit. p.149.
25 Ibid, p.149.
26 Royal Commission on Environmental Pollution (1976) *Fifth Report, Air Pollution Control: An Integrated Approach*, London, HMSO, Cmnd. 6371, p.8.
27 OECD (1980) 'Public participation and environmental matters', *Science and Public Policy*, December, pp.448-469.
28 Goodin, R. E. (1976) op. cit. p.177.

29 Sandbach, F. (1982) op. cit., Chapter 6.
30 Alfandary, A. (1977) 'Air trade-offs: attempting to reconcile industrial growth and clean air in California', *Bulletin of Governmental Studies*, Public Affairs Report, Vol.18, No.5, Oct. University of California, Berkeley.
31 Russell, C. S. (1981) 'Controlled trading of pollution permits', *Environmental Science and Technology*, The American Chemical Society, Vol.15, No.1, January, pp.24-28.
32 Introduction to State of California, Air Resources Board, *Air Conservation Programme*, p.7.
33 Asimow, M. (1981) 'Delegated legislation: United States and United Kingdom', draft paper p.3.
34 Wood, C. (1982) 'Local planning authority controls over pollution', Paper presented to conference on Environmental Pollution and Planning, Institute of British Geographers, Southampton, p.3.
35 Hill, M. 'Air pollution control in Britain', Unpublished paper, p.13.
36 Rhodes, G. (1981) *Inspectorates in British Government* London, Allen and Unwin; Ashby, E. and Anderson, M. (1981) *The Politics of Clean Air*, Oxford, Clarendon.
37 Royal Commission on Environmental Pollution (1976) Fifth Report, op. cit. p.47.
38 Ibid, p.46.
39 Bennett, G. (1979) 'Pollution control in England and Wales: a review', *Environmental Policy and Law*, 5, p.95.
40 Sandbach, F. (1982) op. cit. p.100.
41 Vogel, D. (1980) 'Coercion versus consultation: a comparison of environmental protection policy in the United States and Great Britain', Paper to British Politics Group of the American Political Science Association Annual Convention, Denver, Colorado, pp.46-7.
42 Asimow, M. (1981) op. cit. p.19.
43 Department of the Environment (1981) *Clean Air*, Circular 11/81, HMSO, London.
44 Wood, C. (1980) 'Environmental impact assessment, pollution control and planning', *Clean Air*, Vol.10, No.3, pp.71-80; Williams, R. H. (1982) 'EEC envrionmental programme and pollution control', Paper for Conference on Environmental Pollution and Planning, Institute of British Geographers, Southampton.
45 The theoretical problems with Crenson's analysis are explored in Chapter 6, pp.228-238.
46 Bartlett, R. V. (1980) *The Reserve Mining Controversy*, Bloomington, Indiana University Press.
47 Ibid, p.4.
48 Goodin, R. E. (1976) op. cit.
49 Bartlett, R. V. (1980) op. cit. p.78.
50 Ibid, p.157.
51 'Pollution politics' *The Economist*, 263, 30 April, 1977, p.39.
52 From an article by Walt Anderson: 'Goodbye, Dow Chemical, you sure taught us a lesson'. The cases considered here are based on various reports, letters and Press articles.

53 Summary statement on the Dow Petrochemical Project issued by Dow Chemical, 24 January, 1977, p.8.
54 State of California, Air Resources Board (1977) 'Air pollution consequences of the proposed Sohio-BP crude oil transfer terminal at Long Beach, California', 14 July, p.61.
55 Press statement by Standard Oil Company of Ohio, Cleveland, 13 March, 1979.
56 *The Enterprise*, 16 March, 1979.
57 Quoted in Chapter 5.
58 Vogel, D. (1982) 'The political impact of the modern corporation: a case study of Clean Air legislation, 1967-1977', paper prepared in connection with the Project of the Large Corporation, sponsored by Columbia University School of Law.
59 The British Thermal Unit (BTU) is a measure of the amount of energy released by coal when burned.
60 Ackerman, B.A. and Hassler, W. T. (1981) *Clean Coal/Dirty Air*, New Haven, Yale University Press.
61 Vogel, D. (1962) op. cit. p.86.
62 Ibid, p.96.
63 Navarro, P. (1980) 'The politics of air pollution', *Public Interest*, 59, pp.36-44.
64 Ibid, p.36.
65 Salamon, L. M. and Siegried, J. J. (1977) 'Economic power and political influence: the impact of industry structure on public policy', *The American Political Science Review*, Vol.71, pp.1026-1043.
66 Waller, R. E. (1982) 'Air pollution and health', paper presented to conference on Environmental Pollution and Planning, Institute of British Geographers, Southampton.
67 Sandbach, F. (1982) 'Pollution control: in whose interest?' paper presented to conference on Environmental Pollution and Planning, Institute of British Geographers, Southampton, p.3.
68 Ibid, p.14.
69 For instance the Californian Air Resources Board (See note 54) estimated that Sohio's total expenditure for air pollution control would be less than 1.5 per cent of the Alaskan oil project costs.
70 Stretton, H. (1976) *Capitalism, Socialism and the Environment*, Cambridge University Press; Schnaiberg, A. (1980) *The Environment: From Surplus to Scarcity?* New York and Oxford, Oxford University Press.
71 Vogel, D. (1980) 'The inadequacy of contemporary opposition to business', *Daedalus*, Journal of the American Academy of Arts and Sciences, Summer, pp.47-58, p.48.
72 Vogel, D. (1982) 'The power of business in America: a re-appraisal', *British Journal of Political Science*, 13, pp.19-43.
73 Knoepfel, P. et al (1982) 'The environmental quality game: a proposal for an analytical model', International Institute for Environment and Society, Berlin.
74 Schnaiberg, A. (1980) op. cit. p.304.
75 Bartlett, R. V. (1980) op. cit. p.80.
76 This was the Stoddard Report, *Summary Report on Environmental Impacts of Taconite Waste Disposal in Lake Superior*, referred to in Bartlett, R. V. op. cit.
77 Vogel, D. (1982) 'The political impact of the modern corporation: a case study of Clean Air legislation, 1967-1977', op. cit. p.623.

78 OECD Environmental Directorate (1977) 'The OECD programme on long range transport of air pollutants: summary report', Paris.
79 Ashby, E. and Anderson, M. (1981) op. cit. pp.152-3.
80 For example the transfer of pollution from the USA into Canada. On the geographical extent of the problem, see *Environmental Review*, Citizens for a Better Environment, March, April, 1981; Californian Air Resources Board, 'The phenomenon of acid precipitation and geographical extent'; and Pearce, F. (1982) 'The menace of acid rain', *New Scientist*, 12 August, pp.419-424.
81 Elstow, where the brickfields conflict began in 1978 was, in the autumn of 1983, the scene of a new conflict of far reaching implications. The Nuclear Industry Radioactive Waste Executive (NIREX) were proposing to use the land near the village, owned by the Central Electricity Generating Board, as a repository for low and intermediate level nuclear waste. The site was on the Oxford Clay, land that in the longer term could be used for clay extraction for brickmaking, on which London Brick applied for planning permission in 1984.
82 Advertisement published in *The Observer*, 15 January, 1984.
83 *The Guardian*, 21/1/84.
84 *Bedfordshire Journal*, 1/3/84.

Sources

The material for this case study of London Brick was gathered from a variety of published and unpublished sources. Over the years Bedfordshire County Council has published a number of policy documents on the brickfields. These include: *Report on Atmospheric Pollution in the Brickfields Valley* (1960); *Bedfordshire Brickfield* (1967); *Minerals Aspect Report* (1972); *Minerals: appraisal and issues* (1978); and *Oxford Clay Subject Plan*, the final version of which was published in 1984. In addition the minutes and agenda reports of the County Council, Environmental Services Committee, Planning Advisory Group and the Brickfields Sub-Committee contain detailed information and analysis of the various stages of the conflict and are referred to in the footnotes. Among the other local authority reports relevant to the study are those of Cambridgeshire County Council, North Bedfordshire Borough Council, Mid-Bedfordshire District Council and Fenland District Council.

Various planning permissions and applications formed the substance of the conflict. Among the main sources used here are the post-war permissions and redevelopment plans submitted by the company. Central government sources include the various letters from ministers who refer to the controversy, reports of the Alkali Inspectorate, and major reports such as those of the Royal Commission on Environmental Pollution. Other issues which impinged on the conflict included the Vale of Belvoir Inquiry.

During the period of the conflict there were two major reports on atmospheric pollution. One was by Bedfordshire County Council's consultants Cremer and Warner and the other by the Department of the Environment. The Fletton Brickworks Liaison Committee, comprising several local authorities in the area and other bodies, produced reports on fluoride levels and monitoring. Other sources on pollution are the Warren Springs Laboratory and the Annual Reports of the Alkali and Clean Air Inspectorate.

Information was also gathered from the participants in the conflict, from reports, surveys and correspondence, meetings and at interviews. London Brick PLC's *Annual Reports and Accounts* and its house journal, *London Brick Review*, provided background material, and the company's case was put in various documents and interviews. The environmental arguments were presented by various local pressure groups such as Public Review of Brickmaking and the Environment (PROBE), Bedfordshire Action Committee Against Pollution (BACAP), Cranfield Action Committee (CAC), Group Action to Stop the Pit (GASP), and the

Bedfordshire Preservation Society. The local branch of the National Farmers' Union (Bedfordshire and Huntingdonshire Branch) provided survey information, and the brickworkers' perspective on the drama was gained through meetings and interviews with trade union officials. Throughout the conflict the attitudes of decision makers were canvassed through discussions and interviews with local politicians and council officials.

The conflict was prominent in the local Press, particularly in the *Bedfordshire Times*, *Bedfordshire Journal*, *Bedfordshire on Sunday* and the *Bedford Record*. Among the national newspapers to feature the story were *The Guardian*, *The Sunday Times* and *Private Eye*. There were a number of local TV reports and a feature programme by Thames TV which suggested the title for the book.

As the story unfolded, the shifting events, changing attitudes and external pressures were recorded in a diary. This helped me to connect the events and interpret the evidence. The story is reconstructed on the basis of all the available evidence and provides the substance of the empirical chapters. My interpretation of those events forms the theoretical chapters which conclude the book.

Books and Periodicals

Ackerman, B. A. and Hassler, W. T. (1981) *Clean Coal/Dirty Air*, New Haven, Yale University Press.

Agate, J. N. et. al. (1949) 'Industrial fluorosis: a study of the hazard to man and animals near Fort William, Scotland', A Report to the Fluorosis Committee, Medical Research Council, Memorandum 22, *Industrial Fluorosis*, London, HMSO.

Alexander, A. (1982) *Local Government in Britain since Reorganisation*, London, Allen & Unwin.

—— (1982) *The Politics of Local Government in the United Kingdom*, London, Longman.

Alfandary, A. (1977) 'Air trade-offs: attempting to reconcile industrial growth and clean air in California', *Bulletin of Governmental Studies*, Public Affairs Report, vol. 18, no. 5, October, University of California, Berkeley.

Allison, L. (1975) *Environmental Planning*, London, Allen & Unwin.

Ashby, E. and Anderson, M. (1981) *The Politics of Clean Air*, Oxford, Clarendon Press.

Asimow, M. (1981) 'Delegated legislation: United States and United Kingdom', draft paper.

Bachrach, P. and Baratz, M. S. (1962) 'Two faces of power', *American Political Science Review*, vol. 56, pp.947-52; also in Castles, F. et. al. (eds.) (1971) *Decisions, Organizations and Society*, Harmondsworth, Penguin, pp.376-88.

Bachrach, P. and Baratz, M. S. (1970) *Power and Poverty*, New York, Oxford University Press.

Balbus, I. D. (1971) 'The concept of interest in pluralist and Marxian analysis', *Politics and Society*, 1:2, pp.151-78.

Barr, J. (1964) 'Napoli, Bedfordshire', *New Society*, 2 April.

Bartlett, R. V. (1980) *The Reserve Mining Controversy*, Bloomington, Indiana' University Press.

Batten, P. (1974) 'Economics and the Environment', Unit 16c in *Microeconomics*, Open University Course D222, pp.59-69.

Bealey, F. (1982) 'Changing patterns of business leadership in local parties in Britain and the USA', paper for the Political Studies Association, Canterbury.

Bedfordshire Brickfield Conference, (1968) transcript of proceedings, Bedfordshire County Council, 8 January.

Bedfordshire County Council, (1952) *County Development Plan, Written Analysis*.

—— (1960) *Report on Atmospheric Pollution in the Brickworks Valley*, (The Brothwood Report), Health Department.

—— (1967) *Bedfordshire Brickfield*.

—— (1972) *County Review Minerals Aspect Report*, Consultation Draft, March.

—— (1978) *Minerals: Appraisal and Issues*, Public Consultation, March.

—— (1978) *Minerals: Appraisal and Issues*, Public Consultation, March to July.

—— (1979) *Pollution in the Marston Vale*, Report of the County Planning Officer, 11 January.

—— (1980) *County Structure Plan*.

—— (1982) *Oxford Clay Subject Plan*, Consultation Draft, May.

—— (1982) *Oxford Clay Subject Plan, Results of Public Consultation*, June/July.

Bennett, G. (1979) 'Pollution Control in England and Wales: A Review', *Environmental Policy and Law*, 5, pp.93-9, 190-3.

Benton, T. (1981) ' "Objective" interests and the sociology of power', *Sociology*, 15, pp.163-84.

Blakemore, F., Bosworth, F. J. and Green, H. H. (1941) *Proceedings of Royal Society of Medicine*, 34.

Blakemore, F., et. al. (1948) 'Industrial fluorosis of farm animals in England, attributable to the manufacture of bricks, the calcining of ironstone and to enamelling processes', *Journal of Comparative Pathology*, 58, pp.267-301.

Blowers, A. T. (1977) 'Checks and balances: the politics of minority government in Bedfordshire', *Public Administration*, Autumn, pp.305-16.

—— (1980) *The Limits of Power*, Oxford, Pergamon Press.

—— (1981) 'The Administrative Politics of Planning', *Policies, People and Administration*, Open University Course D336, paper 14.

—— (1982) 'The perils of being hung', *Local Government Studies*, vol. 8, no. 4, July/August, pp.13-20.

—— (1984) 'The triumph of material interests: geography, pollution and the environment', *Political Geography Quarterly*, vol. 3, no. 1, January, pp.49-68.

Bollard, A. E. (1982) *Brick Work: small plants in the brick industry, Alternative Industrial Framework for the UK'*, Report No. 3, Intermediate Technology Development Group.

Bradshaw, A. (1976) 'A critique of Steven Lukes' "Power: A Radical View" ', *Sociology*, vol. 10, pp.121-7.

Braybrooke, D. and Lindblom, C. E. (1963) *A Strategy of Decision*, New York, Free Press.

Brough, A., Parry, M. A. and Whittingham, C. P. (1978) 'The influence of aerial pollution on crop growth', *Chemistry and Industry*, 21 January, pp.51-53.

Brown, J. (1970) *The Un-melting Pot*, London, Tavistock.

Buchanan, S. (1982) 'Power and planning in rural areas: preparation of the Suffolk Structure Plan', in Moseley, M. (ed.) *Power, Planning and People in East Anglia*, Centre for East Anglian Studies, Norwich.

Bugler, J. (1972) *Polluting Britain: a report*, Harmondsworth, Penguin, p.115.

—— (1975) 'Bedfordshire Brick' in B. J. Smith (ed.) (1975) *The Politics of Physical Resources*, Penguin.

Bulpitt, J. G. (1967) *Party Politics in English Local Government*, London, Longman.

Burns, K. N. and Allcroft, R. (1964) 'Fluorosis in cattle: occurrence and effects in industrial areas in England and Wales', *Animal Disease Surveys Report, no. 2* pt.1, Ministry of Agriculture Fisheries and Food, London, HMSO.

Buxton, R. (1973) *Local Government*, Penguin, Harmondsworth.

California, State of, (1977) Air Resources Board 'Air pollution consequences of the proposed Sohio-BP crude oil transfer terminal at Long Beach, California', 14 July.

—— Air Resources Board, *Air Conservation Programme*.

—— Air Resources Board, 'The phenomenon of acid precipitation and geographical extent'.

Carson, R. (1965) *The Silent Spring*, Harmondsworth, Penguin.

Castells, M. (1977) *The Urban Question*, London, Arnold.

—— (1978) *City, Class and Power*, London, Macmillan.

Cawson, A. (1978) 'Pluralism, corporatism and the role of the state', *Government and Opposition*, Routledge & Kegan Paul (draft chapter).

Clarke, A. J., Lucas, D. H. and Ross, F. F. (1970) 'Tall stacks—how effective are they?', Central Electricity Generating Board, Paper to Second International Clean Air Conference, Washington, December.

Clarke, J. and Costello, N. (1982) 'The production of social divisions', *Social Sciences: a foundation course*, Unit 13, The Open University, p.55.

Clayton, P. (1970a) 'Brickwork odours—a subjective evaluation of a removal process', Warren Springs Laboratory, Department of Technology, LR 131 (AP).

—— (1970b) 'Brickworks odours: a laboratory investigation of their production, evaluation and removal', Warren Springs Laboratory, Department of Technology, LR 122 (AP).

Clegg, T. (1982) 'Social consumption, social investment and the dual state: the case of transport policy in the Paris region', paper for the Political Studies Association, Canterbury.

Coing, H. (1966) *Renovation Urbaine et Changement Social*, Paris, Les Editions Ouvrières.

Collier, L. J. (1963) 'The world's largest brickworks', *Bedfordshire Magazine*, vol. 9, no. 65, Summer, pp.18-20.

Connolly, W. E. (1972) 'On "interests" in politics', *Politics and Society*, vol. 2, pp.459-79.

Countryside Review Committee (1976) *The Countryside—Problems and Policies*, London, HMSO.

—— (1978) *Food Production in the Countryside*, London, HMSO.

Cox, A. (1979) *Brickmaking: A History and Gazeteer*, Bedfordshire County Council and Royal Commission on Historical Monuments (England), Survey of Bedfordshire.

Cremer and Warner (1979a and b) *The Environmental Assessment of the Existing and Proposed Brickworks in the Marston Vale, Bedfordshire* (a: General Appraisal; b: Main Report), Consulting Engineers and Scientists, London and Cheshire.

—— (1980) 'Comments on the London Brick Company Research Laboratories', Memorandum (no.RM564) on the Assessment and Implications of the Cremer and Warner Report prepared for Bedfordshire County Council, March.

—— (1982) 'LBC emissions—predictions of current dispersion pattern and resultant concentration at ground level', Report no.82066, 18 June.

—— (1983) 'The January 1983 proposals by London Brick Company for developments in the Marston Vale and their effect on improvements in air quality in the area', Report no.83839, p.12.

Crenson, M. (1971) *The Un-Politics of Air Pollution: A Study of Non-Decisionmaking in the Cities*, Baltimore, The John Hopkins Press.

Crewe, L. (1974) (ed.) *Elites in Western Democracy*, London, Croom Helm.

Crosland, A. (1974) *Socialism Now*, London, Jonathan Cape.

Crossman, R. (1975) *Diaries of a Cabinet Minister*, Hamish Hamilton and Jonathan Cape, vol. 1.

Dahl, R. A. (1957) 'The concept of Power', *Behavioural Science*, 2.

—— (1958) 'A critique of the Ruling Elite model', *American Political Science Review*, 52.

—— (1961) *Who Governs? Democracy and Power in an American City*, Chicago University Press.

Davidoff, P. and Reiner, A. (1962) 'A choice theory of planning', *Journal of the American Institute of Planners*, vol. 28, May.

Davidson, J. and Wibberley, G. (1977) *Planning and the Rural Environment*, Oxford, Pergamon Press.

Davies, J. C. and Davies, B. S. (1975) *The Politics of Pollution*, 2nd ed., Indianapolis, Pegasus.

Dawes, R. M., Delay, J. and Chaplin, W. (1974) 'The decision to pollute', *Environment and Planning*, A. vol. 6, pp.3-10.

Dearlove, J. (1973) *The Politics of Policy in Local Government*, Cambridge University Press.

—— (1979) *The Reorganisation of British Local Government*, Cambridge University Press.

Department of the Environment *102nd Annual Report on Alkali, and C. Works, 1965*, London, HMSO.

—— *107th Annual Report on Alkali, and C. Works, 1971*, London, HMSO.

—— *108th Annual Report on Alkali, and C. Works, 1970*, London, HMSO.

—— (1980) *Air Pollution in the Bedfordshire Brickfields*, Directorate of Noise, Clean Air and Waste 6/80.

—— (1981) *Clean Air*, Circular 11/81, London, HMSO.

Domhoff, G. W. (1978) *Who Really Rules?*, New Brunswick, N. J., Transaction Books.

Donaldson, R. J. (1974) 'Air Pollution and health', Medical Officer of Health, Teeside Health Department, Spring.

Douglas, J. W. B. and Waller, R. E. (1966) 'Air Pollution and respiratory infection in children', *British Journal of Preventive Social Medicine*, 20(1), pp.1-8.

Dow Chemical (1977) Summary statement on the Dow Petrochemical Project, 24 January.

Dunleavy, P. (1980) *Urban Political Analysis*, London, Macmillan.

—— (1981) *The Politics of Mass Housing in Britain, 1945-1975*, Oxford, Clarendon Press.

—— (1981b) 'Alternative theories of liberal democratic politics: the pluralist-marxist debate in the 1980s', paper for Open University Social Sciences Foundation course.

—— (1982) 'Perspectives on urban studies' in Blowers, A. et. al. (1982) (eds.) *Urban Change and Conflict*, London, Harper & Row.

Easton, D. (1965) *A Framework for Political Analysis*, Englewood Cliffs, Prentice-Hall.

Eckstein, H. (1960) *Pressure Group Politics*, London, Allen & Unwin, p.15.

Ecologist, The (1972) 'A Blueprint for Survival', vol. 2, no. 1, Harmondsworth, Penguin.

Economist, The (1977) 'Pollution politics', 263, 30 April.

Elcock, H. (1982) *Local Government*, London, Methuen.

Elkin, S. (1974) *Politics and Land Use Planning*, Cambridge University Press.

Elliott, B. and McCrone, D. (1982) *The City: patterns of domination and conflict*, London, Macmillan.

Flynn, R. (1983) 'Co-optation and strategic planning' in King, R. (ed.) *Capital and Politics*, Routledge & Kegan Paul.

Foljanty-Jost, G. and Weidner, H. (1981) 'Environmental disruption: government policy and the anti-pollution movement in Japan', Paper presented at the European Consortium for Political Research, Lancaster.

Forestry Commission (1980) Mr D. F. Fourt, Proof of Evidence, Vale of Belvoir Inquiry.

Friend, J. K. and Jessop, W. N. (1969) *Local Government and Strategic Choice*, Tavistock, London.

Gaventa, J. (1980) *Power and Powerlessness: Quiescence and Rebellion in an Appalachian Valley*, Urbana, University of Illinois Press.

Gilbert, O. L. (1971-9) 'Tree growth in the vicinity of the Ridgmont Brickworks Bedfordshire' (unpublished).

Gladwin, T. N. (1980) 'Patterns of environmental conflict over industrial facilities in the U.S., 1970-8', *Natural Resources Journal*, vol. 20, no. 2, April, pp.243-74.
Goldsmith, M. (1980) *Politics, Planning and the City*, London, Hutchinson.
Goodin, R. E. (1976) *The Politics of Rational Man*, London, Wiley.
Gregory, R. (1969) 'Local elections and the rule of anticipated reactions', *Political Studies*, vol. 17, pp.31-47.
—— (1971) *The Price of Amenity*, London, Macmillan.

Hardin, G. (1968) 'The tragedy of the commons', *Science*, 162, pp.1243-8.
Hase, T. (1981) 'Japan's growing environmental movement', *Environment*, vol. 23, no. 2, March, pp.14-36.
Heclo, H. H. (1969) 'The councillor's job', *Public Administration*, vol. 47, pp.185-202.
Hill, D. M. (1974) *Democratic Theory and Local Government*, London, Allen & Unwin.
Hill, M. J. (1972) *The Sociology of Public Administration*, London, Weidenfeld & Nicholson.
—— 'Air pollution control in Britain', unpublished paper.
Hillier, R. (1981) *Clay that Burns: a history of the Fletton brick industry*, London Brick Company Ltd, Collier.
Hindess, B. (1971) *The Decline of Working Class Politics*, London, MacGibbon & Kee.
—— (1982) 'Power, interests and the outcomes of struggles', *Sociology*, vol. 16, no. 4, November, pp.498-511.
Hunter, F. (1953) *Community Power Structure*, Chapel Hill Books.

Jack, M. (1974) 'Elite theory: ideological, tautological or scientific?' in *Elites in Western Democracy*, edited by I. Crewe, British Political Sociology Yearbook, vol. 1, London, Croom Helm.
Jones, C. (1975) *Clean Air: the policies and politics of pollution control*, Pittsburgh, University of Pittsburgh Press.
Jones, G. (ed.) (1980) *New Approaches to the Study of Central–Local Relationships*, SSRC, Gower.

Kasper, R. G. (1980) 'Perceptions of risk and their effects on decision making', in *Societal Risk Assessment*, Plenum Press, pp.71-84.
Kimber, R. and Richardson, J. J. (1974) *Campaigning for the Environment*, London, Routledge & Kegan Paul.
Kirk, G. (1980) *Urban Planning in a Capitalist Society*, London, Croom Helm.
Knoepfel, P. et. al. (1982) 'The environmental quality game: a proposal for an analytical model', International Institute for Environment and Society, Berlin (unpublished).
Kvartovkina, L. K. (1968) 'Effect of discharges from an aluminium works on health of children' *Hyg. Sanit.*, English Edition 33 (4-6), pp.106-8.

Lee, J. M. (1963) *Social Leaders and Public Persons*, Oxford, Clarendon Press.
Lewanski, R. (1981) 'Environmentalism and new values in Italy: new skin for an

old ceremony?', paper presented at the European Consortium for Political Research, Lancaster.

Lindblom, C. E. (1977) *Politics and Markets: the World's Political–Economic systems*, New York, Basic Books.

Lipset, S. M. (1981) 'Whatever happened to the proletariat?', *Encounter*, June, pp.18-34.

London Brick Company Limited (1979a) Planning Application for New Brickworks at King's Dyke, Whittlesey to replace existing Brickworks known as Central 1 and 2 and C.B. 1, July.

—— (1979b) Planning Application for Brickworks at Stewartby and associated mineral working and landscaping, August.

—— (1979c) New Stewartby and Ridgmont Works. Outline Landscape Report.

—— (1979d) *Brickworks Redevelopment Plan*, London Brick Company Research Laboratories, Assessment and Implications of the Cremer and Warner Report prepared for Bedfordshire County Council.

—— (1979e) *Report and Accounts*.

London Brick Landfill Limited (1980) *North East Leicestershire Prospect*, Public Inquiry, Proof of Evidence, January.

Lunn, J. E. et. al. (1967) 'Patterns of respiratory illness in Sheffield infant school on children', *British Journal of Preventive Social Medicine*, 21, pp.7-16.

Lukes, S. (1974) *Power: a Radical View*, London, Macmillan.

Marx, K. (1969) 'Theses on Feuerbach' in K. Marx and F. Engels *Selected Works*, London, Lawrence & Wishart.

Meadows, D. L. et. al. (1972) *The Limits to Growth*, London, Earth Island.

Michels, R. (1915) *Political Parties*, New York, Free Press, 1959.

Miliband, R. (1969) *The State in Capitalist Society*, London, Quartet Books.

Ministry of Housing and Local Government (1965) *Derelict Land*, Circular 68/65, October.

Monopolies and Mergers Commission (1976) *Building Bricks: A report on the supply of building bricks*, London, HMSO.

Muchnik, D. N. (1970) *Urban Renewal in Liverpool: A Study of the Politics of Redevelopment*, Occ. Papers on Social Administration no. 33, G. Bell.

Murphy, D. C. (1976) *The Silent Watchdog*, London, Constable.

Navarro, P. (1980) 'The politics of air pollution', *Public Interest*, 59, pp.36-44.

Newby, H. (1980) *Green and Pleasant Land?*, Harmondsworth, Penguin.

Newton, K. (1976) *Second City Politics*, Oxford, Clarendon Press.

O'Connor, J. (1973) *The Fiscal Crisis of the State*, New York, St. Martin's Press.

OECD (1977) 'The OECD programme on long-range transport of air pollutants: summary report', Environmental Directorate, Paris.

—— (1980) 'Public participation and environmental matters', *Science and Public Policy*, December, pp.448-69.

Ogus, A. I. and Richardson, G. M. (1977) 'Economics and the environment: a study of private nuisance', *Cambridge Law Journal*, 36(2) pp.284-325.

344   Something in the Air

Olives, J. (1976) 'The struggle against urban renewal in the Cité d'Aliarte (Paris)', in Pickvance (ed.), *Urban Sociology: critical essays*, London, Tavistock, pp.174-97.

Open University (1975) 'Planning and Pollution, Areas of Concern', *Environmental Pollution and Public Health*, Open University Course PT272, Unit 16.

O'Riordan, T. (1976) *Environmentalism*, London, Pion Press.

Pahl, R. (1977) '"Collective consumption" and the state in capitalist and state socialist societies' in R. Scase (ed.), *Industrial Society: aspects of class, cleavage and control*, London, Allen & Unwin.

Parry, G. and Morriss, P. (1974) 'When is a decision not a decision?' in *Elites in Western Democracy*, edited by I. Crewe, British Sociology Yearbook, vol. 1, London, Croom Helm.

Pearce, F. (1982) 'The menace of acid rain', *New Scientist*, 12 August, pp.419-24.

Petrilli, R. L. (1960) 'Epidemiological studies of air pollution effects in Genoa, Italy', Arch., *Environmental Health*, 12, 733-40.

Plamenatz, J. (1954) 'Interests', *Political Studies*, vol. 2, pp.3-17.

Polsby, N. W. (1963) *Community Power and Political Theory*, New Haven, Yale University Press and 2nd edition, 1980.

Porteous, A., Attenborough, K. and Pollitt, C. (eds.) (1977) *Pollution: The Professionals and the Public*, Air Pollution and Visual Amenity, The Open University Press. See esp. article 3, 'An account of the public inquiry into the appeal by Redland Bricks Ltd.', prepared by The Woburn Sands District Society.

Presthus, R. (1971) 'Pluralism and elitism' in Castles, F. et. al. (eds.) *Decisions, Organisations and Society*, Harmondsworth, Penguin, pp.331-9.

Raine, J. (ed.) (1981) *In Defence of Local Government*, Birmingham, INLOGOV.

Reade, E. (1976) 'An attempt to distinguish planning from other modes of decision making', Seminar Paper, University of Manchester, 24 November, pp.8-9.

—— (1982a) 'The British planning system', Unit 19 of *Urban Change and Conflict*, The Open University Press.

—— (1982b) 'Section 52 and corporatism in planning', *Journal of Planning and Environmental Law*, January, pp.8-16.

—— (1982c) 'Officers and councillors, "facts" and "values"', paper presented to Urban and Regional Studies Unit, University of Kent, Canterbury.

Rhodes, G. (1981) *Inspectorates in British Government*, London, Allen & Unwin.

Richards, P. (1973) *The Reformed Local Government System*, London, Allen & Unwin.

Royal Commission on Environmental Pollution (1971) *First Report*, London, HMSO, Cmnd.4585.

—— (1974) *Fourth Report, Pollution Control: Progress and Problems*, London, HMSO, Cmnd.5780.

—— (1976) *Fifth Report, Air Pollution Control: An Integrated Approach*, London, HMSO, Cmnd.6371.

Russell, C. (1981) 'Controlled trading of pollution permits', *Environmental Science and Technology*, The American Chemical Society, vol. 15, no. 1, January, pp.24-8.

Salamon, L. M. and Siegried, J. J. (1977) 'Economic power and political influence: the impact of industry structure on public policy', *The American Political Science Review*, vol. 71, pp.1026-43.
Sandbach, F. (1980) *Environment, Ideology and Policy*, Oxford, Blackwell.
—— (1982) 'Pollution control: in whose interest?', paper presented to conference on Environmental Pollution and Planning, Institute of British Geographers, Southampton.
—— (1982) *Principles of Pollution Control*, Harlow, Longman.
Saunders, P. (1974) 'They make the rules: political routines and the generation of political bias', *Policy and Politics*, 4, pp.31-58.
—— (1980) *Urban Politics: a Sociological Interpretation*, Harmondsworth, Penguin.
—— (1981) *Social Theory and the Urban Question*, London, Hutchinson.
—— (1982) 'Why study central–local relations?', *Local Government Studies*, May/June, pp.55-66.
Schattschneider, E. E. (1960) *The Semi-Sovereign People: A Realist's View of Democracy in America*, New York, Holt, Rinehart and Winston.
Schnaiberg, A. (1980) *The Environment: from surplus to scarcity*, Oxford University Press.
Self, P. (1971) 'Elected representatives and management in local government: an alternative analysis', *Public Administration*, vol. 49, Autumn.
—— (1972) *Administrative Theories and Politics*, London, Allen & Unwin.
Sharpe, L. J. (1960) 'The politics of local government in Greater London', *Public Administration*, vol. 38, pp.157-72.
Shoard, M. (1980) *The Theft of the Countryside*, London, Temple Smith.
Skellington, R. (1978) *The Housing of Minority Groups in Bedford*.
—— (1980) *Council house allocation in a multi-racial town*, The Open University, Faculty of Social Sciences, Occasional Paper Series.
Slovic, P. and Fischoff, B. (1979) 'How safe is safe enough?' in C. Pollitt et. al. *Public Policy in Theory and Practice*, Hodder & Stoughton, pp.42-64.
Stevens, Sir Roger (Chairman) (1976) *Planning Control over Mineral Working*, London.
Stretton, H. (1976) *Capitalism, Socialism and the Environment*, Cambridge University Press.

Vale of Belvoir Inquiry (1980), Transcript of the Proceedings, 27 February, p.51.
Vogel, D. (1980) 'Coercion versus consultation: a comparison of environmental protection policy in the United States and Great Britain', Paper to British Politics Group of the American Political Science Association Annual Convention, Denver, Colorado.
—— (1980) 'The inadequacy of contemporary opposition to business', *Daedalus*, Journal of the American Academy of Arts and Sciences, Summer, pp.47-58.
—— (1981) 'How business responds to opposition: Corporate political strategies during the 1970s', unpublished draft.
—— (1982) 'The political impact of the modern corporation: a case study of Clear Air legislation, 1967-1977', paper prepared in connection with the Project of the Large Corporation, sponsored by Columbia University School of Law.

—— (1982) 'The power of business in America: a re-appraisal', *British Journal of Political Science*, 13, pp.19-43.

Waller, R. E. (1982) 'Air pollution and health', Paper presented to conference on Environmental Pollution and Planning, Institute of British Geographers, Southampton.

Weber, M. (1947) *The Theory of Social and Economic Organizations*, New York, The Free Press.

Westergaard, J. and Resler, H. (1975) *Class in a Capitalist Society*, London, Heinemann.

Wildavsky, A. (1973) 'If planning is everything, maybe it's nothing', *Journal of Policy Sciences*, vol. 4, no. 2, pp.127-53.

Williams, R. H. (1982) 'EEC environmental programme and pollution control', Paper for Conference on Environmental Pollution and Planning, Institute of British Geographers, Southampton.

Winkler, J. (1977) 'The corporate economy: theory and administration' in R. Scase (ed.) *Industrial Society: class, cleavage and control*, London, Allen & Unwin.

Wolfinger, R. E. (1972) 'Non decisions and the study of local politics', *American Political Science Review*, vol. 65, pp.1063-80.

Wood, C. (1980) 'Environmental impact assessment, pollution control and planning', *Clean Air*, vol. 10, no. 3, pp.71-80.

—— (1982) 'Local planning authority controls over pollution', Paper presented to Conference on Environmental Pollution and Planning, Institute of British Geographers, Southampton.

Wragg, R. and Robertson, J. (1978) *Post War trends in employment*, Research Paper no. 3. Department of Employment.

Principal Actors

In all the indexes, page numbers in italics refer to chapter end notes.

Aldridge, James (Chairman, Bedfordshire Preservation Society)   *160*, 172, *206*

Andrews, Councillor Tom (Labour)   197

Atherton, Dr Howard (District Alkali Inspector)   77, 84, 100, (*see also* Alkali Inspectorate)

Ball, Councillor Kenneth (Conservative)   156

Barber, Trevor (Chairman, CAC)   69, *109*

Benyon, William, MP   136, 160

Blowers, Councillor Andy (Labour Group Leader)   76, 89, 101, 123–5, 132–4, 138–40, 142–3, 151, 154, 156, *160*, 165, 169, 173–4, 181, 186–7, 189, 191–4, 196–8, *207*, 225, 227, 248

Borland, Mr (farmer)   41

Branston, Frank (journalist)   70, 195, 224

Bristow, J. (Senior)   104

Bristow, James (Managing Director, London Brick Company)   14, 42, 76–7, 104, 121, 146, 162, 169, 182, 184, 191, 203, 224–5, 266, 285, *295*

Brothwood, Dr (former Medical Officer of Health)   77

Campbell, Lord (Chairman, Milton Keynes Development Corporation)   144

Causer, Wally (trade unionist)   191

Chapman, Councillor Allan (Conservative)   76, 89, 101–2, 116, 120, 123, 132, 139–40, 143, 151, *160*, 165, 169, 174

Clarry, Stan (District Officer, Transport and General Workers' Union)   181, 186–7

Cook, Councillor Charles (Independent)   132, 156, 185

Cowley, Geoffrey (County Planning Officer)   73, 75, 87

Dawson, John (Deputy County Secretary)   75, 113–14, 116, 119, 132, 164–5, 188–9

Dixon, Councillor Ian (Conservative)   138–40, 144, 152, 154

Dunkley, Mr (farmer)   42, *54*

Elven, John (Chief Executive, Bedfordshire County Council)   196

Everard, Councillor Cyril (Conservative)   101, 133, 183, 189, 195

Farley, Councillor Mick (Labour)   139, 153–4, 156, 186, 269, *293*

Fox, Marcus, MP (Minister for the Environment)   136, 143, *160*, 169, *206*, *294*

Gershon, Councillor Phyllis (Conservative)   132, 151

Gibbons, Councillor Brian (Liberal)   156, 197

Goode, Peter (farmer, Secretary of PROBE)   70–1, 76–7, 88–90, 105, 107, 111, 120–1, 134, 142–4, 146, *159–60*, 169, 183, 197, 221

Griffin, Tony (County Planning Officer)   75, 79, 93–4, 114, 118–19, 123, 132, 140, 146, 151, 183

Harris, Ian (Cranfield Institute of Technology)   80, *109*

Hastings, Stephen, MP   136, *160*, 169, *206*

Hendry, Councillor Philip (Conservative Group Leader)   58, 74–6, 89, 100–1, 105–6, 116–17, 121, 123–4, 132, 134, 138–40, 143–4, 151–4, 156, 163–6, 169, 173, 187, 191, 194, 197–8, *206*, 221, 225, 227, 246, 268–9, 274, *293–4*

Heseltine, Michael, MP (Secretary of State for Environment)   143–4

Hillier, Councillor John (Conservative)   133, 174

Holloman, Dr Derek (Rothamsted Institute)   122

Humphries, Councillor Edward (Conservative)   132, 154, 156, 165

Jones, Miss Emily   87, *109*

Keens, Bryan (trade unionist)   187, 192, 198, *293*
Kemp, Councillor Michael (Conservative)   76, 79–80, 100–1, 117, 138, 140, 183, 188, 196, 198, 221, 227, 246, 268
Keyes, Hon. Miss Elizabeth   87, 221

Lawther, Prof. P. J. (Medical Research Council)   36, 77, 83–4, 279
Lennon, Councillor Janice (Liberal)   140, 151, 154, 156, 174, 197
Lobban, Dr Alfred (Medical Officer of Health)   36, 106, 279
Loxham, Prof. John (PROBE member)   89
Lucas, Mr D. H. (CEGB)   78, 80, *109*

Meier, Stuart (External Relations, LBC)   *160–1*, 191

Needs, Bill (London Brick Landfill)   118–19

Parish, David (PROBE member)   89
Patrick, Mr George (farmer)   41
Payne, Richard (Secretary local National Farmers' Union)   144, 169, 170, *206*

Rhodes, Dr David (GP, PROBE member)   89, 134
Rice, Mr A. P. (Cremer and Warner)   129
Rowe, J. W.   *14*
Rowe, Jeremy (Chairman, London Brick Company)   90, 144–5, 167–8, 173, 183, 225, 266

Shaw, Councillor Mrs (Cambridgeshire County Council Planning Committee)   179
Shepherd, Councillor Marion (Conservative)   197
Skeet, Trevor, MP   134–6, 169
Skelton, Jack (trade unionist)   181
Smart, Prof. Gerald   144
Smith, R. G. (CAC)   *109*
Sollars, Councillor Roy (Conservative)   133, 140, 144, 151–3, 157, 183, *207*

Stanbury, Anthony (PROBE member)   89, 120, *160*
Stewart, Halley (founder London Brick Company)   4, *14*, 266
Stewart, Sir Malcolm (first Chairman, London Brick Company)   4, 5, *14*, 266
Stewart, Sir Ronald (former Chairman, London Brick Company)   *53*, 266

Tagg, Roger (member PROBE)   86, 89, *109*, 160
Tavistock, Marquis of (Chairman, PROBE)   89, 105, 120, 134, 143–4, *160*, 169, 172, *206*
Thornley, Councillor Martin (Labour)   196

Whitbread, Councillor Samuel (Conservative)   144, 152, 154, 268
White, Councillor Keith (Conservative, Chairman, Environmental Services Committee)   59, 76, 79–80, 101, 124, 140, 145–6, 151–4, 165–6, 172, 174, 176, 180, 183, 187, 189, 191, 194–5, 196–8, *206*, 227, 269, 274, 286, 293–5
Wickson, Councillor Diana (Conservative)   174
Witherick, David (Vice-Chairman, local National Farmers' Union)   170
Wix, Dr Paul (South Bank Polytechnic)   88, 109
Wootton, Councillor Edward (Conservative)   152, 157, 197
Wright, John (Estates Manager, London Brick)   77, 182, 195, 225
Wright, Michael (Deputy Chairman, London Brick)   183

Young, Ray (Chairman, GASP)   68, 73–4, *108*, 218, 236, 258

General Index

abstention   230–1, 234–5
acid rain   85, 95, 132, 135–6, 144, 280,
    305, 326–7
Ackerman, B. A. & Hassler, W. T.
    319–20, *332*
actors
    role   74–7, 227, 249, 253–4, 291, *see*
    separate index
administrative politics   270–5, 278, 281,
    286, Fig. 7.1, 289
Agate, J. N. et. al.   *53, 110*
agriculture
    landscape   30
    farming in Marston Vale   38, 40–1, 86,
    145
air pollution
    effect on animals   37–8, 40, 83, 97, 99,
    149, 279, 303
    control   33–4, 39, 43, 59, 63, 68, 71,
    84–5, 92, 98–9, 102, 106, 114, 126–9,
    153, 156, 163, 167, 173, 179
    effect on crops   38–9, 149, 279, 303
    problems of evidence   36–7, 40,
    see also pollution
    effect on health   35–7, 72, 82–3, 87–8,
    97, 99–100, 105–6, 148–9, 151, 153,
    279–80, 303
    as issue   4, 32–43, 49–50, 67–8, 81–90,
    130, 153, 176, 199–202, 264–5
    monitoring   43, 46–7, 82, 88, 96–7,
    100, 114, 129, 149, 151, 201
    pollution levels   82, 84, 96–8, 148–9,
    Fig. 4.4, 153, 201–2
    research on control   43, 94, 102, 114,
    131, 153, 167, 188, 201, 219, 247
    effect on vegetation   39, 97, 99
Alaska   317
Alexander, A.   *294*
Alfandary, A.   *331*
Alkali Inspectorate
    criticism of   35, 39, 43, 72, 84, 279
    and London Brick   46–7, 49–50, 63,
    67–8, 79–80, 86, 106, 122, 125–6,
    131, 136, 149, 167, 179, 201, 219,
    233, 247–8, 280, 300, 303–4, 325
    role in decision making   34, 67, 82,
    101, 134, 136, 276, 278, 281, 309–11
Alkali Acts   34, *109*, 309

Allison, L.   220, *256*
ambient air standards   307, 319
amenity   264, 283, 284, 289, 304–5, 312
Ampthill (Beds.)   121, 225
Anglesey   83
anticipated reactions   230–1, 234–5
Area Health Authority (Beds.)   36, 88,
    126
asbestos   315, 323
Ashby, E. and Ashby, M.   *259, 331, 333*
Asimow, M.   311, *331*
Aspley Guise (Beds.)   5, 76, 283
Association of Professional & Executive
    Staff (APEX)   190–1

Bachrach, P. and Baratz, M. S.   230,
    255, 257
Balbus, I. D.   241, *258, 295*
Banbury Alton   51
Bartlett, R. V.   6, *15*, 216, *256, 258*, 281,
    294, 314–17, *332*
Batten, P.   *330*
Bealey, F.   276, 294
Bedford   1, 3–5, 44, 98, 268
Bedford, Duke of   41
Bedford Record   70, Fig. 4.3, *111, 160*,
    205, 207
Bedfordshire Action Committee Against
    Pollution (BACAP)   58, 68, 220
Bedfordshire Brickfield   14
Bedfordshire Brickfield Conference
    44–5, 47, *55*, 56, 118, 216, 220, 246,
    282
Bedfordshire County Council
    decision April 1980   138–142
    decision July 1980   152–6, 173, 226
    decision December 1980   172–6
    decision April 1981   197–8
    and E.S.C.   12, 58, 193, 196–7, 225–7,
    274–5
    and 'L' field   58
    and pollution control   46, 82
    role   12, 14, 45–6, 58, 85–7, 122–4,
    138–9, 157, *206*, 225
Bedfordshire County Development Plan
    (1952)   33

Bedfordshire County Structure Plan
    (1980)   33, 45, 55, 204, 278, 282
Bedfordshire Journal   70, *108, 110, 160,*
    161, 205, 333
Bedfordshire Minerals Appraisal and
    Issues (1978)   33, *52, 55*
Bedfordshire Minerals Aspect Report
    (1972)   33, *52, 55*
Bedfordshire on Sunday   53–4, 70, 79,
    108–10, 135, *160–1,* 195, *205–8,* 224
Bedfordshire Oxford Clay Subject Plan
    (1982)   45, *52,* 55, 65, *108,* 200,
    208, 278
Bedfordshire Preservation Society   121,
    126, 135, 142, 144, 170, 172, *206,* 236
Bedfordshire Times   54, 70–1, *108–11,*
    122, 124, 135, 145–6, *159–61,* 166,
    181, 187, 194, *205–7,* 224
Belvoir, Vale of   25, Fig. 2.7, 32
    inquiry   117–20, 156, *159*
    and remote disposal in Bedfordshire
    208, 247, 329, *333*
Bennett, G.   *53,* 310, *331*
Benton, T.   *15, 258*
'best practicable means'   34, 309
Birmingham   95
Blakemore, F. et. al.   *54*
Bletchley   2
Bletchley brickworks   1, 196, *206*
'Bletchley disease'   106
Blowers, A. T.   55, *108, 159*
    role, in case study   x, 10–11, *15, 108*
Bollard, A. E.   *14, 51*
Bradshaw, A.   229, *257*
Braybrooke, D. and Lindblom, C. E.
    293
bricks   17, Fig. 2.3, 19
brickmaking
    decline   283
    economics of   16–24, *51, 103,* 184–5
    Fletton process   1, 16, 84, 215
    history   16–17
    non-Fletton industry   17, *51,* 203, *208*
    process   59, Fig. 3.1, 163, *see also*
    Hoffman Kiln, tunnel kilns
    production   17, Figs. 2.1, 2.2, 181
brickworks   Fig 2.4, *see also* separate
    works and London Brick
brickworks consultation area   67
Brickfields sub-committee   113, 123,
    159, 207–8

British Broadcasting Corporation (BBC)
    TV   95, 105
Brogborough (Bedfordshire)   4, 67, 79,
    93
Brogborough Hill   74, 77, 329
Brogborough No. 1 (pit)   31–2
Brogborough No. 2 (pit)   1, 31–2, 52,
    200, 329
Brothwood Report   36, *53,* 97, 234, *257,*
    279
Brough, A. et. al.   *54, 258*
Brown, J.   *55*
Buchanan, S.   *294*
Buckinghamshire   1, 168, 179, 196, 245
Bugler, J.   *14,* 42, *54*
Bulpitt, J. G.   *293*
Bunyan, John   4, 56
bureaucracy   270–2
Burns, K. N. and Alleroft, R.   *54, 257*
business
    cycle   19, 24
    and government   276–8
    as interest   210, 215–17, 241, 323
    power   47, 239–40, 263–4, 275–6,
    281–2, 303, 316, 321–4, 326
Butterley (brick company)   17, 203
Buxton, R.   *293*

cadmium   303
California   303, 317–18, 323, *331*
callow   31, *208*
Calvert brickworks (Bucks)   1
Cambridgeshire
    contrast to Bedfordshire   180, 283,
    314, 324
    new brickworks in   91, 93–4, 104, 120,
    168, 173, 177–80, 183, 196, 199, 242,
    245, 248, 285, 301
Cambridgeshire County Council   177
    planning committee decision   178–80,
    206
Carson, R.   *333*
carbon dioxide   305
carbon monoxide   307
case-study approach   9, 10, 212, 254
    American case-studies   312–22
Castells, M.   *259,* 264, 284, *292*
Cawson, A.   *254*
Central 1 and 2 brickworks (Cambs.)   91,
    178

Central Electricity Generating Board
    (CEGB)   31, *53*, 84, 109, 154, *333*
chairman–chief officer relations   273, 289
Cheshire County Council   273
chimneys
    and new works   59
    and pollution control   84, 94, 153,
        163, 178, 202, *208*, 276, 279–80, 300,
        303, 309, 321
    effect on siting of new works   78–81,
        97–8
    effect on trans-boundary pollution   85,
        95, 122, 136
Clarke, J. & Costello, N.   *15*
class
    conflict   238, 251–2, 262–7
    interests   240–2, 251–2, 284
clay pits
    problem of filling   24–27, Fig. 2.7
    landscaping   25, 29–30, 45–6
    low-level restoration   92, 115–16, 199
    restoration   25, 30–32, 45–6, 65–7, 91,
        115–16
Clayton, P.   *54*
Clean Air Acts (UK)   280, 290, 309, 322,
    330
Clean Air Acts (USA)   305, 307, 317, 319
Clegg, T.   285, *292*, *295*
coal
    effect on pollution   322
coal-fired power plants
    UK   327
    USA   318–22, 326–6
coal interests and alliances
    USA   319–21, 324–5
Coing, H.   *259*, *292*
Collier, L. J.   *14*
collective consumption   284, 289
committee system   273–4
concepts   287–90
    environmental   264, 287
    mediating concepts   211, 261–2, 287
conflict   ix, 6–7, 30, 50, 58–9, Chapters
    6–8
    confrontation   56, Chapter 4
    locational   282
    negotiation   Chapter 3, 156, 232
    over time and space   282–6
    active phase   48–9, 232
    dominant phase   47, 232
    passive phase   47–8, 232

political   125, 267–70
resolution   Chapter 5
Connolly, W. E.   241, *258*
Conservative group   76, 143, 197–8, 290
    split   124–5, 138–9, 151–2, 157, 174,
        268–70, 276
    and trade unions   187–8, 222
    and business   268, 320
control of Pollution Act (1974)   57
Coronation brickworks (Beds.)
    new works   203–4
    old works   3, 22, 327
Coronation pit   2, 80, 91, 203–4
corporate power   *see* business, industry,
        London Brick
corporatism   229, 277–8, 281, 285, 287,
        Fig. 7.1, 290, 325
cost/benefit of decisions   242–3, 286,
        297, 299–302
council meetings
    role   226
councillors
    attitudes to conflict   Fig. 4.3, 138
    role   123, 132, 151, 174, 226–7
    voting intentions   Fig. 5.1, 268
    voting patterns   Fig. 4.5, 156, 157,
        174, Fig. 5.2, 268
    see individual actors
Counter Press, Milton Keynes   71, 108
Countryside Review Committee   52
Cox, A. J.   *51*, *55*
Cranfield (Beds.)   4, 61, 67, 69, 76, 79,
        81, 88, 126, 183
Cranfield Action Committee   69, 74, 77,
        79–81, 91, 93, 95, *109*, 121, 218, 220,
        244
Cranfield Institute of Technology   4, 80
Cremer and Warner (Consultants)   *53*,
        85–6, *110*, 126, 131–2, 145, 148–9,
        151, 158, *159*, 161, 201, *208*
    attitude to London Brick   126–130
    recommendations   99–100, 116, 167,
        178, 200
    report   95–100, 215, 279–80, 303, 316
    reactions to report   100–5

Dahl, R. A.   209, 213, 220, *255–6*
Davidoff, P. & Reiner, A.   *293*
Davies, J. C. & Davies, B. S.   *330*
Dawes, R. M. et. al.   300, *330*
Dearlove, J.   223, *256*, *293*, 294

decision making   40, 47, 56, Fig. 7.1,
    289
    and role of expertise   76
    and uncertainty   123, 136, 138, 157,
        172, 199
    and pluralist theory   214, 222–7,
        252–3, 275
    and elitist theory   229–32, 252–3, 325
    and structuralist theory   244–8,
        252–3, see also theories
dental mottling   36, 77, 83, 97
    caries   149
Department of the Environment, see also
    Environment   53, 57, 94, 154, 156,
    331
    Report on Air Pollution   86, 88, 94,
        106, 123, 138–41, 143, 145, 148–52,
        158–9, 161, 177–8, 201, 226, 247–8,
        279–80, 302, 316, 325
Department of Health and Social
    Security   83
Deposit of Poisonous Wastes Act (1972)
    107
dereliction   4, 9, 24–32, 44–5, 49, 61,
    65–7, 81–2, 156, 199–200, 246–7,
    265, 304
derelict land   31, 53
distributional effects of decisions, see
    pollution
District Council
    powers over pollution control   309
Domhoff, G. W.   255
Donaldson, R. J.   97, 110
Douglas, J. W. B. & Waller, R. E.   110
Dow Chemical   317–18, 323, 326, 332
dual-state thesis   277–9, 285, 287,
    289–90
Dunleavy, P.   9, 15, 211, 251, 255,
    257–9, 273, 291, 293–5
Dunstable Gazette   160
Dutch elm disease   30

East Chicago   230, 233, 237, 313–14
Easton, D.   15
Eastwoods (brick company)   52
Eckstein, H.   15
Ecologist, The   330
Ecology Party   144
economic factors
    role in conflict   141–2, 162, 176,
        180–3, 186, 227, 238, 243, 265–7, 277

economic interests   289, Fig. 7.1, 296,
    323
economic issues   265–7, 287, Fig. 7.1,
    289–90
Economist, The   332
ecosystem   305
Elcock, H.   294
elite pluralism   251
elitist theory
    character   9, 209–10, 228–38, 249–50,
        261, 283–4, 287, 291, 296
    and concentration of power   228
    and corporatism   229, 236
    criticism of   231–2, 250–1, 261
    and dual state thesis   277
    systems of government   310–12
    and interests   231, 236–7, 251, 323
    and issues   228–9, 231–5
    and non-decision making   229–35,
        261, 325
    and privileged access   229, 235–8, 275,
        278, 326
elections   176, 192, 213, 223
    effect on decision   194–5
    1981 council elections   198, 290, 295
Elliott, B. & McCrone, D.   292
Elstow (Beds.)   4, 56–8, 68, 220, 268,
    333
Elstow pit   57, 327
Elstow brickworks   3, 22, 33
Elstow storage site   327, 333
emission banking   307–8
employment issues   176, 187, 193, 196,
    199, 262, 265–7, 270, 286, 316, 329
Environment, Secretary of State for   117,
    133–4, 164
    attitude to public inquiry   87, 94, 136,
        141, 151, 160, 169, 275–6, 276–7, see
        also Fox, M. and Heseltine, M.
Environmental Health Departments   309
    awareness   44, 297, 302–4, 312
environmental impact assessment
    311–12
    interests   43, 45, 50, 176, 217–20, 241,
        252, 287, 296, 304–5, 319
environmental issues   7, 156, 226, 262–5,
    264, 270, 283, 289–90, 297, 304–5,
    312, 315–16
    movement   49, 303, 305, 318, 323–4
Environmental Protection Agency
    (EPA)   305, 307, 315

Environmental Services Committee
(ESC) *107–9, 158–9, 206–7*, 225
and Cambridgeshire works 179,
183–4, 191
and Chairman of London Brick 166–9
and Cremer and Warner Report
100–1
role in decision making 123–4, 139,
157
and Department of Environment
Report 151–2
and final decision 188–9, 196–7
and planning permission 125–33,
151–2
and pollution control 165–6
and closure of Ridgmont 183–4
and site of Ridgmont works 78–80
and Section 52 Agreement 116
see also Beds. County Council
environmentalism 216, 305
evidence
and theory 211–12, 231–2, 250–1,
260–1, 272, 287, 296–8
expertise 262, 271–2, 289, 325
externalities 216, 298, 301, 306, 322

false consciousness 231, 235
farming interests 265, 301
Fenland District Council 94, *110*, 177–8
Fletton (Cambs.) 1
Fletton Brickworks Liaison Committee
(FBLC) 46, 70, 85–6, 88, *109*, 201,
208, 248
fletton process
see brickmaking
Flixborough 303
fluorides 35–8, 45, 50, 72, 83–4, 88,
95–8, 100–5, 107, 154, 164, 173,
200–2, 234, 247, 315
fluoridisation of water 87, 95
fluorosis 37–8, 41–2, 56, 72, 87–8, 106,
121, 281, 321
Flynn, R. 278, *294*
Foljanty-Jost, G. and Weidner, H. *330*
Forestry Commission 118, *159*
Fort William 37, *53*, 83, 97
Friend, J. K. & Jessop, W. N. *293*
fullers' earth 76

Gary (Indiana) 6, 40, 229, 232, 237,
313–14

Gaventa, J. 6, *15, 292, 295*
geography
aspects of conflict 177, 254, 282–6,
302, 308, 323, 325
Gilbert, O. L. 96, *110*
Gladwin, T. N. *15*
Goldsmith, M. *255*
Goodin, R. E. *292*, 304, 315, *330–32*
Greater London Council (GLC) 57, 90,
108
greenhouse effect 305
Gregory, R. *207, 256, 259*, 265, *292*
Group Action to Stop the Pit (GASP)
68, 73–4, 92, 121, 218, 220, 236
Guardian, The 70, 72, 95, 102, *108–9*,
135, 145, *205, 207, 333*

Hanson Trust 203
Hardin, G. 299, *330*
Hase, T. *330*
health
see air pollution, medical evidence,
public health
Heclo, H. H. 226, *256, 293*
Hertfordshire County Council 31
Hill, D. M. *293*
Hill, M. J. 273, *294, 331*
Hillier, R. *14, 51*
Hindess, B. *15*, 253, *259*, 269, *293*
Hoffman Kiln 16, 59, 85, 99, 103, 116,
129, 131, 154, 167, 219, 248
Houghton Conquest (Beds.) 4, 41–2,
67–8, 73–4, 92–3, 133, 151, 218, 220,
328
pit 68, 74, 81, 92–3, 220
Hunter, F. *255*
hydrocarbons 307

Ibstock Johnsen (brick company) 17,
203
ideology
and theory 210
individuals
see actors
industry and government 281, 309, 311
information
role in decision making 279–81,
315–16, 325
interests 7, 176, 209, 215–22
in pluralist theory 213–14, 291
in elitist theory 284, 291

in structuralist theory   240–2, 291
  class   210, 251–2
  material   252, 284 *see also* business,
    economic, environmental
investment withdrawal   199, 244, 267,
    276, 318, 326
  issues   7–8, 49, 56, 65, 94, 156, 176, 198,
    263–7, 287, Fig. 7.1, 296
  see also air pollution, dereliction,
    economic, employment, Ridgmont
    site
Italy   303

Jack, M.   *255*
Japan   303, 305, 318
Jones, C. O.   231, *257*, 264, *292*
Jones, Miss Emily   77, *109*
Jones, G.   *294*

Kasper, R. G.   *331*
Kempston (Beds.)   4, 41
Kempston Hardwick Works   3, 17, 22,
    25, 204, *207*, 327
  closure   198, 201, 203–4
kilns
  design   99, 116, 153–4, 163–4, 167,
    178, 188, *see* Hoffman kiln, tunnel
    kilns
King's Dyke Works (Cambs.)   19, 91,
    93–4, 177, 184, *207*, 245
Kimber, R. and Richardson, J. J.   *258*
Kirk, G.   *257–8, 292*
Knoepfel, P. et. al.   325, *333*
Kvartovkina, L. K.   *110*

'L' field   31, 56–8, 68, 90, 200, 217, 220,
    235, 247, 303, 327
Labour group   76, 125, 133, 138, 143,
    152, 157, 174, 197–8, 290, 320
  and trade unions   147–8, 181, 186–7,
    190, 222, 268–70
  and County Labour Party   187
labour
  working conditions   5, 147, 266
  countries of origin   44, 266, *see also*
    employment, London Brick, trade
    unions
Lake Superior   216, 314–17, 323
law of anticipated reactions   223
lead   95, 307
Lee, J. M.   273, 293

Leicestershire   200
Levanski, R.   *330*
Liberal group   138, 157, 174, 197
Lidlington (Beds.)   4, 17, 36, 41, 67, 76,
    79, 98, 126, 183, 329, *see also* Marston
    works
Lindblom, C. E.   6, *15*, 235, *258*
Lipset, S. M.   264, *292*
Lloyd, W. F.   299, *330*
London Brick Company
  application for new works   59, 90–3,
    110, 116, 121, 130–1, 133, 247–8
  case study   Chapters 2–5
  response to Cremer and Warner   1,
    102–5
  reactions to Council decisions   162–6,
    182, 285
  response to D.o.E. report   151
  impact on economy   6, 14, 157, 301,
    321
  and environmental issues   27, 30–1,
    39–40, 43–7, 72, 86, 102–5, 118–19,
    145, 157, 167–8, 201–2, 216, 246–7,
    301, 315–16
  and farming   41–3, 106–7, 234
  and government   285, 321
  abandons investment   183
  origin and growth   1, 4, 17–19
  and planning agreement   113–14, 246
  and planning officials   235–6, 267–8
  early planning permissions   27–31, 33,
    233
  and politicians   166–9, 182, 268,
    273–4, 324
  attitude to pollution conditions
    163–6, 201, 247–8, 315
  power of   215–17, 222, 234, 239–43,
    266, 285, 290–1, 321
  production and profits   19–20, 22–4,
    Fig. 2.5, 134, 146, *160*, 181, 203
  and public image   5–6, 43–4, 71, 76,
    104, 146, 224–5, 266
  closes Ridgmont   184–5
  and new Ridgmont permission   190–2,
    195–6
  and site of Ridgmont works   77, 81
  switch to Stewartby   203–4
  strategy   86–7, 104, 162, 164–5, 168,
    176–80, 202–4, 244–6, 282, 285–6,
    290–1, 318, 323
  compared to US cases   314–22
  weakness of   215, 266

and workforce   5, 44, 147, 185, 203, 266–7, 275
London Brick Engineering   51, 208
London Brick Farms   22
London Brick Landfill   22, 31, 51, 118, 159, 247
London Brick Property   51, 208
London Brick Products   51, 208
LBC Review   160, 192, 195, 206
LB works (Cambs.)   91, 178
Long Beach (California)   317, 324
Lunn, J. E. et. al   110
Lukes, S.   210, 255–7, 259
Luton (Beds.)   195, 198, 268
Luton News   143, 160–1
Luton Post   145, 160

Marston (brickworks)   3, 22, 329
Marston Moreteine (Beds.)   4, 67, 69, 76, 79, 81, 126, 183, 192, 225, 329
Marston Thrift (site for brickworks)   67, 69, 77, 81, 91, 93, 126, 131, 218, 220, 244, 258, 271
Marston Vale (Beds.)   1, Fig. 1.2, 5, 14, 30, 33, 39, 41, 47, 61, 65, 72, 74, 79, 83, 85, 96, 102, 113, 117–19, 125, 167, 184, 197–200, 202, 204–5, 217–18, 283, 327–9, Fig. 8.1
Marston Valley Brick Company   4, 17, 41–2, 51–2, 56, 185
Marx, K.   255
Marxist theory   209–10, see also structuralist theory
Meadows, D. L. et. al.   330
media   13, 70, 224, see also Press
medical evidence
    on pollution   32, 36–7, 70, 72, 83, 105, 279
mercaptans   35, 84
mercury   303
Mesabi (Lake Superior)   315
Michels, R.   270, 293
Mid-Bedfordshire District Council   77, 125–6
middle class   264–5, 283
Miliband, R.   259, 292–3
Millbrook (Beds.)   126
Milton Keynes Express   160
Milton Keynes Gazette   106
Minamata (Japan)   303
Minister of Housing and Local Government (formerly Town and

Country Planning)   27, 29–31, 33, 52–3, 119
Ministry of Agriculture, Fisheries & Food   38, 279
Minnesota   314, 317
mobilisation of bias   230–1, 234–5
Monopolies and Mergers Commission   17, 22–3, 51, 184, 207–8
multinationals   282
Muchnik, D. N.   256
Murphy, D. C.   256

National Ambient Air Quality Standards (NAAQS) USA   307
National Coal Board   17, 32, 117, 119, 200
National Farmers' Union (NFU)
    and Conservative Group   147
    as an elite interest   236, 251
    opposes London Brick   106–7, 142, 144–5, 170–2, Fig. 5.1, 186, 198, 206
    settlements with London Brick   42–3, 106–7
    role   43, 126, 148, 160, 170, 178, 221–2
national interest   47, 276, 284
National Survey of Air Pollution (UK)   83, 96, 109
Navarro, P.   320, 332
negative decision making   229, 233–4
neo-elitist theory
    see elitist theory
neo-marxist theory
    see structuralist theory
neo-pluralist
    see pluralist theory
neo-Weberian theory   260
Newby, H.   52, 292
New Saxon Works (Cambs.)   19, 91
New Source Performance Standards (NSPS), USA   307
Newton, K.   256–8, 294
nitrogen oxide   307, 326
Northamptonshire County Council   31, 57
North Bedfordshire Borough Council   126, 159
Norway   95, 143, 327
Nottinghamshire   32, 118
nuclear industry   303
Nuclear Industry Radioactive Waste Executive (NIREX)   333
nuclear waste   58, 327

Observer, The   95, *333*
O'Connor, J.   *292*
odours (from brickworks)   35, 39, 78,
    84, 88, 97–9, 102, 116, 127, 131, 149,
    163, 167, 201–2, 247–8, 259, 321
OECD   95, 326, *331, 333*
offsets   307–8, 317
Ogus, A. and Richardson, G. M.   *330*
Olives, J.   *292*
ombudsman   198, 221
'Operation Landfill'   90, 224
'Operation Oberon'   166, 224
O'Riordan, T.   *229*
outcomes   8, 205, 287, Fig. 7.1, 290, 302
    and action   253–4
    and pluralism   214, 253
    and policy   296
    and structuralism   239, 242–3, 253
overpopulation   299
Oxford Clay   1, Fig. 1.1, 16, 25, 45, *51*,
    65, 67, 99, 200, *333*
ozone   299

Pahl, R.   263, *292*
Panama   317
Parry, G. and Morriss, P.   *256–7*
participant observation   10–11
parish council   13, 69, 126, 221
particulate   307
Pearce, F.   *333*
Peterborough   1, 17, 19, 31, 42, 91, 147,
    184, 187, 200
Peterborough Community Health
    Council   178
Petrilli, R. L.   97, *110*
Pitsea (Essex)   58, *108*
Pittsburgh   264
place
    role of   262, 282–6, Fig. 7.1, 290, 318
Plamenatz, J.   *258*
Planning Advisory Group (PAG)   65–8,
    78, 85, *108–9*, 164–5, *206*
planning controls and pollution   311
planning and corporatism   278
planning and industry   311
planning permission (original)   27–31,
    Fig. 2.8, 33, 45, *52*, 118–19, 276, 283,
    see also London Brick
Planning Officer (County)   *108–9*, 158,
    159, 163, *see also* Cowley, G. and
    Griffin, T.

planning officials   13, 30, 47, 61, 63, 73,
    75, 93, 119, 271–3, 289
    and developers   278
    and expertise   271–2, 289
    and relations with London Brick
        Company   246, 270–1, 275
    and politicians   272–5
    and privileged access   235–6
    and Ridgmont site   77–81, 131, 244,
        271
pluralist theory
    character of   8–9, 125, 209–10,
        212–27, 283, Fig. 7.1, 291
    criticisms of   228–9, 250–1, 261
    and decision making   214, 222–7
    and dual state   277
    and government system   310–12
    and interests   213–22, 251
    and interpretation of case study
        212–27
    neo-pluralists   270–72
    and role of officials   270-2
    and participation   220-2
    and power   213–14, 215–17, 220–2
policy
    and consequences   297–8, 308, 312–22
    and decision making   296–7
    and theory   Chapter 8
political culture   313–14
political environment   11–12, Fig. 1.3,
    122–5, 176, 197, 224, 235, 253–4
political organisation   11–12, Fig. 1.4,
    253
political process   287, Fig. 7.1, 289
politics
    administrative   270–5
    and conflict   262, 267–70
    local   223, 313, Chapter 6
    pluralist   125, 268, 270, 274, 323–5
politicians   12–13, 194, 223–4, 226–7,
    237, 252–3, 268
    and officials   270–5
    see also councillors
pollution
    case studies   312–22
    control   298–314, 319–21
    definition   298
    distributional effects   297–9, 301, 308,
        312, 319–20
    export   300–1
    levels   298–302, 320, 322

regulation   306–12, 318, 322
see also air pollution
pollution havens   308, 326
Polsby, N. W.   209, 213, 230, *255–7*
Porteous, A. et. al.   *55, 294–5*
positional goods   264–5
power   6, 7, 27, Chapters 6 and 7
reputation for   40, 313–14
concentration and dispersal   252–3
see also theories
powerlessness   284
praxis   210
Press   68–71, 102, 107, 120, 142, 145–7, 224
Presthus, R.   *256*
pressure groups   13, 68–9, 73–4, 220–2
Prevention of Significant Deterioration (PSD)   308, 319
Private Eye   143–4, 160, 192, *207*
professionals   270–1
Public Review of Brickmaking and the Environment (PROBE)   *15*, Fig. 3.6, 95, 100, *109–11*, 116, 122, 126, 132–3, 139–40, 146, 151, 182, 187, *206*, 269
and Cremer and Warner Report 105–6
as elitist group   236, 251
formation   89–90
strategy   120–2, 134–5, 156–7, 169–70, 221–2
public concern   32, 35, 44–6, 48–9, 56, 69–71, 304, 312, 315, 322
public consultation   126, Fig. 4.2, 45
public health   264, 283, 289, 304–5, 312, 315
Public Health Acts   309
public inquiry   79, 105, 120, 131, 134, 138, 140-1, 147, 151, 154, *160*, 169, 173, 191, 279, 311
public interest   270, 278, 311
public opinion   13, 30, 47, 68, 71–4, 105, 121–2, 191–2, 213, 224, 233, 270, 283

Quest pit   80, 104, 188, 191, 195, 245, 328
quiescence   263

Raine, J.   *294*
rationality   299, 301–2
Reade, E.   *255, 272, 293–4*

recession   176, 180–2, 184, 202–3, 215, 267, 290, 303
Redlands (brick company)   17, 44, *54, 208*
Reserve Mining Company   216, 314–17, 323–6
revocation of planning consents   92, 114
at Ridgmont   204
Rhodes, G.   *331*
Richards, P.   *293*
Ridgmont (Beds.)   76, 120, 172
Ridgmont works
old works   1, 3–4, 17, 21–2, 25, 35, *52*, 59, 77, 79, 93, *207*, 329
site for new works   61, Fig. 3.4, 67, 71, 74, 77–81, 86, 93, 98, 107, 126, 131, 133, 204, 218, 244–6, *258*, 265
new works   91, 104, 131, 183–4, 188–9, 196, 203–4, 227, 245, 274, 287, 323
closure of old works   184–5, 187, 189, 199, 201, 203–4, 222, 227, 318
Riseley (Beds.)   36
risk   303–4, 316
Rookery pit   2–3, 80, 327–8
site for new works   204, 328
Rothamsted Experimental Station   38, 83, 122, 279
Royal Commission on Environmental Pollution   82, *109*, 310, *330–1*
Russell, C.   *331*

Salaman, L. M. and Siegfried, J. J.   *332*
Sandbach, F.   *257–8, 292*, 303, 306, 322–3, *330–2*
San Francisco   317
Santa Barbara   303
Saunders, P.   8, 211, 226, 250, *255–9*, 277, 284, *292, 294*
Saxon Works (Cambs.)   184, *207*
Scandinavian Countries   85, 95, 122, 135, 280, 285, 326–7
Schattschneider, E. E   230, *257*
Schnaiberg, A.   292, 325, *333*
scientific evidence   32, 36, 95–6, 280
Scottish bricks   17
Section 52 Planning Agreement (Beds.)   61, 71, 73–4, 87, *108*, 113–17, 123, 131, Fig. 4.1, 156, *158*, 165, 167, 197, 204, *206*, 218–19, 246, *259*, 274, 278, 300
(Cambs.)   179, 183, 204

Self, P.   273, *293*
Seveso   303
Sharpe, L. J.   226, *256*
Shoard, M.   *52*
Skellington, R.   *55*
Slovic, P. and Fischoff, B.   *331*
smoke   102, 309
social consumption/investment   263, 277, 279, 285, Fig. 7.1, 289–90
Sohio   317–18, 323–4, *332*
"Something in the air" Thames TV   72
Stand-off zones   61, 67, 69, 74, 92, 114, 200, 218, 220, 265
standards, pollution control   307, 312, 315, 317–19, 322, 327, *332–3*
state
  role   238, 262–3, 275–81, 285
  central/local   262, 275–81, 290
State Implementation Plans (SIPs)   307
Stevens (report)   *108*, 113–14, *158*
Stewartby (Beds.)   4, 67, 69, 75, 188, 194, 268, 327
Stewartby works
  in Coronation Pit   91, 202–4
  existing works   2–3, 21–2, 25, 35, 52, 56, 59, 80, 86, 96, 98, 126, 202–4, *207*, 328
  new works   Figs. 3.2 and 3.3, 104, *108*, 116, 120, 130–1, 152–4, 156, 179, 182, 184, 195–6, 203–4, 245, 286, 323
  in Rookery Pit   204, 328
Stewartby Lake   2, 31
Stoddard report   *333*
Streetley (Brick Co.)   17
Stretton, H.   *292, 332*
structuralist theory
  character of   9, 210, 238–50, 261–2, 291
  criticisms of   250–1, 261–2
  and interests   240–2, 251–2
  and interpretation of case study   244–8
  and outcomes   242–3, 246
  and power   239–40, 243, 252–3, 321, 323, 326
sulphates   320
sulphur dioxide (SO$_2$)   34–7, 39, 45, 78, 82–5, 88, 96–8, 100, 102–3, 148–9, 154, 162, 164, 173, 201, 234, 280, 307, 319–20, 326
Sunday Times   *207*

Sweden   95, 122, 135, 143
systems approach   11

taconite   314–15, 317
taxation (on pollution)   306
Texas   317
Thames TV   72
theory   x, 8–11, Chapters 6, 7 and 8
  evaluation of   210–11, 242, 249–55, 260–62, 287
  see also elitist, pluralist, structuralist and evidence
Three Mile Island (Penn.)   303
Times, The   143–5, 183
titanium   95
Torrey Canyon   303
Town and Country Planning Act
  (1947)   27
  (1971)   *108*, 113
toxic waste   56–7, 94, 98–9, *107*, 217, 220, 303, 305
Toyama (Japan)   303
trade unions
  and Conservative Group   267
  as interest   242, 251–2, 265–7
  and London Brick   181-2, 190, 266–7, 275
  and Labour Group   76, 147–8, 181, 186–7, 190, 222, 267–70
  role   13, 19, 142, 185–8, 190–1, 221–2, 237, 265–7, 319–20
"tragedy of the commons"   299–301
Transport and General Workers' Union (TGWU)   190
trees
  planting   30, 114
  effect of pollution   39
tunnel kilns   98, 100, 103, 116, 129, 131, 147, 149, 167, 188, 196, 201, 247

United Kingdom Atomic Energy Research Establishment (UKAERE)   57–8
USSR   97
United States   70, 83, 282, 305
  case studies   313–22, 326–7
  approach to pollution control   307–12
United States Steel   40, 229–30, 233, 237, 313–14, 325
urban protest movements   262–3, 284
urban studies   260

values   210, 216, 234, 272, 283, 296–7, 302, 315-16, 329
Vogel, D.   49, 55, 217, 239, *255*, *258*, 282, 294, 310, 319, 322–3, *331–3*

Waller, R. E.   *322*
Warren Springs (laboratory)   43, *208*, 279
waste disposal   56–7, 90
Water Pollution Control Act US   315
Weber, M.   270, *293*
Westergaard, J. and Resler, H.   *258*, 268, *293*
West Germany   306
Whittlesey (Cambs.)   17, 42, 91, 93–4, 177–8, 180, 225

Wildavsky, A.   *293*
Williams, R. H.   *331*
Windscale   303
Winkler, J.   221, *256*
Woburn (Beds.)   176
Woburn Abbey   120, 134, 236
Woburn Sands (Bucks.)   5, 44, *54*, 76, 282–3
Wolfinger, R. E.   212, *255*, *257*
Wood, C.   309, *331*
Wootton (Beds.)   4, 75, 93, 126
working class   263–4, 289, 301
Wragg, R. and Robertson, J.   *51*

Yokkaichi (Japan)   303